Bill and Hillary

WILLIAM H. CHAFE

Farrar, Straus and Giroux

New York

Bill and Hillary

THE POLITICS
OF THE PERSONAL

Farrar, Straus and Giroux
18 West 18th Street, New York 10011

Distributed in Canada by D&M Publishers, Inc.
Printed in the United States of America
First edition, 2012

Library of Congress Cataloging-in-Publication Data
Chafe, William Henry.
    Bill and Hillary : the politics of the personal / William H. Chafe. — 1st ed.
      p.   cm.
    Includes bibliographical references and index.
    ISBN 978-0-8090-9465-3 (alk. paper)
    1. Clinton, Bill, 1946–   2. Clinton, Hillary Rodham.   3. Presidents—
United States—Biography.   4. Presidents' spouses—United States—Biography.
5. United States—Politics and government—1993–2001.   I. Title.

E886 .C47 2012
973.929092'2—dc23
[B]

                                   2011041302

Designed by Jonathan D. Lippincott

www.fsgbooks.com

10 9 8 7 6 5 4 3 2 1

FOR LORNA,
WHO HAS BEEN THERE FOR
THE WHOLE JOURNEY

Contents

Preface

At first glance it might seem strange that I am writing this book. I started off as a women's historian, writing primarily about the experience of housewives and working women, the suffrage movement, and the impact of the Great Depression, World War II, suburbanization, and latter-day feminism on different groups of women. Hand in hand with that, I pursued a commitment to tell the story of the civil rights struggle from the bottom up, using community studies of ordinary people—not heroes or heroines—to fathom the persistent struggle for social equality among black Americans. But at the foundation of all this was a belief, nurtured by growing up in a socially conscious church, that individuals could make a difference by engaging in the cause of social justice.

One theme running throughout my work is the tension between reform and radicalism in movements for social change. I came of age in the 1960s, when a generation changed every two years. Had I been born a few years later, I would have become a radical. But as it was I grew up with a belief that one could create change by working *within* the system, not by trying to *overthrow* it. Still, I was fascinated by the hair's-edge difference between being an ardent reformer and a confirmed radical. How far could a reformer push the envelope before it broke open?

To better understand that conundrum I undertook my first biography, a study of the quintessential liberal reformer Allard K. Lowenstein. As a leader of the National Student Association, Lowenstein became the young activist who first thought of bringing white civil rights supporters to Mississippi for the Freedom Vote campaign of 1963. He then moved on to become the architect of the Dump Johnson campaign of

1967–68. Lowenstein personified the dilemma I was trying to understand. How did a liberal construct his world? What stopped him from becoming a radical? When I started the biography, I had no idea of the tortured personal roots of Lowenstein's choice to become a liberal crusader. Only when I got inside his life did I discover how profoundly his personal experiences shaped his public life. The principal reasons that Lowenstein pursued his peripatetic lifestyle of reform activism went back to his ambivalence about being Jewish, his anguish after discovering that his real mother had died when he was one, and, above all, the realization that he was attracted sexually to boys. It was from these personal experiences that he could "never stop running"—away from the truth about himself, toward hopping the next airplane and taking on the next crusade. That insight provided the book with its title.

So it turns out that there is a line that directly connects a scholar passionately committed to studying issues of race and gender equality from the bottom up and a scholar who writes about the private motivations of individual men and women and how their private experiences end up shaping their political activities and public lives. It seems appropriate that Bill and Hillary Clinton came to political consciousness and maturity in the same decade I did, with the same focus on race and equality. And that subsequently, the struggle for women's liberation played a central role in their lives, as it did in mine and that of my family. Thus there is a logic to this journey, a roundedness. And rather than being strange, it seems natural to be writing this book about "the politics of the personal."

William H. Chafe
Georgetown, Maine

Bill and Hillary

Introduction

In the 1960s, the women's liberation movement introduced a new phrase into the national vocabulary: "The personal is political."

The slogan had its origins in thousands of consciousness-raising groups around the country where women talked about growing up in a society full of sex stereotypes. Cultural norms defined what was "feminine" behavior and what was "masculine"; what women could do, what men could do; how life could be compartmentalized into gender-labeled categories. American life was full of such categories. What was "public" differed from what was "private." "Political" issues defined one arena of life experience. "Personal" issues occupied a totally different realm.

Feminists disagreed. What went on in the bedroom or the kitchen, they pointed out, reflected patterns of power that pervaded Wall Street and the government as well. The tone of voice one adopted, the household roles one played, the assertiveness or passivity one displayed— all of these reflected a deeper truth: that the private and the public, the personal and the political, were connected. Who did what around the house spoke to a larger system of how power was apportioned, what opportunities did or did not exist. The conclusion feminists drew from this was simple and revolutionary: If relations between women and men were to change, *everything* had to change.

Since the 1960s we have learned to translate the insight of feminists into a larger understanding of what defines history, and of what animates politics. Public figures are shaped by private experiences. Their political behavior reflects personal values and choices as well as issues of public policy. Personal experiences infuse and inspire the choices that political figures make. What goes on in the family where a child grows up helps define in fundamental ways how that child responds as an adult to moments of political or moral crisis.

By now that insight has extended into our study of people in power. We know that understanding the presidency of Franklin Delano Roosevelt requires understanding his relationship with his mother, his aristocratic roots, his marriage to Eleanor Roosevelt, and perhaps above all his experience of being a victim of polio. Similarly, we cannot understand Eleanor Roosevelt without knowing about her alcoholic father, her experience of intellectual awakening in an English boarding school under the tutelage of a strong feminist, her engagement in social activism through networks of women reformers, and the crisis of her learning of her husband's infidelity. The personal is political. The private and the public are deeply connected. Wives affect husbands, and husbands wives.

This book is about two people who even more than Eleanor and Franklin speak to the intersection of the personal and the political. Bill and Hillary Clinton have helped define the political life of a generation. No personalities in recent history speak more compellingly to the importance of understanding that the personal and the political are inseparable.

The entwined personal and political lives of Bill and Hillary Clinton offer new insight into how pivotal it is to understand the personalities of our leaders if we are to understand the politics they have helped shape for us. America provides no clearer example than the Clintons of the consequences of how the forces of the personal and the political are seamlessly connected.

ONE

Bill Clinton: The Early Years

It would be difficult to invent a childhood more bizarre than Bill Clinton's. He was born the son of Virginia Blythe, a nurse proud of her flirtatious nature who spent ninety minutes each morning putting on her makeup. Virginia's husband, Bill, lied serially about his past, and shortly after their marriage during World War II, he went overseas with the army. Five months after returning—and three months before Bill's birth—Bill died in an automobile accident. A year later, Virginia went off to New Orleans to train as a nurse anesthetist, leaving the care of her infant son to her parents. Virginia soon married her second husband, Roger Clinton, whose record of multiple marriages and troubled relationships made Bill Blythe's past look angelic. Soon alcoholism and spousal abuse consumed the Clinton household. Through all of this, Billy Clinton stood as the symbol of hope, the adored special child who would make everything right, the savior of an otherwise unredeemable situation. He emerged as a "family hero" who soon came to see himself, and be seen by others, as destined to become a leader, not just of his family and community but of the American nation as a whole.

Virginia Cassidy, Bill's mother, grew up in a household torn by conflict. Her mother, Edith Grisham, later called Mammaw by everyone, was born poor in rural Arkansas. She craved money and material goods but felt condemned to a life of working in the fields, trying to make ends meet. She married the boy across the road, James Eldridge Cassidy, a sweet, gentle, fun-loving man—not because he guaranteed her a better life, but because he was submissive and she could control him. Virginia's mother demanded that they move in pursuit of more opportunities, so they crated their belongings and settled in Hope, a small city of five thousand. It was big enough to be a stop on the train line and boasted movie theaters, a commercial district, and a greater variety of people. There, Eldridge got a job delivering ice, while Mammaw trained as a nurse through a correspondence course and hired herself out to private patients. She reveled in her status, proudly wearing her starched white uniform and blue cape embroidered with gold initials. Eldridge had fewer pretensions, but he loved gossiping with his customers and making friends.[1]

But it was not a happy home. "My mother created sparks wherever she went," Virginia later wrote, "which meant that my father and I were the ones who got burned the most." Despite her professional pride in being a nurse, Virginia's mother was at heart mean-spirited, showing little affection for other people. "She had hellfire in her," one friend, Margaret Polk, recalled. Virginia agreed. "Her worst trait was her temper," she said, "which was uncontrollable. She was angry somewhere deep inside her, and she took it out on anybody who happened to be around." On the one hand, she enjoyed being able to help those in need. On the other, she could lash out at those who crossed her, stopping "at nothing to undermine them, to hurt them, in terrible ways." It was as if she possessed two personalities. One was the professional helper she showed the public, dressing up in her uniform and making a mask of rouge and lipstick, "like a stylized character in a Japanese kabuki show," in the words of the Clinton biographer David Maraniss. The other, a tyrant, was obsessed with controlling those around her, hiding a vicious streak of sadism. Her husband and daughter bore the brunt of this second personality.[2]

Not surprisingly, Virginia adored her father. "[I loved him] as much as it was possible for a daughter to love her dad," she wrote. "He was kind and gentle, and he loved laughing and fishing and storytelling and people—especially me." Eldridge Cassidy embraced people, reached out to them. When delivering ice, he often stopped off at a customer's home and stayed for a cup of coffee while he sent his coworkers on to the next stop. Some of his coffee companions were his prettiest customers. "He was a ladies' man," Margaret Polk remembered. Later, when Eldridge developed a bronchial condition, he was forced to give up his ice route. Initially, he opened a liquor store, then a small grocery, where, under the counter, he also sold bootleg alcohol. Virginia, whom he called Ginger, loved hanging out at the store, watching her father interact with customers, extend credit to those in need, and laugh with his friends.[3]

Edith—Mammaw—was less appreciative. Hearing stories of Eldridge's "coffee-klatches" with his female customers, Virginia remembered, "she began her nightly screaming fits." Lunging at him, throwing things, and trying to hurt him physically, she accused him of philandering, though Edith herself was rumored to be romantically linked to doctors in town. When the Depression caused them to lose their house, she blamed Eldridge for "failing us." The Cassidy home was neither nurturing nor kindly.

Virginia watched both parents. In early adolescence, she started to emulate her mother's cosmetic habits. She used mascara, eyeliner, rouge, and lipstick, starting a ritual that would become obsessive through the rest of her life. But there could be no question of where her emotional loyalties rested. "Whenever I did something wrong," she wrote, "Mother would whip me furiously." Father, on the other hand, taught her to think the best of people, give them the benefit of the doubt, and reach out a helping hand.[4]

Ironically, the one issue on which both Edith and Eldridge shared a common outlook was race. One might expect that in a Southern small town the habits of generations of white people would prevail, with racism one way that whites could express their need to feel superior. But neither of Virginia's parents succumbed. Her father cultivated a clientele that was both black and white. He granted credit to blacks as readily as, if not more readily than, to whites. Every customer was treated with dignity and fairness. Edith, in turn, expressed horror when one day she heard Virginia use the word "nigger." Often she volunteered her services to black patients in need. It was the Cassidy home's one saving grace.[5]

Virginia took from each parent certain qualities. Like her mother, she became a consummate makeup artist, shaping the image she would present to the world while masking her own agenda. Willful and tempestuous, she had her mother's flair for independence. She insisted on pursuing her individual objectives regardless of what others thought, a trait that would fuel her decades-long campaign against male doctors who she felt stood in the way of her professional development. But beyond those parallels lay a virulent anger at Edith's capricious and selfish behavior. Like the father she worshipped, Virginia chose to see good rather than bad in people. Purposefully, she set aside the unpleasant to focus on the positive. Denying all the negative realities that surrounded her became a habitual pattern of behavior. In her own words, she "brainwashed" herself to be positive. "Inside is love and friends and optimism," she wrote. "Outside is negativity, can't-doism and any criticism of me and mine. Most of the time, this box is strong as steel." It became the normative mode by which Virginia conducted her life—with profound consequences for her marriages and her children. Looking at a photo of herself taken in late adolescence, with her eyes hooded, she subsequently wrote: "By this time, I guess, I had already learned to keep my dark secrets to myself."[6]

Having finished high school, Virginia set off to realize her dreams, almost immediately engaging in a love affair that dramatically underscored her penchant to "brainwash" herself. Already known for being flirtatious and different, she left Hope to go to Shreveport, Louisiana, to train as a nurse anesthetist. That she was "going steady" with a boy back in Hope posed no problems at the Shreveport hospital the night she encountered Bill Blythe, a twenty-five-year-old who had brought another woman to the hospital for treatment. When he asked Virginia what that "ring on her finger" meant, she replied "nothing." "There *is* such a thing as love at first sight," she later wrote. And the moment she laid eyes on Bill Blythe, "all the rules were out the window." Like her father, Blythe seemed to love everybody. He told Virginia he was in sales, and she believed him. Charming, funny, ebullient, and, like Virginia, an ardent fan of dancing and a good time, Blythe won her heart immediately. "We talked fast," Virginia recalled, "[we] played fast [and we] fell in love fast." Virginia introduced him to her parents, who also were charmed. Two months after they met, the two married, and five weeks later, Bill Blythe went off to Italy to serve as a mechanic in the U.S. Army.[7]

What had transpired was a triumph of fantasy over reality and a

profound testimony to Virginia's instinct for seeing only her own version of what was true. In fact Bill Blythe was not a car salesman. All
during the time they were seeing each other—on a daily basis—he was
already in the army. Beyond that he came from a large family she knew
little about. Most important, she had no notion that he had been married three times before, had divorced all three (and perhaps four) previous wives, had fathered at least one (and perhaps two) children, and in
one of the legal cases preceding a divorce had been declared by a judge
to be "guilty of extreme cruelty and gross neglect of duty." Everything
about Bill Blythe, David Maraniss has written, "was contradictory and
mysterious. He constantly reinvented himself, starting over every day,
the familiar stranger, an ultimate traveling salesman, surviving off
charm and affability." That Virginia did not discover the full story until
more than four decades later highlights the absurdity of what had taken
place. More telling was her blind-faith assertion that she could "go to
my grave knowing that I *was* the love of his life."

When Blythe returned to Shreveport in the fall of 1945, he and
Virginia talked about moving together to Chicago, where he had a job
awaiting him as a salesman. They envisioned a life in which they could
raise a family and live out the American dream. For three months, the
reunited couple lived together in a hotel in Illinois while waiting until a
house in Forest Park opened up. That process took longer than expected,
and after she discovered she was pregnant, Virginia went back to Arkansas to wait. Shortly afterward, Blythe set out to drive through the night
to spend the weekend with her in Hope. Driving too fast, he passed a
car, then on the next curve, hurtled off the road and hit a tree. Though
he managed to extricate himself from the car, he fell into a ditch full of
water and drowned. Three months later his son Bill was born.[8]

Perhaps. Bill Blythe was still in Italy nine months before his son's
birth, making it unlikely that he was the father of a child carried to full
term. Virginia would later claim that Bill had been born prematurely.
But during the period when she was writing her own book, Virginia
never mentioned to her collaborator and coauthor that doctors had recommended an early, induced delivery—the story that she subsequently
brought forward. Moreover, the birth was not typical of premature deliv-
eries. Bill weighed six pounds eight ounces at birth, a weight not unusual
for a full-term delivery. In his speech explaining his decision not to run

for president in 1988 in order to spend more time with his daughter, Chelsea, Bill Clinton said: "I made a promise to myself a long, long time ago, that if I was ever lucky enough to have a child, she would never grow up wondering who her father was." To Maraniss, the use of the word "who" suggested doubts in Clinton's mind about the true circumstances of his birth.[9]

Yet the story was about to become even more complicated. After giving birth to her son Bill on August 19, 1946, Virginia returned to her parents' home in Hope. Almost immediately, a war started between Virginia and her mother about who was going to raise—and control—the child. Before long, the winner became clear. As long as Billy was in her home, Mammaw would be in charge. To the exacting daily schedule Mammaw set—when Billy was fed, when he took his naps, what time he went to bed—there would be no exception. The few good moments of mother and son getting to know each other faded before the omnipresent power of her mother, who insisted on "monopolizing him." There was no place to go. Escape became the only option.[10]

After only one year of being a mother, Virginia went off to New Orleans, intent on securing the credentials to become a full-time nurse anesthetist. It was in many ways the only answer—fleeing an untenable family environment where humiliation and resentment were rampant, seeking the skills that would make possible an independent life, and doing so in a city perfectly suited for a girl who loved to flirt, dance, and gamble. As Bill Clinton noted in his memoirs, New Orleans was "an amazing place after the war, full of young people, Dixieland music, and over-the-top haunts like the Club My-Oh-My where men in drag danced and sang as lovely ladies. I guess it wasn't a bad place for a beautiful young widow to move beyond her loss." Yes, she sorely missed her son. He always remembered her kneeling by the train crying as she waved good-bye to him after one of his visits to see her. But compared with the misery of her mother's total domination back in Hope, this was liberation.[11]

In the meantime, Bill Clinton had to survive on his own the contested world of his grandparents, torn between the regimented authoritarianism of Mammaw and the warm embrace of his grandfather. Mammaw ran a tight ship, with clear destinations in a narrow sea lane. As he was eating, a friend of Mammaw said, "she was showing him flash cards . . . [The coffee table] was filled with kindergarten books . . . She had him reading when he was three." At some level, Bill appreciated her dedication. "I knew the poverty of my roots," he later wrote. "I was raised by people who deliberately tried to disabuse me [of the] idea [that I was inferior] from the time I was old enough to think."[12]

He also appreciated the tortured dynamics of his grandparents' relationship. They loved him, he remembered, "much better than they were able to love each other, or, in my grandmother's case, to love my mother." Mammaw was "bright, intense and aggressive [with] a great laugh, but she also was full of anger and disappointment and obsessions she only dimly understood." Instead of dealing with her inner demons, she took out her pathology in "raging tirades against her husband and her daughter." Like his mother, Bill needed to escape, and as it had been for his mother, his outlet was his grandfather's store, where he went every day to play, eat chocolate chip cookies, and revel in the warm embrace of someone who clearly worried about the needs of others more than he worried about his own. In language almost identical to his mother's, Bill Clinton later wrote: "I adored my grandfather." He described him as "an incredibly kind and generous man."[13]

Among other things, Eldridge Cassidy taught his grandson Bill the meaning of racial equality—the natural gift of relating to black Americans, even in a racist Southern state, as friends and equals. "It was rare to find an uneducated rural southerner without a racist bone in his body," Clinton remembered. "That's exactly what my grandfather was." His grandson learned the lesson. He was "the only white boy in that neighborhood who played with black kids," said the daughter of a black customer who remembered what it was like to have fun with a white boy. So even as he squirmed under his grandmother's ironclad tutelage at home, Bill blossomed under the inclusive warmth of his grandfather at the store.[14]

In the end, Bill was shaped by that difficult family dynamic in ways remarkably like his mother. He chose to believe that people were more good than bad, to look on the bright side, to be positive and deny negativity. "A lot of life," he wrote, "is just showing up and hanging on; that laughter is often the best, and sometimes the only response to pain.

Perhaps most important, I learned that everyone has a story—of dreams and nightmares, love and loss, courage and fear, sacrifice and selfishness." His grandfather's store had provided a democratic space where he could learn to look on the positive side of human experience and not be possessed by the demons of negativity. "When I grew up and got into politics," he would state, "I always felt the main point of my work was to give people a chance to have better stories."[15]

Those lessons would become important far sooner than either Bill or his grandfather could have anticipated. Virginia had always been a party girl. She sported a dramatic white streak down the middle of her dark brunette hair, carefully crafted false eyebrows, and a face heavily made up with rouge and lipstick. Dressed to the nines in sexy outfits, she loved going to local nightclubs, even venturing on stage with the entertainers. "I pranced up there to [the stage] to hog the spotlight," she wrote. "In case you hadn't already figured it out . . . I might already have had a cocktail or two." Needless to say, Virginia soon found a series of male counterparts equally dedicated to the fast life. One of them was Roger Clinton, a local Buick dealer who knew her father because he had supplied Eldridge with bootleg whiskey. With dark curly hair and known as Dude, he dressed like a Las Vegas gambler, doused himself in aftershave, and was the life of the party. Soon he became Virginia's boyfriend. She knew he lived on the edge, sometimes got drunk and started fights, and often skirted the law. But "back then . . . getting drunk and crazy was considered cute," she pointed out. Needless to say, Mammaw detested him. When Virginia left town, she was delighted. She would now have total control over Billy, and Roger would be miles away from Virginia.[16]

But before long, the relationship became an item in its own right. After Virginia moved to New Orleans, Roger would come to visit; and he even paid for Virginia's return to Hope to see Billy. Perhaps most important, Roger seemed devoted to Billy, taking him to ballgames, bringing him special treats like a train set, making him feel important. Roger's evident love for both mother and son, of course, enraged Mammaw, who saw him as the ultimate threat both to her need to possess Billy and to her notion of a stable family life. This time, when Virginia announced her intention to wed Roger, there was no joy. Neither Eldridge nor Edith came to the wedding. Indeed, Mammaw became so hateful that she tried to secure legal custody of Billy and prevent him from living with Virginia. "She was willing to rip this family apart," Virginia wrote. "I remember thinking that the blackness inside of her had finally taken over and there was nothing left but the blackness itself." For nearly three years, Billy had endured being pulled and hauled between a controlling grandmother and a free-spirited, loving grandfather. Now he would enter another family dynamic.[17]

Virginia Blythe's marriage with Roger Clinton was, in Yogi Berra's words, "like déjà vu all over again." She knew he drank a lot and partied. That was one of the reasons she was attracted to him. She also was aware that he was a womanizer. On one occasion before they were married, when he was supposedly out of town, she saw his car, went to his apartment, and found the lingerie of another woman strewn about. (She hung it outside to embarrass him, and her.) But the full story of Roger Clinton was far worse, to the point where he made Bill Blythe seem like a saint.[18]

Like Blythe, Roger Clinton had been married a number of times. Indeed, he was still married the day he betrothed Virginia. He owed his wife child support and was more than $2,000 behind in his payments. Far worse, Roger Clinton had been accused repeatedly of spousal abuse, including beating his wife with his fists and attacking her with the heel of her shoe. Notwithstanding his warmth, charm, humor, and party personality, Roger Clinton contained a streak of venal misogyny that more often than not was out of control. Feeding all this was the fact that Roger was an alcoholic.[19]

It was the drinking that fed—and highlighted—Roger's underlying pathology. "Drinking had been so much a part of Roger's and my relationship," Virginia later recounted, "that I really hadn't worried about his excesses in any sustained way." Ever the willful optimist, Virginia either did not see or chose to deny the dangers lurking just beneath the surface. But a routine developed. Virginia and Roger would go to a nightclub. Roger would gamble and drink too much. Virginia would have too many cocktails. Then she would flirt with her companions and Roger would erupt in anger. Over time, the drinking and fighting became the norm, not the exception. They screamed at each other, Roger accusing Virginia of trying to seduce and sleep with other men, Virginia upbraiding Roger for being out of control all the time. It was just like her mother and father, Virginia wrote, each partner berating the other with accusations of infidelity. Roger even took to following Virginia when she went off to work, convinced that she had scheduled a rendezvous with some unknown lover.[20]

The situation worsened. Roger owned a Buick dealership in Hope, purchased for him by his richer, more established brother. (It was viewed by most as inferior to the other major dealership in town, owned by the McLarty family, whose son Mack was a buddy of Bill's in kindergarten.) With declining money and status, Virginia and Roger decided to leave Hope when Billy was seven and move to Hot Springs. According to some, Roger lost his dealership in a crap game. According to others, he simply chose to sell. Besides, Hot Springs was a town more conducive to the couple's lifestyle. The tourist capital of Arkansas, it was famous for its nightclubs, casinos, and racetracks. All these soon became familiar haunts for Roger and Virginia. Now, with a new job at his brother's car dealership, Roger seemed settled financially. His brother also helped Virginia secure a job as a nurse anesthetist, though from the beginning she waged war with her fellow practitioners, especially the men whom she believed conspired against her because she was a woman.[21]

But whatever the economic stability they now enjoyed, the cancer at the heart of their relationship kept growing. Roger's drinking accelerated. The shouting matches became a nightly ritual. Physical violence reared its head. Once, back in Hope, Roger had become enraged when Virginia told him she was going to take Billy to visit her dying grandmother. He took a pistol and shot a bullet through the wall above her head. The police were called, and Roger spent the night in jail. There were no more such episodes. But in Hot Springs, with Roger drinking whiskey from tumblers, matters rocketed out of control. In 1959, when Bill was thirteen, Roger threw Virginia to the floor, and as she later reported, "began to stomp me, pulled my shoe off, and hit me on the head several times." Bill was home and called the family lawyer to report the episode. The next year, Bill heard his parents engaging in another nightly feud, with Roger, consumed by rage, accusing Virginia of seeing other men. According to Virginia's account, Bill rushed in and said

"Daddy, stand up. You must stand up to hear what I have to say . . . Hear me, never . . . *ever* touch my mother again." Bill himself later told a slightly different version. "I grabbed a golf club," he wrote, "and threw open their door. Mother was on the floor and Daddy was standing over her, beating on her. I told him to stop and said that if he didn't I was going to beat the hell out of him with the golf club. He just caved, sitting down in a chair next to the bed and hanging his head. It made me sick." Virginia called the police and Roger spent another night in jail.[22]

By then, Bill had a younger brother, named Roger after his father. One night Roger, five years old, heard "a strange noise—a sort of soft thud." He went into his parents' room and saw his father grabbing Virginia by the throat, with a pair of scissors in his other hand. Rushing next door, he called his brother: "Bubba, come quick! Daddy's killing Dado." When Bill arrived, he subdued his father and said, "You will never hurt either of them again. If you want them, you'll have to go through me." The sickness, however, would not go away. Eventually, Virginia sued for divorce, stating that "[Roger] has continually tried to do bodily harm to myself, and my son Bill." Bill himself told the court that "for the last four or five years, the physical abuse, nagging and drinking has become much worse." By that time, young Roger later said, his father was drunk 90 percent of the time.[23]

Tragically, the divorce lasted only a few months. Downtrodden and humiliated, Roger repented. He became deeply depressed, lost more than thirty pounds, went back to church, and every night found a way to sleep outside or on the front porch of the new home Virginia had purchased. He pleaded for forgiveness. Virginia called a family meeting to discuss what to do. "In my opinion," Bill told her, taking him back "would be a mistake." But caught up once more in her commitment to the positive and her denial of the negative, Virginia acquiesced, and the couple remarried. Predictably, the old patterns reasserted themselves—not the violence this time, but the verbal abuse, the drunkenness, and the jealousy.

Ironically, it was during the time Virginia and Roger were divorced that Bill decided to change his name legally to Clinton. Virginia saw it as a statement about "family solidarity," an extraordinary gesture both toward his younger brother, with whom he would now officially share a name, and "to big Roger, [whom Bill always called Daddy and] whom Bill loved and never stopped loving." Not only was the timing strange; so, too, was the motivation, particularly given Bill's opposition to Roger and Virginia's getting back together. But there was a brother named Roger Clinton. Perhaps more important, there was also an actual person named Roger Clinton. It would no longer be necessary to explain who Bill Blythe was.[24]

All these events shaped Bill Clinton in pivotal ways. It would be impossible to grow up in such a turbulent household without experiencing extraordinary trauma. The impact was even greater since for such a long period of time he was the only child. Already the focus of enormous emotional energy from his grandmother and grandfather, he became the idol of his mother, the single redemptive feature of her life, the vessel into which she could pour all her hopes and aspirations. He even played the same role for Virginia's husband, Roger, who—for all his faults—nevertheless cared deeply for his stepson.

But the pressures placed on Bill Clinton by virtue of his being the "special" son were only compounded by the experience of being the child in an alcoholic family where abuse was the order of the day. How to make things right? How to act in ways that would save the situation? What to do when buffeted by angry voices, with people unable to contain their emotions, people out of control? As David Maraniss has pointed out, Clinton's circumstances fit perfectly the literature about alcoholic families. If you are the only person sane enough to see the havoc being wrought, the only defender able to inject stability into chaos, you bear an excruciatingly heavy burden. You are the only anchor the family has, you are the one who bears the responsibility for making things better, you are the protector who can salvage the unsalvageable. You become the *family hero*, the person who can take charge, who everyone recognizes as the sole source of rescue, the emissary to the outside world who can make things right by bringing credit and praise to a family otherwise lost. Thus brother Roger described Bill as "my best friend, my guardian, my father, and my role model." Virginia observed that "even when he was growing up, Bill was father, brother, and son in this family. He *took care* of Roger and me . . . [He] was a special child . . . mature beyond his years." And Bill himself said, "I was the father."[25]

Through his own initiative, Bill started going to church at the age of eight, recognizing that people who were in need must seek help. Almost instinctively, he sought to garner attention and praise, becoming the centerpiece of every gathering he entered. While a student for two years at a Catholic school in Hot Springs, he tried to speak so much that a nun gave him a C for being a busybody, and when he moved to a public school, one classmate observed, "he just took over." He was the golden boy, the center of his family's hopes for rescue. His mother gave him the master bedroom in the house she moved to when she left Roger, his own car to drive to school each day, the veneration one would usually reserve for a box office idol. The adulation was welcome, but the burden was almost suffocating.[26]

To an extraordinary degree, Bill Clinton was aware of the trap in which he was caught. Writing an autobiographical essay in his junior year in high school—while the family drama raged around him—he noted: "I am a person motivated and influenced by so many diverse forces I sometimes question the sanity of my existence. I am a living paradox—deeply religious, yet not as convinced of my exact beliefs as I want to be; wanting responsibility, yet shirking it; loving the truth but often times giving away to falsity . . . I detest selfishness, but see it in the mirror every day." Caught between competing forces, he struggled to find a path to redemption for his family as well as fulfillment for himself. "Most of the time I was happy," he later said, "but I could never be sure I was as good as I wanted to be."[27]

These were penetrating observations for a junior in high school. Even more insightful were his reflections more than four decades later in his memoir, *My Life*. "We all have addictions," he once told Carolyn Staley, a next-door friend from childhood, but for the Clinton family growing up, alcoholism dominated all others. It was strange, the way it worked, Clinton wrote. "The really disturbing thing . . . is that it isn't always bad." Weeks could go by where "we'd enjoy being a family, blessed with the quiet joys of an ordinary life." During those times, it was easy to forget about the pain, or deny its impact. Clinton even acknowledged erasing from his memory the details of episodes in which he had been intimately involved, including when his mother called the police to

have Roger put in jail, or when Bill called the family lawyer after another episode of abuse. "I'd forgotten," he wrote, "perhaps out of the denial experts say families of alcoholics engage in when they continue to
live with [the disease]." Roger's alcoholism not only terrorized the family, it also induced a kind of schizophrenia, with family members pretending it did not exist when it was not in full display, or repressing its
fearsome reality lest it prove too much to cope with. In retrospect, Bill
Clinton wished fervently that he could have found someone to talk with
about what was happening. "But I didn't, so I had to figure it out for
myself."[28]

Perhaps that was the beginning of what became Bill Clinton's obsession with the "secrets" in his life. He never told anyone—even those
closest to him—what was taking place in his family, because these
were "the secrets of our house." But he did reflect at length on how central his secrets were to his entire personality. "They make our lives
more interesting," he wrote in his memoir. "The place where secrets are
kept can . . . provide a haven, a retreat from the rest of the world, where
one's identity can be shaped and reaffirmed, where being alone can
bring security and peace." But there was another side, too. "Secrets can
be an awful burden to bear, especially if some sense of shame is attached to them." Thus the pivotal experience of growing up in an alcoholic home generated in Clinton a lifelong conundrum: how to deal
with that which others did not know about you, how to deal with your
own feelings about those secrets, and perhaps above all, how and whether
ever to confront openly the presence of the unspeakable.

In a dramatic display of insight, Clinton shared with the readers of
his memoir his retrospective memory of how from the age of thirteen
on he dealt with these dilemmas. "I know," he wrote, "that it became a
struggle for me to find the right balance between secrets of internal
richness and those of hidden fears and shame, and that I was always
reluctant to discuss with anyone the most difficult parts of my personal
life." "Some of what came into my head," he recalled, "scared the living
hell out of me, including anger at Daddy, the first stirrings of sexual
feelings toward girls, and doubts about my religious convictions." But he
also recognized that his struggle resulted from "growing up in an alcoholic home and the mechanisms I developed to cope with it. It took me
a long time just to figure that out. It was even harder to learn which

secrets to keep, which to let go of, which to avoid in the first place. I am still not sure I understand that completely."[29]

If the secrets Clinton kept became one abiding theme of his life, they led directly to a second: his understanding that because of his secrets, he was condemned to living "parallel lives." The first of these consisted of "an external life that takes its natural course," the second "an internal life where the secrets are hidden." Because Clinton had no one to talk with about his internal life, he focused his energies on the external. "When I was a child," he wrote, "my outside life was filled with friends and fun, learning and doing." But his internal life, the one that existed behind closed doors and could never be shared, "was full of uncertainty, anger, and a dread of ever-looming violence." Later in life, Clinton recognized that "no one can live parallel lives with complete success; the two have to intersect." But for the moment, Clinton's two lives—and the secrets they reflected—shaped his adolescence, helping to set in motion the life course that would eventually propel him onto a national stage.[30]

In that process, Bill's mother played an ever larger role. While rarely if ever discussing the problems at home with him, she continued to exude calm, confidence, and the conviction that looking on the bright side of things was always the better option. She reached out to friends, went to the races as often as she could, and continued to party; and when Roger became unmanageable, she could rely on the husband of her best friend, a policeman, to drive him around town until he sobered up and his anger subsided. In the meantime, she taught Bill how to praise and flatter women, particularly the would-be beauty queens. As Carolyn Staley noted, Virginia would come home from a hard day at work and tell Bill, "'You know, nobody has told me all day long how cute I am.' And we would say to her, 'Virginia, you are just so cute.'" How to please and charm women was a lesson Bill would carry with him the rest of his life. And she gave him her own adoration in return, framing his prizes, medals, and photo portraits on a special wall, which his friends called "the shrine."[31]

Bill devoted his energies to achieving the recognition that would bring praise to the family and allow him to feel he was doing his part to make things right. A dominant presence in school, he became president of the Key Club (a kind of junior Kiwanis), a member of the National Honor Society, and an officer in the DeMolay, a sort of junior Masons. (Later he dropped out of DeMolay, a secret society. "I didn't need to be in a secret fraternity to have secrets," he said. "I had real secrets of my own.") "You could argue," Carolyn Staley later said, "that before he even left high school, he knew the leadership of the state." A band member, he played the saxophone, struck up an admiring, nurturing relationship with his band leader, and imagined a time when he might charm women with his playing. "Bill always had this sense about him that he collected girls," Staley told David Maraniss. "He had the eyes for girls everywhere." In all these activities, Staley remembered, Clinton loved to have people around him and would "make crowds happen. He had a psychological drive for it." Another friend, Patty Howe, noted that Bill "has never met a stranger since the day he was born."[32]

Exemplifying all these impulses was Clinton's brilliant campaign to become the state of Arkansas' nominee as senator for a national conference in Washington, D.C., of Boys Nation, the high school version of the American Legion. With single-mindedness, he set out to win the support of his colleagues at the Arkansas state convention of Boys Nation. By the time he had turned sixteen, Clinton later recalled, "I [had already] decided I wanted to be in public life as an elected official." Reading the politics of the Arkansas convention shrewdly, Clinton understood that his childhood friend from Hope, Mack McLarty, had the "governor" slot all wrapped up. But no one had a lock on the senate seat. So Clinton worked the dormitories where his classmates were staying, introducing himself to people, finding out who they were and what they cared about, seeking to develop a personal bond or connection.

But he was not just a glad-hander. The Arkansas meeting consisted of numerous mock debates on issues of national import. One of those was civil rights. Here, Clinton was crystal clear. From the time he hung out at his grandfather's store, he knew he cared about treating black people the same way that white people were treated. In the ninth grade, he had been the only person in his civics class who had supported Kennedy in the Kennedy-Nixon debate, and he became an even more fervent supporter after JFK called Coretta Scott King when her husband, Martin, was sentenced to hard labor in prison just before the election. Now he put those beliefs on the line, arguing courageously in support of a resolution supporting civil rights. His convictions—as well as his politicking—paid off. He won his race to be named one of the two Arkansas senators for the Washington, D.C., national convention.[33]

In yet another indicator of what was to come, Clinton displayed his singularity of purpose when the highlight of the entire D.C. convention took place, a Rose Garden ceremony with President John F. Kennedy. Clinton was determined to be as close to JFK as humanly possible. Already six feet three inches tall at age sixteen, he used his long strides to get ahead of almost all his peers at the White House, ending up only fifteen feet from where the president would speak. At the end of his remarks, JFK hesitated. Then, rather than head straight back to the Oval Office, he moved toward the crowd. Clinton pounced, becoming the first to stand next to the president. There, a White House photographer took the picture that represented the culmination of a perfect expedition—Bill Clinton standing with a beaming smile next to the man whose office he one day aspired to hold. It was the picture he wanted, it was the picture his mother wanted, it was the first step of many to fulfill his dream—of making things right for the Clinton family. A hero in Hot Springs because of what he had done, Billy Clinton now reveled in the honor and praise he received as he worked the lunch circuit of the Elks and other local gatherings to bask in his newfound fame. Whatever his stepfather, Roger, did to overcome his own debilitating disease, Bill Clinton had shown that he was intent on living for the entire family and bringing pride to its name.[34]

If anyone questioned the seriousness of that determination, Clinton's decision to pass up an education at the University of Arkansas to apply to Georgetown University in Washington as his only choice for college should have settled the issue. Clinton had asked his guidance counselor where he could study foreign affairs. The Georgetown School of Foreign Service was the answer. More diverse, less Catholic, and with a substantially higher percentage of women than the larger college at Georgetown, it seemed an ideal fit for Clinton. His mother was making $60,000 a year as a nurse anesthetist, and she was willing to pay for it. So he told Carolyn Staley: "I am going to go to Georgetown, and I am going to go on to grad school, and I am going to get the greatest education

I can and come home to Arkansas and put it to work for the people here." A clear plan, a powerful conviction.[35]

Nor did Clinton waste any time putting himself forward once he got there. A young Protestant southerner from Arkansas might ordinarily have been expected to feel marginal. It was, after all, a campus dominated by Northeastern Catholics. Not Clinton. "Bill fit in perfectly," his roommate Tom Campbell, a conservative Goldwater Republican from Long Island, reported. "Outwardly he bore no signs of homesickness . . . He was exactly where he wanted to be." A serious student, Clinton fit in perfectly with the generally conservative lifestyle of Georgetown. "As a class, perhaps as a generation," Tom Campbell said, "we were attuned to the rules. There were no wild men, alcohol was not a problem, and drugs were unheard of . . . We rarely drank to excess." The match could hardly have been better. Based on his experience at home, Clinton was terrified of alcohol, rarely had so much as a beer, and had never viewed liquor as essential to social interaction. For Clinton, it was peanut butter and banana sandwiches, junk food, and occasionally peanuts dumped into RC Cola that fueled a social gathering.[36]

As if to show how well he fit in, Clinton almost immediately started a campaign to become president of his freshman class. (He probably made the decision before he even arrived.) "Bill . . . wanted to meet everyone," Tom Campbell said, "and to remember their names." He worked the residence halls, learned personal details about the people he met, and pitched his campaign to modest, middle-of-the-road issues like parking and getting involved in student government. Clinton may not have been a carbon copy of the affluent, sophisticated Northeasterners who ran Georgetown's social life, but he turned that fact into a plus rather than a minus. To the surprise of some, but not Bill Clinton, he won election overwhelmingly, and he proceeded to get reelected his sophomore year. Only in his junior year did he lose, having become too well known as a "pol." His opponent that year, a bookish embodiment of an almost anti-Clinton approach, criticized him for being "too smooth," an early version of the "slick Willie" characterization that would later haunt Clinton in the White House. No matter. Clinton had already achieved his goal of becoming known across campus as a student leader.[37]

Clinton also perfected his capacity to cultivate those with power and prestige. In this case that meant the faculty—and later his home state senator J. William Fulbright. He charmed Carroll Quigley, the professor who taught the Civilization requirement, becoming one of only two students out of 230 to receive an A. Quigley told his class that great men slept very little, devoting themselves instead to the larger goals of improving the world; thereafter, Clinton limited himself to only five hours of rest per night. With Quigley, as with others, Clinton displayed an intuitive capacity to discern an instructor's favorite issues and predict the questions they would ask on their exams. Schmoozing with professors became almost as much second nature to Clinton as cultivating political support from his fellow students.[38]

Before long, he had also managed to get a job working on Capitol Hill in the office of Senator Fulbright. He had already met Fulbright at the Boys Nation conference in Washington, but now he wangled an appointment with Fulbright's chief of staff, securing one of the few part-time jobs available. There, too, he used his charm and affability to learn everything other staff members had to teach him. He worked in the documents office, clipped the newspapers, and took maximum advantage of the opportunity to roam the halls of Congress as he delivered messages to various congressional offices. His work complemented beautifully the classes he was taking, such as U.S. History and Diplomacy and Theory and Practice of Communism. Indeed, Clinton was becoming more and more engaged with understanding the lessons of the Vietnam War—soon they would dominate his life—and took pride in working for someone "who doubled the IQ of any room he entered."[39]

The Fulbright experience simply extended Clinton's 100 percent involvement in politics during his time at Georgetown. The previous summer (1966) he had returned to Arkansas to work in a bitterly contested gubernatorial primary between Frank Holt, a dignified, Fulbright-type, civilized politician who believed in playing fair, and Jim Johnson, an Orval Faubus–like segregationist who played dirty and resorted to smear tactics. Clinton spent the summer driving Mrs. Holt and her daughters around the state as they campaigned, talking politics for hours on end. Once Mrs. Holt let Bill make a speech in Hot Springs when his grandmother was present. It was a powerful education in the vicissitudes of campaigning and in the delicate balance that existed between the politics of hope and the politics of fear. Johnson ran a classic racist campaign, and "each day," Clinton would later recall, "we wake up with the scales tipping . . . one way or the other. If they go too far toward hopefulness, we can become naïve and unrealistic. If the scales tip too far the other way, we can get consumed by paranoia and hatred. In the South, the darker side of the scales has always been the bigger problem." Clinton believed that Holt was right to stay above the fray and not get down in the gutter with Johnson. But when Johnson defeated Holt, Clinton learned a harsh lesson.[40]

The depth of Clinton's absorption in the ways of politics grew with each year at Georgetown. "My formal studies increasingly fought a losing battle with politics," he later acknowledged. So much was happening. Clinton's dedication to the issue of civil rights had only intensified. When he had watched Dr. Martin Luther King, Jr., deliver his "I Have a Dream" sermon at the March on Washington, "I started crying," he recalled, "and wept for a good while after Dr. King finished. He had said everything I believed, far better than I ever could. More than anything I ever experienced, except perhaps the power of my grandfather's example, that speech steeled my determination to do whatever I could for the rest of my life to make Martin Luther King, Jr.'s dream come true." Like a plumb line, civil rights ran as a constant through Clinton's life. "Nothing had as profound an effect on Bill's life," his roommate Tom Campbell said, than when Dr. King was assassinated in Memphis. "Bill was more in tune with what King meant to black people than the rest of us." When Carolyn Staley came to visit him the day after the assassination, they drove together to the black neighborhoods of Washington, distributed food and medical supplies to people who had been victimized by the riots, and cried together.[41]

Clinton was also touched deeply by Robert F. Kennedy. Always devoted to the Kennedy family, at Georgetown, Clinton had early become a fast friend of Tommy Caplan, a well-off New Yorker whose family had known JFK and who had done volunteer work at the White House. Caplan took Clinton to meet Evelyn Lincoln, JFK's private secretary, as she was working on the former president's personal papers. If anything, Clinton was even more attached to the president's brother, with his passion for civil rights, for helping the poor, and for providing every American a chance to move forward. "He radiated raw energy," Clinton said. "He's the only man I ever saw who could walk stoop-shouldered, with his head down, and still look like a coiled spring about to release into the air." RFK, he later said, was "the first New Democrat . . . He understood in a visceral way that progressive politics requires the advocacy of both new policies and fundamental values, both far-reaching change and social stability." In fundamental ways, Clinton saw Robert Kennedy as embodying the politics he hoped to practice.[42]

For Clinton as for everyone else, 1968 became a year of destiny. The war in Vietnam deeply troubled him, as much because of its stupidity as because of its betrayal of American values. "His objection," Tom Campbell noted, "was not that the U.S. was immoral but that we were making a big mistake. He wondered how a great nation could admit that and change course. He thought America was wasting lives that it could not spare." At night they would argue about the draft over dinner. Campbell was going to join the Marines after graduating. Clinton supported Kennedy in the Democratic primary contest, viewing Eugene McCarthy, the other antiwar candidate, as someone who would "rather be home reading Saint Thomas Aquinas than going into a tarpaper shack to see how poor people lived." But in all of this, Clinton remained moderate in his political pronouncements.

That would be a Clinton hallmark—to be a player, but not to leave the boundaries of the game. "Though I was sympathetic to the zeitgeist [of 1968]," he later wrote, "I didn't embrace the lifestyle or the radical rhetoric. My hair was short. I didn't even drink, and some of the music was too loud and harsh for my taste. I didn't hate LBJ; I just wanted to end the war, and I was afraid the culture clashes would undermine, not advance, the cause."[43]

In the meantime, he continued the effort to understand what his own life was about and how he could make sense of the secrets he was carrying inside him. Roger Clinton had been diagnosed with cancer. Refusing radical surgery, he reconciled himself to ameliorative care. For her part, Virginia had emotionally distanced herself from the relationship. And as a consequence of the brutal violence toward Virginia that he had seen, his younger brother, Roger, now hated his father. But Bill remained engaged. A part of him had always cared deeply for the man he called Daddy, appreciating those times when he had been a real father, doting on him, taking him to ballgames, showing what a caring parent could mean. Now Bill took over the role of parent.

At one point, after his mother told him the whole family had gone to church, Bill wrote, addressing Roger, to say how much he hoped that practice would continue. "None of us can have any peace, [Daddy]," he said, "unless they can face life with God, knowing that good always outweighs bad." There were two things in particular that he wanted to convey, Bill said in his letter. "1) I don't think you have ever realized how much we all love you. 2) I don't think you have ever realized either how much we have all been hurt . . . but still really have *not* turned against you." "Remember," he concluded, "don't be afraid to look for help *before* you do something you're sorry for—Don't be ashamed to admit your problem."[44]

Roger Clinton's final months brought some form of closure to the relationship that so fearsomely shaped Bill Clinton's life. As Roger's condition grew worse, doctors decided that treatment at Duke Hospital in Durham, North Carolina, offered the best hope for prolonging his life and easing his death. Roger took their advice. Although Duke Hospital was a five-hour drive from Washington, Bill visited his father virtually every weekend. He described those visits as long and languid. He and his father spoke more openly and intimately than ever before. "We came to terms with each other," Bill later wrote, "and he accepted the fact that I loved and forgave him. If he could only have faced life with the same courage and sense of honor with which he faced death, he would have been quite a guy."

The family went to Easter services at Duke Chapel, a magnificent Gothic cathedral, where together they joined in the triumphal hymn "Sing with All the Sons of Glory." While Virginia felt it to be a "healing time," for her son Roger, the death watch was an ordeal. Having prayed for years that his father would stay sober, only to see him turn drunk and violent, he now "prayed for him to die and he wouldn't die. That's when I got sick of praying." But for Bill, his father's death was liberating. The memories remained, the secrets were still hidden, the parallel lives moved forward. But at least there had been a good-bye that permitted some expression of love.[45]

•

Whatever else Roger's death resolved, it never touched the largest legacy of Bill's childhood—his inability to develop a consistent relationship with women. He came close when he first arrived at Georgetown. Shortly after he started classes, he began to date Denise Hyland, whom he asked to the Diplomats Ball months ahead of time. Described by his roommate Tom Campbell as "a statuesque blonde from New Jersey," Hyland might have seemed on the surface to match the "beauty queen" model of the opposite sex that Virginia had taught her sons to seek out. But Hyland was much, much more. Open, inquisitive, engaged with his total personality, Hyland brought out all of Bill Clinton's best qualities— his intellectualism, his spirituality, his enthusiasm for politics and for a life of service. The two dated for his first three years at Georgetown. They spent long evenings together talking about their futures, sometimes on the Capitol steps, sometimes at the Lincoln Memorial. He went to see her family in New Jersey, she came to see his in Arkansas. She even went with him to see his father at Duke Hospital. When they were apart, they wrote long letters daily. "Maybe I am beginning to realize," he wrote her at one point, "that I am almost grown, and will soon have to choose that one final motive in life which I hope will put a little asterisk by my name in the billion pages of the book of life." It seemed the model of a lasting, intimate relationship in which they could tell each other anything and everything. But Bill never spoke a word to her about Roger's alcoholism, his abusive behavior in the family, or the devastating impact all of that had on Bill and everyone else involved.[46]

By 1968, Clinton had broken off his romance with Hyland, though he still wrote to her regularly. Instead, he started playing the field, "like a guy getting out of prison," a friend said. Once it was known he was available, women flocked to him. At the Capitol he was assigned by the Fulbright office to drive Sharon Ann Evans, Miss Arkansas, around Washington. She would be a frequent companion for years thereafter. The following summer, he started a relationship with his oldest and dearest friend from Hot Springs, Carolyn Staley. At Christmas that year she had given him a welcome-home kiss that was different from the usual sisterly peck on the cheek. "My God, where did you learn to kiss like that?" he had asked. But Staley wanted a serious relationship, not just to be one of a posse of girlfriends. She soon discovered that that was not in the cards. When she came to Washington to visit Clinton at the time of the King assassination, Clinton had already started to date another woman, Ann Markusen, who also wanted and expected a serious relationship. "The guys at the house were furious with Bill for not being honest," Staley said. "I would be in the house [with Bill] and he would be on the phone with Ann."[47]

The pattern of multiple simultaneous relationships not only continued, it got worse. That summer he was dating three women at the same time and writing Denise Hyland daily. Staley remained deeply interested, but one day she went next door to Bill's house after church, and looking through the window saw him kissing Sharon Evans passionately. "I needed honesty," she said. "He hadn't ever said to me, 'I'm going to start dating Sharon now, so you're not my girlfriend anymore.'" Staley—who remained Clinton's devoted lifelong friend— thought long and hard about whether there was any future with this man she loved. In the end she decided the answer was no. "I always had been living in the world of monogamous relationships," she said, "and that was my ideal. And with him, I couldn't have real peace about whether that would be." Clinton would never be faithful. He now openly displayed a system of behavior full of dishonesty and egomania. He compartmentalized the women in his life, sequestering them into different categories, while feeling no compunction to reconcile his emotions into a coherent whole. This new penchant for multiple relationships fed a life of secrecy and reinforced his instinct to live parallel lives.[48]

The one consistent feature of Bill Clinton's maturing years was the steadiness of his climb to fame. A renowned campus figure, he knew countless politicians, including his home state senators, Fulbright and John L. McClellan. He had already told Carolyn Staley that he would go to graduate school before returning to Arkansas to serve the people there. But where to go? Why not Oxford, he decided. Fulbright had been a Rhodes scholar in the 1930s, and he encouraged his protégé to pursue the same course. Clinton was bright, curious, willing to take on any challenge. He had just written a 28-page paper on the Gulf of Tonkin resolution with 92 footnotes. And most important, he knew how to game the system. He understood how much his chances were improved because he was a southerner and from a small state. All he needed to do was to burnish his credentials. Although a record as an athlete was not a prerequisite for a Rhodes, some association with sports could not hurt. So Clinton became chair of the Student Athletic Commission at Georgetown. He performed brilliantly in his state interviews, then aced the regional finals in New Orleans. Crying, wishing his father could have lived to see this, he called Virginia and said, "Well, Mother, how do you think I'll look in English tweeds?" With an almost flawless track record, Bill Clinton had moved one more step toward fulfilling the role of family hero.[49]

It had been an extraordinary journey, shaped by three primary forces distinctive to the Clinton family.

The first had been the death of Bill Blythe. It is impossible to read the words of Bill Clinton, then and now, without being overwhelmed by a sense of mortality—and ambition—that came from being born without a father. To be sure, his grandfather had filled that role admirably for a period, but he, too, died early. While campaigning for Frank Holt in Arkansas in 1966 with Holt's wife and daughters, Clinton took them to visit Bill Blythe's grave. In a note to Denise Hyland describing the experience, he wrote, "It was a good reminder that I have a lot of living to do for two other fellows who never even got close to the average lifespan."[50]

Over and over again, Clinton returned to this theme, never more poignantly than in his memoir. "My father," he wrote, "left me with the feeling that I had to live for two people, and that if I did it well enough, somehow I could make up for the life he should have had. And his memory infused me, at a younger age than most, with a sense of my own mortality." There was no actual memory of his father, of course, except in the remembrances passed down through his mother. But the import of the message was clear: "The knowledge that I, too, could die young drove me both to try to drain the most out of every moment of life and to get on with the next big challenge. Even when I wasn't sure where I was going, I was always in a hurry." Thus the impulse to live fully, to waste not a moment, to squeeze from each day every drop of learning and gratification he could find, all traced back to his desire to redeem the life of the father he had never known—before his own life was taken away.[51]

The second force shaping Clinton arose from his experience growing up in a home racked by alcoholism, child and spouse abuse, and the tyranny of marital jealousy. Over and over again, Clinton talked of his love for his stepfather and his gratitude for the moments of affection, attention, and nurturance that Roger had offered. He would never have called him Daddy with such warmth if there had not been a core to the relationship. But that core was eaten away so persistently by Roger's binge drinking, the cruelty of his jealous rage toward Virginia, and the violent explosions that rocked their home that barely a remnant still existed. It was enough to sustain a measure of affection and care, never more visibly demonstrated than in Bill's repeated trips to Durham to see his dying stepfather. In the end, though, the experience with the ravages of alcoholism created a personal dynamic in which Bill Clinton felt called upon to rescue his family, make it whole, and turn the world right again. Like a religious compulsion, this mission consumed Clinton's life, adding depth, focus, and intensity to the passion he already felt for living life for both his lost father and himself.

The third, and perhaps most important, force shaping Bill Clinton's life was his mother. "It was she," he wrote in his memoir, "who taught me to get up every day and keep going; to look for the best in people even when they saw the worst in me; to be grateful for every day and greet it with a smile . . . to believe that, in the end, love and kindness would prevail over cruelty and selfishness . . . if God is love, she was a godly woman."[52]

But she was more as well. A striking individualist, she consistently refused to be confined to a niche. From her ninety-minute-per-day sessions putting on makeup to her brazen contempt for old-fashioned deference to medical professionals, she set her own path. She cared little whether others joined or followed her. When her mother imperiously seized control over raising Virginia's new infant son, Virginia bolted to New Orleans, intent on becoming an independent professional in her own right. She was strong-willed and impetuous. In each of her first two marriages, she ignored, denied, or did not care about evidence that the men she was marrying had lied to her. Refusing to acknowledge or recognize that which she did not wish to see, she helped encourage her two sons, as well, to avoid confronting the implications of living in a dysfunctional family. Her own inability to deal with the secrets of her life, and her commitment to pursue her own parallel lives, helped make the same pattern a central theme of Bill's life.

Nor were her personal choices of dress, presentation, and behavior irrelevant to the way Bill learned to view women. In addition to her passion for makeup—the symbolic equivalent each day of putting on a multilayered mask that would prevent people from seeing the real person underneath—she insisted on playing the role of a coquette, flirting outrageously, getting up on stage after a couple of drinks to take her place among the performers, living the high life of gambling, partying loudly, and letting everyone know that she set her own rules. When working in the garden outside at home, she dressed in a sexy tube top with short shorts, daring neighbors to be scandalized by her appearance. Beauty queens, she wrote, represented "the image of womanhood my boys grew up with—starting at home with their coiffed and painted mother, and extending to the girls they squired to the proms." Growing up in a household dominated by such a female presence could not help but have an impact on the kind of women Bill Clinton was attracted to and how he behaved with them. By the time he finished Georgetown, he had already embarked on his own version of placing women into two categories—those who fit the "beauty queen" image he had learned at home, and those he saw as serious lifelong companions. Although Denise Hyland, Ann Markusen, and Carolyn Staley fell into the second category, he now seemed unwilling or unable to avoid mixing those relationships with women in the first category, the various beauty queens and "hot babes" he dated. The problem was that to persist in such behavior, he would have to compartmentalize his relationships, keep them from intersecting with one another, not see them as part of an integrated life. They would have to remain "secrets," part of his parallel lives. The only thing that was clear, even then, was that the person he asked to be his wife would have to be in the group who qualified as lifelong companions.

"The woman I marry," he told Carolyn Staley during his senior year in college, "is going to be very independent. She's going to work outside the house. She needs to have her own interests and her own life and not be wrapped up entirely in my life." It was a prophetic statement, but not

one that prevented Clinton from embarking on a life of relating to
women that could only be described as schizophrenic and that in profound ways continued to reflect the influence of his mother.[53]

The Bill Clinton who graduated from Georgetown and headed off
to Oxford was not a simple personality. The only feature that was abundantly clear from Boys Nation to the Rhodes fellowship was his commitment to be the "best in his class," in David Maraniss's words. Nothing
would stand in Clinton's way as he cultivated friends, organized supporters, and networked with people of influence to put in place the
foundation for his quest to make a difference, both for the people he
hoped to serve and for his own family's reputation and well-being.
Deeply conscious both of his own mortality and his need to live for two
people, he understood instinctively how to ferret out the path to power.
Even as a senior in college, he had impressed his classmate Jim Moore
with his insight into Arkansas politics. Intimately familiar already with
the courthouse networks, he told Moore that the best way to proceed
was to be elected attorney general of Arkansas and then governor. From
Moore's perspective, the only thing that remained unclear was how
Clinton would define his challenges as he moved forward. Even then,
his friends—male and female—freely predicted that he would become
president.[54]

Less clear was how Clinton would grapple with the more complicated legacy of his youth. The path to political power offered the most
accessible way to bring honor to his family, to make right all that was
wrong about his adolescent years. But the principal influences animat-
ing his quest remained largely unexamined and unresolved—how to fill
the void left by an absent father, how to address the secrets generated
by growing up in a family torn by jealousy and alcoholism, how to bring
integration to a pattern of living separate and parallel lives. At Georgetown he had made a start toward preparing "for the life of a practicing
politician." Now, at Oxford, he would try to find a path that would allow
him to bring personal conviction into balance with "the pressures of
political life."

TWO

Hillary Rodham:
The Early Years

Hillary Rodham grew up in Park Ridge, Illinois, a middle-class suburb of Chicago. It was Republican and it was white. No black families lived there, no Asians, no Jews, no Hispanics. Everyone went to church, paid their taxes, voted conservative, and lived a respectable life of conformity. Most households fit the picture of bourgeois comfort associated with the iconic portrait of suburbia in television sitcoms of the 1950s. It was a town, a subsequent *Washington Post* article said, where the children "were all running in and out of one another's back yards, selling lemonade . . . playing Parcheesi and checkers," and going to amusement parks. It was seemingly idyllic, and Hillary Rodham portrayed it as such. In her memoir, *Living History*, she recalled that she "adored" her father and every night would run down the street to greet him as he came home from work. "I grew up in a family that looked like it was straight out of *Father Knows Best*," she wrote in *It Takes a Village*.[1]

But in the view of many, the realities of the Rodham family profoundly contradicted that idealized portrait. Far from nurturing an environment of love and mutual support, the family often was dominated by hostility and authoritarianism. Rather than provide a model of mutual affection, it frequently degenerated into a brittle verbal truce between avowed combatants. If Bill Clinton's family experience growing up featured physical abuse on a regular basis, Hillary Rodham's family experience witnessed psychological abuse, more subtle perhaps, but no less consequential in its impact.

At the heart of the Rodham household was Hillary's father, Hugh. The son of Welsh immigrants, he had worked with his father in the coal mines near Scranton, Pennsylvania, and then later in the lace mills where they made drapes and curtains. Attending the University of Pennsylvania on a football scholarship (he was third string), when Hugh graduated, he returned to the lace mills. Soon he started to sell drapes. Eventually, he developed his own business, a one-man show. He would solicit orders from theaters or offices, return to his business to make up the drapes, then go back and hang them. He eventually added a secretary (subsequently his wife) and, later in life, a black handyman whom he did not treat well. Tough, thrifty, and hard-headed, Hugh was a throwback to a different age. When almost every man in Park Ridge commuted to the city to work for some large corporation, Hugh was on his own.

He was proud of his home, and he insisted on buying a new Cadillac each year as a sign of his success, but otherwise he had almost nothing in common with the other fathers—and families—who lived nearby. Neither outgoing nor affable, he came across as a loner without social skills. Depression ran through his family. A brother tried to commit suicide. Hugh often sat through an evening by himself, saying nothing. According to Carl Bernstein, author of a biography of Hillary, he "seemed to push through adulthood in a fog of melancholia."[2]

Most distressing, he often treated his children with a condescension that bordered on contempt. His son Hugh, Jr., described him as "gruff . . . confrontational, completely and utterly so." If a child left the cap off a tube of toothpaste, Hugh would throw the cap out the bathroom window into the bushes below—even if it was snowing—and order the child to go get it. His overall demeanor was perhaps best summarized by his iron rule that no matter how frigid the Illinois winter night might be, he would always turn off the heat before going to bed. In his better moments, he played pinochle with the children. He also taught Hillary to read the stock tables on the financial pages. But in general, he stinted on praise and verged on excess in exhorting his children to do better. When Hillary came home with a report card of all A's and one B, he focused on the B. "You did well," he would tell her, "but couldn't you do better?" And when her brother, playing quarterback for the Park Ridge team, had a stellar night completing ten of eleven passes, Hugh berated him for not having completed all of them. In the view of Carl Bernstein, Hugh's rigid authoritarianism "was mitigated only by the distinctly modern notion that Hillary would not be limited in opportunity or skills by the fact that she was a girl." Picking up on the latter point, Hillary's younger brother said "Little Hillary could do no wrong. She was Daddy's girl." But the historian Roger Morris, writing in his book *Partners in Power*, was less kind. "Among both relatives and friends," he said, "many thought Hugh Rodham's treatment of his daughter and sons amounted to the kind of psychological abuse that might have crushed some children."[3]

Dorothy Rodham, Hillary's mother, represented the polar opposite of her husband. Dorothy's own experience growing up could hardly have been bleaker. When she was born, her mother was fifteen, her father seventeen. At age eight, her parents abandoned her, sending Dorothy and her three-year-old sister on a cross-country rail trip—alone—to stay with their grandparents. Dorothy's grandmother treated her cruelly, worked her to the bone, and confined her to her room when she had finished her tasks. Somehow she survived, and six years later she managed to get a job as a nanny with a family that treated her warmly. Eventually, she moved back to Chicago, where her mother had remarried. But her mother, like her grandmother, wished for her only to be a housemaid, so she left. It was at that time she secured employment with Hugh Rodham as a secretary. Dorothy's stepfather, Max Rosenberg, helped Hugh with his business, and eventually Hugh married Dorothy and they moved to Park Ridge, where they soon started their own family.[4]

Dorothy's greatest passion was to make sure that Hillary encountered none of the debilitating disadvantages that had made her years of growing up so painful. She encouraged Hillary's aspirations—she urged her to be the first woman Supreme Court justice—and instilled in her the teachings of the Methodist church, where Dorothy was a devoted Sunday school teacher. She insisted as well that Hillary learn to stand up for herself. In what she called the "defining story of [Hillary's] childhood," Dorothy recounted the time when Hillary came home complaining of being bullied by a neighborhood girl. Dorothy told her, "You're going to have to [fight back]. The next time she hits you I want you to hit her back." Which in due course Hillary did, socking her young friend, then running home to tell her mother, "I can play with the boys now." Which she did. "She just took charge," her mother said, "and they let her."

Hillary became very assertive, insisted on talking about politics, not just "girl" things, and soon she was leading the pack. Above all, Dorothy taught Hillary never to underestimate her talents, her potential, or the value of her education. Going to school, Dorothy told her, was "a great adventure . . . She was going to learn great things, live new passions." Hillary embraced her mother's motivation, and with a zest that could only make her mother burst with pride, she seized every opportunity to surge to new heights of achievement and recognition.[5]

Yet Dorothy's greatest task was to prevent her children from being repressed by the rigid authoritarianism of Hugh, and by his persistent disrespect for her. Frequently they argued at the dinner table. Often in the evening they could be heard yelling at each other. When Dorothy would stand up for herself, Hugh's typical response was, "[Now] where did you come up with such a stupid idea, Miss Smarty Pants?" He could be nasty with his words to the point of cruelty. When she threatened to leave, he would say contemptuously, "Don't let the doorknob hit you in the ass on the way out." One of Hillary's school friends, Betsy Ebeling, was appalled at Hugh's disrespect for his wife and the verbal abuse he subjected her to. She wondered how Dorothy could stay married to such a bully. Ebeling found Dorothy to be sad, beaten down, and isolated, living through her children: "It was very important to her that her children be happy. I don't think she thought she could be happy." Dorothy called Hugh "Mr. Difficult," but she determined that rather than leave the marriage, she would stick with it, make the family work, and through her persistence and strength, enable her children to thrive rather than go through the suffering she had experienced with a broken family.[6]

In the end, Dorothy instilled in her daughter, as well as in the larger family, the pivotal importance of getting their priorities straight. For her, there could be no higher priority than keeping the family intact. "The more Hugh Rodham disparaged and heaped scorn on his wife," Carl Bernstein wrote, "the more she resolved to stay out of his way and ignore his provocation." Dorothy had a higher goal—the well-being of her children, and giving them an unbroken pathway to fulfillment. Over and over again, Dorothy's daughter-in-law Nicole Boxer noted, "It was drummed into me by Dorothy that nobody in this family gets divorced . . . She'd say, 'You can work it out. Don't give up on him. *You do not leave this marriage.*'" Hillary watched and listened and learned. She would find a way to live with her father and put aside his negative behavior while focusing on the ways she could win his respect and affection. Her mother's example inspired and shaped her own way of dealing with adversity.[7]

Family togetherness, Hillary wrote in *It Takes a Village*, was paramount. "Children without fathers, or whose parents float in and out of their lives after divorce, are precarious little boats in the most turbulent seas." Her mother had taught her the importance of maintaining equilibrium. Using a carpenter's level as her instructional tool, Dorothy told Hillary, "Imagine having this carpenter's level inside you . . . Try to keep that bubble in the center. Sometimes it will go way up here, and you have to bring it back." Keeping the family together was key to holding the bubble in the center. Hillary would never forget that.[8]

In the meantime she soared in her appointed role to make the most of all her talents. Although Hillary knew she might not be the very brightest student in her class, she was determined to be the most active, the most visible, and the most accomplished. Hillary mastered the art of student participation. A teacher's pet, she volunteered for countless assignments. As a Girl Scout, she piled up badges one after the other. As a student athlete, she played the gamut of sports from softball to tennis to soccer. She was a superb debater, a member of the student council and prom committee, a leader in student politics, and a writer for the school yearbook and the student newspaper. In the summer, she became a junior lifesaver and learned how to manage a canoe.[9]

How she dealt with being female in the male-dominated culture of adolescence in the early sixties proved particularly revealing. A classmate described Hillary as "womanish," not "girlish"—perhaps an appropriate distinction for one who held a clear sense of her own equality with boys and persisted with an inner determination never to play a feminine, subordinate, or "sexy" role just to secure male attention. Hugh's parsimony probably helped. He refused to buy her expensive or stylish clothes, and even for the prom, her dress was modest at best. Hillary was attractive, but not beautiful. She never slaved over her appearance, shunned makeup, and had a head of hair that, according to her friend Betsy Ebeling, had "a mind of its own." Making fun of her, the school paper predicted that she might become a nun and dubbed her "Sister Frigidaire." Hillary Rodham was a figure unto herself, one who expected to stand on her own, to be open about her nascent feminism. When she was fourteen, she anounced her desire to become a

female astronaut. After she was defeated for the presidency of her senior class, she blamed "dirty campaigning" by her male opponents, and
she was outraged when one boy declared that she "was 'really stupid if
I thought a girl could be elected president.'"[10]

Probably the most important influence on Hillary Rodham during
her adolescent years was the Methodist church she attended, especially
its MYF, the Methodist Youth Fellowship. In countless communities
across America, such youth fellowship groups helped galvanize a social
conscience among young people. Dorothy Rodham had already made
the church a central part of Hillary's life through her own teaching.
Dorothy organized a special summer project to work with Mexican
American migrant families and help provide child care for them. Far
more liberal than Hugh, she was the first to introduce Hillary to the
notion of living one's faith. As Hillary later said, her family "talked
with God, walked with God, ate, studied and argued with God."[11]

But the critical figure in that transformation was a young youth
minister named Don Jones. Arriving in Park Ridge from the seminary
in 1961 in his bright red Impala convertible, Jones took the MYF group
by storm. His goal was to make the youth group a study of "faith in action." It was a total immersion in the theology of the social gospel.
Jones had the students read selections from the theologians Reinhold
Niebuhr and Paul Tillich, study literature by E. E. Cummings and T. S.
Eliot, and learn the meaning of sacrifice by examining the life story of
Dietrich Bonhoeffer, the German minister who led the resistance
against Adolf Hitler and was executed when his campaign of political
activism failed. This was heady stuff, enough to turn a young person's
life around and create a whole new vision of what it might mean to be
a servant of God. Dorothy Rodham loved Jones. She regarded him as
truly her "brother in Christ," and for Hillary, he became the same—a
second father figure, a source of abiding inspiration.[12]

With Dorothy's complete support, Hillary joined Jones on a series
of trips to the inner city of Chicago, where she encountered firsthand
the meaning of the social gospel. Jones took the youth group to black
and Hispanic churches where they could meet young people their
own age but with an experience dramatically different from theirs.
On one occasion he had the youth groups from the suburbs and the inner city look together at Picasso's painting *Guernica*, with its harrowing

depictions of civil war and terrorism in Spain. Not surprising to Jones, perhaps, but very surprising to others, the inner city young people saw features of the painting that the suburban kids never did. To one young black girl, the painting evoked all too powerfully her encounters with violence in her own neighborhood.[13]

Jones also took the young people to hear Martin Luther King, Jr., preach in South Chicago. Interestingly, Hillary heard King twice that year because her grandfather, Dorothy's stepfather, Max Rosenberg, who thought of himself as progressive, also took her to hear King at the Chicago Sunday Evening Club. But the Jones-sponsored trip was the more memorable. King had different sermons he preached around America. One was "Saint Paul's Letter to the Church in America," in which he imagined what the apostle Paul would say to the body of Christ in America, which was the "most segregated institution in the country." But another—and the one Hillary heard—was entitled "Remaining Awake Through a Great Revolution." Using a Rip Van Winkle introduction, King asked his congregations not to sleep through the greatest challenge in their history. He concluded with the peroration, "The end of life is not to be happy, but to do the will of God come what may." Hillary thought she understood what those words meant.[14]

Hillary's encounter with Don Jones did not immediately transform her political perspective. The other major focus of her extracurricular life in high school was the social studies club she attended, led by her civics teacher, Paul Carlson. Like so many high school teachers at that time, Carlson warned of Communist infiltration everywhere, told students to be sure to turn in those who were suspicious, and venerated people like Senator Joseph McCarthy and General Douglas MacArthur. Every other week or so, Carlson held meetings of his social studies club to help inculcate into his students the conservative values he prized so highly. Consistent with those values, and with her father's politics, Hillary became a "Goldwater Girl," and as she got ready to graduate from high school, she took to the streets to canvass for the Republican nominee for president in 1964.[15]

But on balance, the influence that stayed with Hillary Rodham the longest was that introduced by Don Jones and her mother. Appropriately, *motive* magazine, the publication of the youth division of the Methodist church, remained one of her guiding inspirations as she prepared for college. A subscription was given to her by Don Jones, with whom she remained in touch for years to come (he was eventually forced out of her church for being too radical). As with much else, Hillary did not go to extremes in her religious life. There were no dramatic conversions, no epiphanies. Rather, she focused on the moral dimensions of every-day experience, the degree to which good works fit the scheme of God for moral salvation. As one of her later aides said, "Hillary's faith is *the link* . . . It explains the missionary zeal with which she attacks her issues . . . And it also explains [her] really extraordinary self-discipline and focus." Religion would remain at the core of who she was, the north star of her moral compass. "Some people go to shrinks," the aide contin-ued; "she does it by being a Methodist."[16]

Now in the top 5 percent of her class, one of eleven finalists for a National Merit Scholarship, and voted by her classmates the person "most likely to succeed," Hillary Rodham headed off to Wellesley Col-lege. Her mother had succeeded in her fondest ambition. Hillary had survived the family trauma, made strong by her mother's faith and above all by her willingness to sacrifice her personal feelings for a higher pur-pose. Wellesley may have been an elitist institution that catered to the upper crust of society. But it was also a women's college that preserved at its core a commitment to the life of the mind and to the equality of women with men. As one of her boyfriends during the college years noted, she had "grown up and out of the materialistic mind set which is typical of affluent suburbs . . . She was not interested in making money . . . [Rather, she was] a progressive, an ethical Christian, and a political activist." Dorothy Rodham and Don Jones had done their job well.[17]

When Hillary arrived at Wellesley, she came with an agenda, a mo-dus operandi well established in high school. She would use these four years, as she had used her years in high school, to be a moral leader—on her own terms—but within the mainstream community, not outside it. The tone of her approach was perhaps best summarized in a letter she wrote to Don Jones. Is it possible, she asked, to be "a mind conservative and a heart liberal?" Initially discomfited at being a simple midwest-erner in a preppy, sophisticated, and highly elitist environment full of private school graduates, Hillary soon gave up her immediate impulse to go home and instead threw herself into campus politics. Although she was already liberal on race, and concerned about the Vietnam War, one of her first steps was to get elected as president of the Wellesley Republican Club. (Her father was already concerned about her reading *The New York Times* and leaning toward feminism.) That way, she could preserve her relatively conservative base while moving outward to more liberal concerns. A fan of Nelson Rockefeller and New York's new mayor, John Lindsay, her political instincts were right of center, but in flux.[18]

That fall, Hillary started to date Geoffrey Shields, a Harvard student, also from Illinois, whom she saw every weekend throughout her first three years in college. Carl Bernstein, who read the correspondence between the two, has written that "her letters to him . . . reveal her to be soft, thoughtful, alive with the possibilities of youth, dreamy, romantic, passionate." Those were the days of strict parietal regulations at women's colleges. Men might visit on Sundays from 2:00 to 5:30, but the door must always be open, and the "two feet" rule (two feet always on the floor and visible through the partially open doorway) made even heavy petting fairly difficult. But theirs was a strong, healthy, and intimate partnership, reinforced by shared intellectual concerns and a commitment to social issues. "The thing I remember most were the conversations," Shields said. They would go to Beatles parties at Winthrop House, a Harvard residence, but always end up talking about morality. People must act, Hillary would say, quoting *Doctor Zhivago*: "Man is born to live, not to prepare for life."

None of these issues was more important than civil rights. Shields had a black roommate at Harvard, and very often they would end up in intense discussions about the civil rights issues with which Hillary had first become engaged in Illinois through Don Jones. Hillary retained a strong commitment to racial equality, reflected in her highly self-conscious decision to bring a black girl to a local church with her (well advertised by telephone calls in advance) and then to undertake a volunteer tutoring program in the predominantly black Roxbury neighborhood of Boston. But at a time of increased tension within the civil rights movement between radicals and moderates, Hillary retained her commitment to the more reformist positions advanced by Dr. Martin Luther King, Jr., rejecting the "extremism" of Stokely Carmichael. Continuing with her movement toward more liberal causes, she spent the summer after her first year conducting research for a former Wellesley professor who was writing a book on Vietnam.[19]

Throughout this period, Hillary Rodham retained that equilibrium her mother so prized—the bubble at the center of the political terrain. Warm, generous, and attentive to others, she navigated the shoals of campus politics with poise and confidence. Sometimes she would use people, such as the student newspaper editor, to help promote her agenda. But, the editor recalled, "she had a wonderful way of doing that . . . She did not . . . leave you in shreds [or] . . . make you feel like a pawn. It was an empowering process." Another classmate described Hillary's "particular charisma. Her ability to focus and her maturity made her stand out even in a place of very, very talented women." Certainly there were times when she overstepped. According to Wellesley's president, Ruth Adams, Hillary was "not always easy to deal with if you were disagreeing with her." Strong-willed, she did not easily take no for an answer or brook dissent. Nor did she spontaneously disclose her innermost self—many commented on the degree to which she kept her private life private. But her "even keel," which made such personal revelations unlikely in the first place, helped to sustain a slow and steady course. As one of her political science professors said, "She was very organized and articulate and goal-oriented. She knew what she wanted to accomplish and how to go about doing it."[20]

Hillary's political tendency of hewing to the middle revealed itself most clearly following Dr. King's assassination. Devastated by the death of her hero, she came into her room, trembling at the news, and hurled her textbooks against the wall. Once she calmed down, she called her black friends to share their sense of loss. She also participated in the large demonstrations that were organized in the immediate aftermath of King's death on the Wellesley campus. But eschewing more radical demands, she sought successfully to keep channels of communication open between the demonstrators and the administration, focusing on constructive actions that could be taken both within the college and in the Wellesley community to open more opportunities to blacks. She lobbied effectively for the appointment of more black faculty members, the recruitment of more black students, and the development of more Black Studies classes. Of equal importance, she always did her share of the scut work. Geoffrey Shields commented that her primary concern was not simply to be on the "moral" or "right" side of an issue. "She was more interested in the process of achieving victory than in taking a philosophical position that would not lead anywhere. If challenged philosophically, she [would say], 'You can't accomplish anything . . . unless you win.'" The president of Wellesley summed it up best: "She was interested in effecting change," Ruth Adams observed, "but from within rather than outside the system."[21]

In the summer of 1968, Hillary stuck to her middle-of-the-road politics, for the last time officially identifying herself as a Republican. Although she had worked for Eugene McCarthy in his antiwar campaign against Lyndon Johnson in the February New Hampshire primary, she accepted an internship in June, July, and August with the House Republican Conference in Washington, D.C. There she took on an assignment for Melvin Laird, a member of the Republican leadership, writing a position paper on options that America faced in Vietnam. Entitled "Fight Now, Pay Later," it criticized LBJ's failure to calculate the human and financial costs in his strategy of escalation. "She presented her viewpoints very forcibly," Laird later remarked, "always had ideas, always defended what she had in mind." After that assignment, she went to Miami to work on behalf of Nelson Rockefeller at the 1968 Republican convention. As if to ensure that, once again, she would witness firsthand all sides of that summer's struggles, she then returned to Illinois and with her close friend Betsy Ebeling drove three nights in a row (unbeknownst to her parents) into the heart of Chicago, where police were beating up demonstrators who had come to the Democratic convention there to protest the war. "We saw kids our age getting their heads beaten in," Betsy later said. "Hillary and I just looked at each other. We had had a wonderful childhood in Park Ridge, but we obviously hadn't gotten the whole story." The most searing lesson the two took from their experience was the realization, in Ebeling's words, "that our government would do this to our own people."[22]

That same summer, Hillary Rodham discovered her second serious boyfriend. A young man named David Rupert from Georgetown University (he was not part of Bill Clinton's circle of friends), he, too, was a "pretend" Republican, also working on an internship for the party, in his case with the liberal Republican congressman Charles Goodell from New York. They had "an intense love affair," Hillary's college friend Nancy Pietrafesa said, also noting that "Hillary was always attracted to arrogant, sneering, hard-to-please men like her father." After they met at an internship mixer and had talked for a while about their political perspectives, Rupert allegedly exploded, "You're not a Republican. That's a bunch of crap. Why are you playing that game?" (Hillary was probably asking herself the same question.) When he subsequently discovered that Hillary was writing a paper for Laird on the war, he responded: "That's bullshit, you're against the war." For almost three years, from Hillary's senior year at Wellesley well into her second year at Yale Law School, theirs was a full romantic and intellectual partnership. Although he took a different path than she—he became a conscientious objector after graduating from Georgetown and moved to Vermont, where she visited him on weekends in the commune where he lived—they shared common values, she introduced him to her parents as her boyfriend, and he clearly represented a "significant other" at a critical time in her life.[23]

This was a period when Hillary weighed other options as well. In some ways the contemporary "hippie" culture appealed to her. She acknowledged feeling alienated from the "entire reality of middle-class America," in particular the lifestyle and values of her hometown. In the summer and fall of 1968, she seemed to consider greater rebellion against the mainstream and more extreme political options. But in the end, she returned to seeking equilibrium—the bubble in the carpenter's level—choosing a middle path of working inside the system, albeit for significant change, rather than attacking the system and seeking to replace it. Hence, in her last two years at Wellesley, she aspired to, and won, appointment as a Vil Junior, an honorary leadership position. She was chosen president of student government, and over and over again she opted to work for change that was acceptable to the college's leadership. While increasingly committed to the antiwar movement, she chose the tactic of "teach-ins" rather than militant confrontations. As with her work on behalf of ending mandatory prayers in the dining halls, supporting more widespread use of a pass-fail grading option, and boosting the number of black undergraduates at Wellesley, her approach was one of reform, not revolution. It promised greater results and recognition.[24]

Hillary Rodham returned to campus in the fall of 1968 to undertake a senior thesis on the value of community action programs in achieving dramatic social change. She had read and heard about Saul Alinsky, the intellectual radical from Chicago who had helped revolutionize neighborhoods there with the tactics of a community organizer. Alinsky recommended organizing working-class communities and churches around bread-and-butter issues. They could then fight against the established political leadership and force social changes of their own devising. Believing that such activities might be the secret to the kind of far-reaching reforms she advocated, Hillary went to Chicago and did on-the-ground research, investigating the philosophy of "Maximum Feasible Participation" that was so crucial to many of the antipoverty efforts then being carried out, especially through Community Action Projects (CAPs). In the end, she was disappointed. Her lengthy thesis suggested that more structure and traditional leadership were needed for meaningful change to occur and that a simple formula like Maximum Feasible Participation was not enough by itself to make more than a marginal difference. A brilliant study, its conclusion was completely consistent with where Hillary ended up in her own way of thinking, oriented by her own gyroscope. She would focus on pragmatic reform, not utopian visions, working to change those already in power rather than seek revolution by ousting them. "She is by far the most outstanding young woman I have taught at Wellesley College," her professor concluded.[25]

It was no surprise, then, when Hillary Rodham was chosen to speak at Wellesley's commencement in 1969. A student speaker had never before been part of graduation ceremonies. But this was a new generation. The civil rights movement, the antiwar movement, the rebellion of college students throughout the country—above all, the traumatic events on college campuses as diverse as Columbia, Berkeley, Wisconsin, and Duke in the late sixties—all created pressures on academic administrations to give students a role in their own graduation rituals. Hillary Rodham seemed the ideal candidate for the task at Wellesley. Student body president, activist reformer on issues ranging from civil rights to the war, well-recognized participant in myriad campus activities, she seemed a natural. Even Ruth Adams, the college's president, felt that if anyone could do the job responsibly, it would be Hillary.

The event turned out to be far more dramatic than anyone had anticipated. Hillary and her friends felt keenly the importance of making the speech notable, both for what it said and what it represented. Many of Hillary's closest colleagues contributed to polishing her remarks. But everything changed on the day of graduation. The primary speaker at the convocation was Senator Edward Brooke, the only black member of

the U.S. Senate. A moderate to liberal Republican, Brooke would ordinarily have been one of Rodham's political heroes. But that day he gave
a speech that seemed disconnected to the turmoil sweeping the nation's
campuses. Barely critical of the war or of racial injustice, he seemed
glibly—and all too comfortably—to accept the conventional way of doing things. Almost condescendingly, he dismissed the distinctive sensibility of his audience. While expressing "empathy" with student
perspectives, Brooke seemed to disparage their seriousness.

Courageously—audaciously—Rodham decided on the spur of the
moment to comment on both the tone and content of Brooke's remarks.
Speaking directly to him, she declared: "Part of the problem with empathy with professed goals is that empathy doesn't do anything." "We've
had lots of empathy," she said, but it was the "indispensable task" of her
generation to engage in critical and constructive protest that extended
beyond empathy. "[For] too long our leaders have used politics as the art
of the possible. And the challenge now is to practice politics as the
art of making what appears to be impossible possible." There it was.
Boldly, directly, Wellesley's student graduation speaker had taken on a
United States senator and the politics of civility. It was not a radical
challenge. The rest of her prepared speech read much like a typical
proclamation from the counterculture. "We are all . . . exploring a world
that none of us understands," it said. "We're searching for more immediate, ecstatic and penetrating modes of living . . ." But the first part—
the direct retort to Senator Brooke—garnered national headlines.
Before long Hillary Rodham, with her Coke-bottle glasses, long hair,
and aura of intellectual bravado, appeared in a *Life* magazine story, a
symbol of the new generation coming of age in America.[26]

It had been the kind of four years that Dorothy Rodham could only
have dreamed of. Her daughter was fulfilling all her own dreams and
suppressed desires. (Later, Dorothy would go back to college and get
her own degree.) Hillary learned to explore a new world. She trod down
paths that were different, even deviant, from those she had known
while growing up. Occasionally, she even contemplated becoming the
rebel some hoped she would turn into. But in the end, she retained the
moral core given to her by her mother and by Don Jones. With her own
distinctive form of courage, she hewed to the path of working inside, not
outside—of keeping her equilibrium, with the bubble in the middle.

THREE

Oxford and the Draft:
A Test of Character

If a single period in an individual's life can illuminate his entire character, the two years Bill Clinton spent at Oxford offer an ideal prism through which to understand who he was and who he would become. As he embarked on his journey to England in 1968, Clinton believed he was about to complete the intellectual training necessary to prepare himself for a life of public service. Instead, he experienced a moral crisis that galvanized his self-doubt, refined a capacity for manipulation that proved a harbinger of things to come, and crystallized a conflict between moral conviction and political accommodation that would accompany him the rest of his life. The issue was the Vietnam War; the question, how to respond to it in a manner consistent with personal honor, moral integrity, and authentic self-interest. Even as Clinton's time abroad highlighted other character traits, the way he grappled with whether and how to serve his country established both the depth and the ambivalence of his moral sensibility.

Clinton's "class" of Rhodes scholars reads like a Who's Who of subsequent stars of the political and academic world. Mostly from Ivy League schools, they had already registered their genius. Strobe Talbott was the editor of the *Yale Daily News* who later became a *Time* magazine editor and deputy secretary of state. Four years after going to Oxford, Rick Stearns would help manage the presidential campaign of George McGovern. Others ended up as authors, cabinet members, and witty savants. It was a cohort, said Robert Reich (later secretary of labor and national news commentator), "ready to launch their careers [as]

ambassadors or presidents or university professors." Clinton fit in perfectly, immediately starting, in Daniel Singer's words, to seek out
"everybody that he thought was informative and valuable." Nor was he
shy about his own aspirations. "I remember . . . him telling me within
forty-five minutes," Rick Stearns said, "that he planned to go back to
Arkansas to be governor or senator and would like to be a national
leader someday."[1]

Denise Hyland, still a close friend, took Clinton to the SS *United
States* to see him and his buddies off. "I knew where the huge ocean
liner was headed," Clinton later recalled, "but I had no idea where I was
going." The expectation for Rhodes scholars was that the trip across the
ocean would provide a time for bonding. The best and the brightest
could learn how really good they were, separate the stars from the
superstars, and create the magical chemistry of becoming a community
of caring brothers. (There were no women Rhodes scholars at that
time, although on board the ship were a number of women college students going to spend time abroad.) A few got seasick right away, Robert
Reich and Daniel Singer among them. But even that helped cement the
group as those more able to tolerate the ocean's turbulence helped care
for the less well off. It was a voyage that fulfilled its traditional mission.
"Most of us," Clinton wrote, "were so earnest we almost felt guilty about
enjoying the trip." Clinton himself continued one pattern of behavior
while setting aside another. Having said good-bye to his former girlfriend Denise Hyland, he started a shipboard love affair with the writer
Martha Saxton. And for the first time in his life, he sampled alcohol,
trying scotch, bourbon, and vodka (not all at the same time). While
never a good drinker (he got red in the face after one cocktail), he had
now left behind his days as a teetotaler.[2]

The single theme that most united this diverse class of thirty-five
was their shared sense of anxiety about the war in Vietnam. They all
had lived through the traumas of early 1968. In almost staccato fashion,
crisis after crisis rocked the country. First had come the Tet offensive in
January and February; then Eugene McCarthy's near defeat of Lyndon
Johnson in the New Hampshire primary in March; Robert F. Kennedy's
entry into the presidential race shortly thereafter, followed by LBJ's
shocking withdrawal from the contest just three weeks later. Then the
horror of Martin Luther King, Jr.'s assassination in Memphis on April 4,

with rioting occurring in every major city; then students taking over the main buildings of Columbia University in May; and finally, Robert F. Kennedy's assassination in June. It was all too much. Everything felt as if it was falling apart. Even political conventions could not meet without massive violence. As student protestors gathered in Chicago at the Democratic convention, baton-wielding police sheared their ranks and beat their heads. The year 1968, Clinton later wrote, transformed the political landscape. It was the time "that conservative populism replaced progressive populism as the dominant political force in our nation," forming "the arena in which I and all other progressive politicians had to struggle over our entire careers."[3]

Not one of the Rhodes scholars was a radical. Most would have called themselves "establishment liberals" of moderate political persuasion. But all were obsessed with the war, which lay at the heart of all the traumas of the past year. "All of us," Strobe Talbott had told his Yale graduating class, "are in a sense already veterans of the war in Vietnam. We are certainly veterans of that dimension of the war which has brought such frustration and intellectual if not literal violence into our country, into our homes, and into our lives." And now they were embarked on what should have been a free-spirited, luxurious intellectual journey. Except that every one of them felt besieged by a sense of fear. As one Smith graduate on board the SS *United States* observed, "All the boys were scared stiff because of the draft. Some didn't know whether they should have left at all. Some were wondering whether they should ever go back. Everyone was trying to figure out how to manage the dilemma." No Rhodes class before them, or after, had ever experienced such a profound sense of collective anxiety.[4]

Before long, they had settled into their lodgings, grouped in threes and fours at different colleges in Oxford. Clinton found himself at University College, together with Robert Reich, John Isaacson, and Doug Eakeley. The pivotal local figure at each college was the porter who presided over the lodgings. Not an academic, but rather a kind of blue-collar residential patriarch, the porter could make a student's life happy or miserable. Robert Reich, the feisty, energized spark plug of the group—who was only four feet six inches tall—found himself instantly the target of what passed for satirical humor from the University College porter. "They told me I was getting four Yanks," he sputtered, "and here they send me three and a half. You're the goddamn bloody shortest freaking American I've ever seen."[5]

Almost immediately, Clinton distinguished himself as the social and intellectual butterfly of the cohort. "[He] was always the character who wanted to do one more thing," his classmate Doug Paschal said, "go one more place, stay up one more hour . . . He came across as somebody with a great appetite for life." Not surprisingly, Clinton zeroed in on the University College porter, Douglas Millin, as central to his freedom and comfort at Oxford. Neither shy nor intimidated, Clinton cultivated Millin as if he were the decisive voter in a deadlocked election. Schmoozing endlessly, he became Millin's intimate buddy, discussing everything from the war in Vietnam to the porter's favorite pub and where the best-looking girls could be found. The two got on like buddies who had spent a lifetime together, "two bull-shitters swapping stories," John Isaacson, another University College classmate, said. After that, anything Clinton wanted to do was fine.[6]

Academically, the Oxford system was unlike anything members of the group had ever seen. Instead of classes or seminars, there were tutorials. An individual student was responsible for setting up readings with a particular scholar, working out a program of consultation and writing that would eventually lead to a series of papers, and perhaps even a dissertation, depending on the degree being pursued. Clinton started off with a concentration in politics, philosophy, and economics, but failed to put together a comprehensive program of tutorials and readings. Instead, he shifted to a Bachelor of Philosophy emphasis, supposedly with a weekly tutorial and bimonthly papers that would eventually lead to a degree. While he wrote a few papers focusing on the Soviet Union (one on Kremlinology, for example, another on the Totalitarian School), in fact the academic side of the program never took off for Clinton. His intellectual life would more often consist of reading classic novels, books of philosophy, and meditations on politics. Nor were the other Rhodes scholars much better. Only nine of the thirty-five ever received degrees, the lowest in the history of Rhodes scholars.[7]

The reason, in large part, was that other issues weighed more heavily on their minds. Almost nightly they would gather in one of their rooms, the subject of the draft never far from their concern. The floating gathering might take place in Clinton's room or that of his close friend Frank Aller. The topics varied, from the latest developments in the presidential election campaign between Richard Nixon and Hubert Humphrey to the devastating repression of Czechoslovakian freedom fighters by Soviet soldiers in Prague. But inevitably it returned to the war. At Christmastime, Clinton made a surprise journey home to attend the wedding of his mother. She was getting married for the third time, to a hairdresser named Jeff Dwire (although family members tried to get Bill to dissuade her because Dwire had served a prison term for stock swindling and was still not finally divorced from his current wife). While there, Clinton had talked to Dwire about his draft status, and after consulting members of the local draft board, Dwire had reassured Clinton that whatever happened with his draft classification, he would be able to finish the year at Oxford. Others in the group had received similar assurances. But that did not minimize the imminence of the issue, or the fact that each of them understood it was only a matter of time before he would have to make a life-changing decision on how to respond to a draft call. For Clinton, that moment got closer when he received orders to take his draft physical in London in January. Writing to Denise Hyland, he indicated he expected to be drafted by March 1, 1969. He passed the physical with no problem.[8]

It was the personal dimension of these challenges that most troubled Clinton and his classmates. Most had gone to school and played with friends who were in Vietnam. These were flesh-and-blood companions, not statistics, people with whom Clinton and friends shared a common and cherished past. Before going to England, Clinton recalled seeing the name of his high school classmate Tommy Young on a list of casualties. That experience, he noted, "triggered the first pangs of guilt I felt about being a student and only touching the deaths in Vietnam from a distance." The awareness that "it could have been me" brought the issue down to a profoundly personal level. It was no longer an abstraction. As a result, Clinton said, "I briefly flirted with the idea of dropping out of school and enlisting in the military . . . I didn't feel entitled to escape even a war I had come to oppose." By the time he got to Oxford, two members of Clinton's high school class had already died in the war. The message was further driven home when he received a letter from an old friend who was serving in Vietnam and who wrote eloquently about the futility of the war effort. At no point did the personal dimension become more real than when Clinton learned that one of his closest childhood friends, Bert Jeffries, had been killed. "I cried for my friend," he recalled, "and wondered again whether my decision to go to Oxford was not motivated more by the desire to go on living than by opposition to the war." After his friend's death, Clinton wrote in his diary that "the privilege of living in suspension . . . is impossible to justify."[9]

But it was not just the deaths of his high school classmates that captured Clinton's emotions. It was also the agony that he saw his closest friends at Oxford endure as they contemplated what choices *they* would make when faced with the decision of whether to say yes to a draft notice. Nowhere was this more manifest than in the case of Frank Aller, with whom Clinton shared so much. As Clinton prepared to journey back to America for his surprise visit to his mother's wedding, Aller received his draft notice. For hours on end in the fall, the two had counseled and comforted each other as they contemplated what they would do. Others came to the two of them seeking advice and asking for help in preparing to become a conscientious objector. Aller had journeyed to England already committed in his own mind never to say yes to a draft notice. Nor would he apply to become a CO. Such a declaration required, in his mind, that a person be opposed to *all* wars, and Aller did not count himself in that category. He believed that World War II had been a just war, and that if given the opportunity, he would have fought then. But *this* war, he believed, was evil.

In so many ways, Aller and Clinton seemed alike—almost like brothers. Both were brilliant, each reached out and tried to understand the experience of others, both wrestled with how to find a political solution to the problems they faced. But they were also different. Clinton was outgoing, happy-go-lucky, almost always taking the upbeat, positive view on issues. Aller was more intellectual, sad, given to irony and a sense of tragedy. When his draft notice came, he immediately prepared to go home and alert his parents and girlfriend to the fact that he was going to become a draft resister and stay in England. But he discouraged Clinton from pursuing a similar course, because he believed Clinton "had the desire and ability to make a difference in politics," an opportunity that resisting the draft would destroy. But in the end, that advice rendered the dilemma all the more acute. "His generosity only made me feel more guilty," Clinton wrote, "as the angst-ridden pages of my diary show. He was cutting me more slack than I could allow myself." Clinton was reminded of the autobiographical essay he had written about himself in high school, fixated on the self-disgust "that storms my brain." Now, he said, "[those same] storms were really raging." The day that Aller declared his intention to resist, all his Rhodes colleagues threw a party in his honor. He had "put his money where his mouth was." So they gathered in John Isaacson's room at University College to salute their brother. They listened to the music of Judy Collins ("Who Knows Where the Time Goes?") and Leonard Cohen ("Suzanne" and "Hey, That's No Way to Say Goodbye"). Then they raised a glass to toast their dear friend, his conscience, and his conviction. None would ever forget the evening.[10]

Just a couple of months later, Bill Clinton received his own draft notice. The date was April 30. Although during a political campaign he would later claim that he could remember neither the draft notice nor the day it arrived, nothing could have been further from the truth. Immediately he called home to get advice from his mother and Jeff Dwire on what his next steps should be. They told him to remain in England until his normal return date, then come home. His induction date had been set for July 28.

Why Clinton dissembled about these facts—he freely acknowledges them in his memoir—remains a mystery. As late as 1991, Clinton told a *Washington Post* reporter that although he had expected his draft board to call him, "they never did"—a blatant lie. The only answer that makes sense is that Clinton was so transfixed by the news of his induction notice—and then the elaborate machinations he engaged in to circumvent it—that he wished at all costs to avoid a public examination of his response.

In fact, the entire episode highlights just how tormented Clinton was by the war, how he struggled to come to grips with his options, and how glaringly his reactions spoke to the deepest insecurities of his character. One night after receiving the draft notice, Clinton went to a friend's room to talk about the news. When there was no answer to his knock, he simply sat on the stairs and wept.[11]

In truth, Clinton had few options. He could go ahead and join the armed forces, as countless others—including his college roommate

Tom Campbell, and his many high school classmates—had done. He could choose the path of open resistance to the draft, as his Rhodes soulmate Frank Aller had done. Or he could find some other way to play the system to avoid the immediate draft, yet still claim to be operating within the rules of the game. Clearly, resistance was not a viable choice if he expected to pursue a political career. For a long time in June and early July he seemed resigned to accepting induction, even as he sought a way out. While still in England, he had contacted Cliff Jackson, another student from Arkansas and a Republican, to ask whether he could get the Arkansas governor, Winthrop Rockefeller, to help. He also investigated the ROTC option at Yale, only to find it was a dead end. The National Guard in Arkansas was full, and Clinton flunked the physical exams for both the naval and air force reserves. There seemed no alternatives left, and on July 8 he wrote to Denise Hyland. "Every day it becomes clearer the draft is the only way," he told her. "There isn't much else to say. I am not happy, but neither was anyone else who was called before me, I guess."[12]

Then, within a week, everything had changed. Almost as if he had awoken one morning with an infusion of energy and a whole new outlook, Clinton turned the entire situation around. He began by renewing his outreach to Cliff Jackson. It became one of the strangest ironies of both men's political lives. Jackson was the exact opposite of Clinton. A staunch conservative, he had stayed home to go to college, rejecting the out-of-town option. While he, too, had taken the opportunity to attend Oxford, he was offended by what he saw as Clinton's phony charm offensives. Whereas Clinton saw everyone as a potential ally, Jackson dealt in a world of clear-cut enemies. Clinton was open and embracing, Jackson a rigid control freak. Yet they were intrigued by each other, even drawn to each other by some sense of mutual respect. Both were concerned about Vietnam. And now Jackson enlisted in the Clinton cause, asking his friends to get an appointment for Clinton and himself with the head of Selective Service. When it turned out the National Guard was not an option, Jackson helped arrange for Clinton to be accepted into an ROTC unit at the University of Arkansas Law School. He even intervened with Colonel Holmes, the ROTC commander, to help make possible Clinton's deferring his ROTC service until the next year. Only years later, when Jackson became

Clinton's ardent right-wing enemy, would the ironies begin to come home.[13]

In the meantime, Clinton pulled other strings. His old friends from Fulbright's Senate office weighed in, Lee Williams contacting Colonel Holmes to lobby the ROTC head to allow Clinton to join the ROTC the following year. After Clinton met with Holmes to explore the possibilities, the Fulbright team ratcheted up the pressure. All this within one week's time. Soon, Colonel Holmes had agreed to Clinton's coming on board with the ROTC the following summer (1970), and the draft board had issued a new classification. Clinton would become 1-D, not 1-A, deferred from immediate service because he was now a reservist. "It's all too good to be true," Clinton wrote Denise nine days after his first letter telling her he was going to be drafted. The boy wonder had done it again. From the depths of despair, he had worked a miracle, using all his charm and connections to escape what had only days earlier seemed an inevitable and early departure to serve in Vietnam.[14]

And yet even at the height of his joy, Clinton's conscience continued gnawing at him. In the same letter to Denise proclaiming his disbelief that it had all turned out so well, he wrote that "there is still the doubt that maybe I should have said to hell with it, done this thing, and be free." Had his cleverness and charm won him a prize that he neither deserved nor could live with? Yes, he had won. But he could not avoid knowing how he had done it, and how high the price was. He understood that he now had a chance to avoid Vietnam, "but," as he wrote in his diary, "somebody will be getting on that bus in ten days [the time of his supposed induction] and it may be that I should be getting on it too." Deep in his soul, Clinton appeared to struggle with the outcome of a process he had himself initiated. What for most would have represented a happy end to a torturous experience turned out instead to be only the beginning of a process of introspection that would become a defining moment in his life.[15]

The passage of time did not abate Clinton's unhappiness. Instead, his despair intensified. "As the summer wore on," he later wrote, "I felt worse and worse about my decision to join the ROTC and go to Arkansas Law School." Unable to sleep, he wrestled with his conscience, talking to friends who were nearby, reaching out to others in writing. One person told him to forget about the deferment, join the Marines, and learn something about life. Another told him to just be happy and accept the ROTC resolution of his dilemma. As days passed, the whole process of wrenching ambivalence started to feed on itself. Looking back, Clinton recalled how much time he spent "thinking about death at an early age" and how much he felt captive to "unrelenting anxieties." "I searched my heart," he said, "trying to determine whether my aversion to going was rooted in conviction or cowardice." There seemed no way to resolve the issue. Indeed, "given the way it played out," he said, "I'm not sure I ever answered the question for myself."[16]

Things only got worse. Writing to Rick Stearns, his Rhodes classmate, Clinton seemed almost out of control, as if his brain were a pinball bouncing off the sides of the draft deferment issue, desperately trying to find a resting place. "My mind is every day more confused," he wrote Stearns. "Nothing could be worse than this torment." Being at home only complicated matters. "Everyone else's children seem to be in the military," he noted. Here, the empathy he had always shown toward others deepened his ambivalence, especially in light of his intense self-consciousness about those friends who had gone to serve and already died. On the one side, he understood the advantages of the deal he had struck. "I look forward to going to the U of A," he wrote Stearns, "the thing for aspiring politicos to do—and going to ROTC . . . [but] in between then and now I have this thing hanging over me like a pall."[17]

In the end, Clinton drilled to the core of the issue, "One of the worst side effects of this whole thing," he said, "is the way it's ravaged my own image of myself." How could Clinton live up to the role he had assigned himself if he felt himself to be less than a hero, a step below the ideal son and citizen? The whole dilemma of what to do about the draft crystallized Clinton's ultimate self-doubts—"whether I was, or could become, a really good person." It was all about his soul, the root of his being, what made him a distinctive human being who was good and cared for others. And now in the face of the draft crisis and the war in Vietnam, "I was afraid . . . that I was losing it."[18]

As if all this were not enough, Clinton also had to deal with how much he really wanted to go back to England for the second year of his Rhodes fellowship. It was not simply whether to enroll in law school at the University of Arkansas and the next summer enter the ROTC. His decision would also determine whether or not he could fulfill his passion for being a citizen of the world, staying with his class of the best and the brightest at the world's premier university, following the star that seemed destined to guide him all the way to his grandest aspirations. Could he give that up? "I want so much to tell you we're going back to England," he wrote Rick Stearns in the same *sturm und drang* letter where he bemoaned his hopeless confusion about what to do with regard to the draft. Yet wasn't going back to England the most egocentric thing Clinton could do? Was it not confirmation that he was putting his selfish self ahead of his soul?

In another rush of activity, Clinton sought in early September to bring some order to the chaos of his conflicting ruminations. He did so by pursuing two opposite choices simultaneously. His first act was to write a letter renouncing the arrangements he had just made to go to law school at the University of Arkansas and join the ROTC the following summer. That month, Clinton had been reading David Halberstam's book on Robert F. Kennedy, which reminded him—as if he needed to be reminded—that "I don't believe in deferments . . . I cannot do this ROTC." Staying up all night long, he wrote William Armstrong, the chair of the draft board, that he had never really been interested in the ROTC and requested that he be reclassified 1-A. Through the act of composing that letter, it seemed as though Clinton had finally resolved his dilemma. Except that he never sent it.[19]

Shortly thereafter, Clinton went to see Colonel Holmes. In that meeting, he raised the question of whether he might go back to Oxford and finish his second year, then join the ROTC the following summer and enter the University of Arkansas Law School the following fall. Grudgingly, Holmes agreed to Clinton's request. But Holmes did not tell his colleagues, who were dismayed when they learned that Clinton failed to enroll at the law school. "All we knew is that Bill Clinton did not show up," one staff member said. "We didn't normally have people promise to do something and not do it." Cliff Jackson, who had played such a central role in making the whole arrangement possible, was also angry. "Bill Clinton [was just] trying to wiggle his way out of the 'disreputable' Arkansas Law School," he said.[20]

Although Clinton may have clarified his choices in his own mind by pursuing two contradictory options in September, he clearly had not come to any final resolution. What he *had* done was clear the path for his return to England—the most self-interested and gratifying result possible. But the fundamental dilemma continued to gnaw at his soul, and he continued to obsess about it, "feeling more and more uncomfortable with the way I'd handled it." If anything, Clinton compounded the dilemma by identifying more openly with the antiwar movement. Before returning to Oxford, he attended a meeting of the Vietnam Moratorium Committee and joined a gathering on Martha's Vineyard of antiwar activists, where he carried on intense conversations with people like David Mixner, a prominent leader of the student left, who was engaged in an internal struggle over whether to let people know that he was gay. Letting his own internal debate surface, Clinton asked Mixner, "Are you embarrassed when you go home and meet someone who's in the service?" to which Mixner responded, "Yeah, I try to avoid them."[21]

Finally, in October Clinton cut the Gordian knot. The decision was perhaps precipitated by an antiwar demonstration that was planned for London in midmonth. Painfully aware of the ethical conflict inherent in openly expressing antiwar views while holding a reservist's deferment and planning to join the ROTC, Clinton concluded that his time had run out. He had to act, and decisively. Sometime between October 1 and October 15 he made the decision to tell the draft board to reclassify him 1-A, calling Jeff Dwire to ask him to transmit the decision immediately and then conveying it himself by mail. The letter he had drafted on September 12 remained unsent, but the gist of its contents was now confirmed. His conscience now clear, Clinton joined the antiwar movement. His long nightmare was over.[22]

Except that it contained one last act, perhaps as convoluted and revealing as anything Clinton had done up to this point. Clinton felt compelled to put down on paper a tale of his tortured deliberations and send it to Colonel Holmes, the man who had made it possible for Clinton to enroll in law school at the University of Arkansas, join the ROTC the following summer, and in the meantime to go back to Oxford. A person of authority, but also kindness and sensitivity, Holmes had listened to Clinton, understood where he was coming from, and conferred on Clinton the prize he had so avidly sought. This man surely deserved an explanation of what had taken place.

Clinton began by thanking Holmes for his kindness. He then launched into a sometimes hyperbolic account of his own evolving viewpoint. Ever since working for Fulbright, he explained, he had devoted himself to "working every day against a war I opposed and despised with a depth of feeling I had reserved solely for racism in America before Vietnam." (Not exactly true, since Clinton had never been known as a radical, had abstained from antiwar protests at Oxford, and only in the last month had marched with unfurled banners against the war.) He then recounted his longtime criticism of the draft. World War II, he acknowledged, was an exception "because the life of the people collectively was at stake," but that was not the case in Vietnam. Recounting the story of his many friends who had become COs or draft resisters, his words suddenly became brutally candid. "The decision not to be a resister and related subsequent decisions were the most difficult of my life," he said. "I decided to accept the draft in spite of my beliefs for one reason: to maintain my political viability within the system. For years I have worked to prepare myself for a political life characterized by both practical political ability and concern for rapid social progress."

Why, then, had he come to see Holmes in July? Because "ROTC was the one way left in which I could possibly, but not positively, avoid both Vietnam and resistance." But as soon as he had entered into the agreement, "I began to wonder whether the compromise I had made with myself was not more objectionable than the draft would have been." Brutally candid once again, he declared: "I had no interest in the ROTC program and all I seemed to have done was to protect myself from physical harm." Just as important, "I began to think I had deceived you," and all of what followed had caused "the anguish and loss of my self regard" that had led him to this moment. In the end, he declared, it was better to come clean, to thank Colonel Holmes for his generosity, and to seek reclassification as 1-A and take his chances on being drafted.[23]

The same week, Clinton submitted his application to Yale Law School.

It had been an amazing drama, with a degree of documentation and reflection rare in any historical narrative, in particular one revolving around a decisive moment in the life—and character—of a future president. Not surprisingly, it has also given rise to dramatically different interpretations of who Bill Clinton was and how and why he acted as he did.

One perspective—totally consistent with a lifetime of calculated political behavior—was that throughout the process, Clinton was driven by pure self-interest. Impelled above all by the desire to protect himself and "stay clean," he played the system with a stunning degree of finesse and shrewdness. Clinton, according to this view, cleverly dissected the odds of his being drafted at every stage of the process. Thus he knew there was no chance of his being drafted while he was still in England, because Richard Nixon, on October 1, had announced that any student already in graduate school would be permitted to finish out the academic year before being enrolled in the armed services. Furthermore, a few weeks earlier, Nixon had announced a series of troop reductions in Vietnam—the beginning of the "Vietnamization" process whereby more and more of the fighting would be turned over to the Vietnamese army while American troops came home—and further declared that the October draft call of 29,000 would be extended over a three-month period. Perhaps most important, Nixon also declared that he supported a lottery system in which the eligibility of any individual being considered for the draft would be determined by the number associated with his birth date in a random process. Moreover, no individual would be subject to the lottery more than once.[24]

According to this perspective, Clinton had scoped out the entire situation and concluded that the odds of his being drafted were limited in a worst-case scenario, and slim to none in a best-case scenario. At the very least, he knew that he would remain in England until July 1970, that draft calls were likely to diminish dramatically, and that the once-a-year lottery greatly bettered the odds of his not getting called. All of this, the skeptics suggest, support the notion that Clinton was convinced that the chances of his being drafted in the near future were minimal, and hence that he could reclassify himself 1-A with a high degree of confidence that he would come out looking clean and yet not have to serve in Vietnam. From a political science viewpoint, this was a "rational actor" scenario, meaning that anyone who checked out all the probabilities would agree it was an intelligent gamble to make.

Stated more bluntly, Clinton had gamed the system, retaining his "political viability" while avoiding having to fight in an ugly war. Those arguing this case point triumphantly to the fact that when the lottery actually took place on December 1, Clinton's birthdate came in at number 311, a virtual guarantee he would never have to fight. He had won it all. He did not have to resist; he avoided three years in ROTC; and he could go to Yale, not the University of Arkansas. "He fretted and planned every move," David Maraniss has written, "he got help from others when needed, he resorted to deception or manipulation when necessary, and he was ultimately lucky."

Perhaps most tellingly, Clinton wrote his letter to Colonel Holmes on December 3, two days after the lottery number had made him un-draftable. Now, more than ever before, he could afford to express himself fully.[25]

But what of all the hand-wringing? What of the soul-searching, the late-night phone calls, the desperate letters full of anguish? Were these all phony, part of a carefully plotted effort to pad the historical record to make the "hero" look better? Was Clinton that much of a fraud? A liar who besieged his friends—almost all of whom believed he was genuine—with pleas for help and understanding simply as a cover so that future historians would defend his integrity and accept his protestations of ambivalence?

There are no simple answers. But on balance, the evidence suggests that at least a part of Clinton was sincere in his protestations of anguish. First, there appears to be an interior logic to the progression of his concerns. The conversations he had with friends at Georgetown, his work on the Fulbright staff, and the nonstop focus on Vietnam during the trip to England suggest a natural unfolding of worries. Probably the most critical moments in that process came with the combat deaths of his high school friends, and with Frank Aller's struggle over whether to resist. Aller's injunction that Clinton not follow his own path of resis-tance, because Clinton was destined for a political future in which he could actually change things, provides a coherent context for all of Clinton's deliberations, especially his calculation of the odds of whether he might be drafted.

Second, the sustained ambivalence of Clinton's reflections over time indicates the degree to which he saw this choice as central to his own sense of self. Just as coming to grips with Roger Clinton's alcoholism and abuse defined Clinton during his adolescence, his desire to "get it right" on Vietnam—and knowing in his heart of hearts that there was no real "right"—constituted *the* test of his character as a young adult. It was about his soul, about whether he could reconcile his image of himself in the future with his behavior in the present. Without question, the shift in government policies on the draft shaped the calculations that went into his final decision, but that did not mean that all the anguish he experienced was contrived.

Finally, the second thoughts that besieged Clinton after his helter-skelter rush to avoid the draft in July highlight the degree to which he remained confused. Panicked by the realization that time was running out on every option, Clinton poured every resource he could mobilize—including his relationships with Cliff Jackson and J. William Fulbright—into a last-minute surge of activity to avoid a worst-case scenario. But as with all such efforts, a decisive movement in one direction inevitably provokes second thoughts. In that light, Clinton's persistent ruminations ring true to human experience. In a letter to Denise Hyland, he even expressed in the same sentence both euphoria at having escaped the draft and the gnawing doubt that perhaps he had done an unethical thing. In the end, both perspectives ring true. It *was* a brilliant manipulation of the system. And he *did* remain troubled by what that said about his true inner soul.

Clinton's experience at Oxford represented a critical test in his life. Although there were many moments of pointed and sustained ethical anguish to come, these two years possessed a focused and intense quality that helped shape patterns that would persist through the rest of his career.

The Oxford years did not bring much intellectual stimulation to Clinton. His academic workload was slim at best. He fell in love with England, had a good time traveling to its high points, and met a group of friends who would be with him for the rest of his life. Now boasting a beard and curly hair, he looked more like a "hippie" by the end than an "establishment" graduate of Georgetown. Consistent with his former life, he continued to charm people, make friends, ingratiate himself with natives of the different countries he visited, and arrange to get free meals and lodging from many. On a "grand tour" of Norway, Finland, and Russia toward the end of his time abroad, he broadened his exposure to the world enormously.

Significantly, he continued to have difficulty sustaining relationships with women. He was in love with Ann Markusen, a classmate from Georgetown whom he had dated periodically—and intensely—both in his final year in college and during his first year at Oxford. But she was feisty, intellectually independent, and wary of the more manipulative side of his charms. During his spring break from Oxford, Clinton traveled to Germany, where he went to Cologne Cathedral ("I felt close to God in that cathedral," he later said) and also to see Markusen. But the relationship ended because, Clinton said, he was unable to sustain a commitment to one person. The same could be said of the rest of his ties with women while abroad.[26]

But the heart of his experience there was his struggle with the war. Years later, Clinton made a direct connection between his time in England and the "parallel lives" he had come to accept as central to his existence, most notably the conflict between his external public life, filled with "friends and fun, learning and doing," and his internal private life, "full of uncertainty, anger, and a dread of ever-looming violence." That was the life "where the secrets are hidden." As he thought back over his time in London, he reveled in its good side; "I had traveled a lot and loved it." But he also reflected on the downside; "I had also ventured into the far reaches of my mind and heart." In that context, he wrote, "the draft dilemma brought back my internal life with a vengeance. Beneath my new and exciting external life, the old demons of self-doubt and impending destruction reared their ugly heads again."

All that he wrote and talked about as he wrestled with the draft spoke to this inner self—perhaps above all, "the difficulty I've had in letting anyone into the deepest recesses of my internal life." Clinton's ruminations—to himself, to his classmates, to his closest friends—revealed more of what was going on in those deep recesses than he allowed perhaps at any other time in his life. They helped make this one of the decisive moments of his young existence, one that would define his person, and his way of dealing with truths he wished to avoid, for decades after.[27]

FOUR

Hillary and Bill at Yale: Two Destinies Intersect

When Bill Clinton arrived at Yale in the fall of 1970, one thing was clear: Politics would be the singular focus of his life. Far less clear were his other priorities. He continued to exude charm and affability, drawing to himself potential political allies, personal friends, and devoted acolytes. But what about his intellectual life? Did academics matter? Should he prepare for a professional career if politics did not work out? More important, would he be able to reconcile his parallel lives? In particular, how would he resolve his persistent inability to sustain a long-term relationship with a woman? Repeatedly, he had commented on his lack of commitment to others. His relationship with Ann Markusen—whom he first started to date at Georgetown—had broken off, even though he said he loved her, because he could not bring himself to say yes to a long-term relationship. It was a story repeated again and again, throughout his stay in England and now on his return. Instead of sustained commitments, he had begun a chronic pattern of carrying on multiple relationships marked by no honest communication with the various women involved. Where would all that lead?

At Yale, Clinton found an answer—another person, equally bright, just as driven to break barriers and change the world. She was almost as complicated as he was—perhaps even more so—with a family history that came close to his in its crazy dynamics. Hillary Rodham would change his life. He would change hers. And from the moment of their meeting, they created a partnership, both political and personal, that helped shape the course of the country.

•

For Hillary, going to law school represented the next logical step in her trajectory to make a difference in the world and be one of a new generation of women out to break traditional barriers. Wellesley had been a perfect choice for her, providing what she called in *Living History* "the psychic space" to be who she wanted to be, unintimidated by men or patriarchal folkways.

With her stellar record at Wellesley, going to a premier law school should have been easy. But the time was 1969. Even given the birth of the National Organization for Women in 1966, the popularity of Betty Friedan's *Feminine Mystique,* published in 1963, and the birth of a new generation of young activists who supported women's liberation, it was still a time of traditional stereotypes and deep-seated resistance to women in the professions. As late as 1965, fewer than 5 percent of the students entering American law schools, medical schools, and business schools were female. Indeed, when Hillary Rodham explored the possibilities of going to Harvard Law School, she rejected the option immediately because a male professor there opined that "we don't need any more women."[1]

But Yale was different. Dynamic, vibrant, and progressive, it had for years thrived on a reputation for innovation, critical thinking, and community outreach. Yale was not a law school that celebrated rote learning. It gave no prizes for being able to recite the greatest number of Supreme Court decisions. Instead, it nurtured independence, encouraging students to branch out and do volunteer legal work on their own. Above all, it embraced free thinking, intellectual exploration, and critical engagement with diverse legal and political perspectives. In a typical law school, the best students were known for being able to cite conflicting precedents on a legal doctrine when they were called on in class. At Yale, the best students were those who were not in class—at least not at *every* class—and who instead were off trying to change the world. Although she was one of only 27 women in a cohort of 235, this was probably the best place she could imagine being.

When she first got to Yale, Hillary was invited to a League of Women Voters conference to talk about the future of politics in America. Peter Edelman, a former aide to Robert F. Kennedy, had seen her picture and story in *Life* and had invited her. At the conference she met people like Vernon Jordan, soon to become president of the Urban

League (and a pivotally important friend), and David Mixner, a student antiwar activist about to come out of the closet and lead the gay rights movement. Hillary joined the LWV's Youth Advisory Committee and, most important, was introduced to Peter Edelman's wife-to-be, Marian Wright, a civil rights activist about to create the Children's Defense Fund, perhaps the most important activist agency Hillary Rodham would be identified with for years to come. *That* was what it was like to be a Yale law student.[2]

New Haven that fall was like another planet. The previous spring, Alex Rackley, a local Black Panther leader, had been murdered—allegedly because he was a police informer. He had been put on trial by his fellow Panthers and subsequently executed. That summer, indictments were handed down and a slew of Black Panthers were put on trial for his murder, including Bobby Seale, the nationally known Black Panther leader. The entire community was consumed by political agitation. Black Panthers and other activists were everywhere. The occupation of Columbia University's academic offices had occurred just the year before, and tensions ran to extremes as people feared student revolts, Panther violence, and civil chaos. Kingman Brewster, the president of Yale, publicly doubted "the ability of black revolutionaries to achieve a fair trial anywhere in the United States." The Black Panther David Hilliard taunted student activists who were allegedly on his side: "You're a goddam fool if you think I'm going to stand up here and let a bunch of so-called pacifists, you violent motherfuckers, boo me without getting violent with you." His tirade was emblematic of the confrontational tone that pervaded New Haven, and the country, that fall.[3]

Hillary Rodham, though, kept her cool. Retaining her penchant for moderate actions inside the boundaries of acceptable behavior, she joined the law students who took part in monitoring the trial, helped to schedule students for different movement activities, and encouraged constructive dialogue. Hillary, a dean said, "somehow managed to keep the discussion calm." She moderated a large student meeting on whether to engage in a general campus strike and made sure to keep her lines of communication open with both the school administration and the demonstrators. Greg Craig, a fellow student who would become a lifelong friend, described Hillary as "a mainstream, conscientious, politically astute person who still believed in American institutions." Which in the environment of Yale in the early seventies "meant she was conservative."[4]

Hillary also joined the staff of a new journal designed to be an alternative to the *Yale Law Journal*. Hillary was named associate editor of the *Yale Review of Law and Social Action* and helped supervise a whole issue on the Panther trial, all the while continuing her work as a mediating force. "Hillary did what would nowadays be called international summitry," her classmate Kristine Olson said later, "flying back and forth between both sides . . . She's always been the one who sees the need for balance."

The *Review* also became involved in other kinds of social questions such as children's and spousal rights. Hillary's interest in these issues caused her to reconnect with Marian Wright Edelman in the spring of 1970. Edelman had no money to pay staff, so Hillary persuaded the Law Students Civil Rights Research Council at Yale to give her money to work as an intern for Edelman's Washington Research Project, the immediate predecessor of the Children's Defense Fund, where she spent the first part of the summer researching the living conditions of migrant farmers before returning to work at the Yale Child Study Center on family law issues. Eventually she became a research assistant for a book on children being edited by Anna Freud, and she helped write an article advocating for neglected children, arguing that under the Constitution, children enjoyed citizenship rights just as adults did. In a subsequent *New York Review of Books* essay, Garry Wills called her "one of the more important scholar activists of the last two decades." It had been a productive—and not at all atypical—first-year experience at Yale Law School.[5]

But year one was just the beginning. Because, as she wrote in *Living History*, in year two "I was about to meet the person who would cause my life to spin in directions that I never could have imagined."

Bill Clinton had chosen Yale because he wished to continue being surrounded by the brightest, most talented, most compelling members of his generation. Some of his closest friends among his Rhodes classmates were joining him there, including Doug Eakeley and Robert Reich. Like them, and like Hillary Rodham, he knew Yale provided a milieu that would feed his political passions while preparing him for a life of independent thought and intellectual exploration. The summer before he enrolled, he continued his antiwar work. When fall came, Clinton smoothly segued into another full-time political role, becoming an organizer for the U.S. Senate campaign of the Reverend Joe Duffey. A professor of ethics at Hartford Seminary, Duffey was also president of Americans for Democratic Action (ADA), one of the oldest liberal groups in the Democratic Party.

It was a campaign full of enthusiasm, notoriety, and naïveté. Co-chaired by the actor Paul Newman, it sought to win a majority in an almost impossible three-way race with the sitting senator Thomas Dodd (pro-war) and the liberal Republican Lowell Weicker. Quickly, Clinton worked his charm. As a newcomer from Arkansas and England, he successfully organized a series of urban neighborhoods and found a mother figure in virtually every community who would feed him and give him a place to sleep. All the way through the November election, he worked full-time on the campaign. As expected, Duffey lost, coming in second to Weicker. But Clinton was doing what he had come to Yale to do—following his instincts and his passions.[6]

All this time, of course, Clinton was enrolled in classes—which he never attended. Like Hillary Rodham in her first year, Bill Clinton followed his own agenda. When he returned to campus after the campaign, his fellow student Nancy Bekavac said to him, "Where the hell have you been? We've been here since September." "[Why], I've been running the Joe Duffey campaign," he responded. He then asked if he could borrow her notes. Back on campus, he rarely attended class, though he did just fine on his exams. As another student with a similar attitude to Clinton's explained, "[At Yale], the concern was more whether you could get the policy argument right than get the [correct] citations in a case. So for people with conceptual minds, like Clinton, it was pretty easy." Clinton's roommate would often come home late at night to find Clinton immersed in a book—but it was most often a novel, not a law text, and the next morning, after doing an all-nighter, he would still be reading the novel. The law books could wait.[7]

Meanwhile, he acted in classic Bill Clinton fashion. At Yale, as at most American universities in the early 1970s, black students ate together at what became known as the "black table" in the cafeteria.

Virtually every other student respected that space. Except for Bill Clinton. Bill Coleman, one of his black classmates, described how one day, this "tall, robust, friendly fellow with a southern accent and a cherubic face [ambled over and] unceremoniously violated the unspoken taboo by plopping himself down [next to us]." He then had the chutzpah to act "oblivious to the stares." A gifted storyteller, Clinton had mastered the ability to get people to talk about themselves. Because of his lifelong experience of relating easily to black people, this moment was just another in a long tradition of open communication. "By simply being himself," Coleman said, "Bill Clinton dissolved the unspoken taboo and became a regular and welcome member of the table." Soon Coleman joined Clinton as a roommate in a beach house that four Yalies rented outside New Haven.[8]

As long as politics was the issue, Clinton seemed fine. When it came to women, however, he persisted in developing multiple relationships, with no center or focus. Using his charm, he easily started conversations with women. Often he used the ploy of seeing a woman reading a book, then going over to her and saying, "Hey, that's one of *my* favorite books, too"—a terrific "breaking the ice" line. Nancy Bekavac noted that Clinton always remembered "some human fact" about people's lives, "not unrelated to sentimentality and emotionalism," that constituted a tie to them. (Sometimes Clinton's folksiness went too far. Once when Clinton was playing up his "poor kid from Arkansas" line, Bekavac injected: "Now, Bill, it wasn't Oxford, Mississippi, where you were a Rhodes scholar, was it?") While living with Coleman at the beach house, Clinton dated three or four women simultaneously, including at least one African American woman. Bekavac could not believe his "fitting them all . . . into one semester." But there was no sustained gratification. In his memoir, Clinton recalled his personal life at the time as a "mess." One relationship ended when the woman decided instead to marry an old boyfriend. On another occasion, he "had a painful parting with a law student I liked very much but couldn't commit to." Commitment—a critical issue, then and for a long time thereafter.[9]

There were two ways of reading Clinton's first few months at Yale. One was to see him as fulfilling the Yale norm, thriving in an environment that prized independence, encouraged entrepreneurial outreach, and celebrated political activism. In such an interpretation, Clinton's absorption in the Duffey campaign, his exploration of existential literature such as the novels of Albert Camus, his flamboyant lifestyle, and his general indifference toward academic studies represented a logical extension of the Yale ethos. Arguably, Hillary Rodham's involvement in political and social issues during her first year represented a similar experience—except that she had a center to her life, continued to pursue academic excellence, and found ways to make her various activities fit a coherent scheme.

A second interpretation of Clinton's early time at Yale is to see it as a time of restless searching. Yes, the political focus was consistent with all his prior activities. He was simply extending into new territory a passion that was his lifelong guiding star. But his indifference to academic work, and above all his penchant for multiple relationships with women, suggest someone who lacked focus and was profoundly unsettled. Behind his series of narcissistic pursuits—from novels to women—Clinton craved some kind of anchor. The comment about the "mess" of his personal life in the memoir suggests a desire for greater substance and meaning.

Which interpretation was correct remains an open question. Both can be supported. But in the end Bill Clinton wished the Yale experience to be more than simply a series of momentary encounters. This is where Hillary Rodham entered.

There are multiple stories about how the two met. The classic version, told repeatedly, is that they had noticed each other early on. She was in her second year, he in his first. But rather than start a conversation, they circled each other warily, each sizing the other up. Then one day in the library, after Bill kept gazing at Hillary down at the other end of the Gothic-arched room, Hillary strode up to him and said, in effect, "Look, if we're going to spend all this time staring at each other, we should at least get to know who the other is." And the rest, supposedly, is history.

Robert Reich claims to have introduced the two at the beginning of the semester. But nothing happened. In Bill Clinton's memoir, he says that he saw Hillary for the first time in a class on political and civil rights. "She had thick dark blond hair," he wrote, "and wore eyeglasses and no makeup. But she conveyed a sense of strength and self-possession

I had rarely seen in anyone, man or woman." Still another version has Bill following Hillary around campus. At the time, she was still dating David Rupert. He caught up with her on her way to registration and joined her in the line, even though he had already registered. Then the two went off and talked their way into the Yale Art Museum, which was closed, but which had a special exhibit on Mark Rothko that they both wanted to see. In this story, according to Bill's memoir, she sat down in the lap of a Henry Moore sculpture, and he sat beside her. "Before long," he wrote, "I leaned over and put my head on her shoulder. It was our first date."[10]

Whatever the sequence, a spark had been struck. Clinton phoned Hillary soon after the museum experience and discovered she was sick. Immediately, and unbidden, he went to her house with orange juice and chicken soup. Clinton's courtship had commenced. Electricity was in the air.

Clinton, a friend of Hillary's said, was "the wild card in her well-ordered cerebral existence." She had charted a well-organized campaign to achieve her ends in her own way, and now a new and powerful presence was scrambling her best-laid plans. "He was the first man I'd met," she told one interviewer, "who wasn't afraid of me." For someone whose head had always ruled her heart, a new element had entered the equation. She admired his brains and his commitment, but also his physicality. In her memoir, she talks about the "shape of his hands. His wrists are narrow and his fingers tapered and deft, like those of a pianist or a surgeon." Clinton marshaled all his resources to keep his advantage. He lobbied his housemates to "make nice" to Hillary. If they could impress her, she might think better of him. "I'd never seen anyone with that much focus," Nancy Bekavac said. Hillary was deeply impressed by how much he cared about his origins and how much he was committed to going back to Arkansas to make a difference. Although he did not say it, she and all her friends quickly got the message about the ultimate potential of Bill Clinton. More than twenty years before it happened, they were already talking about his becoming president of the United States. "Absolutely," Bekavac said. "I don't think I knew him two hours before it dawned on me." In addition to his intellectual and physical attractiveness, Clinton's charisma clearly made an impact as well.[11]

Bill and Hillary brought out the best in each other. She helped impart discipline and rigor into his quest for making a difference. He helped soften and humanize her. "He saw the side of her that liked spontaneity and laughter," her friend Sara Ehrman noted. "He found her guttural laugh [appealing]: it's fabulous—there's nothing held back. The public never sees that side of her. When she's laughing, that's when she's free."[12]

They also learned how effectively they could complement each other. Bill was gentle, affable, averse to conflict, and loath to attack people. Hillary was tough, direct, willing to fight and take the battle to the other side. "Clinton had the charm and sex appeal," their friend Steve Cohen said, "whereas Hillary . . . was straightforward, articulate and self-possessed." Sometimes the contrasts led to exchanges that were humorous as well as telling. "They were funny together," Clinton's roommate Don Pogue recalled. "Hillary would not take any of Bill's soft stories, his southern boy stuff. She would just puncture it, even while showing real affection. She'd say, 'Spit it out, Clinton!' or 'Get to the point, will you, Bill!'" Nowhere were the differences, or complementarities, more evident than when the two served as cocounsel in the Prize Trial, held before the entire law school, with opposing sets of law students trying to win a case before a distinguished judge, in this instance the former Supreme Court justice Abe Fortas. While Bill sought to win over the judge and jury with his charm—and brooded when their side lost a difficult procedural ruling—Hillary was all business. As Nancy Bekavac noted, "Hillary was very sharp and Chicago, and Bill was very *To Kill a Mockingbird.*" Stated another way, to Bill's soft, stereotypically "feminine" qualities, Hillary brought tough, classically "masculine" traits.[13]

The only problem was that more often than not, their complementary differences also generated outright conflict. Just as often as the two cooed and flirted, they fought viciously, using their superintelligence to rip each other apart. Neither was weak-willed, but given their other qualities—his affability and charm, her assertiveness and strong-mindedness—she was more likely to go on the attack, and he was more likely to be on the defensive. And more often than not, in a confrontation, she would be the victor and he would have to pay the price.

Nevertheless, the attraction was sufficiently strong that from that semester forward, Bill Clinton and Hillary Rodham were inextricably linked. "She was in my face from the start," Bill Clinton recalled, "and, before I knew it, in my heart." Hillary, in turn, remembered that "falling in love with Bill Clinton" was the most exciting thing to happen to her in the 1970s. For Bill, Hillary was something different. Other women had embodied some of what he now found with Hillary. His lifelong friendship with Carolyn Staley was always more substantive than romantic. For three years, he combined romance and friendship in his relationship with Denise Hyland. But that dynamic had less of a cutting edge, fewer direct challenges. Ann Markusen at Georgetown was the closest he had come to being involved with a person like Hillary. But she was perhaps too independent, too "in his face," too unwilling to accommodate his style and find a modus vivendi that would allow them to develop as a couple. Hillary was different. While clearly unwilling to be submissive, she was sufficiently enchanted that, arguably for the first time, she considered melding her own ambitions to change the world with those of someone else in a joint endeavor. In his memoir, Bill declared he simply liked being around Hillary "because I thought I'd never be bored with her. In the beginning I used to tell her that I would like being old with her." An interesting perspective. Not romantic. Not impetuous. Rather, a vision over time—a long time.[14]

Soon enough they became a couple, with Bill moving into Hillary's limited quarters. Interested in continuing the relationship and apprehensive about losing her if they were apart, he asked if he could go with her to California in the summer of 1971. She was going there to intern with an Oakland law firm—Treuhaft, Walker and Bernstein—notorious for its left-wing political associations. It was an interesting choice, part of Hillary's balancing act between her "conservative mind and liberal heart." She had taken a law course with Thomas Emerson, also known for his left-of-center proclivities, and he provided the connection to the Oakland firm, two of whose partners had been Communist Party members.

In a significant gesture of faith in their future, Hillary agreed to let Bill come along. Hillary was moving in her political agenda, now much more focused on her liberal instincts. Bill had helped in that process. His activism, openness, and warmth had clearly nudged her in new directions. The fact that she was willing to entertain this level of commitment conveyed its own message. Traveling with someone to California suggested something more than a campus relationship.

Bill, too, had changed. For someone deeply disturbed by his inability to make commitments to women, Hillary had introduced a new dimension. As he wrote, she was someone he could not get out of his head. Nothing illustrated the change more than his decision to bring her into his family sphere, an act of commitment on his part that he must have known would not be smooth. When Bill's mother came to Yale to see her son, Virginia met Hillary for the first time. It was not a successful encounter. "With no makeup, a work shirt and jeans, and bare feet coated with tar from walking on the beach at Milford," Clinton recalled, "she might as well have been a space alien." But at least the initial contact had now been made. Hillary reciprocated, taking Bill to Park Ridge to meet her parents. He immediately bonded with her mother, Dorothy, while making no connection at all with her father, Hugh.

Both continued to learn about each other that summer. "He's more complex [than I had thought]," Hillary said, "there's lots of layers to him . . . The more I see him, the more I discover new things about him." Bill seemed to feel the same. "When the summer ended," he later wrote, "Hillary and I were nowhere near finished with our conversation, so we decided to live together back in New Haven, a move that doubtless caused both of our families concern." It was an interesting way to summarize their time away from Yale.[15]

Upon their return to New Haven, the two moved into an apartment near the law school where their mutual friend Greg Craig had lived. Each carried on a busy independent life. Bill was now going to class more than before; Hillary was fully involved in her clinical work on children's rights. But the most important event to take place that fall rocked Bill Clinton, called into question all his previous assumptions, and in the end may have played a crucial role in bonding their relationship.

It all went back to Bill's time at Oxford and the intense and intimate relationship he had developed with Frank Aller. Shortly after he returned from California with Hillary, Bill received a phone call. Frank Aller had committed suicide.

Aller had gone back to California to face the consequences of his decision to resist the draft. He turned himself in to the authorities, prepared to go to jail. But then he failed the army physical. Suddenly, what had begun as a long journey to martyrdom and prison became a roller-coaster ride to liberation. Aller was a free man. Yet when Clinton visited him in early 1971, he reported that he still "seemed caught in the throes of a depression." Aller was spending the year writing an autobiographical novel about the life of a draft resister. "It was an exciting but also sobering experience," Aller wrote a friend, "as I tried to assess what the decision meant after two years of living with it and what it was likely to mean in the long run. At the end of the period when I was actively revising the second draft . . . I realized that I was being led toward another decision just as difficult as the first one, if not more so." It was an ominous sign.[16]

Brooke Shearer, a woman friend from Oxford and the partner of his Rhodes classmate Strobe Talbott, was the one who called Clinton with the news. She had been one of the last people to see Aller. On the surface, everything seemed to be rosy. The *Los Angeles Times* had just offered him a job as a correspondent in Southeast Asia, writing about the war he hated. Yet something did not feel right to Shearer. A few days later, Aller put a gun to his head and pulled the trigger. His friends— soulmates, really—were devastated. They had lived through the traumas of his resistance decision, providing the support he so desperately needed. And now, just as things turned right, they went horribly wrong. It seemed, his Rhodes classmate John Isaacson said, that Aller "needed the war to stay alive. He needed the external crisis to avoid the internal crisis." Another friend, Mike Shea, believed the resistance had given him something to live for. Now there was only nothingness—and the "other decision" Aller had referred to.[17]

Clinton was devastated. Aller and he had lived through the drama of the draft decision together. It had been Aller who told Clinton he must not choose the path of resistance because he had so much to offer as a political figure. They had pondered, struggled, explored, and finally come to resolution together. Now his closest existential partner during this struggle was gone. Clinton began once again to question his own choice, the very purpose of his existence. "I am having trouble getting my hunger back up," he wrote Cliff Jackson, "and someday I may be spent and bitter that I let the world pass me by." The optimist became a skeptic, the do-gooder a naysayer. Greg Craig remembered a paper Clinton wrote during this time that questioned the worth of the entire social system and condemned the life of politics as inherently corrupt. "It was . . . an angry, hostile period of his life," Craig said, "consistent with what a lot of us felt."[18]

Writing more than three decades later, Clinton reflected further on his friend's suicide. "As I learned on that awful day, depression crowds out rationality with a vengeance. It's a disease that, when far advanced, is beyond the reasoned reach of spouses, children, lovers, and friends . . . After Frank's death, I lost my usual optimism and my interest in courses, politics, and people."[19]

It was in that period of crisis that Hillary came through for him. She had lived through her own periods of self-doubt and confusion. Despite being one of the most inner-directed and self-motivated students at Wellesley, she had experienced bouts of ennui, reluctance to get out of bed in the morning, alienation from the tasks before her, and a pervasive case of the "blahs." In February of her junior year at Wellesley, and then again for a brief period at Yale, she felt doubt about the meaning of it all and wondered whether anything could make commitment and hard work worthwhile. Now, during these darkest days with Bill Clinton, she shared that part of her inner self. "She opened herself to me," Clinton wrote. It was almost as though he were seeing a different person, less rock-hard, straight-ahead, and singularly focused than the one he had first encountered. Her willingness to be vulnerable, to share, to reveal her most private self "only strengthened and validated my feelings for her." And in doing so, Hillary helped remind Clinton "that what I was learning, doing, and thinking mattered."[20]

Having come through a personal crisis together, they resumed—indeed, in some ways, initiated—their political life together. Although they held common views on the war in Vietnam, racial inequality, and Democratic politics, each had pursued his or her own public activities. Now, as the 1972 presidential race loomed, they came together in common cause to elect George McGovern. Bill Clinton came out early for McGovern in Connecticut. The South Dakota senator had been one of the first to denounce the war; Clinton had worked in the summer after

Oxford to build support for the McGovern-Hatfield amendment, which called for ending funding for Vietnam; and his good friend from Oxford Rick Stearns was McGovern's deputy campaign manager. Hillary started the summer working for Marian Wright Edelman, then followed Bill to the campaign, recognizing that no other candidate so thoroughly mirrored her own political views. She threw herself into the work with almost religious fervor, seeking to fold together her Methodist commitment to making the world right through good works and her now thoroughly ingrained liberal political ideology. Significantly, she carried her Bible with her everywhere, reading and marking it as she went.[21]

Gary Hart, McGovern's young campaign manager, assigned Clinton to Texas, where he would be responsible for running the campaign with Taylor Branch, a University of North Carolina graduate introduced to antiwar politics by the liberal gadfly Allard Lowenstein. Local politicians in Texas could not believe the youth of the so-called campaign managers. "One of them looks ten, the other twelve," said Billie Carr. (Clinton was the ten-year-old.) Clinton and Branch had first met at Martha's Vineyard at a gathering of antiwar activists the summer before Clinton's departure for Oxford. Now they roomed together in Austin, joined on a regular basis by Hillary, who had been placed in charge of voter registration in San Antonio. On one level it was a hopeless campaign. A conservative state, Texas was never likely to embrace a stridently antiwar Democratic candidate whose nomination took place at a convention intent on reversing the politics of the 1968 convention by mandating certain percentages of black delegates, women, and other underrepresented groups. But in many ways, that made Texas an ideal place for young activists to learn the political game.[22]

Clinton worked wonders with the Democratic political apparatus. He proved especially good at getting minorities involved and bringing together different, often conflicting factions of the party. Although plans for a dramatic endorsement ceremony for McGovern at the LBJ ranch fell through (LBJ delivered his endorsement in a tepid letter to a local paper the day before), the management team hung in there. Branch was particularly impressed by Clinton's instinctive ability to size up political personalities. "He was Johnsonian in that sense," Branch said, "knowing how to read [people]." Scouring the state, he built up networks of supporters, carefully compiling phone numbers, addresses, and critical talking points on cards that he filed away for future use.[23]

It was Hillary, however, who in many ways made the greater impact. She inspired many of the women in the campaign. They saw her as personifying the new, vibrant role of women in politics, reflected in their own experience in the campaign of Sissy Farenthold for governor of Texas. Fearlessly, Hillary knocked on door after door in the toughest neighborhoods of San Antonio, trying to get as many Hispanic voters as possible to go to the polls. She teamed up with Sara Ehrman, a nearly middle-aged Jewish woman from Brooklyn. "Hillary," Ehrman recalled, "came into headquarters a kid—in brown corduroy pants, brown shirt, brown hair . . . no makeup . . . her Coke-bottle glasses . . . She looked like the campus intellectual she was." Yet the two "oddballs," as Ehrman dubbed the team, made a great combination.[24]

Almost every weekend Hillary went to Austin to stay with Bill and Taylor Branch. She and Branch got along well, and they often focused on "the grand cosmic questions." Recently separated from his wife, Branch recalled "feeling rootless and unhinged, and it was easier to talk to Hillary about those things than to Bill." In fact, Bill and Hillary spent a good portion of their time arguing, often vigorously. It was nothing new—they did it all the time back in New Haven—but there must have been a special intensity to it in Austin, because after a while they decided to stop seeing each other. A Latino labor organizer finally got them back together ("You really saved our relationship," Bill told him). But the tensions remained.[25]

Whatever was behind their brief hiatus, it evidently did not involve Bill's penchant for womanizing. While he exuded his usual charismatic charm and "all the women thought Bill was absolutely adorable and precious," he remained to all appearances faithful. From Clinton's perspective, there just was not much opportunity to pursue his wandering eye. "Gol dang," he said, "I couldn't do something if I wanted to." Hillary was present more than she was absent. But whatever they were fighting about, it was a period of stress as well as cooperation, reflecting the degree to which underlying issues in their complementary relationship persisted and remained unresolved.

Perhaps the most important consequence of their being together in Texas was the emergence of a new and critical figure in their lives—a young woman named Betsey Wright. Coming out of the Sissy Farent-hold gubernatorial campaign, Wright was excited about the possibilities of women in politics, and Hillary fit her profile. The two worked closely together, spending hours discussing their enthusiasm for the young feminist movement and the books they had read by Simone de Beauvoir and Germaine Greer. "Women were the ethical and pure force" that would change American politics, Wright believed, and no one was better suited to bring that revolution to fruition than Hillary Rodham. "I was obsessed with how far Hillary might go," she said, "with her mixture of brilliance, ambition, and self-assuredness . . . [I couldn't stop thinking] about all the incredible things she could do in the world." Hillary shared Wright's enthusiasm, and she was so impressed by her ability that after McGovern's defeat she persuaded Wright to move to Washington to work for the National Women's Political Caucus.[26]

Betsey Wright thereafter became a fixture in the lives of Bill and Hillary. Bill, Wright thought, was attractive and charming, but Hillary was the person she wanted to put her money on to become the first female president of the United States. Ironically, it was Bill she glommed on to first. In 1982 she became Governor Clinton's chief of staff. It was there that Wright made her major political contribution to the Clintons' political future. But no one came into the vortex of that relationship understanding better the personal as well as political dynamics between Bill and Hillary. Moreover, no one made more astute and consequential observations about their partnership.[27]

Bill Clinton drew his own conclusions from the McGovern campaign. Clinton, David Maraniss observed, learned "the lesson of not being caught too far out on the left on defense, welfare, crime. From then on he would take steps to make sure those were marketed in a way to appeal to conservatives and moderates." Bill's classmate Nancy Bekavac agreed. Deep in his bones, Clinton learned from Texas that "the Age of [the New Deal] Titans" had passed, and how difficult that would make his own climb to political credibility in a southern state with many of the same conservative tendencies as Texas. "He had been part of the largest, most lopsided defeat in American politics," she said. "The meaning of that was not lost on him."[28]

Hillary and Bill returned for their final year at Yale wiser and more seasoned. Hillary had tasted the rich possibilities of feminist politics and the opportunities that could be seized by the right person at the right time. Bill had learned even more about the politics of grassroots networking and organizing, and he had come to understand the limitations that the politics of his region placed on how far a candidate could go in expressing liberal ideas. They also remained together, though in tension over multiple issues that divided them. The next year would help establish the boundaries of those tensions and determine whether and how they could be lived with.

Once again, Bill did not attend his first class of the fall semester until mid-November. He stayed on in Austin to do cleanup work for the McGovern campaign and organize all the file cards he had generated over the course of the summer and fall. Once again, he passed his courses with solid grades. But mostly he devoted himself to thinking about the future. He intended to go back to Arkansas and get into politics. But a person did not just jump into the political arena from nowhere, especially if the nowhere was New Haven, Connecticut. So Bill spent part of his spring semester working his connections at the University of Arkansas in hopes of securing an appointment there as professor in its law school. He contacted the appropriate deans, gave a talk to the faculty, and walked the halls using his charm to persuade his future colleagues that he would be a positive addition to their ranks. Yale's letter saying he had a "very good but not outstanding record" seemed good enough for Arkansas. The only question the faculty had was whether he really wanted to teach law or just wished to use a faculty position as a stepping-stone to politics. Clinton responded, in a fashion with which people would become familiar over the years, "I have no plans *at this time* (italics added) to run for public office." Perhaps most strange, Clinton portrayed his appointment at Arkansas subsequently as a "pure accident" prompted by a phone call from a desperate dean who needed his help, when in fact Bill had initiated and orchestrated the entire process. Here, as in the case of the draft, it was as if he wished to rewrite what actually happened and minimize the degree to which it was the result of calculated planning.[29]

Hillary, in the meantime, spent much of her fourth (and additional) year at Yale pursuing her passion for children's law issues. She worked with the Yale Child Study Center and the Carnegie Foundation's Council on Children. The project was headed by the noted child psychologist

Kenneth Keniston. She helped to write an article for the *Harvard Education Review* that focused on the need to treat children as people, not just dependents, and liberate them from the legal constraints created by their being subject to the "empire of the father." Clearly, she intended to make a career of work that joined her legal expertise with her commitment to prevent child abuse. Indeed, by the time she graduated in 1973, she had already accepted a job in Cambridge at Marian Wright Edelman's Children's Defense Fund.[30]

That, of course, ran counter to Bill Clinton's plan. While he understood fully the sacrifice he was asking Hillary to make, he hoped very much that she would decide to come to Arkansas with him and be part of a political team that would ascend the heights, first of state politics, then perhaps more. In effect, he was asking her to forgo a wealth of other opportunities, from being a premier young associate in the most prestigious law firms of Washington, New York, or Boston to fully committing herself to public service on behalf of children and families in nonprofit organizations full of exciting people who could help her establish her own independent career in political and public service.

To celebrate their graduation, the two went to England, where Bill showed Hillary his old haunts. He took her to the great sites of the hill and lake country as well as to the theaters and art galleries of London. It was during their time in the lake country that Bill asked Hillary to be his wife. "I couldn't believe I'd done it," he said. "Neither could she. She said she loved me but couldn't say yes." Bill couldn't blame her. There were so many conflicting options, two worlds of vastly different possibilities, not to mention the abiding tensions in their relationship, and the magnetic appeal Hillary herself possessed as a political star and a potential national figure. Still, after saying no to Bill's proposal, she agreed to come to Arkansas in June so they could take the Arkansas bar examination together. Bill was determined not to lose her as Hillary was weighing her options and their consequences.[31]

To his friends, Bill had described Hillary as his future wife. "She has the biggest heart, the most beautiful eyes. Her middle name is Diane—that means loving and gorgeous." Not in the eyes of Bill's friends and family. In the gendered Southern culture of Arkansas she came across as plain, unattractive, and uninteresting. One summed it up simply, noting "No makeup." More important was the response of the family. "I thought her hair was silly and hated her Coke-bottle glasses," Bill's brother, Roger, said. "Mother and I looked at her, then looked at each other, surprised because Bill usually dated Barbie doll types. Hillary was different, indeed." Bill's mother, with her bright red lipstick, heavily rouged face, and white skunk stripe down the middle of her black hair, wished she could sit Hillary on the edge of a bathtub "and give her some makeup lessons." Hillary seemed the exact opposite of what Virginia had hoped for. This was a Yankee who cared not a whit about her appearance—in fact, she seemed to *try* to be plain. Hillary was "too busy getting educated and doing good things like starting youth-advocate programs," Virginia noted, to devote any time to making herself pretty. She found Hillary to be "quiet, cool, unresponsive. Maybe she was reflecting back the vibrations she felt from us. Or maybe she was as confused by us Arkansans as we were by this Chicagoan." It was not a visit full of promise for the future.[32]

Bill was apoplectic. He unloaded on his mother for the coolness she had shown Hillary, her disrespect for her. He told his mother to pray for him. "Pray that it's Hillary. Because I'll tell you this. For me it's Hillary or it's nobody." Clearly two irreconcilable forces had collided. Virginia Clinton and Hillary Rodham were as close to Bill Clinton as any two persons could be. Yet they were total opposites, each detesting the values, lifestyle, and appearance of the other. Their confrontation carried lessons. Hillary had gained a firsthand understanding of Bill's character that she may never have fully grasped before; and Bill, perhaps for the first time, fully comprehended the nature of the conflict that existed between the kind of male-female relationships he had grown up with and those he had encountered with Ann Markusen and Hillary Rodham. Unsurprisingly, Hillary's trip south resolved nothing, and for the moment, Bill and she simply returned to their respective new lives, one as a neophyte law professor quietly exploring the political waters of Arkansas, the other as a crusading lawyer contemplating her future as an advocate for children and an agent for social change. Each had much to think about.[33]

On one level, Bill Clinton appeared to be proceeding with his non-stop success story. On another level, he was someone whose life as a late adolescent and early adult consisted of nothing but crises. First he had tried to deal with the history of child and spousal abuse and alcoholism at home, then with the death of the only father he ever knew.

After that there came the two-year struggle over the draft and the soul-searching anguish of trying to find an answer, and finally, the restlessness of his first year at Yale, followed by the horror of having to deal with Frank Aller's suicide.

It was in the midst of that maelstrom that Hillary Rodham had entered his life. A compelling, committed, and above all distinctive personality, she brought together in one person virtually all the attributes Clinton most needed. Sui generis, she offered strength of character, discipline of personality, moral direction, and the poise of a self-certain political actor that complemented all of Clinton's own qualities, and also helped fill the void in his emotional life. At a time when his personal life was a "shambles," she presented the opportunity to achieve wholeness, a moral center, and beyond that, an ongoing reason to take on the next challenge.

Hillary, in turn, came from her own complicated past. Growing up in a household in some ways as dysfunctional as his, she took her cues from a mother who courageously chose to hold the family together despite her husband's gruffness, authoritarianism, and capriciousness. But because of the strength of her mother, Hillary developed the ego, the moral center, and the religious commitment necessary to transcend the dilemmas of her childhood. There was a strength and consistency to her moral vision that gave her that equilibrium, that carpenter's-level center, that carried her through the tough times. She was demanding, provocative, challenging, and rarely satisfied—not an easy person to live with—but also possessed by a sense of calm and self-certainty that made disrupting her journey forward difficult to attempt.

To Bill's charm, outgoingness, political charisma, and intellectual genius, she brought direction, stability, discipline, and a personal center. To Hillary's intense journey of individual leadership for social good and political change, he brought humor, softness, and a sensitivity to human frailty and complexity. By definition, their personal attributes created a perfect formula for conflict and tension. How could she live with someone who was so indirect, winsome, and circuitous? How could he live with someone who was so directed, controlled, and task-oriented? Yet they also presented an ideal example of how traits that were opposite could be complementary, and how divisions that sometimes could paralyze were also ones that enabled achievements otherwise unimaginable.

FIVE

The Arkansas Years, Part One: 1973–80

Bill started to teach in the Law School at the University of Arkansas with the same casual style that had characterized his three years at Yale. Rather than give pedantic lectures studded with references to legal precedents, he treated his classes as conversations about interesting subjects. He enjoyed interacting with his students, but he rarely if ever devoted much time to getting ready for class or grading tests. Indeed, in one famous moment, he "lost" all the exams of his students from one class and sought to strike a deal with them, giving everyone a high passing grade without having them retake the test. His approach, as one colleague said, was "off the cuff."[1]

Not surprisingly given his history, he proved particularly effective with black students. Clinton made them feel at home in his classroom, befriended them, and signaled his commitment to their success. In return they called him "Wonder Boy." "It was a miracle the way he was," one of his students later said. "Fayetteville and northwest Arkansas was a white enclave [but] Wonder Boy did not waver in respect to his conduct with African Americans."[2]

The time Bill Clinton did not spend on preparing lectures he spent riding around the state with his political buddies to scout out the most appealing territory in which to make his first bid for office. Although during his recruitment visit to Fayetteville he declared that he had no "plans" to run for office, that was true only in the sense that he had not identified the particular place where he would launch his first campaign. From his work with Senator Fulbright and his summer-long involvement in the gubernatorial campaign of Frank Holt, Clinton already had numerous political allies. Despite being an academic town, Fayetteville was also a great place for political networking, and he had already become a fast friend to Rudy Moore, one of the liberal state legislators who knew the state's party politics inside out. The local political guru Carl Whillock, who had card files on local counties that were beyond belief, took Clinton on a tour of rural towns—"retail politics," he called it. Rudy and his other friends, including Paul and Mary Fray, discussed ad nauseam Bill's next move. All agreed that running for the state legislature or senate was small potatoes and made no sense.

Gradually, they zeroed in on the Third Congressional District, where a Republican, John Paul Hammerschmidt, had been in office for years. (He had won 77 percent of the vote in 1972.) But this was the time of Watergate. The nation was up in arms at the increasingly transparent dirty tricks that Richard Nixon had arrogantly played on the American political system during the 1972 presidential election. Like most Republicans, Hammerschmidt had tried to defend Nixon, and the more he did so, the more he lost popularity. So Clinton, with the help of people like Fray, Moore, and Whillock, concluded that this was the place to run. If Bill simply met enough people, with that winsome charm of his he could defeat Hammerschmidt.[3]

Clinton embarked on his campaign with a terrific staff of local politicians and a $10,000 campaign fund provided by his uncle Raymond, the car dealer, and Raymond's good friend Gabe Crawford, also a close associate of Bill's mother. Bill went into every café and country store he could find and came out ahead in the first Democratic primary with 44 percent of the vote. He won the runoff with 69 percent, but was still behind in the polls against Hammerschmidt by a two-to-one margin in September. But Clinton kept up his personal visits, raised enough money to do TV and radio ads, and, for the first time in his political life, endorsed national health insurance, as well as arguing for more aid to education, a more equitable tax structure, and better jobs for the average working person. Without too much trouble he won endorsements from a variety of groups, including teachers, local labor unions, and the national AFL-CIO.[4]

In Cambridge, Hillary continued to work for the Children's Defense Fund, but as Bill was considering his political future, she also was considering her options. Above all, she was grappling with the question of whether to move to Arkansas and marry Bill Clinton. When she flew to Arkansas for Thanksgiving, they ruminated on their future together. In a beautiful Frank Lloyd Wright–type house Bill had rented by a river, he acknowledged that being married to him "would be a high wire operation." She, in turn, acknowledged that it might be better for her to go her own way. They would meet again at Christmas to talk further.

It was during that visit that John Doar, former deputy attorney general under Robert F. Kennedy and now head of the task force investigating the possible impeachment of Richard Nixon for the House Judiciary Committee, called Clinton to ask him to join his team. Clinton, having already cast his lot with Arkansas politics, declined, but he strongly recommended Hillary, who was also on Doar's short list. Doar quickly called her to offer the position, and she accepted, letting Marian Wright Edelman know the news while she was still in Arkansas with Bill. Shortly thereafter, Hillary moved to D.C., taking up a life full of secrecy, critically important investigations, nonstop work—with national implications—and little if any social life. It suited her ideally.[5]

In Washington, Hillary Rodham was surrounded by colleagues as intense, bright, and committed as she was. By definition, everything the team did was classified. Her task was to be part of the smaller group who investigated the meaning of the phrase "high crimes and misdemeanors." Did it mean that an actual criminal offense had to have been committed? What was the history? Working with a scholarly team headed by the Yale historian C. Vann Woodward, Hillary's group dug into that background, concluding that "to limit impeachable conduct to criminal offenses would be incompatible with the evidence concerning the constitutional meaning of the phrase." Doar prized Hillary's work, considering her one of his stars. She got along well with her colleagues, one of whom—Terry Kirkpatrick—told her that if she did decide to go to Arkansas to practice law, she would have to be three times as good as any man to succeed. But, he added, "you can be a big fish in a small pond."[6]

Everyone on the staff knew about her relationship with Bill Clinton. When he called, or came to Washington, her "face would change. It would light up." She was "besotted," one said, "absolutely, totally crazy" about him. One evening she was driving home with her colleague and close friend Bernard Nussbaum, a New Yorker who was working on the impeachment investigation with her. She told Nussbaum that Bill was going to run for Congress, then governor, and that before long he would become president of the United States. "Hillary," he said, "that's the most ridiculous thing I've ever heard. How can you tell me that your boyfriend is going to become president of the United States? That's nuts." Hillary was not charmed. "You asshole, Bernie," she responded, "you're a jerk. So don't pontificate to me. He's going to be president of the United States." It took days for their relationship to return to normal. Although Hillary had not yet made up her mind about moving to Arkansas, her leisure hours were dominated by thoughts about what was going on there.[7]

Indeed, once Clinton became an active candidate, Hillary became an active player, even if from a distance. People in the campaign already knew about her. Rudy Moore recalled, "We all had a good feeling about her because he talked so lovingly about her as a person and as an intellectual partner." But once the campaign was launched, she became more intrusive—and less popular. For long periods, she called the campaign staff daily, offering advice, giving instructions, conveying from her office in Washington what she saw as the do's and don'ts for Bill to follow. Many staff members came to resent her, and she them, especially when they failed to follow her instructions.[8]

Hillary also picked up on the fact that Bill was seeing other women during the campaign. Betsey Wright noted that "there were girls falling all over him like he was a rock star." When, in response, Hillary supposedly told him that she was considering sleeping with someone in Washington, Clinton went crazy, and according to one campaign aide "about broke down and cried." But that did not stop Clinton from pursuing the other women. Betsey Wright, probably the longest-term observer of these tensions, translated Bill's actions as saying, "Hillary is a very important person to me . . . She is one of the most incredible people I've ever known. And hey, isn't this girl falling all over me cute [as can be]."[9]

All of this came to a head when suddenly, in midsummer, the impeachment process in Washington reached a climax. Prosecutors, authorized by a Supreme Court decision to listen to all the tape recordings that Nixon had made of his White House conversations, quickly "found the smoking gun." Nixon had explicitly told his aides to cover up White House involvement in the Watergate break-ins, ordering that "hush money" be delivered to potential informants and that the FBI quash its own investigation. Within days, Nixon was forced to resign, the work of

the Doar task force was over, and Hillary faced the most critical decision of her life—to go or not to go to Arkansas. Her friend Sara Ehrman
told her "You are crazy" if you go. Knowing that Hillary had already approached the University of Arkansas Law School about a teaching position, Ehrman asked, "Why on earth would you throw away your future"
on what she characterized as a "hillbilly law school." Was Hillary sure
this was the right move? Hillary replied, "No, but I'm going anyway."
Subsequently, she acknowledged the doubts that plagued her. "My
friends and family thought I had lost my mind," she said. "I was a little
bit concerned about that as well."[10]

In fact, her decision was carefully thought through. In light of all the
rumors about Bill's multiple flirtations, she had urged her father and
brother to go to Arkansas and volunteer in the campaign. One day they
simply showed up at headquarters, asking to be told what to do. But in
the eyes of many, their primary task was crystal clear—to monitor Bill's
romantic activities and keep him under control. One woman in particular, called "the College Girl," a campaign staffer, had become Clinton's
favorite erotic interest. Even when Hillary arrived from Washington, he
showed no indication of—or interest in—ending the relationship. Rather,
he gave explicit instructions to his staff to keep an eye out for Hillary's
arrival at headquarters each day, and then to act accordingly. "There were
times," one staffer said, "when Hillary would be coming in the front door,
and we'd be hustling the College Girl out the back. It was sad. It was
horrible." Eventually, Bill moved to get her out of the office by having the
wife of another campaign staffer, Paul Fray, hire her as a babysitter, but
only when the young woman realized there was no future with the candidate did she decide to go off with an old boyfriend and get married.[11]

The tension between Hillary and Bill during this time was palpable. "They would constantly argue," one of Hillary's Wellesley friends,
Nancy "Peach" Pietrafesa said, "and the next thing you know, they'd be
falling all over each other with 'Oh my darling . . . come here baby . . .
you're adorable,' then throwing things at each other." It was an emotional
roller coaster. At the same time, Hillary's style alienated many of the
campaign workers. Hillary "managed to antagonize the entire staff,"
Clinton's press secretary wrote to him. After her arrival, Clinton's campaign manager declared, the whole organization "went to shit." Yet on
virtually every occasion, Bill sided with Hillary when his campaign

managers disagreed. Despite her tone and unpopularity, he was afraid of her. At some point during their time at Yale together, he had decided that he needed her, and although that never stopped his predilection for living parallel lives, the fear of losing her ultimately became the critical variable in his response to their conflicts. He would not go against her wishes or alienate her.[12]

It all came to a head on election eve. In a critical last-minute decision, the campaign had to decide whether to send $15,000 to Fort Smith, where the race was predicted to be close and manipulation of voting data was common. The money would go to assist with "voter turnout." It was a classic political and moral dilemma. Clinton remained quiet. Hillary reportedly said, "No, you don't want to be a party to this . . . I don't want to win this way." She made the call. The election was incredibly close. Fort Smith went to Hammerschmidt by a much higher margin than predicted. The difference between defeat and victory was only six thousand votes, making the Clinton campaign's decision not to send money to Fort Smith a pivotal call. According to some, election night turned into a nasty brawl. When Paul Fray accused Hillary of having cost Bill the election, Hillary retorted by accusing Fray of having found "Bill a bedmate while I was in Washington."[13]

Despite the conflict in his campaign and the loss, Clinton had transformed Arkansas politics. From being down more than 30 percentage points two months before the election, he had come back to lose by only two. No one had ever turned an electorate around like that. His future would be bright. But in the process, the political partnership of Bill and Hillary had endured heavy seas, setting patterns of behavior and response that were in many ways prophetic. What they would learn from the experience, and how it would shape their future, occupied their attention for much of the ensuing six years.

The most important development was Hillary's decision to take the leap and marry Bill Clinton. It was not a simple decision. She knew by now exactly what she was getting into. Nor did she come to it quickly, first wrestling with whether to move to Arkansas at all. But once she made her decision, Hillary was committed to sticking to it—a lesson she had learned from her mother.

The first stage of the evolving drama was Hillary's application for a teaching position in Fayetteville at the University of Arkansas Law School. She was singularly impressive in her interviews—poised, direct, sharp, incisive. In the classroom, she displayed a teaching style diametrically opposite to that of Bill. While he was conversational, informal, open, and easy, she was demanding, tightly organized, structured, and efficient. As one friend noted, when Hillary strode into class, "she neither talked nor dressed like she was from Arkansas . . . If she seemed a little out of place, it was also abundantly clear that she was tough, intelligent and articulate." At the university, as in the campaign, "people were never indifferent about Hillary." She cared less about charming people, far more about eliciting their respect. In the end, almost everyone respected her—and those that did not were at least afraid of her.[14]

Arkansas was different from any other place Hillary had ever lived. The culture shock was evident. In Fayetteville, the only place to eat downtown was a cafeteria. The football game on Saturdays represented the social highlight of the week, for which people both dressed up and yelled "sooo-*eee*" for the Arkansas Razorbacks. To some, at least, Hillary just did not fit in and was perceived as arrogant, "above it all." "I never knew from one day to the next how I was going to be received by Hillary," Carolyn Staley said. She also conveyed signals that were off-putting. "You're either useful or extraneous to her," Staley said. "Look, Hillary is as tough as nails." On the other hand, she bonded closely with her few other female colleagues at the university. Hillary and Diane Kincaid from Political Science (soon to be Diane Blair) formed a bond that would last a lifetime. Still the questions remained: Was she willing to commit to Bill, and how long would Arkansas remain the place she wished to be, given all the options that remained open to her?[15]

Hillary understood that she could not postpone this decision forever. As much as she appreciated the risks in marrying Clinton, she also grasped the uniqueness of what Bill had to offer. She was in love, he had unlimited potential, he *would* make a difference, and she could be part of that. Moreover, how much longer would he remain the long-suffering suitor? At what point would he tire of her repeatedly saying no, not yet? One day, as Bill was taking Hillary to the airport for an out-of-town professional trip, they passed a house that she admired with a "For Sale" sign on it. When Hillary returned, Bill drove her to the house again and told her he had just bought it, but it was far too big and expensive for him alone. She must marry him so they could live in it together. This time she said yes. Looking back on the whole experience, Hillary told the author Gail Sheehy: "I kept struggling between my head and my heart." Should she pursue her ambitions as an independent woman and change the world, or take the chance that this partnership with Bill might be the best path to her larger goal?

The decision to stay in Arkansas was ultimately a leap of faith. But it was more than faith alone. Love and calculation went hand in hand, leading to her conclusion that this relationship might be the most realistic way to achieve what her heart told her to do and also what her mind wanted. "Bill's desire to be in public life was much more specific than my desire to do good," she said, and that fact, in combination with Hillary's desire "to be part of changing the world," made the difference.[16]

And so the die was cast. It was not a decision that she or others took lightly. Paul Fray, the local politician who had helped run his campaign, predicted to Bill: "Hillary will be your Waterloo." Betsey Wright, the Texas woman who once envisioned Hillary as the first woman president, "was disappointed when they married." Most of Hillary's close friends advised her to reclaim her own life and not subject herself to the whims of someone notorious for having a wandering eye. Even Bill acknowledged doubts. Despite being an indefatigable suitor, he recognized how difficult it had been for him ever to make a commitment to a woman. "For the longest time," he reflected in his memoir, "I'd thought I'd never get married." Proud of Hillary and convinced their marriage "felt right," he also recognized that it rested on "a relationship that might not ever be perfect, but would certainly never be boring." A mixed recipe for marital bliss.[17]

Only family and friends were present for the marriage ceremony, which took place not in a church but in their home. On the eve of her wedding, Hillary still did not have a bridal gown. She and her mother hastened to the biggest department store in town to buy one—off the rack. The morning of the wedding, Bill broke the news to his mother that Hillary would keep her own name and not become Mrs. Clinton. Virginia broke down, infuriated at what she took to be a profound insult. After the wedding, Ann Henry, a good friend and colleague of them both, hosted a reception at her home for all their friends in Fayetteville.

As an almost symbolic coda to the pervasive sense that this was a marriage very much out of the ordinary, the newly married couple did not go on a honeymoon. Instead, weeks later—accompanied by the entire Rodham family—they journeyed to Acapulco on a special package that Dorothy Rodham had dug up. On their wedding night itself, Bill was rousted from bed twice to go downtown and bail out guests who had gotten too rambunctious and been detained by police. Thus did the Arkansas years of Bill Clinton and Hillary Rodham as husband and wife commence.[18]

Within six months, Bill and Hillary made their second big decision. He would run for attorney general. It made perfect sense. He was an attorney, a professor at the state law school, and someone who had shown spectacular promise by almost defeating an entrenched congressman who earlier had won by 77 percent. Moreover, this was a statewide office, and hence a natural stepping-stone to the governorship. Bill Clinton was twenty-nine years old, he had come home to serve the people he loved, and he already had a finely tuned courthouse network. Indeed, his 1974 campaign aide Rudy Moore had developed a computerized file of people throughout the state who would support Bill. While in his congressional race Clinton had taken traditional liberal stands on most issues, he now moved toward the center, focusing on consumer interests. For example, he was unwilling to support repeal of the state's right-to-work law, a litmus test for organized labor. Hence he lost their endorsement. But he went on to win 55.6 percent of the vote in the Democratic primary, and from there moved to an overwhelming victory in the general election. So secure was his victory that he and Hillary spent much of their summer working for Jimmy Carter's presidential campaign, Bill running the effort in Arkansas, Hillary in Indianapolis.[19]

Strategically, Clinton could not have made a wiser move. While the attorney general's office had statewide visibility, it rarely became involved in divisive partisan squabbles. Rather, the attorney general looked out primarily for the rights of average citizens demanding fair treatment at the hands of government and corporations. Clinton embraced that role avidly. He spent most of his time seeking to regulate utility rates so that power companies could not squeeze excess profits out of public resources; and he actively opposed telephone companies when they tried to raise their prices, particularly on pay phone use. He also dedicated himself to improving the quality of nursing home care. In addition, Clinton followed his longtime personal instincts, substantially diversifying the staff of the attorney general's office, making it 25 percent female and 20 percent African American. At the same time, Clinton used his statewide visibility to increase his political reputation. Having worked hard as a couple for the election of Jimmy Carter to the presidency, Bill and Hillary soon appeared on Carter's invitation list to prominent Washington social functions. Thus both in his new elected office and as an increasingly visible national presence, Clinton brought pride to his home state. If in 1974 his political opponents in the congressional race could claim that Clinton lacked political experience, serving as attorney general, his friend Doug Wallace observed, helped "provide a proving ground for the future."[20]

Moving to Little Rock also meant new opportunities for Hillary. Looking for a prestigious legal position, she soon joined the Rose law firm, the most highly regarded in the state. With a wide variety of clients, and connections to major national companies with offices in Arkansas, she found herself part of a network of powerhouse figures. Not every lawyer in the firm was enthusiastic about this young woman from Yale. As one of her close associates said, in Little Rock "Rule Number One might well have been: Little Rock women don't have careers." Some secretaries joined in the criticism of Hillary, making pejorative remarks about her hair and clothes (sometimes she did not wear nylons). "There wasn't one stereotypically womanly or feminine thing about her," her own secretary commented. In return, and displaying characteristic self-confidence, Hillary never held her tongue or played the game of being deferential.[21]

Her salvation was the fact that she quickly became a close ally of two of the most powerful and respected members of the Rose cohort, Webb Hubbell and Vince Foster. Hillary became particularly close to Foster, a childhood friend of Bill Clinton's. Like Hillary, Foster seemed almost preternaturally mature and middle-aged. Taciturn, handsome, and brilliant, he possessed a charm almost directly proportionate to his shyness. The two shared a passion for books and topics of philosophical gravitas. The first to recommend her to the firm, Foster developed a special relationship with Hillary that was both personal and collegial. Hillary showed a sense of humor with Foster not seen in her other

associations, calling him Vincent Fosterini and hiring a belly dancer to
celebrate his birthday at an office party. Even Hubbell, the third in the
"team" dubbed the "three amigos," felt sometimes like an outsider in
the presence of the other two. Although it has been suggested by some
that Foster and Hillary carried on a sexual affair, there is no evidence
for the allegation, and most commentators have dismissed the idea out
of hand. But no one underestimates the importance of the relationship,
or the degree to which Hubbell and Foster made possible a professional
life for Hillary in Little Rock that provided a foundation for her political
and social initiatives both inside and outside the state.[22]

Perhaps the most significant long-term relationship Bill Clinton
and Hillary Rodham developed during their early years in Little Rock
was with a young political operator from New York City named Dick
Morris. Almost exactly the same age as Clinton, Morris experienced
the same kind of single-minded and purposeful trajectory as Clinton,
only in political management. Bright and aggressive, Morris read *The
New York Times* from front to back from the time he was eight, and
early on became involved in canvassing for Democratic candidates in
Manhattan, whether they were running for City Council, State Assembly, or Congress. As a student at Columbia University in the mid-
sixties, Morris created one of the most effective political machines that
the Democratic Party on the West Side of Manhattan had ever seen.

The reform wing of the New York Democratic Party had started a
series of political clubs throughout Manhattan dedicated to electing
public officials who would toss out the old guard of Tammany Hall.
Morris volunteered the services of his young army of college activists to
the cause. Their techniques were tactically brilliant and politically simple. Dividing up every precinct and every block, teams went into apartment and tenement buildings to knock on each door. They would then
initiate ten-to-fifteen-minute conversations, asking (not telling) the
residents about which issues concerned them, what they thought were
the city's biggest problems, and how they felt the political system could
best develop solutions that they would support. They engaged in no
campaigning per se, only information gathering. Armed with their
notes, the team would later determine which concerns had the greatest
priority for each voter. At that point, an individualized letter would be
sent to the person, linking their concerns to the platform of a local can-

didate and urging support. Follow-up visits would then be made, with the team rating the odds on whether given voters were favorable or un-favorable to their candidate and how likely it was that they would go to the polls. With that information as a base, students were mobilized to run "get out the vote" campaigns on election day.

The system worked miracles. Party leaders were thrown out and new reformers installed. An anti–Vietnam War candidate achieved the unheard-of moral victory of coming within one percentage point of de-feating a multiterm pro-war congressman—this at the very beginning of the antiwar movement. New reform members of the State Senate, the State Assembly, and the City Council were chosen. And Morris deserved a substantial amount of the credit. Well-organized, disci-plined, and loyal, Morris's activists, dubbed the "Junior Mafia," united behind his ironclad leadership. This was a modern-day version of the old Democratic machine, but with a scientific expertise and hands-on process for sifting and calculating the language of political appeals that made it seem almost revolutionary.[23]

A decade later, Morris had put together a political consulting busi-ness that he was marketing around the country. Of the sixty campaigns he approached in his first year on the national market, he found only three clients, with Clinton's being the first. Though they were com-pletely different from each other in mood, affect, and style, the two hit it off. Clinton was easy, charming, and outgoing; Morris was direct, controlled, and short-tempered. Later, Clinton summarized Morris's personality. "[He's] a brilliant, abrasive character," Clinton wrote, "brim-ming with ideas about politics and policy. He believed in aggressive, creative campaigns, and was so cocksure about everything that a lot of people, especially in a down-home place like Arkansas, found him hard to take. But I was stimulated by him . . . I refused to be put off by his manner, partly because I had good instincts about when he was right and when he wasn't. One thing I really liked about him was that he would tell me things I didn't want to hear." That was Dick Morris.[24]

The New York tactician came to Clinton at exactly the right time in Clinton's political decision-making process. He had been a wunderkind as attorney general, pleasing almost everyone and alienating few. But what was the next step on the political ladder? John McClellan, the se-nior U.S. senator from Arkansas, had decided to step down, completing

his final term in 1978. Although an old conservative with views drastically different from those of Clinton, he knew and liked the young attorney general and strongly urged him to run for his now vacant Senate
seat. The governorship—Clinton's other option—McClellan dismissed
as a minor office by comparison. Most important, McClellan did not like
the ex-governor David Pryor, the other potential candidate for his seat.

McClellan hit the nail on the head. Should Clinton go for the
enormous prestige of the United States Senate at the age of thirty-one,
pitting himself against a candidate who had been the governor and possessed a substantial political following; or should he let Pryor run unop-
posed in the Democratic primary for the Senate and choose instead to
be a candidate for governor? These were the kinds of questions Morris's
methods were primed to answer. In lieu of high school and college students going door to door to find out what constituents were thinking,
Morris used public opinion polls, but not the kind that simply asked a
respondent who they were going to vote for or how they felt about war
or a piece of legislation. Rather, Morris's polls asked carefully calibrated
questions designed to tease out the same kind of nuanced political information that his old student canvassers had sought in their open-
ended dialogues.

Morris was hired to help answer the basic question of whether
Clinton should run for the Senate or the governorship. They were both
fanatics about the process. They talked for hours, winnowing questions, refining language, figuring out which queries would produce reli-
able data. The focus was issues, not image. "We were a match," Morris
later wrote about the relationship. "I had found a client who could delve
into the strategy with me." After seeing the basic data, Morris and Clinton arrived at the same conclusion. Yes, Clinton might well win the
Senate seat, but it would be a difficult race and against someone with
whom Clinton shared a basic constituency and similar points of view.
The governor's race, however, would be much more an open-and-shut
case. Clinton could win easily, and do so without alienating one of his
closest potential allies. After Clinton told Pryor of his decision, he
urged him to use Morris's skills to defeat his own opponent, Congressman Jim Guy Tucker. Which Pryor promptly did.[25]

Morris had been correct about the gubernatorial race. It was a
landslide. Clinton won with 63 percent of the vote. He had broadened

his political message again, speaking to multiple constituencies. Education, he argued, was the state's top priority. Arkansas ranked next to last in per capita school expenditures and student test scores. No issue was more critical, he said, as an avenue to economic growth and a higher standard of living. He also focused on tax reform—another populist issue that affected virtually every resident in the state—and the need for more monies to go into public works such as roads, sewers, and bridges. Blasting the Republican Party for having done nothing, either in Washington or Little Rock, for average workers, family farmers, or the poor, he wrapped himself in the traditional imagery of a Franklin Roosevelt Democrat who cared about the everyday citizen down the block.

Notable during the campaign was the way Clinton handled the criticisms against him and against Hillary. For the first time—but not the last—his opponents charged him with draft evasion. But they lacked the evidence to prove that Clinton had manipulated the Selective Service process, and he simply referred them to Colonel Holmes, who at the time remained neutral and nonresponsive on the issue. When Hillary was portrayed as a "hoity-toity" Yankee with strange ideas and manners alien to people in Arkansas, Clinton rallied to her defense. Hillary, he said, was "old-fashioned . . . in every conceivable way." Along with being hardworking, no-nonsense, and intelligent, he extolled her for not seeing "any sense in extramarital sex" and not caring "for drink." It could hardly have been a more fervent affirmation of Hillary—yet with a strange selection of qualities for an Arkansas audience to relate to.[26]

At the same time, the Hillary-Bill dynamic continued to play out in the internal politics of the campaign. Just as she had with Clinton's 1974 campaign for Congress and the 1976 race for attorney general, Hillary played the role of number one adviser. No one could supplant her, go around her, or ace her—especially when the issue was critical and she felt strongly about it. Rudy Moore, who had been with Clinton since 1974 and now managed his gubernatorial campaign, described exactly why Hillary was so important: "Bill sees the light and the sunshine about people," Moore said; "Hillary sees their darker side. She has much more ability than he does to see who's with you, who's against you, and to make sure they don't take advantage of you. He's not expecting to be jumped, but she always is." Protective and tough, she was the one always ready to strike back. Bill not only recognized that he needed Hillary's discipline and toughness, he also knew that without it he could never maximize his potential. As a later pollster for Clinton described it, Bill "was conflict averse . . . and by nature uncomfortable attacking," while Hillary possessed a "fierceness" that put steel in his spine.[27]

Dick Morris saw the same qualities—from the beginning. Like Richard Nixon, he wrote, "she definitely has a streak of ruthlessness and paranoia . . . When she's mad at you she doesn't talk to you for months and months [and unlike Bill], she believes in always taking the fight to the other side." The same roles that they played in the moot court appearance at Yale Law School were again evident: He was the feminine voice of the two, she the masculine. As partners they were clearly unique. Only rarely did they show affection toward each other. As the reporter Roy Reed noted, "their romance is not showy. In public he calls her Hillary, not Honey. She calls him Bill, not Darling. But they manage to leave no doubt that each is the most important person in the other's life." Usually the two roles complemented each other, Bill's winsomeness and charm smoothing over and making more palatable her directness, her discipline giving focus to his otherwise all-inclusive outreach for approval.

When the two were working as a team, they were virtually unbeatable. When they came into conflict, however, the battle took precedence over cooperation. One person had to win, and the victor would not be Bill. Hillary wielded the ultimate power, because in the end, Bill was afraid of what would happen if he lost her. Thus, when she turned on him in anger, he capitulated.[28]

In the election of 1978 the chemistry worked perfectly and the young couple swept to victory. Bill Clinton was the youngest governor ever elected in the United States. Just thirty-one years of age, he had achieved virtually all the goals he had set for himself up to that point in life. Not only was he the family hero, he had delivered on his promise to come back to the United States from England and serve the people of Arkansas whom he loved.

Clinton's inauguration summed up the emotional exhilaration of the triumph. All his old friends from Georgetown and Oxford gathered for the ceremony. Greg Craig and Steve Cohen were there, the latter having just finished four years of service in government that had eroded his faith and undermined his optimism. But now, suddenly, he felt as if his generation had its chance to take its place in the sun. "I feel two emotions in this room [right now] that I haven't experienced in a long time," he said, "pride and hope."

The next day Clinton rang the chimes on Cohen's choice of words. Pride and Hope became the theme of his inaugural address. "For as long as I can remember," he declared, "I have believed passionately in the cause of equal opportunity, and I will do what I can to advance it. For as long as I remember, I have deplored the arbitrary and abusive exercise of power by those in authority, and I will do what I can to prevent it . . . For as long as I can remember, I have loved the land, air and water of Arkansas, and I will do what I can to protect them. For as long as I can remember," he concluded, "I have wished to ease the burdens of life for those, who through no fault of their own, are old and weak or needy, and I will try to help them." All he had learned from his grandfather he now would seek to put to work for the people of Arkansas, black and white, rich and poor, pledging to provide every citizen "not a hand out, but a hand up."[29]

A long distance had been traveled. A new partnership had been formed. A sense of promise was everywhere.

It did not last long. Clinton's list of objectives for his administration was as long as his arm—education, health care, roads, taxes, energy, economic development. But there was little focus, no sense of priorities. The average citizen was frustrated by the absence of a sense of what really came first. But instead of choosing education or jobs Clinton went for everything at once. After Dick Morris polled the voters of the state, he concluded that Clinton had proposed "a program that was thoroughly admirable but indescribable." While the new administration's ambitions were seemingly unbounded, the absence of discipline and order undermined any efforts to move forward.[30]

Nor did the confusion end with Clinton's legislative aspirations. Much more dangerously, it pervaded his staff and the way they undertook the tasks of administration. Clinton chose to run his office with a troika. Instead of there being one chief of staff to whom various deputies reported, he and Hillary decided that three people should share that role—Rudy Moore, who had played a major role in all of Clinton's political activities; Stephen Smith, an "idea" man who had served with him in the attorney general's office; and John Danner, the husband of Nancy "Peach" Pietrafesa, who was an old friend of Hillary's from Wellesley. All held equal status, and no one called the shots.

If Bill Clinton had imposed order on his staff, coherence might have emerged. But Clinton himself was totally disorganized. Rather than take charge, he always wanted to be on the road, meeting people. "Stop at that grocery store," he would order the trooper driving his car. The hour or so of schmoozing that followed automatically made him late for his next appointment. If someone told him about a problem they were having, he would tell them to stop by his office to see him. When voters followed up on his invitation, they would arrive without an appointment, and the governor's office would be full of people waiting to see him. It drove his staff to distraction.[31]

Clinton's penchant for making everyone feel good simply compounded the problem. It was "Bill's nature," Rudy Moore said, "to trust everyone and to want everyone to like him." His goal was to find a "magic consensus." Given this natural tendency, Moore observed, Clinton hated to say no to anyone. "The chief criticism of him was always that he told people what they wanted to hear and didn't follow through on his commitments . . . So people would leave his office thinking that they had a commitment when he had only been understanding and cordial." It was a political style that sowed the seeds for widespread discontent. Implied promises were not kept, and favor seekers suddenly found themselves on the short end of the stick. An old-time political figure in Arkansas asked whether it was really possible for "a man so sweetly disposed to everyone to play tough with friends as well as foes."[32]

Worst of all, too many of Clinton's key appointments were both young and from out of state. The Arkansas press had already portrayed Clinton in cartoons as a child riding a tricycle. Now he surrounded himself with people who looked as inexperienced as he did. All the members of his troika sported beards, none dressed in conventional suits and ties, and their style of interacting with each other and the public gave off an air of general indifference to traditional norms of behavior for a gubernatorial staff. "My conservative critics in the legislature had a field day with them," Clinton later wrote. Clinton not only created new departments such as Energy and Economic Development; he also imported outsiders to run the Department of Health, the Department of Human Services, the Department of Education, and the Department of Energy. It was not a good way to please the locals. The impression that Clinton left was one of arrogance, of an intent to impose ideas on Arkansas' citizens whether they were ready for them or not.[33]

A revolt soon broke out on Clinton's staff against two people who symbolized the "foreign" invasion. John Danner and Nancy "Peach" Pietrafesa were Californians. He was one of the "young beards," she a Wellesley classmate of Hillary's with an acerbic wit who held a more minor staff position. Both were close to Bill and Hillary. When Danner failed to fit in with the rest of the troika, a "gang of five" of the senior members of Clinton's staff came to Rudy Moore and demanded that he intervene. As requested, Moore went to the executive mansion to deliver the complaint. To Moore's amazement, the Clintons then asked *him* to go back and fire Danner and Pietrafesa, unable to bring themselves to do the deed. "It was the worst thing I ever had to do," Moore said. "That was a terrible way to handle the termination of jobs that were based on personal friendship, but at that time, he simply couldn't do it." Clinton later acknowledged his shame at how the episode had been handled. "Our relationship never recovered," he wrote. "I doubt that they ever forgave me for not handling it myself." Of greater concern was how it represented a pattern. Clinton always tried to avoid offending people or breaking off difficult personal relationships.[34]

Unfortunately, the staff imbroglios represented only the first of a series of political embarrassments. On the long list of legislative options he had proposed, one soon ascended to the top. Arkansas roads were in atrocious condition. The state's largest industries—Wal-Mart and Tyson Poultry, among others—lambasted the government for not modernizing its highway system and its rules for regulating long-haul heavy shipping. Recognizing the problem, Clinton acted with dispatch to get a highway bill before the state legislature. The problem was how to pay for the expensive improvements the legislation mandated. From the point of view of many, big business, the chief beneficiary of the changes, should foot the bill. But they had powerful lobbies and argued that they could not produce new jobs if their taxes soared. A second option was to raise the fees for renewing vehicle registrations. The increase Clinton proposed was 100 percent, or double the existing cost. Dick Morris polled the issue and assured Clinton that 53 percent of the state would be fine with that outcome. But then a new and untested variable entered the equation. It was proposed that vehicle owners be charged on the *weight* of their car, not its value or age. Unforeseen by many, that meant that people with older, heavier cars ended up paying much more than people with newer, lighter ones.

As the meaning of the new tax hit home—each month, one-twelfth of the drivers in the state were obliged to drive to their county seat to reregister their vehicles—a grassroots revolt began. Arkansas was not a cash-rich state. Owners of old pickup trucks and worn-out clunkers often came to the motor vehicle registration office only to find out that they had not brought enough money to pay the state for reregistering their vehicles. So they had to go home to get more cash—in one person's words, giving them "approximately six hours" back and forth to think about how much they hated this young whiz kid who was wrecking their lives. At a time when oil shortages had already caused long lines at the pump as well as raising gas prices, this tax increase made it all intolerable. "They're killing me out there," Clinton told Rudy Moore. "I go into these factories where people have always been kind to me and they tell me I kicked them in the teeth . . . when they were down." A decade-old Ford cost as much to register as a brand-new Cadillac, inflation was soaring, the economy was going to hell in a handbasket, and Clinton had the nerve to double motor registration fees. "It was the single dumbest mistake I ever made in politics until 1994 when I agreed to ask for a special prosecutor in the Whitewater case," Clinton later wrote.[35]

In a two-year term—the duration of Arkansas' governorship at that time—one such mistake was often sufficient to doom a reelection bid. But there was more. At the end of the 1970s, a massive exodus of Cuban refugees arrived in the United States. Fidel Castro had encouraged political dissidents to leave, and they poured into Florida. The Carter administration saw no easy solution and chose to send the refugees, for the time being, to a variety of federal facilities. The largest group was assigned to Fort Chaffee in Arkansas, in the middle of the state. But nothing was done to address the refugees' underlying problems. They were penned up, given minimal food and supplies, and left to fester.

Increasingly frustrated and angry, the refugees at Fort Chaffee stormed out of their confinement and threatened an insurrection. Clinton responded decisively, calling out the National Guard and quickly reasserting control as well as securing a promise from Carter not to send any more refugees to Arkansas. But Carter then reneged on his promise, and in the summer of 1980 remanded *all* the refugees at that time in Wisconsin, Florida, and Pennsylvania to Fort Chaffee. It was a stunning blow, not so much because the refugees represented any direct threat to Arkansas citizens as because their very presence suggested a state government out of control.[36]

Clinton refused to denounce Carter in public. While he was furious with the administration, both for its lack of a coherent policy on dealing with the refugees and for going back on its word, Clinton believed it would be historically unacceptable and politically reckless to go after Carter. The infamous insubordination of Orval Faubus toward Dwight Eisenhower in 1957 during the Little Rock school desegregation crisis still rankled Clinton and was a source of ongoing shame to the state. (After promising Eisenhower his cooperation in enforcing a federal court order to desegregate the schools, Faubus had instead incited white racists in Little Rock to block the entry to Central High School.) Clinton was not about to fall into that historic trap. In addition, he chose to stand by Carter in his election-year primary contest with Ted Kennedy. If nothing else, Clinton knew that aligning himself with a northeast liberal like Kennedy would be political anathema in Arkansas. So Clinton absorbed the refugee blow, defended (appropriately) his own strong response to Carter, and simply hoped the damage could be contained.[37]

Amid the tumult, the "best" thing that ever happened to him—Bill's words—occurred when Chelsea Clinton was born early in 1980. The Clintons had long wanted to have children. They actually came up with the name Chelsea for a daughter while walking through London and recalling the lyrics to Joni Mitchell's song "Chelsea Morning." Bill and Hillary had had difficulty conceiving and were about to consult a fertility expert in California. Both had problems, Bill a low sperm count, Hillary endometriosis, a condition that can cause extreme pain during and after intercourse. (As many as 40 percent of women with endometriosis cannot have children.) In some ways, then, it seemed like a miracle when Bill and Hillary returned from a vacation in Bermuda to discover that she was pregnant. Bill joined Hillary in Lamaze classes, in which the couple learns to be a team, with the husband joining his wife in regulating her breathing as contractions increase in frequency during the labor process.[38]

As it turned out, Bill never got to put his Lamaze training to work. Hillary's pregnancy became increasingly difficult, and three weeks before she was due to give birth, doctors performed a cesarean section. With Hillary still knocked out from the anesthesia, Bill was the first person to see Chelsea. "I knew then that being a father was the most important job I'd ever have," he wrote. "[She was] the world's most wonderful baby. I talked to her and sang to her. I never wanted that night to end." Arriving at the hospital, Diane Blair observed the scene. Holding his infant daughter, Blair noted, Bill "was absolutely overcome with adoration and gratitude." For someone who had felt during his entire life the absence of his own father, the moment was ecstasy. Clinton recalled saying to himself that night, thinking of Bill Blythe, "Well, here's another milestone he didn't reach." Clinton became a doting father, reading to Chelsea each night, tossing her in the air, playing with her on the floor. This, to him, was the meaning of family. It was for Hillary, too. "I don't think I could ever be a woman without having a child," she said later. It was a high point in both their lives.[39]

Two other portentous events took place on the eve of and during Clinton's first term as governor. The first involved a simple word: Whitewater. It was the name of a potential resort in the hill country of western Arkansas that Jim McDougal and his wife, Susan, hoped to develop into a multimillion-dollar real estate deal. Bill had known Jim McDougal since his days working for J. William Fulbright. A combination of hustler, reformed alcoholic, and manic-depressive, McDougal had come back from Washington to teach at Ouachita Baptist University, where he met, fell in love with, and married a beautiful student named Susan. Together, they dabbled in real estate while Jim kept his hand in politics by working with Clinton. One night at dinner, McDougal suggested that Bill and Hillary join them as partners in buying a beautiful parcel of land where soon, they predicted, people would flock to build weekend homes overlooking water rushing over rocks. Clinton, who cared little about money or investments, seemed indifferent. Hillary responded with excited interest. It seemed too good a deal to pass up. They would not have to put up any cash, only cosign for a loan from a local bank. Then people would rush to buy a lot, and they would become rich. The deal was done without the Clintons' ever seeing the land now called Whitewater.[40]

The second event was Hillary's decision to play the financial market, specifically cattle futures. Hillary had always been the one to care about the Clintons' financial future. Even with her partnership in a prominent law firm, the rent-free executive mansion with servants, and Bill's salary as governor ($35,000), they were not well off. So Hillary became increasingly interested in private investment possibilities, particularly after talking at length with their family friend Jim Blair, a bold high-stakes gambler. Blair held a prominent position in a finance company, was well connected with Tyson Poultry, and was predicting a bull market in cattle futures. Hillary decided to invest $1,000. When she pulled out of the market ten months later, her account was worth $100,000.

How did it happen? The question remains unanswered. According to Hillary, she had always loved following the market, having learned to read stock tables at her father's side. Using computer models and the expertise of Blair and his friends, she simply "lucked out," then withdrew from the market when she was well ahead. The story is more complicated, with Blair at its center. He controlled the company through which their funds were channeled. He also secured for Hillary the same privileges that he enjoyed. These included not having to pay "margin calls"—the money due from a client when a speculative investment goes bad. So at one point when Hillary was $60,000 in the red, with only $40,000 in her account, no funds were demanded of her. Soon thereafter the market turned in her favor. Despite her claims of actively managing her own account, it turns out that on the three days when her trading was most active, she was involved in all-day meetings out of town. Hillary's incredible good fortune in the investment world, it would seem, had a lot more to do with her close connections with Jim Blair than with anything she accomplished on her own.[41]

The biggest problem besetting the Clintons reflected the ongoing parallel lives Bill Clinton continued to pursue. Despite his devotion to Hillary and becoming a father, Bill lived a second life full of risky liaisons with young, attractive women. "Bill was like a kid with a new toy," one associate said, describing Clinton's life as governor. "The perks, the mansion, having the most powerful people in the world paying court to you. And he always had a weakness for bleached blonds with big jewelry, in short skirts, their figures shown off to best advantage." As victory approached in the 1978 gubernatorial race, Clinton was more and more careless, cruising nightclubs with attractive women hanging all over him. Although Chelsea's birth transformed his life, it did not alter his extracurricular behavior. Clinton seemed unabashed about flirting openly—even with Hillary present. Nor were others unaware. He allegedly talked openly with state troopers about his encounters with attractive women; Nancy Pietrafesa told people that Clinton had an unerring eye for two kinds of women: those he could tell were having marital problems, and heavily made-up blondes.[42]

Although the full extent of Clinton's philandering during this period may never be known, there seems little doubt that Hillary was aware of it. She had lived with Bill's wandering eye for years. Although Rudy Moore, one of Clinton's closest aides, believed the stories of Clinton's sexual activities at this time were exaggerated, he also recognized that the stories were rife and that Hillary knew about them. How she dealt with the rumors with Bill no one knows. But in the eyes of some, a clear pattern had emerged. From the very beginning of his relationship with the Clintons, Dick Morris observed "a mutual pattern of enabling and concealment between [Hillary and Bill]. Neither asked the other probing questions. Each looked the other way." As long as an affair was not public, Hillary would go along with the behavior, however egregious it might be. The writer Gail Sheehy saw the same pattern of denial. "The dark side of her husband's soul was not a territory she cared to explore," she wrote. "Hillary's choice was not to know what she knew."[43]

In the midst of all this, Clinton came up for reelection. It had been a lightning-fast two years, both nationally and in the state. Inflation was at record levels. Mortgage rates soared to near 20 percent; Iranian revolutionary students had taken over the U.S. embassy in Tehran in the fall of 1979; the Soviet Union had invaded Afghanistan; Jimmy Carter was in big trouble. And so was Bill Clinton. Some of his problems resulted from natural disasters. Tornadoes swept the state in 1979 and '80. A record heat wave in 1980 buckled state highways, while an outbreak of fires killed more than a hundred people. Clinton had little control over the Cuban refugee crisis. Nor was he responsible for the explosion of a Titan II ballistic missile near Damascus, Arkansas, which terrified people fearful of a nuclear accident. But he *was* responsible for the car tag scandal, he personally created the chaos on his staff, and he deserved blame for the failure to define priorities for his governorship. As a result, Clinton said, "it was painfully clear that thousands of people thought I'd gotten too big for my britches, too obsessed with what I wanted to do, and oblivious to what they wanted me to do." Or, as Carl Whillock, a Clinton aide, put it, all the frustrations of the late seventies translated into a "vague discontent which focused on the young governor."[44]

Stepping into that vacuum was Frank White, a former conservative Democrat now turned Republican. White brilliantly capitalized on Clinton's weaknesses, focusing his advertising campaign on both the car tag issue and the Cuban refugee dilemma. In a clever ad (Hillary called it unabashedly racist), White showed dark-skinned refugees bolting out the doors of Fort Chaffee, theoretically threatening the safety and well-being of all "native-born Arkansans," presumably white. Clinton's opponent also helped promote the widespread rumors that existed about Hillary—her career, her insistence on being Hillary "Rodham," her feminism, and her independence. "People thought even his [own] wife didn't like [Clinton] enough to take his name," one columnist wrote. Then there were the "young beards" who in ordinary times might simply have been dismissed as the political baggage of a too-youthful governor but who now were scapegoated as part of a generalized disaffection with the candidate's style.[45]

In the end, the registration fees and refugees proved decisive. On election day, Clinton (and Carter) received only 48 percent of the total vote, White 52 percent. Of those who switched sides from two years earlier, 12 percent said it was because of the car tags, 6 percent because of the Cuban refugees. Clinton carried only twenty-four of the sixty-five counties in the state, almost a complete reversal of what had occurred in 1978. Significantly, the person whose advice had been most instrumental in Clinton's first gubernatorial victory had been dismissed from the governor's entourage. Clinton had gotten tired of Dick Morris and, in the political consultant's own words, had come to think of him as "something dirty, that he didn't want to touch without gloves." No longer able to marry idealism to pragmatism, and unwilling to rely any longer on the "out-of-stater" who had helped engineer his political success, Bill Clinton had lost his way.[46]

The now-defeated governor was devastated. "God, I'm an idiot," Clinton said at the time, "I should have seen it coming." Hillary did, and she called Morris at the last minute, seeking to rescue the unrescuable—but it was far too late. Clinton described his own reaction: "I was full of self-pity and anger, mostly at myself." On election night, Bill was so overcome with depression he could not even rally himself to make a concession speech. Instead, he sent out Hillary. "Bill's eyes were puffy and his voice was hoarse," Webb Hubbell commented. "Hillary had dark circles under her eyes. Both of them looked more fragile than I'd ever seen them." The next day, Bill and Hillary had lunch with their friends Jim and Diane Blair. Clinton was morose. Sitting at a table in a downtown juke joint, he said he did not know whether to laugh or cry as they listened to the country song "I Feel So Bad I Don't Know Whether to Kill Myself or Go Bowling." David Maraniss, the biographer of Clinton's early years, gave perhaps the most telling assessment. "At thirty-four," Marannis wrote, "[Clinton] fit the ironic description of the quintessential Rhodes Scholar: someone with a great future behind him."[47]

In the end, the 1980 election defeat had as much to do with the complex intertwining of Bill's and Hillary's narratives as with the immediate issues of the campaign. Appropriately, it represented a culmination of all that had taken place in their lives during the previous six years. It also offered a prism through which to understand the internal dynamics that were shaping their fate, and would continue to do so—who was in control, how did they complement or not complement each other, was there a balance or an imbalance in their partnership?

Rudy Moore expressed some of the mystery surrounding the campaign. Clinton, he noted, was no longer the same person psychologically by 1980. "It must have been something personal, perhaps in his relationship with Hillary, but he was ambivalent and preoccupied. Those fantastic political insights had abandoned him." Not only did Clinton have people "running the campaign who had no experience running a statewide race. There was bickering, organizational work wasn't being done, decisions weren't being made, and most important, the charges being made by his opponent weren't being answered. Bill never demanded of that campaign what he had demanded before, and what he has demanded since. He wouldn't make decisions that would bring the campaign out of its lassitude." Significantly, Moore noted the same attitudinal breakdown in Hillary. She just did not seem to be involved. "She was ordinarily a perfect balance to Bill, who tended to trust everybody . . . She saw the dark side of events, and she could see that certain ideas and programs wouldn't work . . . But she, like the governor, did not seem to be fully engaged in the campaign of 1980." In short, the absence of the complementary strengths that had produced success earlier offered the best explanation for their failure this time.[48]

So what was going on? Although there is no way of knowing with certainty, it appears that these were years of considerable instability in their personal relationship—not surprising given Hillary's prolonged uncertainty about moving to Arkansas and her long-standing awareness of Bill's womanizing. In Hillary's own life, there were tensions between her role at the Rose law firm and her responsibilities as First Lady of the state. To whom did she owe primary loyalty? Her law partners, or her husband's political image? Simultaneously, she sought to shape public policy, build her law business (including bringing state business to the law firm, which raised some eyebrows), and avoid all those official functions like presiding over "ladies' lunches." As one columnist wrote, "She just went her own way . . . A lot of people thought she was remote, distant." On the other hand, she continued to come under pressure from her law partners to do more for the firm. Only the steadfast support of Webb Hubbell and Vince Foster—both had been asked to persuade her to leave—enabled her to stay.[49]

Even more troubling was Bill's ongoing pattern of living dual lives. He had started a relationship with the singer and model Gennifer Flowers in 1977, which would become headlines during the 1992 presidential campaign. Rumors were rife about other affairs, including some that were more than one-time flings. None of this escaped Hillary, who faced the infinitely delicate task of negotiating the terrain of her own personal independence, her professional career, her political aspirations, and her family responsibilities. It would be unusual for confusion and conflict not to reign in such a situation.

But Bill seemed equally confused. Like a random set of firecrackers going off on the Fourth of July, he lit up the sky in multiple ways, shooting off flares in a hundred directions. Rather than define a few priorities, he pursued multiple paths simultaneously. His (and Hillary's) decision to have three de facto chiefs of staff rather than one suggested a dangerous incapacity to decide. Ordinarily in such a situation, Hillary—the "tough," hard-nosed disciplinarian—would have stepped in to impose order. But in this instance, John Danner and Nancy Pietrafesa were her friends, and Bill was trying to satisfy Hillary while not alienating Rudy Moore or Stephen Smith. The same incapacity characterized his initial legislative program. He paid some attention to education, some to highways, some to rural health, some to job creation. But there was no clear-cut order, no priority list of "must do's."

All of this "deciding by not deciding" mirrored what was going on in their personal lives. Were they happy or unhappy in their relationship? Could Bill contain his extracurricular interests? And if he persisted with those, what was the effect on his ability to stand up to Hillary, or overrule her if he thought she was wrong?

The birth of Chelsea both complicated and simplified everything. It was a lifelong dream come true. He was now what he had never had in his own life, a real father. No role mattered more, no person counted as much. But how would that affect his political aspirations? And what would it mean for his personal choices and how he dealt with his own "secret" life? Almost as though he were reflecting on all these dilemmas, Bill told a political science class of Diane Blair's a few months after his defeat that the lives of political figures were a combination of darkness and light. Only in great leaders, he concluded, did the light triumph.

Now Bill and Hillary would be forced to struggle with their respective demons and decide how to play out the tortured dynamics of their personal relationship. How they negotiated that terrain would help determine not only their personal history over the ensuing years, but the political history of the state and country they hoped to serve.

SIX

The Arkansas Years, Part Two: 1980–91

From out of nowhere came somewhere. After moping for weeks, Clinton was determined to stop feeling sorry for himself. He still approached people on the street or at the supermarket to ask what he had done wrong. But deep down he knew the answers. He had failed to listen, he had failed to communicate, he had failed to lead. Beneath it all, he had lost his political gyroscope. To be sure, the chaos in his personal life underlay much of the rest of the confusion. That problem he would have to deal with in his own way, with Hillary or without her. But he could not abandon the one career path that had been his lodestar since he went to the White House with Boys Nation. "It's the only track I've ever known," he told Diane Blair's political science class. But how could he put back together what had fallen apart so quickly?

The answers would not come easily. Nor would they be clear-cut, or without obstacles. Hillary and Bill needed to make pivotal decisions, about both their personal life and their political partnership. How would they proceed as a team? What rules and regulations would undergird their relationship? Could they sustain success politically if they failed in their marriage? As Bill and Hillary assessed the damage in the weeks after the 1980 election, they began a process that promised recovery on the one hand but ongoing pain on the other. It was a tension that would never go away. Triumph and despair existed side by side, the one emerging almost immediately after the other, as night follows day.

With shrewd insight, Bill Clinton recalled in his memoir how decisive his loss in 1980 had proven to be for the rest of his political career. "If I hadn't been defeated," he wrote, "I probably never would have become President. It was a near-death experience, but an invaluable one, forcing me to be more sensitive to the political problems inherent in progressive politics: the system can absorb only so much change at once; no one can beat all the entrenched interests at the same time; and if people think you've stopped listening, you're sunk."[1]

The first thing Clinton did was to examine carefully why and how he had so badly wrecked his political operation. From being one of the most effective in the country, it had deteriorated into dysfunctionality. Three things struck him immediately. He desperately needed Hillary to be his cocaptain, to steer the ship, to deliver unwelcome news, to balance his optimism with her realism. More than that, he needed someone by his side who could discipline the crew, keep people operating from the same navigation chart, and make sure that their efforts blended rather than devolving into conflict. Finally, he needed a master strategist, someone who could test the waters, propose a course to follow, then modify whatever approach he was taking as events unfolded. Three necessities, three people—Hillary Rodham, Betsey Wright, and Dick Morris.[2]

Hillary was the first among equals. She understood the meaning of the loss. She had committed her life, energy, and extraordinary talents to achieving her dream of helping to change the world. Now, all of that seemed in peril. As one adviser wrote, "the experience of watching Bill screw up made Hillary realize she [must] jump into the breach." From that moment forward, she took charge, creating a new sense of order in his life, classifying his associates into "good guys" and "bad guys," and making sure that the good guys were in place and the bad guys got short shrift. Recognizing the degree to which her own role—or at least the way that role had been caricatured in the campaign—had contributed to Bill's defeat, she quickly made corrective changes. She accepted Bill's last name as her own, suddenly becoming Mrs. Clinton. She adopted contact lenses to replace her thick eyeglasses, straightened her hair, became more blond, started to dress in fashionable styles, and adopted the manners of a supportive spouse. As one Clinton aide noted, "she conformed, eyes batting. She hated it, for a while resented it no end, but she became what Arkansas wanted her to be."

Most important, she rearranged her priorities, giving the political partnership—and its success—her greatest attention. It was not easy. The days before and after the election were fraught with tension. Bill and Hillary screamed at each other in the executive mansion. Friends recalled Bill playing on the floor and tossing Chelsea up and down, riffing on the Tammy Wynette song, "I want a div-or-or-ce, I want a div-or-or-ce." But Hillary kept her eye on the prize, and despite Bill's self-pity, depression, and ongoing recklessness with other women, she made the decision to hang in there and rebuild their political future. No one was more grateful than her husband. "Hillary was especially good to me in that awful period," he later wrote, "balancing love and sympathy with an uncanny knack for keeping me focused on the present and the future."[3]

At Hillary's suggestion, Bill rehired both Betsey Wright and Dick Morris. Wright responded immediately to Hillary's request that she come to Little Rock and help Bill dig out of the despair of the last campaign while preparing to do battle in the next. In theory, her task was to organize his papers as he prepared to transition from the governor's office, but in fact her assignment was to put in place the infrastructure for reactivating a statewide political operation, using all the phone numbers, addresses, and politically powerful information she could gather on potential supporters for a race two years hence. When queried by reporters about her role in the governor's office, Clinton resorted to one of his classic acts of dissembling. "There *is* no campaign," he told the press. In fact, Wright was laying the groundwork for an electoral comeback.[4]

Finally, there was Dick Morris. He was as close to Hillary as he was to Bill, perhaps never more so than during this crucial time. Morris also learned how to work well with Betsey Wright. He was "one of the smartest little sons of bitches" she had ever met, Wright said. "Mean. But God he was good." The two were a stunning combination. Morris returned with a scenario he called "the permanent campaign." Its first dictum was to interweave pragmatism and idealism. "When you lead in an idealistic direction," he said, "the most important thing is to be highly pragmatic about it. And when necessity forces upon you a problem of great pragmatism, you need to use idealism to find your way out of the thicket." Balance was the key.

Morris's second and third dicta were even more important. Clinton should use paid media to convey his priorities to the public, he told Clinton, rather than rely on coverage by the press. That way a candidate could send an uninterrupted, unmediated message to the public, circumventing the biases or partial perceptions of a newsperson or commentator.

Finally came the clincher: the use of polling to discern the best way to present a position to voters so that they would respond most favorably. By testing language options with random samples of citizens, Morris—and Clinton—could settle on the best formulation to present as a final product. Clinton loved the idea.[5]

With his team in place, Clinton could now start his comeback. At first he remained depressed. Moving out of the mansion into a far less elegant suburban home, occupying a small office in a large law firm where he served "as counsel," losing all the perks of power—all of these contributed to a feeling of having been demoted. "The image that stays in my mind," Dick Morris recalled, "is of this tall guy, folded into a chair, stuffed underneath a small desk in a small room with the walls crowding him closely, and having to go out to search for someone in the steno pool to do his work . . . He was like a patient afflicted with cancer wondering if he had any chance of survival." But soon Clinton perked up. He had a mission, not simply to recover what he had lost, but to return to the message he had always preached. Above all he was concerned about those who no longer saw any reason to believe in government. In Clinton's view, the task of a "new politics" was to speak to those "who do not care." It was these people who would decide the future, and it was Clinton's goal to "prove to them that we offer more in the way of creative and realistic solutions." He had lost the ability to convey that message in 1980, and now it was time to recover it.[6]

In his gut, Dick Morris knew that the most important way for Bill Clinton to start was to acknowledge to the people of Arkansas that he had screwed up and to apologize. In Morris's view, Clinton was like the prodigal son who had "grown too big for his britches." The election of 1980 had been a "public spanking" from the voters, but now was the time for forgiveness and reconciliation. "Recognize your sins," Morris implored, "confess to them, and promise to sin no more." The key, he insisted, was for Clinton to be genuinely humble and contrite. "You can't be self-justified. You have to say, 'I'm very sorry, ashamed, I know

I did wrong and I'll never do it again.'" But Clinton was always in the process of justifying himself. He hated the very idea of apologizing, or acknowledging that he had done wrong. But Morris would not back off. Moreover, he insisted that this was the time to act on his second dictum and use a paid advertisement to get the message across.[7]

True to character, Clinton took the advice but insisted on giving it his own personal gloss. He would find a way to convey the *feeling* that he was being apologetic without ever using the words "I apologize." The result was brilliant. Taping his advertisement in New York, Clinton acknowledged that "it was a mistake" to raise taxes on driver's registrations "because so many of you were hurt by it." He then went on to give his meditation on the tax "mistake" a personal dimension. "When I was a boy growing up," he told his TV audience, "my daddy never had to whip me twice for the same thing. And now I hope you'll give me another chance to serve as governor because our state has many problems and opportunities that demand strong leadership. If you do, I assure you I won't try to raise the car licenses again."[8]

Clinton's speech was an innovative modification of a strategically shrewd political calculation. By conveying regret—and using the parable of a parental whipping as the instrument—he succeeded in achieving two objectives at once: he personalized his experience in ways that every Arkansas son or daughter would understand, and he inoculated himself against the fresh criticism he would receive for his initial mistake.

Morris and Clinton knew that the tax hike would be just as widely and prominently used in a 1982 race as it had been in the 1980 election. But by "owning" the mistake, Clinton shielded himself against the charge made by his opponents. He had already acknowledged his error, voters would say, so why beat him up for it. The tactic worked. Voters appreciated Clinton's admission of wrongdoing, they forgave him, and they grew irritated at his opposition for "piling on."[9]

With Morris's ploy of "calculated contrition" in place, Clinton announced his candidacy for the governorship on February 27, 1982, also Chelsea's second birthday. Hillary, who had taken a leave of absence from the Rose law firm to run the campaign, marked the occasion by giving Bill a picture of the three of them, with the inscription: "Chelsea's second birthday, Bill's second chance." The first challenge was a primary race with the former congressman Jim Guy Tucker. Predictably, Tucker ran a series of attack ads, but following Clinton's "contrition" ad, they fell flat. Meanwhile, Clinton's ads criticizing Tucker's attendance record in Congress—he was notorious for his absences—resonated. Morris and Hillary complemented each other beautifully. "In meetings," Morris said, "I would urge a fairly aggressive strategy. Clinton would demur, and then Hillary would say, Bill, you've got to do this." Hillary was the one who reinforced the need to run negative ads, to remain aggressive. "Her mental attitude at that point was, This guy is too nice to manage his own life. He doesn't understand how venal people can be. He's not tough enough." With Betsey Wright mobilizing the troops in the field, Clinton swept to a decisive victory over Tucker and prepared to take on White in the general election. Clinton's old foe Jim Johnson had long ago warned about the "Bill and Hillary Clinton" show and the danger of underestimating the talent of these "social manipulators." He could not have foreseen just how right his prophecy was.[10]

This time, Clinton's campaign boasted both focus and discipline. Conscious of all those "left out" by the system, Clinton emphasized his commitment to fair treatment for all, especially minority citizens and the average worker. This time, he secured labor's backing, and emphasized his support for health care, education, and reduced utility rates. In a series of attack ads, he successfully branded White as tied to special interests and having sought to reduce Medicaid against the interests of senior citizens. "Frank White," his lead ad announced, "Soft on Utilities / Tough on the Elderly." White's ads, on the other hand, suffered the same fate as Tucker's. "It got to be almost a joke," Morris said. "We felt like we were behind bulletproof glass."[11]

Clinton also hired three African American campaign workers— ranging from conservative to militant—to get out the black vote. Playing on his longtime support for civil rights, Clinton cultivated the black constituency in Arkansas with a dedicated campaign. It worked. At one voter forum in Forrest City, one of his black supporters galvanized the crowd after Clinton was criticized by an onlooker as "a loser." Before Clinton became governor, the black advocate said, human waste ran in the streets and children were constantly catching infections. "When he left office," on the other hand, "we had a sewer system and my babies wasn't sick anymore . . . Let me ask you something. If we don't stick with folks who stick with us, who will ever respect us again? He may be a loser, but if he loses, I'm going down with him. And so should you." Each Sunday Clinton went to a different black church, and at each, he felt perfectly at home, greeted as a brother and friend.[12]

The result: Two years after being turned out of office in disgrace, Bill Clinton roared back with a stunning electoral victory. He earned 55 percent of the total vote, and what he himself called a "staggering" percentage of the black vote. In almost every instance, he succeeded in winning back the counties that he had lost two years earlier. It was about as thorough a vindication as any aspiring politician could seek. No longer would Bill Clinton be the Rhodes scholar whose best years lay behind him. Once again he became the young man from Hope, destined to carve out a career that would alter the country's future. The combination of Hillary Clinton, Betsey Wright, and Dick Morris had delivered on their promise. The question was whether, this time, Bill Clinton, as governor, could deliver on his.[13]

In many ways, Arkansas had become a different kind of state than the one Clinton had governed two years earlier. Wal-Mart, Tyson Foods, and the Stephens Corporation dominated economic affairs more than ever. A new Indonesian billionaire named Riady had invested heavily in the state, with his son James becoming head of the Worthen Banking Corporation. More than a few times, the Clintons flew on their private planes. Many of their legal fees also went to the Rose law firm, and to an increasing degree, Hillary faced questions of conflict of interest. For his part, Clinton did all he could to encourage industrial development. More than once, he went to bat for these large corporations. And Betsey Wright as his new chief of staff brought order and discipline where once chaos had reigned. Clinton consequently stayed on message and devoted all his energies to the issue on which most people had based their electoral choice.[14]

That issue was education. From day one of the campaign, Clinton insisted he was tired of Arkansas being ranked last or next to last on national standardized tests, teachers' salaries, and per capita pupil expenditures. With admirable speed, he introduced and secured passage of laws establishing universal kindergarten. At the same time he mandated that students could take half their academic courses in neighboring schools if their home district did not offer them. To pay the bill, Clinton asked the legislature to raise taxes on cigarettes, beer, and liquor, with half the proceeds to go to the schools.[15]

But the heart of Clinton's education initiative revolved around the new Education Standards Committee that he created, with his wife as chair. For the third time in four years, Hillary took a leave of absence from the Rose law firm. Clinton created the task force immediately after the state supreme court declared unconstitutional the gross disparity in funding that existed between rural and urban schools. In some areas of Arkansas, teachers were paid only $10,000 a year and lived on food stamps. When he nominated Hillary to chair the centerpiece of his program, Clinton declared: "This guarantees that I will have a person who is closer to me than anyone else overseeing a project that is more important to me than anything else." Hillary threw herself into the task. Her task force met seventy-five times in three months, going to virtually every county in the state and hearing testimony for up to nine hours a day. It was a remarkable expenditure of energy. No longer, the committee declared, should football coaches be considered more valuable than reading teachers. Statewide standards would need to be imposed. At the end of the third grade, the sixth grade, and the eighth grade, pupils would be required to take uniform tests measuring their competency. Each school would be given a scorecard to measure its progress. The task force had discovered glaring weaknesses. Nearly 150 high schools offered no physics classes, 135 no advanced math classes, and 180 no classes in foreign languages. After Dick Morris polled voters to find out the most acceptable way of paying for improvements, Clinton proposed a 1 percent sales tax increase.[16]

Clinton also decided to insist that all teachers in the state take a standardized test to prove their competence. Dick Morris had suggested the measure, arguing that it would appeal to the average voter, prove that Clinton was not a prisoner of special interests, and demonstrate just how serious was his—and Hillary's—commitment to quality teaching in the classroom. Needless to say, the teachers' union was furious. But Morris's polling had shown that 75 percent of the voting population approved, and the additional testing made it nearly impossible for conservatives to oppose reform. Mandatory tests, Clinton insisted, were "a small price to pay for the biggest tax increase for education in the history of the state and to restore the teaching profession to the position of public esteem that I think it deserves."

Crisscrossing the state, Clinton took his commitment directly to the voters. Although opposition was significant, Clinton refused to pull back. Indeed, he said he would forsake the entire legislative package if his mandatory testing provision was not included in the final legislation. It was Clinton's first attempt, Morris gloated, "to merge Democratic compassion with the Republican notion of responsibility." And it worked brilliantly. In a special five-week session of the legislature, every portion of his program was enacted, including hiking the sales tax, equalization of school aid between rural and urban districts, and an increase in teacher pay of $3,000 per year. Newspaper columnists who had excoriated Clinton for having no backbone now hailed his political courage. Paul Greenberg of the *Arkansas Times* wrote, "This was a new Bill Clinton, and let's hope he sticks around."[17]

The Clintons had established a new reputation for discipline, focus, and persuasiveness. Hillary appeared before the state legislature to defend the package of reforms she had come up with. Always in the past seen as something of an interloper from "up there in Yankee-land," this time she wowed the assembled "good old boys." As one of the stalwarts in the State Senate said afterward, "Well, fellas, it looks like we might have elected the wrong Clinton." Without question, the reform package improved Arkansas' low reputation in education. It also advanced Hillary's standing as a serious player, not only in politics but in policy. But most important, it solidified the impression in the minds of citizens in Arkansas and political observers throughout the nation that this Clinton administration was dramatically different from the one that preceded it. These people were serious, and it was time to pay attention.[18]

In the middle of their moment of triumph, the Clintons—and the entire extended family—endured the most traumatic emotional crisis they had experienced since confronting the alcoholism and spousal abuse behavior of Virginia's husband Roger. This time the center of attention was Roger's namesake, Bill's half-brother, Roger Clinton, Jr. In July 1984, state police came to the governor to tell Clinton that his brother had been selling cocaine to an undercover policeman. Roger had started using drugs extensively while a sophomore at Hendrix

College. He soon came to believe he could get away with anything. "I just wasn't mature enough to handle being the brother of the man who ran the state," he said later. For three years, starting in 1981, Roger began to deal drugs on an ever-increasing basis. Working with a big-time dealer with links to Colombian drug titans, Roger would take flights into and out of New York with large packets of cocaine taped to his body. Once in 1983, $20,000 of coke was stolen from his car, and he nearly fell victim to reprisals from within the drug cartel, but Roger played his ace in the hole: he was the governor's brother. He bragged about having sexual liaisons in the governor's mansion, and even suggested that Bill had a hankering for the drug. Eventually, he went too far and took too many chances. Bill Clinton kept confidential the state police intelligence he had been receiving throughout the final days of the investigation until the grand jury indictment was handed down in midsummer.[19]

For the first time in his life, Bill Clinton and his family openly confronted the pathology at the center of their lives. While there had been moments of candor before—as when Bill confronted his stepfather about his violence—"normal" life had quickly resumed with no further discussion of what had occurred. Now the time had come to face up to the history that had brought them to this day.

The first step took place when Bill met with Roger and his mother. Mortified by shame, Roger threatened to kill himself. Bill was outraged, seized him by the shoulders, and shook him. "How dare you be so selfish?" Roger remembers his brother saying. "You're the most precious thing in the world to your mother and me, and you'd dare think about taking that away from us?" Roger said that Bill was crying—he had never seen that before. Nor had he ever witnessed his brother trembling with anger. "Don't worry so much about what other people will think of your life," Bill told him. "You need to be accountable to yourself." It signaled a new stage in the entire family's accepting some level of accountability for their collective fate.[20]

The next step was far more important—a series of family therapy sessions where Bill, Roger, Virginia, and Hillary came together with a counselor, Karen Ballard, to explore the origins of the current crisis and to understand how they all had become enmeshed in a culture of denial. Virginia was at the center of the discussion. As she acknowledged repeatedly in her memoir, she had purposefully followed a philosophy of looking only on the bright side of things and repressing all negatives. She took pride in her sunny disposition, self-consciously using the metaphor of how much time she spent putting her makeup on in the morning as a way of describing how she covered up the aspects of her existence she did not wish to disclose. Now, in the therapy sessions, this pattern of pathological denial was exposed, with a painful revelation of how systematically Virginia—and hence the rest of the family— had suppressed the addictions they all had become victims of. Even more difficult, it was Hillary's observations about the family pathology that brought this pattern to the fore, sending Virginia reeling from the room in angry disbelief.[21]

Bill, especially, was forced to recognize his own habit of following his mother's example—putting the best light on everything, suppressing all the negatives. Hence, he could talk to friends about his birth father's death, but he never confided in anyone about Roger's alcoholism or spousal abuse. Now he appeared for the first time to confront the implications of his denial. He burrowed into the literature on alcoholism, discovering how it affected his life and made him so wary of conflict. "He did a lot of introspection that I had never seen him do . . . before," Betsey Wright said. "He got a much better understanding of why he did things the way he did and . . . why he was always trying to please people." Clinton also reached out to his oldest friends. "I think we're all addicted to something," he said to Carolyn Staley. "Some people are addicted to drugs. Some to power. Some to food. Some to sex. We're all addicted to something." Friends had never seen him so low, so down on himself. But on the other hand, for perhaps the first time, he was talking openly about the source of his personal demons.[22]

It was during this period that Hillary Clinton for the first time entertained the possibility of divorce. Bill's antics with other women had never ceased. And through the counseling sessions over Roger's arrest and its causes, Hillary perceived with new insight the depth and complexity of her husband's personal demons. In addition, it appeared that her voice in the political councils of the administration had begun to diminish. By the mid-1980s, "Bill had begun to chafe under Hillary's domination," Dick Morris observed. "The leash was too tight around his neck." The same seemed to be true of Betsey Wright, whom "he promoted"—read "kicked upstairs"—to the position of state Democratic Party chair.

Yet Hillary was also encouraged by the effect of the family therapy sessions on Bill. He seemed to be taking seriously the nature of the family pathology. By reading in depth the medical literature on what experts called ACOA, the Adult Child of Alcoholics syndrome, he seemed to gain more insight and control over his own emotional behavior. Both Clintons were also rediscovering the importance of religion in their lives. Hillary joined a Methodist congregation and became what one of her pastors called "a model" of making her faith part of her life, traveling across the state to talk to different church groups about social justice and the personal meaning of her religion. Bill, too, joined a church, in his case Immanuel Baptist, where he sang in the choir and developed a close relationship with the minister, Dr. Worsley Oscar Vaught, from whom he sought counsel on issues such as abortion and the death penalty. The therapy and the new role of religion in their lives allowed Hillary to sustain her now decade-long commitment to her partnership with Bill both in politics and in marriage.

Back at the Rose law firm after her leave of absence to chair the Education Standards Committee, Hillary was picking up new business. She also continued her pro bono work on issues of legal aid, children's defense, and child advocacy. And she remained connected to Jim and Susan McDougal. Unfortunately—from the perspective of ten years later—part of that work involved providing legal counsel to Castle Grande, a real estate venture of questionable legitimacy being run by McDougal, and distantly connected to the Whitewater venture where she and Bill were investors.[23]

Politically, the period leading up to the 1986 elections was full of good news. Bill Clinton's only potential rival, Sheffield Nelson, decided to drop out of the primary race, writing that he fundamentally agreed with Clinton's programs on education, energy, and jobs and hoped for only modest revisions. In the meantime, Bill Clinton's national visibility continued to increase. At the 1984 Democratic National Convention, he once again delivered a well-received address on the new politics. Rather than remain embedded in the old ideas inherited from the New Deal and the Fair Deal, he argued, the party needed to get in tune with the modern world, focusing on economic productivity, reducing deficit spending, promoting welfare reform, and improving health care and education. Arkansas' education reforms, he emphasized repeatedly, provided a perfect example of how responsibility and opportunity—themes he returned to again and again—worked together. In early 1985 he was chosen by national party leaders to be part of the team developing the party's response to Ronald Reagan's State of the Union address, and he began to play a leading role in the Democratic Leadership Council, the recently formed institutional voice of a "new politics" in the Democratic Party.[24]

By 1986, Arkansas had finally decided to move from a two-year gubernatorial term to the national norm of a four-year term of office. Clinton was brilliantly situated to seize the opportunity to increase his reputation for leadership within the state while promoting his visibility as a future national candidate. He now had been governor for a total of six years, with the prospect of four more. Notwithstanding the popularity of Ronald Reagan, in Arkansas he had shown voters another path to follow. He combined the Republican themes of fiscal prudence and responsibility with his own focus on opportunity—giving people a "hand up," not a "handout"—and building a sense of community and mutual caring among ordinary citizens. As he ran for another term, Clinton boasted of how effectively he had worked with the private sector to keep firms like International Paper, Sanyo TV, and a local shoe manufacturer from leaving Arkansas while partnering with Wal-Mart on a "Buy American" campaign. As evidence of his national presence, he was chosen chair of the National Governors Association, chair of the Education Commission of the States, and cochair of the Governors' Conference on Welfare Reform. The gubernatorial race was at times harsh and bitter, with allegations made that he had befriended corrupt allies and had associated with drug dealers. But for the most part Clinton remained above the personal fray, adopting a statesmanlike pose. Speaking to a meeting of all the editors of the Gannett newspaper chain, he focused on his new themes: the key to economic growth was investing in human capital; private enterprise and government regulation must work in partnership; and a stronger America required that responsibility, opportunity, and community prevail as the nation's dominant values. It was a formula for success. On election day, Clinton swept to victory with 64 percent of the vote.[25]

•

As his triumphant election victory began to recede into memory, Bill Clinton and his followers focused on the 1988 presidential election. His role as chair of the National Governors Association, as well as his prominence in the Democratic Leadership Council, positioned him ideally to be the spokesman for a "new politics" in America. "Opportunity, Responsibility, Community"—Clinton's new mantra—resonated with all those centrist politicians seeking to fuse the altruism of the old Democrats with the fiscal responsibility of the new. Around the country, Clinton both advocated and advertized his program of education reform, economic development, and remaking the welfare system. Voters looking for a new voice responded. Others in the party were doing the same thing—Gary Hart, senator from Colorado, who appealed to the same audience of "new" Democrats; Dale Bumpers of Arkansas, who had already won the plaudits of those looking for a new kind of Southern Democrat; and Michael Dukakis, governor of Massachusetts, known for his efficiency, his skill at merging technology with a politics of compassion, and his managerial excellence. But Clinton was in the wings, looking for his chance to move forward.

It did not take long. Dale Bumpers announced in the spring of 1987 that he had decided not to be a candidate for the Democratic nomination. Earlier, New York's governor, Mario Cuomo, did the same. Their actions opened the door for Clinton. After setting up exploratory committees to assess his chances and doing random polling across the country, his advisers concluded that he could compete with the remainder of the field. In their assessment, a second-place finish in the New Hampshire primary seemed plausible, and from there, anything could happen.

Then the leading contender for the nomination, Gary Hart, suddenly announced in May that he was dropping out of the race. Reporters in Miami were circulating stories about his extramarital love life. Recklessly, he had challenged them to follow him if they wanted to catch him being a playboy. They did, and he was. Targeting Hart's house in Washington, reporters saw Hart entering at night with Donna Rice, an attractive model, and her leaving in the morning. Subsequently, they found a photograph of Hart and Rice sitting in a romantic pose on a dock near a cabin cruiser in the Bahamas, ironically named *Monkey*

Business. Hart's credibility was shattered. As David Broder, the *Washington Post's* eminent columnist, wrote at the time, "What was at issue was Hart's truthfulness, his self-discipline, his sense of responsibility to other people—indeed his willingness to face hard choices and realities . . . The fundamental character questions raised by Hart's actions [are] vital in judging a potential President."[26]

Hart's implosion created an opportunity for Clinton and simultaneously placed him in imminent peril of the same fate. By now, stories of Clinton's affairs were legion. Although reporters had never done to him what they did to Hart, the possibility of similar surveillance was just around the corner. Clinton gingerly approached others in politics who had similar reputations to seek their advice. He also talked directly with Dick Morris about the problem. How should he deal with the whole "infidelity" thing? he asked his pollster. Morris questioned random samples of voters about the impact of personal scandals involving sex on their decisions in the voting booth. "Sex," he wrote, "loomed large in [Clinton's] consideration. Very large."

Still, the time seemed ripe. Reagan was leaving office. Clinton had a decent chance to secure the nomination. He knew that his own appeal was similar to Hart's—"a brilliant, innovative politician who was always thinking about America's big challenges and what to do about them." How to proceed? After thinking about it, Clinton concluded that there was no way of predicting the future. "Those of us who had not led perfect lives had no way of knowing what the press's standards of disclosure were," he wrote. "Finally, I concluded that anyone who believed he had something to offer should just run, deal with whatever charges arose, and trust the American people. Without a high pain threshold, you can't be a successful President anyway." And so the plans for the campaign proceeded, Clinton called a press conference to announce his decision, and his closest associates, past and present, flocked to Little Rock.[27]

But the story was not yet over. As the press conference approached, two critical interventions occurred. The first originated with Betsey Wright. For years, she had observed Bill and Hillary's relationship. She was keenly aware of his womanizing. As chief of staff, she frequently had tried to call him in the middle of the night while he was on the road, only to get no answer. In an effort to control Clinton's reckless behavior, she often changed the personnel accompanying him, hoping that this would discourage his wandering eye. In her view, Hillary had made peace with Bill's womanizing and decided "that what she wanted out of the relationship was worth putting up with some of that." But Wright was also keenly aware of how politically vulnerable Clinton's extramarital relationships made him. So two days before his public announcement, she openly demanded that he confront the issue and talk about the "huge schisms" in his marriage. Although some sources assert that she brought with her a list of all the women she knew Clinton had been with during his public life, it seems that she simply demanded that he provide her with a list of names. Clinton responded forthrightly. To her surprise, there were women on the list she had known nothing about. "I was horrified because I thought I knew everybody," she said. At the end of the conversation, she told Clinton directly that it would destroy his marriage and his relationship with Chelsea if he was to announce his candidacy for the presidency. All the information about his sex life would then become fodder for the press, she said.[28]

The second intervention came from Chelsea herself. As July 14, the day of the press conference, approached, Clinton initiated a series of conversations with close friends about the pros and cons of running. One night, as Clinton pursued the subject with the political advisers Mickey Kantor and Carl Wagner, Chelsea asked him about their family vacation that summer. Clinton responded that if he was running for president, a vacation might be out of the question. "Well, then," Chelsea responded, "Mom and I will go without you." Although brief, the conversation riveted Clinton, delivering the penetrating message that life with one's child was both invaluable and irreplaceable. In close proximity to Chelsea's comment, Clinton asked Carl Wagner for his personal read on the presidential decision. "Walk into your daughter's bedroom [when you go upstairs]," Wagner responded. "Look at her, and understand that if you do this, your relationship with her will never be the same." Subsequently, Clinton acknowledged that Chelsea's casual comment about the vacation "was the turning point of the conversation."

The next day, Clinton announced to the world that he would not be a candidate for president. He framed his decision in distinctively personal terms. "I need some family time," he told the assembled reporters at his press conference, "I need some personal time [for] renewal." And then Clinton went on to the ultimate motivation. "The other, even more important reason for my decision," he went on, "is the certain impact this campaign would have on our daughter . . . A long, long time ago I made a promise to myself that if I was ever lucky enough to have a child, she would never grow up wondering who her father was." Here, in one brief heartfelt statement, were encapsulated the primary themes of Bill Clinton's life—the centrality of fatherhood, the meaning of the child-parent relationship, the visceral consciousness of mortality and how one spent his hours on this planet. Many considerations influenced Clinton's decision—awareness of his vulnerability on the infidelity issue, knowledge of how difficult the campaign would be in a multitude of ways. But in the end, it was Chelsea who made the difference. "After the decision," he later wrote, "I felt as though the weight of the world had been lifted from my shoulders. I was free to be a father, husband, and governor, and to work and speak on national issues unencumbered by immediate ambitions."[29]

In the aftermath of his announcement, Clinton reaped both the rewards and the penalties of the national recognition that his statesmanlike withdrawal from the race had created. Everyone noted the political significance of Clinton's choice. Massachusetts's governor, Michael Dukakis, now the front-runner, signaled his gratitude by asking Clinton to put his name in nomination.

Never before, aides said, had Clinton worked so hard on a speech. Although he was allotted only twenty minutes, Clinton believed he had packed everything into the speech that any candidate could want, and Dukakis agreed. But when the moment came, everything went wrong. The house lights stayed up, the audience paid no attention, raucous laughter filled the hall, and Clinton gave the worst performance of his life. When the TV networks stopped broadcasting the speech, Betsey Wright declared she was overwhelmed "by a completely helpless feeling." Clinton was flabbergasted. "I felt as if the speech was a two hundred–pound rock I was pushing up a hill," he said. The press and late-night comics agreed. "As Jesse Jackson electrified the hall on Tuesday," the *Washington Post* TV critic Tom Shales said, "Governor Bill Clinton calcified it Wednesday night." Johnny Carson joked that Clinton's speech had just been approved as a "new sleeping aid."

Yet within days, Clinton soared back. Going on Carson's *Tonight* show, he played his baritone sax, then made fun of himself. The speech had been the worst hour of his life, he said—"no," he added, "make that an hour and a half"—and through his own good humor salvaged an otherwise horrific embarrassment. The same Tom Shales who had berated Clinton the day after his speech wrote a column the next week saying he "had recovered miraculously." The "Comeback Kid" had done it again.[30]

But of all the patterns in Clinton's life, perhaps the most telling was the way his moments of triumph led almost inexorably to personal implosions that reflected his capacity for self-destruction. Usually sexual in nature, such episodes spoke to Clinton's ongoing inability to resolve the secrets of his "parallel lives."

Despite Clinton's statement that a huge weight had been lifted from his shoulders by the decision to withdraw from the presidential race, aides noted that he almost immediately went into a severe depression, akin to what he had experienced after his defeat in the gubernatorial election in 1980. "There was an adrenaline cutoff immediately," Betsey Wright observed, "and the funk after that. I mean, he just thought his life was over." With the next rung on the political ladder removed, at least for now, he felt lost, abandoned. "There was nothing else for him to do," Wright noted. "And he was nutty . . . reckless . . . I couldn't get his attention."

Typically in such circumstances, Clinton's wandering eye for other women helped to fill the vacuum. According to Wright, everyone knew Clinton was having multiple assignations. She tried, with no success, to control him. "By the time the whole thing came to a head," she said, Clinton "just went crazy . . . He nearly burned his relationship with Hillary. He burned it with me." The state troopers knew about the affairs, she said, and the staff talked about them all the time. "He was [even] playing some games with some of the women [who worked for me]," she said. Rumors spread of screaming matches between Bill and Hillary at the mansion. Chelsea, too, became more aware of the tensions. There seemed no limit to how badly Clinton was prepared to allow his relationship with Hillary to deteriorate. What was more, according to Wright, "he wasn't doing his job. He wasn't paying attention."[31]

At the heart of the crisis was the fact that Clinton had fallen in love with another woman. She was not another beauty queen or one of the young, attractive groupies who gathered by his side in bars. Rather, she was a divorcee near Bill's age, she had an MBA, and she offered intellectual as well as sexual companionship. Her name was Marilyn Jo Jenkins. A southerner born and bred, she had married a military officer she met in college. Moving around the country and the world with him, she reared two children and then, after fifteen years, decided to file for divorce, get a graduate degree, and return to the South as a marketing manager in a growing company. She was strikingly beautiful, very bright, and appropriately discreet. When they met, she fell in love with Bill, and he with her. Virtually everyone knew it. "Bill," Betsey Wright told him, "you're crazy if you think everybody in this office is oblivious to [what's happening.]" In the past, Clinton might simultaneously have carried on a series of side affairs, but Marilyn Jo Jenkins was different. This was serious.[32]

So serious, in fact, that Bill asked Hillary for a divorce. In light of all the previous affairs, this represented a step that dramatically distinguished the relationship with Marilyn Jo Jenkins from all the others. Bill Clinton now stated openly that he was in love with two women, and that, given a choice, he wished to put his political future at risk by divorcing one and marrying the other.[33]

In a decision comparable in scope and portent to Bill's struggle with the draft, Hillary said no. She chose to remain in her marriage and fight to save it. The decision could not have been easy. Hillary discussed her circumstances with Diane Blair. While not sharing the details of Bill's effort to dissolve their relationship, she worried candidly about her financial resources, especially if she was to become a single parent. She opened up more to Betsey Wright. "There are things worse than infidelity," Hillary told Wright. Probably no two people had observed Clinton's wayward habits more closely, or over a longer time frame, than Wright and Hillary; and although they never discussed the topic in depth, Wright believed that she understood the dynamics behind Hillary's determination to save the marriage. "Hillary had long ago made some peace with the womanizing and the trade-offs," Wright recalled. "[For] what she wanted out of the relationship, [it] was worth putting up with some of that." Hillary understood that this woman was different, yet this made her even more determined to persist.[34]

In the end, it all went back to the advice Hillary had received from her mother. However impossible Hugh Rodham or Bill Clinton might be in his disregard for the sensibilities of his spouse, dissolving a marriage was too high a price to pay. "My strong feelings about divorce and its effects on children," Hillary wrote in a 1992 magazine piece, "have caused me to bite my tongue more than a few times during my own marriage"—as if she were commenting directly on her experience with Marilyn Jo Jenkins three years earlier. Just as her mother refused to permit even the idea of divorce because she wished to protect her children, Hillary argued for the necessity of putting the interests of the whole family before the feelings of any one person. "Regardless of individual feelings," she later wrote, "everyone involved in the process [of marital negotiation], especially a parent, has an obligation to temper the pain children will inevitably experience."[35]

Despite proclaiming his love for Marilyn Jo, Bill also experienced the tenacity of Hillary, continued to love her as well, and in the end determined to find some way to hold the marriage together. With toughness and an indomitable will, Hillary made sure that she kept her family intact. Even as they entered marriage counseling, Bill continued covertly to see Jenkins. He called her repeatedly on the telephone through early 1991, on one out-of-town trip spending more than ninety minutes on the phone with Jenkins while calling Hillary only briefly. But Hillary prevailed. What transpired is anyone's guess. Betsey Wright believed that a "negotiation" occurred. Neither for the first nor the last time, she observed, "Bill had to be a puppy dog and do everything [Hillary] wanted him to do." Once again, Bill's fear of Hillary's power and moral authority kicked in. But the effort at reconciliation succeeded. Bill remained within the marriage. Hillary kept her family—and her dreams of a political partnership—together. Bill held on to his political viability. And the dream of a trip one day to the White House stayed alive. Another pivotal moment of courting disaster had passed. Now all that was necessary was to keep the political train in motion and win the gubernatorial election of 1990.[36]

It would not be an easy task. By 1990, Bill Clinton had served as Arkansas' governor for a full ten years. The time since his withdrawal from the presidential race in 1988 had been chock-full of turmoil, from his initial depression to a series of reckless flirtations to a full-scale affair with a woman he loved. No one counted that time as a high point of his governing. Betsey Wright noted his indifference. Others saw a mood of detachment. As Dick Morris read the political tea leaves, what he found most absent was any sense of mission on Clinton's part. At his best, Clinton was always pursuing "some important, valiant fight for the good of the world to lend coherence and structure to his life." When such a fight was not present, Clinton became sour. "He would eat away at himself . . . become depressed, paranoid, surly." So uncertain was Clinton about running again for governor that Hillary actively considered becoming a candidate to replace him, potentially resuming the independent career in politics that Betsey Wright had envisioned when the two first met nearly two decades earlier. But polls showed that Hillary would elicit little initial enthusiasm from the electorate, and she put the idea on hold.[37]

In the end, Clinton's instincts about his political future were pivotal. As the time for decision approached, the national scene looked particularly unattractive for a Democrat. George Herbert Walker Bush had presided over the end of the Cold War, shown sure-handedness in handling world politics, and seemed relatively uncontroversial on the domestic front. That meant 1996 would be a more logical year to think about a presidential run than 1992. But if Clinton did not run for reelection as governor, that would mean he would have been out of public office for six years, and by then, potentially, a forgotten man. Fellow governors like South Carolina's Richard Riley and North Carolina's Jim Hunt urged him to hang in there, using his reelection to another four-year gubernatorial term as the basis from which to launch a presidential campaign later in the nineties. Literally no one, not even Hillary, possessed a clue as to his final decision.

Somehow, Clinton found the resolve to rejoin the gubernatorial fray. "As dithering and depressed" as he was, in Dick Morris's words, he understood at some profound level that it was now or never. He would run again, find a new idealistic platform to advance, and carry on the dream. "You could have knocked Hillary over with a feather," one of their friends observed. In his own way, Clinton's decision to run again testified to the power of the underlying impulse of his life—to become the "family hero," make things right, and in that process find redemption.[38]

Once he was in the race, a new energy flowed. The contest brought out both Clinton's combativeness and his vision for a different kind of future for the people of Arkansas. Retaining education as his primary crusade, Clinton pledged that under his new administration, every student graduating from Arkansas public schools with a B average would be provided with a publicly funded scholarship to attend college. Anticipating by nearly a decade a crucial issue facing America in the world, he also promised to plant ten million trees in Arkansas to help reduce greenhouse gases.[39]

Appropriately, Hillary assumed command of the campaign, dedicating herself to Bill's victory with a passion and vigor that seemed more intense than ever. When in the middle of the campaign a former state employee charged that Clinton had used public funds to carry on affairs with five women, including Gennifer Flowers, Hillary led the countercharge. Together with Betsey Wright, she mobilized Webb Hubbell and Vince Foster to secure affidavits from the women stating that they had never had sex with Clinton. (Clinton confessed to Flowers in a phone call that he hated having "to deny that.") Hillary was tough as nails. "What Bill doesn't understand," she told one writer, "is you've gotta . . . pound the Republican attack machine and run against the press." Gathering dirt on Flowers, she said, "If we were in front of a jury, I would crucify her." Tellingly, her rage focused on Flowers, not on her husband.[40]

The one casualty of the campaign was Dick Morris. For the second time (but not the last), Clinton repudiated his alliance with, and dependence on, the brilliant political strategist. Morris continued to offer ingenious advice, massaging his polling questions to elucidate the most congenial words with which Clinton could frame his campaign messages. But just as in 1979–80, Clinton seemed to feel tainted by his reliance on Morris and his "permanent campaign." Morris was also working for others in Arkansas, and Clinton resented the apparent diffusion of his energies and attention. The two had a near-violent confrontation, with Clinton accusing Morris of ignoring his campaign and seeking only to make money from it. According to Morris, the governor declared, "I don't get shit from you anymore. You're screwing me. You're screwing me." Already more a consultant for Republicans than for Democrats, Morris simply walked away, saying, in his recollection, "Go fuck yourself. I'm quitting your goddamn campaign, and now I'm a free agent. I can be a fifty state Republican and don't have to take your shit." Whatever the actual words, all accounts agree that the confrontation occurred. Once again, Dick Morris disappeared from Bill Clinton's life.[41]

Despite the fireworks, Clinton—with indispensable support from Hillary—soared to political victory. It was not the largest majority he had ever won (only 57 to 43 percent), but in some ways it was the most important. He continued to score legislative triumphs with his education program, including college scholarships, preschool programs, teachers' salaries, and community colleges; he solidified his reputation as a pioneer in the environmental arena; he appointed more blacks and women to high office than had all previous governors combined; and perhaps most important, he advanced his image as the personification of what it meant to be a "new" Democrat. No role advanced that image more than Clinton's chairmanship of the Democratic Leadership Council (DLC), the institutional voice of innovation in party councils.

Clinton's keynote address to the May 1991 DLC convention provided a stunning opportunity to crystallize the message he hoped to present to the American people. It was time, Clinton declared, to break through all the either/or debates. No longer was the choice between a cleaner environment or more economic growth. These were false choices, Clinton insisted. Instead, he said, Democrats had to embrace ideals that were both liberal and conservative. "Our burden is to give people a new choice rooted in old values. A new choice that is simple, that offers opportunity, demands responsibility, gives citizens more say, provides them responsive government, all because we recognize that we are a community. We're all in this together, and we're going up or down together."[42] Opportunity, Responsibility, Community—the Clinton message for the nineties. Never had Clinton more succinctly articulated the political vision that catapulted him to the forefront of twentieth-century political figures.

The Clintons were ready for the next step. More than at any other time, their fates were not only joined, but reciprocally intertwined. They had just come through hell in their personal lives; but after therapy and near divorce, they felt stronger, ready to move on. Where to remained an open question. But one thing was crystal clear. As the Clintons entered the nineties, their fates were joined.

SEVEN

"There Is a Place Called Hope"

The time had come to choose. Although Bill Clinton had promised Arkansas voters that he would serve a full four years if elected to his fifth term in 1990, it made less and less sense to defer a run for the presidency until 1996. He was at his peak. Nationally known, Clinton had broken into the inner circle of party leadership. As head of the Democratic Leadership Council, he pioneered a new message of how to combine the politics of the center with a commitment to expanding opportunities and entitlements for the middle class. Still young, vibrant, and electric, he risked losing momentum, as well as resonance with the electorate, by waiting another half decade to throw his hat into the ring. Perhaps most important, he and Hillary had just survived the greatest challenge to their two-decades-old relationship. Having chosen not to divorce, they could now seize the moment for realizing their lifelong dream together.

The primary obstacle was that in the summer and fall of 1991, George Herbert Walker Bush seemed unbeatable. The Reagan economic boom remained in full flower. The country still basked in the glory of having "won" the Cold War. Not only had the Soviet Union disintegrated, but George H. W. Bush had brilliantly orchestrated the aftermath of its demise to create a multilateral world order, with the United States at its head. Most important, Bush had presided masterfully over building the thirty-four-nation coalition that took on Iraq's Saddam Hussein after he recklessly chose to invade Kuwait in the summer of 1990. Assisted by the calm genius of his military commander, Colin Powell, Bush orchestrated a nearly flawless assault on Hussein. In three days, Iraqi troops were routed from Kuwait. There was minimal loss of life among allied troops. The next month, Bush's approval ratings soared to 91 percent. How could anyone challenge, let alone defeat, such a president?

But Clinton held a wider and a longer view. He was less sure than others that the Reagan-era economic bubble would persist in light of rising deficits and reduced job creation. Although he could not have anticipated the speed or impact of the 1991 recession (and certainly could never have predicted Bush's fundamental indifference to it once it arrived), Clinton knew the hunger of the American people for programs that would increase their children's chances for a decent education, their desire for greater security in the health care they were offered, and their hope for better employment and income possibilities.[1]

At the heart of Clinton's "new" political philosophy was a flair for fresh ways of responding to voters' instincts. Clinton consciously rejected old-fashioned Democratic ideas in search of a new formulation of political values that spoke to the contemporary conditions of American middle- and working-class families. Almost always, such an approach involved talking about children and education, opportunity and individual responsibility. If "Opportunity, Responsibility, Community" had become the Clinton mantra, the words never seemed hackneyed.

This penchant for new language and new values came to fruition in Clinton's embrace of the Democratic Leadership Council. Although derided by people like Jesse Jackson as a faction more deservedly named "Democrats for the Leisure Class," the DLC spoke to the abiding thirst of millions of Americans for ideas that went beyond traditional Democratic sloganeering. A gifted public speaker, Clinton was always best when he got into a rhythm with his audience, almost as though he were in a black church engaging in the call-and-response dynamic that made him so at home with African Americans. But he could do the same with any group where he let his energies soar, his imagination leap, and his words reach out for new ways of expressing what was happening between him and his audience.

Nowhere did that impulse take clearer flight than in his 1991 keynote address to the DLC. Using a set of twenty-one single-word "cues" to prompt his remarks, Clinton galvanized his audience. They leaped to their feet, convinced that here *was* a new kind of politician, speaking

for a new set of values. "Our burden," he told the assembled throng, "is
to give the people a new choice, rooted in old values, a new choice that
is simple, that offers *opportunity*, demands *responsibility*, gives citizens
more say, provides them responsive government—all because we recognize that we are a *community*. We are all in this together, and we are
going up or down together." One party bigwig called it "the best Democratic speech I've heard in ten years," and the TV commentator John
King—not given to hyperbole—described it as "toe-tingling."[2]

Clinton's words embodied a different way of talking about political
choices. No longer an us-against-them dynamic, this new Democratic
message trumpeted accountability, insisted on individual responsibility
for seizing moments of opportunity, and celebrated a vision of everyone
aboard a common vessel, rising or falling based on their ability to act in
their mutual best interest. If Clinton delayed a presidential campaign,
he took the risk that both his message and the audience it touched
might disappear. If not now, when?

But the most compelling reason for taking the leap was that Hillary
and Bill were ready to take on the challenge together. They had been
through hell. When Bill seemed ready to abandon his partnership with
Hillary—and with it the promise that they might one day occupy the
White House together—Hillary had resisted. They had sought counseling, both spiritual and psychological, and had made a new commitment
to each other. At the heart of the decision to run for the presidency in
1992, therefore, was a renewed dedication to the goal that had given
meaning to their relationship from day one. Neither believed that either
of them alone could reform America. They could only do it together.
This was the time to lay on the line all the dreams they had shared.[3]
If ever the Clinton relationship reached a peak moment of efficiency,
it was at that moment. For most of the 1992 campaign, they were
perfectly aligned.[4]

By nature, Bill was often uncontrollable. Meeting him, his Arkansas colleague David Pryor once said, "was like meeting a jaguar that
was just about to pounce." Some even worried about his emotional stability. Given these proclivities, Hillary had always served as an essential
counterbalance. She disciplined his impulses, honed his political messages, made into a taut political operation what otherwise would have
been an out-of-control, flailing set of instincts. Working with Clinton,

the journalist Carl Bernstein observed, was "like tuning an instrument." Without perfect control of pitch and tone, cacophony was more likely than communication. But with the right kind of tuning, all that energy and brilliance could be channeled into a series of brilliant messages. For nearly two decades—when their relationship was intact—the person most able to strike that balance had been Hillary. Arguably, she alone had the power and ability to control Bill.

He, in turn, provided the most effective vehicle by which Hillary could achieve her lifelong dream to be an agent of transformation. As she noted in her autobiography, "While Bill talked about social change, I embodied it. I had my own opinions, interests and profession . . . I was outspoken. I represented a fundamental change in the way women functioned in our society." With the civil rights movement as a spur, feminism experienced a powerful revival in the sixties and seventies—precisely the era when Hillary's generation came to maturity. She was among the burgeoning group of new women lawyers, and it was no accident that Betsey Wright, her companion and friend in Texas in 1972, fervently believed that Hillary should become the first woman president. Instead, Hillary had made the excruciatingly difficult decision to cast her lot with the man she loved—on the condition that they work as a team of equals to achieve their agreed-upon goals. More than the sum of their parts, they would break new ground as the first-ever "partnership" seeking to occupy the White House and transform the nation. While Eleanor Roosevelt had pioneered an independent role for women in politics during the New Deal and World War II, she never portrayed herself as a coequal with her husband, Franklin. By contrast, Bill Clinton spoke explicitly of his campaign offering "two for the price of one." By his accounting, voters would be getting "far more than Franklin Roosevelt and Eleanor." They were two great people, but on different tracks. "If I get elected," he promised, "we'll do things together, like we always have."[5]

Thus the Clinton campaign consciously represented a brand-new phenomenon in American politics: a modern feminist partnership. The very nature of the enterprise made it revolutionary. Moreover, the notion of coequals was clearly not just a turn of phrase. Hillary, noted Nancy Hernreich, Bill's scheduling secretary, was the most important person in the campaign. "She just had a way of cutting through to the core of [everything]." Whatever others might do, campaign workers understood that Hillary was the master strategist. Not only the last person Bill talked to at night and the first he spoke with in the morning, she also "[grabbed] the reins . . . and was her fiercest and most determined [when trouble arose]," her friend Diane Blair said. "The essential dialogue was between them," Carl Bernstein noted, and "their partnership . . . largely determined the philosophy, strategy, offenses, defenses, sound bites . . . and general health of the campaign."[6]

Not surprisingly, the feminist message conveyed by the Clinton campaign proved problematic for millions of Americans. Many were offended by Hillary's determination to be front and center. In every interview, she used the pronoun "we" to refer to the plans of the administration she and Bill hoped to bring to Washington. To many Americans, it all seemed too much of a calculated business arrangement. In a public opinion poll in March 1992, only 28 percent of the respondents viewed Hillary favorably, and more than half believed that the heart of the Clintons' relationship was a professional pact rather than a loving marriage.

What that perception ignored, however, was the passion underlying Bill and Hillary's commitment to each other. Betsey Wright, who knew them better than most, noted that "they are two of the most passionate people I ever met. They love passionately, they parent passionately, they read passionately, they play passionately." Their entire bearing toward each other suggested ardent feeling rather than calculated prearrangement. "You couldn't sustain that level of irritation if it were an arrangement," one friend observed. For better or worse, the chemistry of this relationship suggested a degree of emotional attachment (and dependency) rarely on display in American public life. It was almost impossible to speak of one of the Clintons without having the other in mind as well.[7]

The reason for launching a presidential race for 1992, therefore, was its timeliness for the Bill and Hillary partnership. They talked it over constantly, weighed the pluses and minuses, considered the options. On almost all counts, the verdict came in as positive. Even if they lost, they would have put themselves forward as potential candidates for 1996, whereas not to move forward at all was to risk being a nonentity in 1996. But above all, they were ready as a team. The chemistry and balance in their relationship seemed ideal. Regardless of what others thought about the idea of a copresidency, Bill and Hillary were on the same wavelength. There could be no better time to proceed.

Thus in October 1991, Bill Clinton announced his candidacy, highlighting the new politics he sought to bring to Washington. Intentionally, he portrayed himself as a link between past and future. He invoked his connection to John F. Kennedy, praised the role his grandparents played in his life, and zeroed in on his commitment to middle America. The "larger cause" to which he committed himself, Clinton said, was "preserving the American dream, restoring the hopes of the forgotten middle class"—a phrase he used fourteen times in the announcement—and "reclaiming the future for our children." It would be his responsibility, Clinton said, to forge a "new covenant" with the American people, based on "more opportunity for all, more responsibility from everyone, and a greater sense of common purpose." One more time: Opportunity, Responsibility, Community.

That night, family and friends gathered to celebrate the announcement. With Carolyn Staley playing the family piano, they sang "Abraham, Martin and John," then ended the evening with Bill's favorite hymn, "Amazing Grace." "How sweet the sound," the group intoned, "that saved a wretch like me, I once was lost but now am found, was blind, but now I see." Bill and Hillary were ready.[8]

Appropriately, the Clintons decided on Little Rock as the home base for their campaign. By remaining in Little Rock, the Clintons hoped to avoid the helter-skelter of Washington and retain enough psychological and physical distance from the 24/7 news cycle that they could still have time for strategic thinking. Bruce Lindsey, one of Clinton's oldest and best friends, was named campaign director. Lindsey knew more about Clinton than he would ever tell, and he understood intuitively how to maximize the candidate's strengths and minimize his weaknesses. Lindsey was always an ally to be trusted, and his discretion—and wisdom—made him an ideal overseer. He was slow to panic, shrewd in his awareness of the personal side of the Clintons' political dynamic, and clear in his understanding of both the strengths and the weaknesses of the Clinton duo.

Soon Lindsey was joined by George Stephanopoulos, a young Greek American and the son of an Orthodox priest. Unlike Lindsey, Stephanopoulos was assertive, full of himself, and on top of every aspect of the campaign. Named communications director, the youthful Stephanopoulos (he started when he was still in his twenties) demonstrated flair bordering on arrogance. The exact opposite of Lindsey, he luxuriated in the "countless stream of consciousness tours across the political landscape" that he engaged in with Clinton every day. It was fun, Stephanopoulos recounted, to work for a boss who "seemed to know something about everything—from the party rules for picking super delegates to turnout in black precincts." The early team was soon rounded out with David Wilhelm, an Illinois professional who understood all the intricacies of campaign organization, and Rahm Emanuel, a Chicagoan who combined brilliance with bravado and chutzpah. Clinton described him as "so aggressive [that] he made me look laid-back." Others quickly signed up—old friends from the Renaissance Weekends that the Clintons had attended on New Years since they were started by Phil and Linda Lader to bring together the best and brightest minds of the new generation; Harold Ickes and Susan Thomases from New York (Ickes was the son of FDR's interior secretary); and a group of economic gurus well plugged in to Goldman Sachs and other New York powerhouses. It was a great start.[9]

One of the Clintons' primary concerns was how to anticipate the issues that would emerge as obstacles. Ironically, Clinton was forewarned about what to expect by the Bush White House aide Roger Porter, with whom he had worked as part of the governors' conference on education. In an otherwise routine phone call, Porter suddenly alerted Clinton to the fact that the White House viewed his potential candidacy with apprehension. If Clinton's candidacy were to emerge, Porter said, the Bush people would seek to "destroy him." As a favor, Porter was giving Clinton "fair warning" not to venture into territory that would lead to devastating results. The Clintons began to prepare their response.[10]

Hillary's record of work in the Rose law firm, particularly those cases in which she may have crossed an ethical line by talking with officials in state government about the interests of her clients, was one area of concern. There had been a number of instances when, knowingly or unknowingly, she had done so. In one instance, her name was all over the file of the Southern Development bank, where records showed Hillary having numerous phone conversations with state officials. Hillary was also gun-shy about disclosing information about the sudden wealth she had garnered from trading in cattle futures under the tutelage of Jim Blair, and she kept secret her tax returns for that year, acknowledging to a friend that it would be hard to "work in Democratic politics again" if such information became public. Most of all, Hillary was secretive about her ongoing relationship with Jim McDougal. Not only had she been part of the initial Whitewater investment; she had also recruited as an ongoing client of the Rose law firm the Madison Guaranty Savings and Loan, which Jim McDougal had started to help finance his sometimes questionable investments. Here, too, Hillary had trodden on dangerous ground when she spoke on her client's behalf with state government officials who were ultimately the employees of her husband, the governor. For the moment, keeping these relationships secret seemed unproblematic, yet their very existence suggested the potentially nasty consequences that might flow when and if a public spotlight was turned upon them.[11]

What everyone realized, of course, was that Bill's history of womanizing was the number one concern. When one campaign worker suggested that Bill preempt the opposition by admitting his shenanigans, Clinton joked, "I can't open my closet . . . I'll get crushed by the skeletons." But no one recognized more than Hillary the need to prepare a defense ahead of time. She insisted that the campaign proactively neutralize the issue, digging for evidence of wrongdoing on the other side and winning over a neutral public by being the first ones to confront the issue openly.

Nothing illustrated this aspect of the Bill and Hillary partnership better than their carefully laid plans to raise with a group of reporters the issue of Bill's sexual history. Godfrey Sperling, *The Christian Science Monitor*'s Washington correspondent, regularly brought together a breakfast group of Washington reporters to meet prominent political leaders. Mickey Kantor, one of Bill Clinton's most experienced political advisers, first proposed that the Clintons seek an invitation to the Sperling breakfast. Hillary eagerly followed up. For days, they rehearsed with aides what they would say. Hillary vetoed the idea of ever using the word "adultery." Bill insisted he would entertain no questions about their private life. Hillary said that was impossible. Over hours of discussion, the couple worked out a game plan. They would acknowledge having encountered problems in their marriage, but that was over now, and they were fully committed to each other and to their daughter, Chelsea.

Awkwardly, when the breakfast took place, none of the reporters raised the issue. So Bill intervened, thanking them for their delicacy in not bringing it up, "but I know all of you are concerned." Soon they were off and running. True to script, Bill acknowledged that "like nearly anybody who has been together twenty years, our relationship has not been perfect or free of difficulties, but we feel good about where we are and we believe in our obligation to each other, and we intend to be together thirty or forty years from now, whether I run for president or not." It was a "boffo" performance, Godfrey Sperling later wrote, to which the reporters present had an "especially understanding and sympathetic response." Hillary was supportive and reinforcing throughout. It had been a brilliant success, and a dress rehearsal for what was to come.[12]

The wisdom of being proactive was clear. Scandals beset the Clinton campaign that even the most gifted fortune-teller could not have foreseen. In late January 1992, a supermarket tabloid blazoned headlines that Gennifer Flowers had carried on a twelve-year affair with Bill Clinton. Two weeks later, the story broke that Bill Clinton had lied about his draft status to reporters and systematically manipulated local draft officials to avoid serving in the Vietnam War. And in early March, *The New York Times* suggested that Hillary Clinton had used her connections in the governor's office to influence state policies affecting her clients with the Rose law firm. Like grenades launched from hidden guerrilla sites, the stories exploded the campaign's momentum and triggered disarray among the staff. More important, they generated a set of responses that provided a lasting model for how the Clintons would handle political conflict, including a process of dissembling, avoidance, and obscuring the truth.

When the Gennifer Flowers story broke, Bill Clinton was riding a wave of positive political news. New Hampshire, as always, was both the first primary and the pivotal place to make a good beginning. Paul Tsongas, senator from the next-door state of Massachusetts, a popular centrist and a cancer survivor, was the odds-on favorite to win. Other competitors were Nebraska's senator Bob Kerrey, a Medal of Honor winner who touted national health care as his primary campaign goal, and Jerry Brown, governor of California, the maverick in the race. (After repeated equivocations, New York's Mario Cuomo at the last minute decided not to run.) Clinton blitzed the state. Performing the same magic with audiences that he had accomplished with Arkansans for over a decade, he attracted larger and larger crowds. By the end of December he was second to Tsongas and gaining. He had also raised more money than anyone else in the field. Everything was going as planned.[13]

Then came the Flowers bombshell. Not only did she claim a twelve-year affair, she also boasted of (and played) a series of tape recordings of conversations with Clinton. In the 1990 gubernatorial race, Flowers had denied having had sex with Clinton, even signing an affidavit to that effect. Now she not only repudiated that affidavit but went on national television to make her claims. Although experts determined that the tapes had probably been doctored, they still contained Bill Clinton's voice making suggestive comments. Moreover, follow-up stories regaled people with headlines like THEY MADE LOVE ALL OVER THE APARTMENT, allegations that Bill would jog over to her apartment for a "quickie," and that he even asked her for sex in the men's room of the governor's mansion while Hillary was upstairs. Even though network television and the mainstream media played down the more sensationalist aspects of the tabloid headlines, it was clear the campaign was in crisis. Clinton's popularity started to plummet. "If we don't turn this [around]," the Clinton staffer Paul Begala said, "we're going down."[14]

Hillary led the counterassault. Once again, her immediate response was to dig up dirt on the attackers and discredit them. As one observer noted, she became "her fiercest and most determined" when it appeared that the Gennifer Flowers story was gaining traction. Quickly, Hillary created a "defense team" to help rebut the allegations and persuade a press corps threatening to get out of control to stay on focus and be fair. Headed by Betsey Wright, the defense team hired a team of private detectives to investigate the nineteen women who had been identified by various tabloids as potential sources and to persuade them to sign affidavits denying they had had sex with Bill Clinton. Betsey Wright, meanwhile, was instructed to go through all the Clintons' legal and personal papers to identify any other materials that might be embarrassing.[15]

Hillary herself defined the tone of the couple's response. "From my perspective," she said, "our marriage is a strong marriage. We love each other, we support each other, and we have had a lot of strong and important experiences together that have meant a lot to us." Acknowledging that, as in all marriages, there had been problems, she asked that people respect their privacy. After all, she said, "Is anything about our marriage as important to the people of New Hampshire as whether or not they will have a chance to keep their families together?"[16]

But Hillary knew instinctively that more was needed. So when George Stephanopoulos, Mickey Kantor, and other staff aides came up with the idea that the Clintons, together as a couple, go on national television, she embraced the idea. It was a critical choice. Arguably, the key moment of the 1992 campaign was Bill and Hillary's appearance on the CBS news show *60 Minutes* to talk about Gennifer Flowers's claims. Coming immediately after the Super Bowl game, the show reached the largest audience of almost any news program in history. Once again, as with the Godfrey Sperling breakfast, the Clintons were perfectly rehearsed. Hillary "steeled herself," their old friend Bob Reich observed, and Bill absorbed her discipline. Using almost the same phrasing he had used at the breakfast, he acknowledged having "caused pain in my marriage." But once more, the Clintons refused to use the word "adultery." When Steve Kroft, the moderator, pushed for more details on the alleged affair, Hillary leaped in: "I don't think that being any more specific about what's happening in the privacy of our life together is relevant to anybody but us." Hillary's defense of the couple's privacy, in tandem with the vulnerability exposed by Bill's confession of "problems" in their relationship, worked perfectly as a way to enlist the audience's sympathies. "Wait a minute," Bill told Kroft when he suggested their marriage was merely an "arrangement," "You're looking at two people who love each other. This is not an arrangement or an understanding. This is a *marriage*." Hardly anyone in TV land could fail to respond, especially when Hillary added that she was there "because I love him and I respect him and I honor what he's been through and what we've been through together. And you know, if that's not enough for people, then heck, don't vote for him." Her delivery was perfect.[17]

Although George Stephanopoulos later called the *60 Minutes* appearance the "media equivalent of experimental chemotherapy," it represented a risk the Clintons felt compelled to take, with Hillary in the lead. By demonstrating total solidarity with Bill, Carl Bernstein noted, she had become his "ultimate character reference." Brilliantly, the Clintons had simultaneously exposed their emotional souls, defended their family's sanctity, and turned a debilitating personal weakness into a political strength. Instead of undermining their credibility, the Clintons had enhanced it, in the process winning the emotional identification of millions of families who had experienced similar moments of stress and pain. It would be hard to imagine a more brilliantly orchestrated response. For the moment, at least, the downward spiral in public opinion had been stemmed—perhaps even reversed.[18]

Two weeks later, the second bombshell dropped. On February 6, the *Wall Street Journal* broke the story that Clinton had been granted a deferment from the draft from August 1969 through late October 1969. The revelation flew directly in the face of Clinton's explicit denial that he had ever received a deferment or a draft notice. Shortly thereafter, Ted Koppel, the host of ABC's *Nightline* news show, called Clinton headquarters to say that he had obtained a copy of Clinton's letter to the Arkansas draft board in which he had explained—at tortuous length—his initial request for an ROTC appointment at the University of Arkansas Law School, and then subsequently his decision to renounce the ROTC appointment and take his chances (admittedly then much diminished) of being selected in the draft lottery. In an extraordinary act of deception, Clinton declared that he had "forgotten all about the letter."[19]

Clinton's dissembling immediately created suspicion on the part of the press that Clinton could never be trusted to tell the truth. The candidate had first raised skepticism in the press corps about his draft status when he told the *Washington Post* reporter Dan Balz that although he had expected to be drafted during his time at Oxford, he had never in fact received a draft notice. "They never did [call me]," he told Balz. Clinton then compounded his initial act of deception by saying, "I wound up just going through the lottery and it was just a pure fluke that

I was never called." Balz found Clinton's use of the word "fluke" strange even at the time. Later—after the revelation about his deferment—Jim Wooten of ABC News asked Clinton directly whether he had received his draft induction notice before applying to the ROTC. Clinton once again lied, declaring no, he had not.

Why Clinton so totally distorted reality remains a mystery. But his decision to lie created a pattern that caused members of the press, especially at the *Post*, to distrust virtually everything he said. When Balz learned from the investigations of the *Wall Street Journal* and the *Los Angeles Times* that Clinton had actually received his draft notice in April 1969, he was "stunned." Clinton had not simply "fudged" the truth. He had "brazenly lied." Reporters now greeted Clinton's ordinary remarks with deep suspicion. When David Broder, one of Washington's most respected reporters, first heard that Clinton claimed to have "forgotten" about his draft notice, he declared: "That's bullshit. Nobody forgets their own draft notice." For Broder, a lightbulb went off: "This is a guy who reconstructs his own history to suit his needs."[20]

Not surprisingly, the Clinton staff experienced its own sense of unease. Through endless discussions of campaign strategy and hours of policy-wonk bull sessions, Clinton had impressed those around him with how articulate he was, how wide-ranging his thought process, how open he was to diverse perspectives. He had also assured his campaign aides that he had shared with them all there was to know about the major controversies in his closet. Now that assurance no longer seemed credible. "How long will people give us the benefit of the doubt?" George Stephanopoulos asked himself. "How much of this stuff can they take? How much more can I take?" Stephanopoulos could not believe that Clinton had kept the existence of his letter to Colonel Holmes a secret. How was that possible from a man running for the presidency?[21]

In the end, the letter itself generated a mixed response. It was so tortured, so full of agonizing, that for some, at least, it exposed not simply a calculating, self-interested political activist seeking to avoid the draft, but also a deeply moral young patriot consumed by doubt and existential anxiety. James Carville, another young aide to Clinton, argued that "this letter is our friend . . . If you read the whole letter, you end up thinking 'I wouldn't mind having a president who could write a letter like that when he was twenty-one.'" The question was whether voters would choose to remember Clinton's lies about his draft history, or the honest ambivalence Clinton (and millions of others) felt about the Vietnam War.

To the amazement of many, the voters of New Hampshire gave Clinton the benefit of the doubt. Although he had clearly lost the momentum that had helped him almost obliterate Tsongas's lead, he returned to campaigning with a ferocious energy to persuade the voters of New Hampshire of his good faith. "I'll tell you what I think the character issue is," he declared. "[It's] who really cares about you." Viscerally, powerfully, Clinton literally grabbed the electorate. If you elect me, Bill declared, "I'll never forget who gave me a second chance, and I'll be there for you 'til the last dog dies." He and Hillary had bonded with the voters, both in their campaigning together and in their 60 *Minutes* performance. Now Clinton was begging for understanding. The voters of New Hampshire would be the judge, and in the end, Clinton triumphed. Although Tsongas secured 35 percent of the vote, Clinton—having sunk below 20 percent in the polls—garnered 26 percent to finish a surprising second. Not for the first (or the last) time, Bill Clinton showed that he deserved to be called the Comeback Kid.[22]

But the season of explosive shocks had not yet ended. On March 7, just six weeks after the Gennifer Flowers story broke in the tabloid press, *The New York Times* raised another series of pointed questions, this time about the ethics and politics of Hillary Rodham Clinton. Written by the reporter Jeff Gerth, the story focused on Hillary's role with the Rose law firm in representing clients who had dealings with the state. It also raised the question of whether the governor and his wife should be in business with people like Jim and Susan McDougal, whose savings and loan was regulated by the state. The Clintons' partnership with the McDougals involved the Whitewater real estate investment, not the Madison Guaranty Savings and Loan company that McDougal subsequently established to help finance his real estate operations. Technically, the two were separate businesses. Yet in practice, the same people were involved, leading to legitimate questions as to whether Hillary Clinton, who had recruited a $2,000-per-month retainer from McDougal on behalf of Madison Guaranty, should have been speaking to state regulators about the affairs of her business associate.

Hillary faced a simple choice: release all her records from the Rose law firm and apologize if they disclosed inappropriate conflict-of-interest activities, or hunker down, deny any and all requests for material, and seek to blow her accusers out of the water. The law of politics should have made the choice easy: Once a person admits to a mistake, it is soon forgotten, while failure to do so almost inevitably leads to greater digging, with the stakes rising higher with each new renewal of the confrontation. Yet in this instance, contrary to her advice to Bill that they go forward at the Sperling breakfast and on *60 Minutes* to face the charges of inappropriate sexual activity on Bill's part, Hillary took exactly the opposite tack. This time it was she who was under attack, and instead of responding with openness, she slammed the door. Already the head of the defense team that had been created to handle the Flowers and draft controversies, Hillary now asserted total control over all responses to the Gerth story. No one was to speak to the press about the allegations without her explicit permission. Meanwhile, Susan Thomases, her most trusted aide, along with Webb Hubbell and Vince Foster, her closest friends and law partners, were instructed to go through all the Rose law firm records, including any contacts Hillary might have had with the state banking commissioner. They were to keep their findings secret, put the files in a secure place, and systematically deny access to all but the most innocuous documents.[23]

Commenting later, Jane Sherburne, one of the lawyers working on the White House team assigned to defend Hillary on Whitewater, observed that "a lot of Hillary's reaction originated with that very private nature of hers. Her attitude was 'What business is this of theirs? We want to be talking about education and health care. Why should anybody care about this?' I don't think she recognized the precancerous nature of the Gerth story." But precancerous it was. Denial fed the appetite of a press convinced that there was something to hide. As the party insider and White House appointee Lanny Davis later noted: "One can speculate that the whole chain of events that led to the Whitewater investigation, then led to [the appointment of Special Prosecutor] Ken Starr, which then led to the investigation of Monica and finally to impeachment can be traced back to the first Jeff Gerth *New York Times* story on Whitewater, and the first instinct—to lock down." Without question, the "Fuck you, Jeff Gerth" strategy, as it came to be called, multiplied exponentially the number of reporters who became convinced that Hillary had something to hide. In effect, she adopted the politically suicidal position of acting as though she were beyond the purview of any investigation.[24]

Soon enough, the Gerth story garnered attention in the presidential race. In a March presidential debate in Chicago, Jerry Brown seized on Gerth's allegations to charge that Clinton was "funneling money to his wife's law firm for state business." Rarely did Bill Clinton totally lose it; on this occasion he flared into instant fury. "I don't care what you say about me," he fumed, "but you ought to be ashamed of yourself for jumping on my wife. You're not worth being on the same platform as my wife. Jerry comes in with his family wealth and his fifteen-hundred-dollar suits, and makes a lying accusation about my wife." Hillary outdid him in her defensiveness. When TV reporters independently pursued the story, she declared, archly: "[Well,] I suppose I could have stayed home, baked cookies, and had teas," but instead she had become a lawyer "to assure that women can make the choices that they should make—whether it's a full-time career, full-time motherhood, some combination." If Hillary was trying to make herself the poster child for her generation, she failed. Thousands of women, homemakers as well as career women, saw her remarks as demeaning. The conservative *New York Times* columnist William Safire called Hillary's comments another outbreak of her "foot-in-mouth disease." Campaign pollsters soon noted public disapproval of Hillary's ambitious reputation, concluding that she should appear more feminine, engage in fewer off-the-cuff remarks, and pursue a schedule that would keep her away from the national press corps.[25]

By mid-April, the immediate contretemps over Hillary and her law practice had cooled. Bill resumed his campaign for centrist votes, armed with the all-pervasive slogan billboarded by his aide James Carville: "It's the economy, stupid!" By the winter of 1991–92, unemployment had risen, the economic growth rate had fallen, and public commentators more and more often invoked the "recession" mantra. With the controversies about their personal lives now muted, the Clintons could shift from crisis mode toward piecing together the winning combinations from New York, California, Illinois, and other key states that would bring victory at the convention. But the six weeks of implosion that had

occurred from late January through early March disclosed patterns
that, while not clearly visible at the time, would shape the future of the
next eight years. The three explosions may have been contained for
now. But the lessons they taught were never heeded, with consequences
that were profound.

The first of these was Bill's evidently incurable passion for extracurricular sex. Repeatedly he vowed to stop, yet he never did. More
than anything else, this behavior would control his political destiny.

Second, Bill's behavior empowered Hillary. The more Bill sinned and
was caught, the greater Hillary's control over their lives became, politically as well as personally. It was no accident when, in the midst of the
Gennifer Flowers scandal, Hillary moved front and center to exercise
damage control, imposing stringent discipline on the entire defense team
that she had created to fight off the charges. Hillary's response reflected
her ability to use Bill's lapses to advance her own agenda. "Hillary has
the most incredible ability to separate her personal hurts, her personal
indignity," Betsey Wright commented, "from a bigger picture, and a bigger goal, and a bigger love for him . . . I could not do it. I'd get so mad at
him . . . yet she could sort through that within a matter of hours." As a
consequence of that decision, she exercised new power. "When Gennifer Flowers appears," the historian Doris Kearns Goodwin has noted,
"and Hillary pulls [Bill] up, she's way at the top and he's down." Looking
at the same dynamic, Dick Morris observed that "it always starts when
Hillary has to rescue her husband from sexual accusations. But, after
the rescue, Hillary assumes greater power over the rest of her husband's
career than she should."[26]

Third, in dissembling about the draft, Bill Clinton displayed his
inability to come clean about personal issues that were at the core of
his identity. Sometimes he outright lied. More often, he shaded the
truth. Always, he seemed to feel entitled to construct events or recall
experiences in ways that worked to his own benefit. A tendency toward
self-congratulation and self-protection may be universal. But Clinton
practiced it in ways that soon became famous. One inevitable consequence was to make his audience, most often reporters, profoundly suspicious. As he came to believe that the press was "out to get him" as part
of a conspiracy to destroy his presidency, Clinton never realized the degree to which he had actually created the problem by evading the truth.

Finally, Hillary Clinton revealed her own fatal flaw in the way she responded to questions about her law practice. Unable to acknowledge her human frailty, she chose to resist disclosure of her personal business records by fighting back. Yet all she did by stonewalling reporters was to inflame their appetite for more investigations. And there was no one in the campaign to take her on. By now, she had so entrenched her own position that even her closest friends and staff aides were afraid to confront her.

Three moments of crisis. Six weeks of finding ways to cope. Eight years of paying the consequences.

For the time being, Clinton, reinvigorated by his comeback in New Hampshire, prepared for the heart of the battle. Clinton fought his opponents to a draw in Colorado, then moved on to a decisive victory in Georgia, backed by the civil rights hero John Lewis, Governor Zell Miller, and Atlanta's mayor, Maynard Jackson. A huge victory in South Carolina soon followed, with Super Tuesday—nine primaries and three caucuses—looming. Clinton hit his stride that day, sweeping six southern states while remaining competitive elsewhere. Immediately showing that he was not just a regional candidate, Clinton went on to win impressive victories in Illinois (52–25 against Tsongas) and in Michigan (49–27 against Brown).

Still, the battle was not over. Jerry Brown became Clinton's new archrival, narrowly defeating Clinton in Connecticut (37–36). Moreover, the Texas businessman Ross Perot decided to toss his hat into the ring as an independent. Immediately, Perot's presence diminished Clinton's appeal in the national polls, making him a third-place choice when compared directly with Bush and Perot. New York became the new test of Clinton's clout. Less attuned to the state's cosmopolitan diversity than he had been to New Hampshire's rural voters or the industrial workers of Michigan and Illinois, Clinton found the Empire State difficult. But then he received endorsements from newspapers as different as *The New York Times*, the *New York Post*, and the New York *Daily News*. Jimmy Carter enthusiastically endorsed him, and in the end, Clinton won New York easily. He then went on to seal the nomination by triumphing in New Jersey, Ohio, New Mexico, Montana, and, perhaps most important, California, where he defeated Brown in his home state by 48 to 40 percent.[27]

In all of this, Clinton displayed the core qualities that had carried him from his small-town birth to a single mother in rural Arkansas to election as the youngest governor in the nation's history and chair of the unorthodox Democratic Leadership Council. Bill Clinton was fresh, he had new ideas, and he understood how to relate to people. Crucially, for him, "opportunity," "responsibility," and "community" were not just words that made up a political slogan; they spoke to a reality he wished passionately to bring to life.

With a host of victories behind him, Bill Clinton, with Hillary at his side, prepared to seize his moment of triumph in Madison Square Garden. Four years earlier, he had earned headlines with the debacle of his forty-three-minute nominating speech for Michael Dukakis. Now *he* was to be the candidate, his name placed in nomination by the greatest orator of the Democratic party, Mario Cuomo. When the time came for his acceptance speech, Clinton reminded people of who he was and what he stood for. Once again he focused on the "forgotten middle class," "those who do the work and pay the taxes" so that their children can enjoy a better life. On a poignant personal note, he recalled the night Chelsea was born. "I was overcome with the thought that God had given me a blessing my own father never knew: the chance to hold my child in my arms." Then he made the link: "Somewhere at this very moment, a child is being born in America. Let it be our cause to give that child a happy home, a healthy family, and a hopeful future . . . Let it be our cause that we give this child a country that is coming together, not coming apart—a country of boundless hopes and endless dreams . . . My fellow Americans, I end tonight where it all began for me: I still believe in a place called Hope." It was as good a place as any to begin a campaign for the White House.[28]

To the lasting advantage of the Democrats, the Republicans offered little that was new or vibrant. Despite George Herbert Walker Bush's successes in foreign policy, his presidency had badly faltered. As recession gripped the land, Bush and his cabinet showed almost no interest in responding. Compounding the error, the Republicans ran a convention seemingly intent on conveying the narrowest, most partisan message. In a concession to his right-wing foes, Bush turned over the opening night to Pat Robertson, the evangelical fundamentalist preacher. Robertson's *Praise the Lord* (*PTL*) TV show specialized in demonizing liberals for their social policies on abortion, gay rights, and children's rights. Now that message became the Republican Party message, as though those were the only issues the party stood for. With the conservative commentators Pat Buchanan and Pat Robertson in the lead, the entire convention took on the air of a culture-war revival meeting. Speakers denounced Bill Clinton as a skirt chaser and draft dodger, Hillary as a nontraditional woman who was unfeminine. The result was to leave the Republicans with a national image as mean-spirited reactionaries with no program for addressing what the Democrats claimed was the number one issue: "It's the economy, stupid!"[29]

Although Clinton initially ranked third in the polls, his campaign soon obliterated that disadvantage. Bush lost more than he gained when his campaign suggested that Clinton's travels to Russia as a student at Oxford were unpatriotic. Meanwhile, Al Gore quickly dispatched Dan Quayle, the Republican vice presidential nominee, in their single debate. But the coup de grâce came in the second presidential debate when a black woman in the audience asked how the national debt had affected each candidate's life. Bush looked frustrated, saying that he did not understand the question. But Clinton walked directly toward the woman, metaphorically reaching out to her while inviting her to join the discussion by saying, "Tell me how it's affected you." As one commentator said, Clinton's "body language" turned the evening around. "The three steps he had taken toward [her] spoke volumes about his empathy, his concern, his desire to respond to the needs of the public. Bush, by contrast, was caught [on camera] gazing at his wristwatch—hoping desperately that this awkward moment would soon be done. And indeed it was. The presidential campaign was, in effect, over."[30]

By Election Day it would have taken a miracle for Bush to recover. Seemingly indifferent to the economy, he also appeared indecisive with regard to his party's message. Clinton meanwhile sustained his "New Democrat" image, rallied minority voters, and reached out to troubled voters with a fresh new message. Election Day was not even close. "This victory was more than a victory of party," Clinton declared, imitating his hero, John F. Kennedy. "It was a victory for those who work hard and play by the rules, a victory for people who felt left out and left behind and want to do better." Clinton secured 43 percent of the vote, Bush only 37 percent. Perot was the difference, with 19 percent—more than any third-party candidate had won since 1912. But in the electoral college, it was all Clinton, 372 to 168, with thirty-two states in his column. Despite the bombshells of January 23–March 7, the Clintons had prevailed. The world had changed. A new team was in the White House.

But the Clintons had won together before. The question was, how would they handle their victory this time? Would the "copresidency" become a reality? If so, who would be in charge? For which programs, which initiatives? Who would be the staff, and who would they report to? What space would they occupy? Above all, who held final decision-making power? And through what process would that power be exercised? As the three months after Election Day quickly demonstrated, the absence of clear-cut answers to such questions proved devastating to the new administration's aspiration for a "revolutionary transformation" in Washington.

The first sign of problems to come was the inability of the Clintons to determine who would be the director of the transition team. Mickey Kantor, a dear friend of Clinton and his campaign chair through the election, seemed the logical choice. A take-charge guy, he assumed he would occupy the position and started to push for decisions right away. Hillary balked. "[She] leveled that cold stare . . . and her face was firm," one aide recounted. "She said to Mickey: 'Don't do that! You're not going to push him! . . . So back off." Fatigued, almost falling apart from the last frenetic days of the campaign, Clinton raised no objection to Hillary's stance. Deeply disappointed, Kantor headed back to California. Instead, Clinton appointed Warren Christopher, a quintessential diplomat who would go to any lengths to keep the peace. But peace was not what was needed. Someone willing to make hard decisions was required. Torn between having a tough guy who could bark orders, or an open process in which everyone could speak with equal time, the Clintons chose chaos over order. "It was a bloody, ugly mess," one staff member said. Stephen Hess of the Brookings Institute echoed the sentiment, calling it the "worst [presidential] transition in modern history."

"The degree of squabbling in the early days of the transition," David Halberstam wrote, was "poisonous."[31]

At the heart of the problem was confusion at the center. Who was going to run this presidency? Bill and Hillary had a pact. They would be copresidents. But no one believed that was workable. More to the point, Hillary had not been elected. Bill had. So, too, had Al Gore, his vice president and the person to whom Bill had promised a preeminent role. Was this to be another troika, with three people signing off on everything? That was absurd on its face. But such was the reality of the early days—three people struggling for power, each committed to playing the decisive role, worming his or her way into the pivotal decision-making slot. Amazingly—and frighteningly—it was a replay of the scene at the governor's mansion after Clinton won for the first time in 1978. No one was in charge, four different aides competed for authority, and helter-skelter was the order of the day.

Hillary was at the center of the controversy. She needed to define her power and role. Talking with Dick Morris, she raised the idea of becoming chief of staff herself, something that *Time* magazine had also mentioned. That would be impossible, Morris responded, because the chief of staff served as lightning rod, taking all the heat for hard, unpopular decisions. What about secretary of education or attorney general, she asked? No, he demurred. There was the question of nepotism. Instead, he suggested, Hillary should think about taking charge of a major domestic initiative such as health care, as she had with the education issue back in Arkansas. After all, it tied directly to issues of children and family, abiding strong points on her agenda. Bill and Hillary had already discussed the possibility. "It felt right," she said, and she could be in the forefront of an initiative that would transform the nation.[32]

But what about Gore? From the very beginning, Clinton had pledged to make his vice president a full partner, consulting him on every decision, giving him special responsibility for issues he cared most about, such as the environment. Ever since Jimmy Carter's experience with Walter Mondale, the vice presidency had grown in stature. Now Gore would raise the office's stature higher yet. Not willing simply to take Clinton at his word about being a partner, Gore immediately rented a suite of offices in Little Rock, intent on playing a pivotal role in every major appointment. He reached out to Clinton's most loyal staffers, such as George Stephanopoulos, urged them to come to see him whenever they had problems (including with Hillary), and sought to develop with the entire White House team a relationship of confidence and trust that would keep him on the inside looking out rather than the outside looking in. Gore aspired to be the steel in Clinton's spine, the last person he talked with before making a crucial decision, the ultimate confidant.[33]

The problem was that there was already somebody in that role, named Hillary. Whatever Bill Clinton had promised Gore, he had committed three times over to Hillary. Not only did Clinton believe she was a genius, according to one staff member, "he thought she had the magic touch." When Hillary came up with the last line of his acceptance speech, "I still believe in a place called Hope," the White House aide Mandy Grunwald noted, "the look he gave her . . . was unforgettable. It was like, 'You *always* know the right thing.'" Added to the power Hillary assumed when Bill needed to be rescued from his sexual peccadilloes, it was hard to imagine anyone getting between her and Bill, or exercising greater influence over his decision making.[34]

Conflict, therefore, was endemic to the new White House team. Hillary and Gore jousted with each other repeatedly, albeit in an atmosphere of civility. But neither willingly gave way. Worst of all, there was no chief of staff to impose order, draw up a set of rules, allocate chores, and insist on a clear-cut division of responsibilities. The absence of a strong chief of staff—echoing the absence of a decisive director of the transition team—turned out to be the most critical mistake of Clinton's preinaugural period. Deeply influenced by Hillary, Clinton eventually decided to appoint his childhood friend Mack McLarty to the post of chief of staff. McLarty was sarcastically dubbed "Mack the Nice." Kind, gracious, and accommodating, McLarty saw his role as easing the process by which others could bring their demands to the troika running the White House. It was a recipe for chaos, an invitation for people to push their agendas at any cost, knowing that there was no policeman managing the Oval Office, regulating access to power. Few decisions would prove more portentous.

The process of choosing a cabinet exemplified all these dilemmas.

For whatever reason, Clinton determined to complete the selection process by the New Year, and to defer until then the naming of his personal staff. Clinton complicated the process by insisting that the cabinet should reflect the diversity of the American people, becoming "the most fully integrated this country has ever seen." However admirable in principle, that idea soon became a straitjacket. It gave the appearance of identifying a particular slot as the "Latino" post, or the "black" position, or the "woman's" office. "Rigging certain departments for a single gender or race," the *New Republic* sermonized, "is an insult to minorities and a depressing sign of the cultural balkanization of our politics."[35]

Choosing an attorney general highlighted the dilemma. One of the top four cabinet posts—the others being secretary of state, secretary of the treasury, and secretary of defense—the attorney general represented prestige, status, and power. The other three posts were all to be filled by white men. Hence, Hillary Clinton was intent that the AG be a woman. Though by prior agreement, all cabinet nominees were vetted by Hillary, Bill, and Al Gore, Hillary took direct responsibility for selecting a woman for attorney general. Unlike the other three "prestige" cabinet appointments, no obvious figure leaped to mind, so Hillary concentrated on talented individuals who had not yet reached the national radar screen. Zoe Baird quickly surfaced. An old Renaissance Weekend compatriot, she served as general counsel for Aetna Insurance and was a personal favorite of Warren Christopher, head of the transition team. Early on, Harold Ickes pointed out a problem. Baird, by her own admission, had hired two Peruvian immigrants for her household staff without paying Social Security taxes for them. Both Hillary and Christopher brushed the concern aside, but soon it came to symbolize the dangers of making a single criterion the sine qua non for appointment to high office. A barrage of protests greeted the revelation of Baird's "immigrant" dilemma, yet Hillary would not back off.[36]

The problem of "identity politics" became even more pronounced when Clinton, in an impromptu exchange with NBC's Andrea Mitchell, briskly declared that he intended to keep "right away" his promise to allow gays to serve openly in the military. Throughout the campaign, Clinton had made overt appeals to the gay community, as he had to other constituencies defined primarily by their racial, ethnic, or sexual identities. But here, he seemed to give priority to a policy that, in the

eyes of most Americans—and even in the eyes of most gays—ranked
far down the list of important initiatives. Rather than create a task force
to make recommendations, or announce that he would address the
question after he first dealt with the economy, he responded reflexively.
In the process he created a firestorm that obscured, for the moment at
least, far more compelling problems of public policy. A strong chief of
staff might have prevented such a gaffe; without question, he would
have insisted that the president stay on message.[37]

What a strong chief almost certainly would not have tolerated was
perhaps the worst decision of the transition process, the determination
that none of the president's personal aides would be chosen until after
Christmas and after the cabinet had been completed—as if the president's personal advisers were less important than a secretary of the
interior. Moreover, Hillary—with her aide Susan Thomases—was given
primary responsibility for choosing those personal aides, albeit with
approval from Gore and Clinton. As a result, David Gergen noted, the
internal White House team was put together "at the last minute. People
didn't know where they would be sitting . . . didn't know what their jobs
would be." It all led, the Brookings Institute scholar Stephen Hess said,
"to a *terribly* shaky start."

Confusion was everywhere. No one knew what he or she would be
doing. Harold Ickes, one of Clinton's closest campaign aides, was assured repeatedly that he would be in the inner circle, only at the last
minute to be told that there was no place for him. Dee Dee Myers, soon
to become Clinton's press secretary, characterized the entire appointment process as "awful." For even the highest-placed people in the
campaign, she said, "there was tremendous uncertainty about our own
jobs."[38]

As if the existing chaos were not bad enough, the Bush administration threw a monkey wrench into the process when in mid-December,
Richard Darman, the budget director, announced that the deficit for
the ensuing year would be 50 percent higher than previously forecast—$387 billion rather than $250 billion. Immediately, the announcement confounded all the hopes Clinton had generated for
domestic policy initiatives, from a middle-class tax cut to health care
reform. The promises Clinton had made in the campaign now came
face to face with the reality that there was no money to pay for them.

His economic team—a brilliant group led by Lloyd Bentsen, the secretary of the treasury, and including Wall Street giants like Robert Rubin—warned that unless Clinton took steps immediately to control the deficit by raising taxes and lowering spending, interest rates would rise and the entire Clinton program would go down the tubes. "You mean to tell me," Clinton asked his financial team, "that the success of my [entire] program . . . hinges on the Federal Reserve Board and a bunch of fucking bond traders?" The answer was yes, and immediately the Clinton team shifted gears to devise a plan that would win Wall Street's confidence and restore faith in a growing economy. Now deficit reduction and a balanced budget took front and center stage, not a middle-class tax cut and health reform.[39]

The bad news on the economic front also had serious implications for Clinton's relationship with Congress and the press. In December, Clinton held a dinner with congressional leaders. The hope was that legislative leaders would come to an agreement with the president on how to proceed to enact the priorities they all agreed upon. Yet at the dinner, Clinton was uncharacteristically subdued. Being in the same room with leaders like Tom Foley and Daniel Patrick Moynihan seemed to intimidate him. The congressional leadership persistently pushed their own point of view, and when there seemed to be a difference of opinion, Clinton deferred to their judgment, suggesting to at least some that he was a pushover. As Moynihan observed, the weeks of late December seemed to echo with "the clatter of campaign promises being tossed out the window."[40]

At the same time, the press more vigorously held Clinton accountable for his campaign promises. When Clinton tried to deny that he had made a middle-class tax cut pivotal to his economic plan, he was met with disbelief. When confronted with his declaration that his economic plan would be announced the day after he took office, he retorted, "I don't know who led you to believe that." On foreign policy questions involving Iraq and Haiti, as well as on domestic issues, Clinton seemed intent on using nuances of language to back off positions he had previously taken. Repeating his experience with the press on the draft issue, Clinton seemed intent on dissembling. He thereby widened even further the credibility gap that already existed. As a result, one *Washington Post* reporter noted, a "peevish spirit" developed among reporters. At an early press conference, he said, "Both the questions and the answers [were] freighted with a suspicion bordering on contempt."[41]

The events leading up to and including the inauguration reflected many of the defining features of the preceding eleven weeks. On the one hand, there remained an almost palpable sense of change, symbolized by the Clintons as a presidential team, their young daughter, the complexity of their relationship, and Bill Clinton's ability to connect almost viscerally with vast segments of the American public. On the other hand, a sense of disarray was pervasive. Many future White House staff aides did not know what they would be doing, where they would be assigned, or under whose leadership they would be working. According to some, Hillary Clinton was still fighting with her husband to make sure that she and her staff would have offices in the West Wing—the first presidential spouse ever to seek working space in the executive mansion's center of power. But what would that do to Al Gore's allocation of precious square feet? Proximity was key. So, too, was the symbolism of who had more room.[42]

Illustrative of the entire transition process was the preparation for Bill Clinton's inaugural address. Clinton, who so excelled at off-the-cuff inspiration, was less good at giving a carefully scripted speech. He had no favorite speechwriter, no one who read his mind as Ted Sorensen had done for Jack Kennedy. And so the day before he was inaugurated, Bill Clinton had no speech. A "committee" of authors, ranging from campaign aides like George Stephanopoulos to old personal friends like Tommy Caplan and Taylor Branch, came forward with various suggestions. But there was no single author, no "voice," no rhythm that bespoke a moving, coherent message. The draft speech was terrible. "Today," it declared, in a vain effort to sound Kennedyesque, "a generation raised in the shadow of the Cold War assumes new responsibilities in a world warmed by the sunshine of freedom but threatened still by ancient hatreds and new plagues . . . We have to march to the music of time, but ours is a timeless mission." If a speech could drown in metaphors, this one would long since have been declared dead.

The speech was still a bunch of unconnected phrases when Bill and Hillary returned from eleven inaugural balls at two in the morning and Clinton sat down with all his "best friends" to slave for the next three hours to come up with a presentable draft. It was all disturbingly

like what had occurred in the preceding weeks after the election—
uncontrolled, undisciplined, unfocused, largely incoherent.

Inauguration Day turned into a mirror of all the good and bad that
had preceded it. First, a rousing church service at a black church, just
five hours after the president-elect had finally gone to bed. Then, in total
violation of protocol, the Clintons arrived at the White House thirty
minutes late, with unannounced guests, to meet Barbara and George
Bush. In a minor miracle, the inaugural address itself was a relatively
successful amalgam of all the last-minute suggestions that had been
made. (Its most memorable phrase was the statement that by their election of Bill Clinton, the American people had "forced the spring.")
Then another round of celebratory events, culminating in another cycle
of inaugural balls lasting until well past midnight. Perhaps appropriately, the most startling event of all occurred the next morning. At
5:30 a.m., the White House staff awakened the Clintons for breakfast,
just three hours after they had gone to bed. Every day George and Barbara Bush had had breakfast at that time, and surely, the White House
staff believed, the new president would wish to get up that early in order to begin a rigorous, disciplined day. The 5:30 a.m. breakfast call
represented a fitting end to a transition process that could only be described as chaotic.[43]

Inauguration Day came almost exactly one year after the Gennifer Flowers story had broken. The intervening period highlighted themes that
dominated the Clintons' relationship: Bill's propensity to dissemble,
and occasionally to lie outright; Hillary's instinctive privacy and wish to
preserve her image as a "good" Methodist; and the evolving chemistry
between the two of them that determined the success or failure of their
personal and political partnership.

The presidential campaign, like much that was to follow, reflected
the roller-coaster life that Bill and Hillary led together. Having survived
a near divorce, they had come to a new understanding. They would work
as partners, acknowledging the fact that each person's strengths and
weaknesses needed to be complemented by the other's. Bill had the energy to burst all boundaries; Hillary had the organizational focus to keep
him grounded. He was reluctant to attack; she was ready, preemptively,

to destroy their enemies. While he fiddled, she cut to the core of an issue and resolved it. At times she could be arrogant and presumptuous. At those times, he needed to introduce an appreciation for ambiguity, a willingness to live and let live.

During the first months of their presidential bid, the team had functioned like clockwork. Hillary knew they had to anticipate attacks about Bill's sexual appetites, and together the two plotted their responses. The combination of her planning skills and his capacity to connect to voters looking for new hope made the initial months of the campaign seem like a cakewalk.

But then came the implosions, predictable and self-induced, but sufficiently dangerous that they threatened to blow the campaign out of the water. Bill's sexual behavior slapped him in the face. Once again, Hillary rose to save him—with her defense team, headed by Betsey Wright, and with her heartfelt affirmation of the love she felt. In her brilliant performance with Bill on *60 Minutes,* she repeated, almost word for word, the script they had agreed upon for the Sperling breakfast, turning a devastating threat into a moment of confident reaffirmation in the strength of their marriage.

What Hillary could not control was Bill's instinct to cover up his own weaknesses. In a remarkable display of his egomania, Clinton seemed to believe he could lie about his past. With total justification, the press asked, "Who does this guy think he is? And if he has lied about this, what more has he been trying to hide?" Stung by his deceptiveness, the press corps now responded with skepticism to any claims he made.

Hillary replicated this penchant for denial. Embarrassed by how many times she had made phone calls on behalf of Rose law firm clients to state officials working under her husband's authority, she refused to make any of her records public. She, too, made the fatal political error of stonewalling the press when they asked to see her files on Whitewater or the billing records of her law firm. In the process, she alienated the press in the same way that her husband had, fueling their disbelief in the couple's integrity.

At the time, the Clintons worked to overcome these negatives. After Bill's comeback in New Hampshire, they rebuilt their momentum. Then, during the crucial transition phase, things started to fall apart. In large part, they did so because of tensions over Hillary's role. What had worked so effectively during the campaign now turned sour. Notwithstanding the talk about a copresidency, they now had to turn words into reality. What did a copresidency mean in practice? How would they deal with a third player, Al Gore, who had every reason to believe that he should be the person closest to the president? Here, the power that Hillary accumulated in light of the Gennifer Flowers scandal helped create an imbalance. Hillary was not about to let anyone else tell her what to do, and with no one in a position to question her authority, her mistakes went unchallenged.

As the Clintons took office, checks and balances had gone away, and no chief of staff was in place to call the house to order. Only time would tell if this brilliant duo could find a way of restoring balance to their partnership.

EIGHT

The First Year

If the first month was any indicator, it was going to be a long, hard slog. With almost lightning speed, everything that could go wrong did, from gay rights to staff disarray, from press fury to failed cabinet appointments. Yet no one seemed in charge, and the idea of an orderly rollout of government goals seemed a romantic throwback to a previous century. Although by late summer and early fall the tide finally turned, the implications of these first-year mistakes would not soon go away. Just as in the transition phase, what was most disturbing was the degree to which the underlying source of the difficulties resided in the personal styles of Bill and Hillary, the dynamic between them, and their inability to find, then restore, the balance that had existed in the early days of the campaign. As one observer noted, most members of the "Clinton team felt as if they were starting their presidency amid a howling gale." The problem was that the gale was of the Clintons' own making.

Although the president-elect for months had told everyone within earshot that he would focus on the economy "like a laser beam" from day one of his presidency—indeed, that he would have an economic plan to offer the American people on day two—the only news headlines on January 22 were about Clinton's commitment to move immediately to allow gays in the military, the troubled nomination of Zoe Baird to become attorney general of the United States, and the astonishing news that the White House press corps had been banned from the White House. No mention of health care, the deficit, the environment, or welfare reform—all the principal issues discussed in the campaign. In his

first press briefing, a brash, slightly overwhelmed George Stephanopoulos found himself bouncing from wall to wall in response to questions.
Yes, the president would sign an executive order on gays in the military
within a week. No, the president still supported the Zoe Baird candidacy despite the uproar in Congress and in newspapers about her hiring
illegal immigrants as household aides and not paying Social Security
taxes for them. The ultimate kicker came from Helen Thomas, dean of
the Washington press corps. "I've been here since [John F.] Kennedy,"
she said, "and the press secretary's office [in the West Wing] has never
been off limits." Why now?[1]

Amazingly, the Joint Chiefs of Staff first learned that Clinton
planned to issue an executive order to permit gays in the military from
newspaper reports prior to their initial meeting with the new secretary
of defense, Les Aspin, on January 21, the day after the inauguration.
They exploded at Aspin and demanded an immediate meeting with
Clinton. But it was not only the military who had not been consulted.
Sam Nunn, chair of the Senate Armed Services Committee, had not
been briefed either. "If there's a strategy there, it hasn't been explained
to me," he commented. How was it possible for a presidential administration to take on such a volatile issue with no strategy for alerting, massaging, and winning over those most involved with implementing it?

Ordinarily, a chief of staff would have been all over the question,
ensuring that every official with a possible interest in the subject had
been talked to. The fact that no one had been approached suggested
the depth of Clinton's problem: There was no discipline, focus, or order
in the entire presidential operation. The gays-in-the-military issue also
provoked a rapid-fire response. Congress was prepared to pass a resolution endorsing existing policy. Nunn took reporters on a tour of a sub-
marine to highlight the close quarters within which soldiers had to
live—thereby raising the specter of unwanted sexual advances. And
Senator Robert Byrd used his rhetorical eloquence to warn that moral
decay could destroy America, just as it had the Roman Empire. Same-
sex marriage and homosexuals in the Boy Scouts might soon follow
acceptance of gays, Byrd suggested.

When the Joint Chiefs met with Clinton on January 25, they ver-
bally acknowledged his authority as commander in chief, and then
took control of the room. The Marine Corps commandant insisted that

homosexuality was a moral depravity, and his colleagues agreed. Colin Powell, chairman of the Joint Chiefs, proposed a political compromise, suggesting that the issue be studied and that instead of outright acceptance of gays, the president consider a policy of simply not inquiring of soldiers whether they were gay. If they wished to keep their sexual orientation to themselves, that would be fine. It was the precursor of the ultimate policy of "Don't Ask, Don't Tell." Democratic members of the U.S. Senate preferred such a stance to outright endorsement of Clinton's original position. The Senate Republican leader, Robert Dole, meanwhile, let Clinton know that under no circumstances should he expect any support from the opposition; indeed, he would prefer that Clinton stick by his guns so that Dole and the Republicans could further embarrass him. As Rahm Emanuel, the sharp young Clinton staff member from Illinois, observed, "if you're trying to [set] a rhythm and a tempo, [this gay issue] totally threw it off."[2]

But it was hardly the only problem. By the end of his first day in office, Bill Clinton was confronted with the unpleasant news that his nominee for attorney general could not be confirmed regardless of his support. Zoe Baird was Hillary's candidate. And that of Warren Christopher—the head of Clinton's transition team as well as his incoming secretary of state. But even the most loyal Democrats in the Senate had qualms about her. Once again, no one on the Clinton team had blown a warning whistle. From the beginning, Baird had told the people vetting her that she had not paid the taxes for her Peruvian household help. Warning bells should have gone off. Instead, Hillary assumed that they had the power to push Baird through, and it took a call from Joe Biden of the Senate Judiciary Committee to convince the Clintons that Baird's nomination was dead in the water. Finally Hillary agreed, and the next day, Baird withdrew her name from consideration, but appropriately, and angrily, she pointed out that she had never lied or tried to cover up her actions. Another embarrassing example of sloppy staff work.[3]

Both stories, about gays in the military and the withdrawal of Zoe Baird's name for appointment as attorney general, hit a press corps still reeling from the door that was shut in their face, literally, when the White House suddenly decided to bar reporters from entering the press secretary's office in the White House. Initially there was no explanation for the new policy. In fact, it was Hillary Clinton's idea, developed in concert with her close staff aide Susan Thomases. Both had nothing but contempt for the press, with its insistence on prying into the First Lady's affairs. Hillary also wanted to use the space freed up by the change to rebuild a swimming pool for the family to use. It would be difficult to conceive a more impolitic thing to do as a new administration took office. Every president wants friends in the press corps. To alienate reporters, who had been able for decades to use access to the press secretary's office as an excuse to conduct sidebar interviews with presidential aides, amounted almost to political hara-kiri.

Perhaps the strangest—but most prophetic—event of the Clintons' first month in the White House was a retreat they sponsored at Camp David so that the White House staff and cabinet could "get to know each other better." Initially proposed by Al Gore, the retreat sought to permit staff members to develop mutual confidence and trust. In one exercise, participants were asked to share with one another something personal about themselves. Bill Clinton started by telling about how humiliated he felt as a child to be called "fat bubba." Faced with what they considered New Age nonsense, older politicians like Treasury Secretary Lloyd Bentsen simply went to their rooms. But the real news of the weekend was how Hillary took over the event and made it the occasion for letting everyone know that she was in charge.

She commandeered the meeting with a noontime speech during which she sought to inspire the White House team to join her (and Bill) in implementing her vision of where the Clinton administration should go. Focusing initially on the fact that the Clintons had tried to do too much in the first term in Arkansas, she emphasized the importance of establishing priorities. Assessing their first week, she noted the danger of getting distracted by side issues and the critical importance of focusing on the "long journey" they had embarked upon together. At the heart of her tough lecture was her insistence on staying with the story of the administration's mission, defining reality in terms of enemies and villains, and rallying people to join the crusade on their side. If they marched together, they would succeed. According to this version of reality, the world was binary; they were on the good side and the Republicans embodied evil. Only when they marched together to this drummer would they succeed. Although Warren Christopher and others questioned her vision, Hillary dismissed the critique, daring people to rise to her challenge. As Carl Bernstein observed, "After less than two weeks in the White House, Hillary had assumed her command as America's first warrior First Lady."[4]

A few days earlier, Bill Clinton had announced that Hillary would chair the administration's task force on health care. Using almost exactly the same language he had used when he placed her in charge of education reform in Arkansas, Clinton declared that it was a sign of his commitment to health care that he had placed responsibility for drafting the plan in the hands of the one person in the world closest to him. Although Vice President Gore had suggested he might be willing to take on the health care assignment, Hillary objected, fearing that Gore would take command of the entire domestic agenda. Having already won the battle to have an office in the West Wing, Hillary's status as one of the troika running the White House was confirmed.

Significantly, Clinton had consulted none of his leading cabinet officers—including Donna Shalala, secretary of health, education, and welfare—about Hillary's appointment. Nor was there any discussion among his economic and domestic policy aides, or congressional leaders, as to whether this was the time to place health care at the forefront of the administration's domestic reform agenda. A working group on welfare reform had already been established. In fact, many believed that welfare reform should come first—a program that could surely win Republican support, thus setting the stage for health care reform. But Hillary wanted health care to go first, and the Clintons together determined that with Hillary in charge, it would be easier to craft a plan that would be responsive to the shifting pressures of politics and the volatile economic environment.[5]

In fact, Clinton's economic team was deeply concerned that the focus on health care might actually undermine their long-range commitment to reducing the deficit and trimming the government bureaucracy. Convinced that their major objective was to persuade Wall Street to give the signal to start investing again, many of Clinton's most powerful economic advisers—including Lloyd Bentsen, Robert Rubin, and Leon Panetta—worried that the focus on creating a huge new federal bureaucracy to resolve health care issues would shatter their credibility. Of course, the economic team—like most parts of the new administration—was sharply divided on how best to proceed. In light of the Bush administration's acknowledgment in December of a deficit 50 percent higher than had been forecast, the economic conservatives on the Clinton team insisted that a credible deficit reduction scheme was the only initiative that stood a chance of securing Wall Street support. On the other hand, Secretary of Labor Robert Reich—and many of Clinton's top personal aides, including George Stephanopoulos, James Carville, and Paul Begala—viewed the Bentsen-Rubin stance as a repudiation of what the campaign had been all about. This was a battle in which Clinton's head was in one place, his heart in another.

Ever since the new realities of the budget hit home, the Bentsen and Reich forces had done battle. The Reich team insisted that more public investment was needed—on jobs, health care, education, and job training. An economic stimulus package, they insisted, was a necessary accompaniment to any deficit reduction legislation. Bentsen, Rubin, and Panetta, on the other hand, believed that if Clinton did not come forward with a compelling plan to cut spending and curtail the federal bureaucracy, the investment community would turn its back on the new administration. In response, Clinton invited all perspectives to the table. "The way Clinton arrived at decisions," the journalist Joe Klein noted, "was . . . he opened the door to *every* approach." One way to see such a modus operandi was as an invitation to totally open debate. Another was to see it as indecisiveness. Even his old friend (and chief of staff) Mack McLarty wondered "how a man with such genius organizing his own thoughts . . . could be so disorganized in managing himself."[6]

In the end, Clinton tried to follow both his heart and his head. As Rubin recalled the meeting where Clinton finally declared his position, the president said: "Look, there are a lot of things that I think we need to do, but the threshold issue is the deficit. Until we deal with that, nothing else is going to work . . . So let's take that as our threshold issue and then, within that context, let's do as much else as we can." A classic Clinton compromise: They would go for a stimulus package, a middle-class tax cut, *and* a deficit reduction package, but the last would be the top priority. What, then, about health care? As Donna Shalala recalled, all the key economic actors believed there were fundamental contradictions between priorities. But then, that was the way the Clinton administration worked, or did not work, in its early days, with little clarity, many contradictions, and above all, a sense of veering this way, then that, in search of a road to follow.[7]

The confusion that bedeviled the administration had many causes, but ultimately, it reflected one fact: The president lacked a clear sense of direction and the discipline to follow it. Central to his style with staff and advisers was to let everyone believe he was on their side. But this approach only fostered factional infighting, which in turn caused key constituencies—Congress, his own advisers, the press—to feel unsure about *anything* he supposedly had committed to. As Leon Panetta later noted, people on all sides, but especially in Congress, "were always nervous; they never quite knew that he would stand by his position." Because he always wanted to please people, no one felt quite sure about where he stood in his own mind. This was particularly true when, after a decision had presumably been made, Clinton would talk to Hillary or Gore and then reverse himself. Lawrence Summers, an economic adviser, observed that "there are three presidents—and two of them know what they want to do! The three being Bill, Al, and Hillary. Al had his agenda. Hillary had her agenda. And Bill had *every* agenda." Joe Klein summed it up this way: Clinton's leadership style was "a consequence of two character traits that his aides found distressing: his inability to deliver bad news [and thus displease somebody], and his inability to make up his mind."[8]

As if to compound the problem, Clinton displayed a temper with his aides that was profoundly unsettling, at least until they recognized that it was a normal part of the president's daily routine. It started off with his "morning roar," as George Stephanopoulos remembered it. Others called it his SMO (Standard Morning Outburst). Clinton's volatility, a veteran Washington observer noted, "was the worst [I had seen] by a magnitude of at least two." If the "morning roar was a way of clearing his throat before breakfast," Stephanopoulos later wrote, it could quickly give way to a "slow boil," an explosion of resentment that had been building up all day, or even for weeks. The day ended with a Clinton "nightcap," a final expression of anger at some conversation that had happened during the day. However exaggerated, Clinton's volatility suggests a White House atmosphere that only reinforced the sense that no one was in control, that the president lacked toughness and resolve, and that, for good reason, no one could ever be sure of what had been decided or what was coming next.[9]

To be sure, there were moments of victory. In early February, Congress passed, and the president signed, the Family Medical Leave Act, permitting employees to take up to three weeks of unpaid leave to deal with family emergencies. As soon as he took office, Clinton also overturned twelve years of Reagan and Bush executive orders prohibiting United States financial support for family planning programs, run by either international organizations or the United States government, that involved disseminating information on either birth control or the termination of pregnancies. The president also sanctioned fetal tissue research on Alzheimer's and Parkinson's disease and on diabetes and leukemia. But ultimately these were exceptions to the larger view that things were badly awry in the nation's capital, and particularly in the inner workings of the new administration.

Ongoing problems at the Justice Department highlighted the abiding sense of disarray. After the Zoe Baird disaster, Hillary's team sought another woman candidate, and they zeroed in on Kimba Wood, a federal district court judge—again, not a household name, but someone with high recommendations. Although she had not been offered the job by the president, a White House staffer leaked her name to the press, setting off another flurry of investigative phone calls. To the humiliation of the White House, it turned out that Wood, too, had a "nanny tax" problem. Her name, too, was "withdrawn," although she had never in fact been nominated. White House leaks (notwithstanding the shutting of the press office door) reflected once more the lack of discipline of the White House staff. With no punishment-exacting chief of staff to snap the whip, people felt free to cultivate their own relationships with the press and thereby to advance the interest of their particular faction within the free-for-all that constituted the White House decision-making process.[10]

The next and final nominee brought forward for attorney general ironically came to Hillary at the suggestion of her brother Hughie, who had dealt with Janet Reno as a prosecutor in Florida. No one seemed to

know very much about her, but as a single career woman, she had
no nanny problem. Hillary's closest friend, Diane Blair, had only good
things to say about Reno, and Florida's senator Bob Graham called her
a "model prosecutor of intelligence, integrity, and drive." Without further investigation, Clinton decided to nominate her. Though he confessed to his close friend Taylor Branch that Reno's aloofness and
independence troubled him, especially vis-à-vis the political side of her
job, there was no chief of staff to ask further probing questions. As a
result, Clinton quickly sent her name forward for one of the four top
cabinet posts, the one historically most involved with sensitive political
questions.[11]

A few weeks after taking office, Reno—with Bill Clinton's support—
ordered an armed raid on a religious sect called the Branch Davidians,
which had sought refuge in a huge house in Waco, Texas, after killing
four federal agents investigating the group on February 28. For more
than a month, the FBI had conducted a siege of the Branch Davidians,
trying by psychological manipulation to persuade them to surrender.
But David Koresh, the sect's leader, refused. Instead, he adopted a
tougher and tougher line. Reno then came to Clinton with the request
that he approve a military-style raid on the house, with tear gas grenades. Initially skeptical, Clinton nevertheless went along. The raid was
a disaster. Either the grenades, or Koresh himself, ignited a fire inside
the house. Eighty people were killed, mostly women and children. Clinton's instinct was to go on television immediately and acknowledge responsibility for the tragedy, but he was dissuaded from doing so by
Stephanopoulos, who wished to wait until more information was obtained. Instead, Reno went on the air to take the blame, immediately
winning praise. Clinton was furious with himself, first because he had
not followed through on questioning the wisdom of the raid, and second because he had allowed Stephanopoulos to dissuade him from assuming public responsibility for the raid's consequences. In both cases,
he later noted, "I had accepted advice that ran counter to my instincts."
In Clinton's mind there was a direct link between his errors in Waco
and the fact that two days later, Congress turned down his economic
stimulus package through a successful Republican filibuster.[12]

But embarrassments at Justice were not yet over. At Hillary's suggestion, he had nominated Lani Guinier as deputy attorney general in

charge of civil rights. An African American scholar who had been a classmate of Bill and Hillary's at Yale Law School, Guinier was bright, gifted, and controversial. She had written a series of law review articles, some of which proposed guaranteeing minority political rights by using proportional representation—as opposed to one person, one vote—as the basis for electing people to governmental bodies. Guinier's suggestion had been prompted by the use of citywide elections to dilute the power of neighborhood or precinct elections in which minorities held a plurality. But by definition, her arguments were provocative. Edward Kennedy had warned Hillary about the nomination, though neither the Department of Justice nor the White House carefully vetted Guinier or checked with Congress on her viability. Guinier's initial interviews went poorly, and soon Kennedy was joined by Carol Moseley Braun, the black senator from Illinois, and by Senators David Pryor and George Mitchell in urging that her name be withdrawn. "You don't have the capital in your bank account to do this," Pryor told his old friend. Finally, Clinton read Guinier's articles, and he concluded that despite his and Hillary's personal affection for her, he must ask her to give up the fight. In a seventy-five-minute meeting with Guinier, in which she angrily resisted his message, Clinton told her that he did not subscribe to her arguments. Once more, the absence of a commanding chief of staff and a disciplined vetting process had made the president look weak.[13]

Even the opportunity to name a stellar nominee to the Supreme Court became more an embarrassment than a boon, with the focus as much on the equivocation of Clinton's decision-making process as on his final choice. When Byron White, appointed by John F. Kennedy in 1962, announced he would step down, Clinton immediately thought of Mario Cuomo as a logical successor. A brilliant orator, statesman, and philosopher, Cuomo had provided the intellectual cutting edge for the party since his famous keynote address at the 1984 convention. Repeatedly rumored to be a presidential candidate, he had always backed out at the last minute, seemingly unwilling to go the final step. Whether out of fear of family revelations, a prying press, or a personal passion for privacy, Cuomo had always come to the starting line, then abandoned the race. But he was a logical choice for the Supreme Court.

Cuomo's equivocation mirrored Clinton's. Initially, he refused to return Clinton's phone calls. Then he said he probably would be interested in being chosen, only to change his mind a few days later. As days, then weeks, passed, Clinton considered other possibilities, but that process, too, took time. Finally, Cuomo's son Andrew, working as secretary of housing in Washington, alerted Clinton that his father was ready to reconsider. An hour before the phone call in which he was to accept Clinton's invitation, however, Cuomo, infuriatingly, once more pulled out. Now, more than two months into the selection process, Clinton finally turned to Ruth Bader Ginsburg, a Jewish woman with a remarkable personal story and a superb legacy of legal accomplishments. But when a proud president introduced her to the press, the first question focused not on Ginsburg but rather on the interminable process through which her nomination had been determined. "I wonder, sir," ABC News's Brit Hume asked, "[about] a certain zigzag quality in the decision-making process here. I wonder, sir, if you could . . . perhaps disabuse us of any notion we might have along these lines." Clinton was enraged, but as George Stephanopoulos noted, "Brit just didn't know how right he was." The dominant story of the administration, highlighted by the length of time it took to come up with a Supreme Court nominee, was that the Clinton administration did not seem to know what it was doing, or how to make timely decisions.[14]

Ever since he had lied to the press about his draft history, a state of simmering war had existed between the Clintons and the media. All too often, he used language with enough ambiguity to permit multiple interpretations. In part it was a question of integrity and credibility. But just as much, the distrust involved the Clintons' relationship with the entire Washington establishment. From the beginning, Bill and Hillary felt alienated from the Washington elite, which in large part revolved around *The Washington Post*.

It all started on inauguration eve. At the gala that evening, the Clintons' first overnight guests at the White House, Linda and Harry Bloodworth-Thomason, showed a video that featured leading journalists making fools of themselves by declaring that Clinton did not stand a chance in the election. It was almost contemptuous, but clearly meant to convey a message. As Harold Ickes, one of those closest to Hillary, later noted, "[the Clintons] really saw themselves as the White Knight and the White Queen coming in to do good." In their view, the press were scandal seekers, going after "character" issues such as Bill's sex habits, or the draft, or whether he had inhaled when he smoked marijuana. "Instead of reaching a hand out to the press," Ickes noted, "[the] olive branch was never extended [and] the press . . . continued to carp."

The hostility was particularly visible in Hillary. "Since she came to the White House," the reporter Helen Thomas noted, "she's had the biggest chip on her shoulder. It's more than just 'blame the messenger.' We never had a chance." Others shared the same impression. "She is the first [First Lady] I have covered," Ann Compton of ABC News said, "who has totally ignored and avoided the White House press corps." But she was not alone. In a sharply barbed joke, Bill Clinton told a White House correspondents' dinner, "You know why I can stiff you on press conferences? Because Larry King liberated me by giving me to the American people directly." No wonder that an adversarial tone became pervasive. Reporters came to view Clinton as someone always trying to "get away" with something. "This president salts his remarks with so many inventions, half-truths, and self-serving exaggerations," Carl Cannon of the Baltimore *Sun* wrote, "that reporters who cover him often have to choose between truth-squadding every speech or ignoring his fibs."[15]

Yet it was not just the press corps that the Clintons were "stiffing." The reporters did not simply represent a small occupational category in a huge metropolis. They embodied the ethos of a larger, more powerful community, the social elite who dined on politics at their evening soirees, who shaped the discourse of the rich and influential, and who determined, in large part, who was up and who was down in the opinion of those who orchestrated Congress and molded the editorial pages of the nation's largest newspapers. To shun the press, therefore, was a signal of disrespect in a community where invitations to dinner, gossip traded over drinks, and simple acknowledgment that someone was important became the currency of triumph or defeat.[16]

The powers that be reached out to the new occupants of the White House to test the waters. Vernon Jordan, one of the Clintons' oldest friends, hosted dinners with Pamela Harriman, wife of Averell and former ambassador to France. Others issued invitations as well. But the key to the city was held by Katharine Graham, publisher of *The Washington*

Post. She hosted a dinner party for the Clintons in December, inviting all the most famous columnists and political figures. Bill made a favorable impression, using his toast to invoke a plea for a higher sense of community and identity in the nation. "I hope to bring more of the country to the capital," he intoned, "and more of the capital to the country."

But Hillary made a less positive impression. Sally Quinn, gossip columnist for the *Post*—hence one of its most powerful figures—noted that while Hillary wowed the guests with her knowledge of the budget, she repeatedly used the pronoun "we" to suggest that she and Bill were coequals. "But Little Rock is not Washington," Quinn commented. "'We' is the kiss of death in Washington." Quinn advised Hillary to "get something outside government in her own field of child welfare, health and education." She should not "attend her husband's meetings" or play too active a role in trying to shape policy. Rosalynn Carter and Nancy Reagan, she noted, had suffered for doing that. Professional women, Quinn concluded, "are watching with a mixture of pride and apprehension to see how she is going to handle the position . . . Many of these women are worried that she has already made a few missteps that could get her off to a troubled start."[17]

Anyone who knew Hillary Clinton understood immediately that Quinn's words were like rubbing salt into an open wound. Understandably, Hillary got her back up. How dare Quinn presume such authority? And why should Hillary reciprocate with social invitations to people who were so small-minded and narrow? At one level, it was like a small-town spitting war, with each side characterizing the other as mean-spirited, venal, contemptible. The words one group used to characterize the other would be reciprocated, almost without the change of a syllable. Each felt a sense of entitlement, each looked at the other with suspicion and derision.

"You know," Hillary told Taylor Branch, "[Sally Quinn] has been hostile since the moment we got here. Why should we invite somebody like that into our home? How could she expect us to?" When her social secretary, Anne Stock, urged her to mollify the Washington "establishment" by asking local charitable donors to White House social events as a step toward bridging the gap, Hillary declined. Nor would Hillary let her name be used by Washington's elite philanthropists to raise money for their charitable causes. Instead, the Clintons turned the social scene at the White House into an arena for political teas and receptions. After a state dinner for the nation's governors in February, no official White House banquets were held for ten months. As a result, Carl Bernstein has written, "the so-called Georgetown set, leading members of Congress from both parties, the city's permanent political leaders . . . and high-level officials lured by the Clintons to Washington . . . were ignored, often studiously." So dogmatic and righteous was Hillary that when she learned that Rahm Emanuel had invited James Baker, the former secretary of state, to the White House for a bipartisan gathering in support of free trade, she rebuked him angrily. "What are you doing inviting these people into my house?" she asked. "These people are our enemies. They are trying to destroy us."[18]

Quinn had warned of the consequences. Back in November, she advised that the Clintons imagine themselves on a plane that crash-landed in a foreign land. "You found yourself surrounded by a curious and possibly hostile tribe. Instead of giving them beads and eating the monkey tongues they offer you, you decide that you don't need their help. Fine, but don't be surprised if you end up with poison darts in your backside. Like any other culture, Washington has its own totems and taboos. It would serve the newcomers well to learn and abide by them." Truer words were never uttered.[19]

If anything could contribute further to the Clintons' sense of alienation from their new home, it was the attitude of the White House ushers, cooks, and servants, and that of the Secret Service. It all began with the 5:30 breakfast the day after the inauguration, and it continued over the following days. From the two Secret Service teams that needed to be on duty in the morning in case the president decided to go out jogging, to Clinton's penchant for playing cards and talking with aides until the wee hours, it all meant longer tours of duty. Not only was the First Couple's lifestyle a problem; so, too, was that of their young staff, who dressed like teenagers, ordered in pizzas all day long, and left the trash cans stuffed with discarded boxes of take-out food. Worst of all, word of the staff's discontent leaked. On February 19, the *Chicago Tribune* even ran a story—evidently based on information from a White House domestic worker—that the Clintons had engaged in a terrible fight, with Hillary throwing a lamp at the president. The Clintons felt under siege. Soon enough, changes were made. The number of Secret

Service agents assigned to the family quarters was cut, while household staff became more accustomed to the new First Family's distinctive lifestyle. Most also seemed thrilled to have Chelsea in the White House, and appreciative of the fact that Hillary made her daughter and friends pick up all the popcorn they had dropped on the floor while they watched a movie. Still, the experience of living in a house that seemed to be occupied by an alien work force only exacerbated the sense of us versus them.[20]

Overreaction on all sides was the result. The press actively looked for evidence of deception; the Clintons in turn saw conspiracies every-where. The natural response was to hunker down and view with suspicion any effort to penetrate the White House walls with Washington "spies." The result, Carl Bernstein has pointed out, was that each side leaped to premature judgments about the other. From the point of view of Washingtonians, the Clintons seemed like an invading army, "sweeping into town like a band of hillbillies with no respect for tradition or what passed in Washington for good breeding or pedigree." From the point of view of the Clintons, on the other hand, the "principal power players in media and politics [who] wined and dined together" stood in the way of "thoughtful policy and new ideas." It all became part of a mutually reinforcing downward spiral that each day widened the gap between the administration and those who reported on its activities.[21]

One consequence was an insistence, by Hillary especially, that the inner staff be dominated by their own people, not Washingtonians. Although George Stephanopoulos, Dee Dee Myers, and Rahm Emanuel came from different parts of the country and represented diverse perspectives, the White House political staff was made up overwhelmingly of Arkansans. Indeed, there was an active prejudice in the beginning against bringing Washington "insiders" onto the Clinton team. Bruce Lindsey, one of Clinton's oldest and most intimate friends, wielded enormous influence. Carol Rasco ran the domestic policy council. Nancy Hernreich oversaw the Oval Office. And Vince Foster and Webb Hubbell, Hillary's closest friends and law partners, played critical roles. All were from Arkansas.[22]

Nowhere was the pernicious chemistry between the Clintons and the culture of Washington more visible than in "Travelgate." In mid-March, the White House decided to fire all seven staff members of the travel office. These were people who for years had handled flight arrangements, ground transportation, and hotels for the White House press corps when the president traveled. Publicly, the rationale for the firings was that the office was mismanaged. In fact, Hillary was the primary actor in the firings, and the real rationale was to put "our people" in charge. Then, in order to cover up the role of the First Lady, extraordinary measures were taken. Deputy White House Counsel Vince Foster sought to erase from the record any evidence of Hillary's involvement. A minor event at its inception, Travelgate eventually became a huge scandal with tragic consequences—a symbol of all that could go wrong in a White House consumed by its own interior dynamic of petty politics and "gotcha" rivalries.

The episode began when Harry Thomason—a close friend of Hillary's and, with his wife, Linda, a frequent overnight guest at the White House—suggested to Hillary that there were serious problems with the travel office involving "gross financial mismanagement." Moreover, Thomason had a replacement travel team to recommend, headed by a distant cousin of Bill Clinton. Hillary responded with alacrity, seeing this as an ideal opportunity to fire inefficient employees, get rid of some of the "old guard," and in the process get some positive press coverage for addressing the alleged mismanagement. Hillary asked Mack McLarty if he was aware of the situation, and when her initial intervention failed to bring immediate action, she went to Vince Foster to demand follow-through.

Clearly, Hillary had issued a forceful mandate, and in the Clinton White House it was a fool who failed to respond. After an audit showed irregularities, especially on cash disbursements, Hillary commented: "We need these people out—we need *our people* in. We need the slots." So clear was her intent that Bill Kennedy, another Rose law firm associate who was working for Vince Foster, called the FBI into the investigation, pointing out that people "at the highest level" of the White House were concerned. (In doing so, Kennedy violated a long-established rule that the White House go through the Justice Department on any issue involving use of the FBI.) Though Foster believed that Hillary was moving too fast, he kept quiet, having already felt her anger after he had urged her to be cautious about getting rid of some old-time Secret Service agents from the White House staff. Now McLarty and Foster acted quickly. Seven members of the travel office were fired peremptorily. They were given no hearing, no opportunity to defend themselves. The whole episode was over, in Washington, D.C., terms, in a millisecond.

Until Andrea Mitchell of NBC News asked, "George, what are you guys doing firing the travel office?" These were the staff who for years had helped the press navigate foreign travel, clear their visa applications, get through customs, bring home gifts, and otherwise make life simpler and easier for the working press. Why would reporters give a positive spin to a story seemingly aimed at hurting their colleagues? An audit? Mismanagement? None of it made sense, and to a press corps already suspicious of the Clintons—and quick to catch on to the fact that the replacement team was rumored to be headed by a Clinton cousin—it smelled funny. Overnight, in George Stephanopoulos's words, the story became not about the travel office's "accounting practices, [but] about our management style." As the presidential chronicler John Harris noted, "the travel office saga was a capsule of all that was maddening about Washington in the Clinton years."[23]

Hillary Clinton was at the center of virtually all the controversies that beset the Clinton administration during these first six months. From Zoe Baird to the Camp David retreat, from denying reporters access to the White House to the Lani Guinier nomination, from relations with the Washington power elite to Travelgate, Hillary played the pivotal role. In doing so, she not only confirmed her powerful position as copresident with her husband, but suggested to at least some that she had become the dominant figure in the relationship, highlighting by her example of decisive, if sometimes ill-informed, leadership the more ambiguous and equivocating style of her husband.

It all began with the issue of her office. Historically, First Ladies had their headquarters in the East Wing, where the family resided. Hillary was determined that hers would be in the West Wing, where the men were, where power resided. Some worried that such a move would spark controversy, feeding Republican efforts to portray Hillary as a man-eating feminist trying to be president. But despite these objections, Hillary and her closest allies, Maggie Williams and Susan Thomases, insisted that the office issue was critical, if for no other reason than it would signal to America how different this administration would be. Hillary was a feminist. She understood that "our society's going through a tricky passage about men's and women's roles, and appropriate partnerships between husbands and wives, and . . . what is being played out in the homes and workplaces of America is now being played out in the White House." Precisely because her office location would symbolize her status, she insisted that she be alongside the vice president as the person with the closest physical proximity to the president.[24]

For the same reason, Hillary pursued a quiet but persistent battle with Al Gore over their respective "turf" and who would exercise the greater influence in the White House. While the two avoided outright confrontations, they were in a constant tug-of-war over administration priorities. Once it was clear that Hillary would take on health care, the vice-president assumed responsibility for the "reinventing government" portfolio. It would be his task to streamline the bureaucracy, eliminate duplication, and abolish unnecessary programs. In addition to his responsibility for environmental policy (his number one passion), Gore devoted most of his supervisory time to the "reinventing" project, ultimately saving the government $157 billion and cutting the workforce by 350,000 people. But there were numerous stand-offs with Hillary. He wanted the "reinventing" project to have priority over health care. They both went forward simultaneously. Gore, along with many other top White House advisers, urged that welfare reform be taken up before health care, arguing that a major step toward efficiency in government would make health care reform more palatable. But he quickly ended up on the losing side. Under no circumstances would Hillary cede dominance to the vice president on her pet project.[25]

In the eyes of at least some, Hillary's pursuit of power reflected her misreading of the election results. Although Bill Clinton had received only 43 percent of the total vote, Hillary saw the results as a mandate to proceed with ambitious plans to transform the nation. She "overstated" the win, one unsympathetic White House source declared, and was intent on showing "the press who's in charge . . . This is our chance to do it all the way. And we've got to seize it." She and Bill believed that the election had been "a cleansing event" in the nation's life that gave them—and her—the authority to do what no presidential couple had ever attempted before. As a result, Hillary assumed an air of entitlement,

reflected in her refusal to talk to the press (except on conditions prear-
ranged to be to her liking), in her attitude toward her physical space,
and in the role she assumed in making appointments.[26]

Health care, of course, most reflected this sense of power and entitlement. From the beginning, leading officials in the administration
looked askance at Hillary's plans to convene a large task force, hold secret hearings, and bring forth a blunderbuss bill that would take on
the entire health care system. Donna Shalala, the secretary of health,
education, and welfare, saw trouble ahead immediately. "People thought
that . . . the whole system Hillary was setting up was crazy," she said.
Lloyd Bentsen, Robert Rubin, Leon Panetta, and Alice Rivlin, Clinton's
chief economic advisers, concurred. Bentsen "thought the president
was taking a hell of a risk appointing his wife," according to Bob Woodward; and Lawrence Summers, still another economic superstar, perceived her appointment as a "disaster."[27]

But none of that mattered. Hillary was copresident. She had total
confidence in herself and the unwavering support of her husband. The
First Lady believed, devoutly, that she could solve any problem. Aware
of the concerns of his advisers, Bill either chose not to act on them or
felt helpless to do anything about them. One aide later explained: "He
was president in no small measure because she stood by him in the
Gennifer Flowers mess. And he had to pay her back." The pendulum
had swung to her side. "This is what she wanted," the aide concluded,
"and he couldn't figure out how not to give it to her. And so he hoped for
the best, and jumped over the side with her." The most he could promise Shalala and his economic team was that the process of dealing with
health care would be "open and participatory."[28]

In the end, the process was anything but. With steely conviction,
Hillary resisted those who questioned her intentions or her plans for
how to proceed. Correctly, the St. Petersburg Times worried that Hillary's "obvious influence with the President could inhibit candid debate
within the administration on issues for which she is responsible." When
Laura Tyson, chair of the president's Council of Economic Advisers,
found the courage to ask a probing question about Clinton's task force
plans, the First Lady cut her off instantly. All those present quickly got
the message. This would be no "open and participatory" process, no
matter what the president said. As one communications staff member

noted, "[Hillary] was the only person in the White House that people were afraid of." The result was a pervasive air of intimidation. "Her position stifled healthy skepticism about our strategy," George Stephanopoulos wrote, "and Hillary became the object of some quiet resentment." But it was a resentment that could never be candidly expressed or discussed in staff meetings.[29]

Understandably, that dynamic created significant staff tensions among those who had different primary loyalties to Bill, to Hillary, and to Al Gore, but especially the first two. Loyalty among Hillary's own staff members was absolute. They all had close ties to her and to liberal causes. Maggie Williams, her chief of staff, came to the White House after many years with Hillary's favorite nongovernmental agency, the Children's Defense Fund. Her deputy chief of staff was Melanne Verveer, who boasted a distinguished record with Common Cause and People for the American Way. Ira Magaziner, her right hand on the health care task force, had been a classmate of Bill's at Oxford and now served her with total devotion, coordinating the twenty-eight committees the two of them set up. In the White House and cabinet, Hillary recruits were everywhere, including Bernard Nussbaum as counsel to the president, Vince Foster as his deputy, Peter Edelman at Justice (his wife, Marian, headed the Children's Defense Fund), and Donna Shalala. It was a tight group, devoted to their leader, brooking no dissent. The First Lady's staff offices in the West Wing were called "Hillaryland," as if to suggest that their space constituted not only a geographical entity but, more important, a culture and a worldview. She worked her team as hard as she worked herself. They embraced the same "Manichean fantasies" that she did about the world outside the White House gates, and they stood by her 100 percent. As Hillary wrote in her memoir, they had their "own little subculture." Her people never leaked to the news media (whom they detested, as did she) and rarely challenged their boss. "No one on her staff ever betrayed her," James Carville commented. "That's all you need to know about her character."[30]

The other side of having such a tight cohort of supporters, however, was to view the president's (and vice president's) side as lesser people, full of flaws—a perspective that came from the First Lady herself and quickly extended to her lieutenants. Hillary blamed Bill's problems on his staff, not the president himself, accusing his aides of serving him poorly. On one occasion she screamed at Bill for forty minutes about just "how shitty his staff was." To those listening, however, it seemed as though she were demonizing his aides as a way to criticize the president himself. "Her words [may have been] about the staff," one associate said, "but it was clear the president was her target." "Just wait and see how much better the health care campaign [will] be," she boasted.[31]

On the other hand, Hillary's staff spent hours trying to prevent her mistakes from seeing the light of day. A "garrison atmosphere" surrounded the First Lady, Joe Klein noted. Endless efforts were made to obfuscate her pivotal role in ordering the press corps cut off from access to the White House West Wing. With Travelgate, the coverup was even more remarkable. Vince Foster went to extraordinary lengths to erase the First Lady's name from the record. If her associates were to be believed, the First Lady had never uttered a word to anyone about firing the travel office staff.[32]

Hillary's siege mentality against the press corps and the Washington establishment briefly receded when, on March 19, her father, Hugh, suffered a stroke and she went immediately to his bedside in Little Rock. Their relationship had been emotional, complicated, and fraught with tension. She never confronted, in her writings or conversations, her father's tyrannical side. But the complexity of the relationship— especially her mother's willingness to tolerate her husband's excesses as the price for protecting her children—helped shape Hillary's entire approach to life. Thus it was with conflicting emotions that she hastened to his hospital room in Little Rock, where her parents had settled in their retirement. Recently, they had been guests at the White House, where the staff had noted Hugh's harsh demeanor. Now he was dying, and Hillary rushed to be with him.

There is no way of knowing what thoughts went through Hillary's mind as she sat at the bedside of her dying father. Did they include digging for a toothpaste cap in the snow in Park Ridge? Or the pride of a man, however gruff, who had achieved so much? During this time, she seems to have returned to her spiritual tradition, far distant from the political battles raging with Sally Quinn or Katharine Graham, closer to the conversations she recalled with Don Jones or her reading of Paul Tillich. She returned to questions about the meaning of life— and death.

We know this because of a speech she gave in Austin, Texas, the annual Liz Carpenter Lecture, in the midst of the times she was at her father's bedside. "When does life begin?" she asked her audience. Then, in a tone even more personal, "When does it end?" While at the hospital, Hillary had been reading the thoughts of Lee Atwater, the Republican tactical genius who had orchestrated George H. W. Bush's pernicious campaign against Michael Dukakis in 1988, including the infamous demonizing of Dukakis as "soft on crime" with an ad depicting the black prisoner, Willie Horton, who was released on weekend parole when Dukakis was governor and then raped a woman. Atwater had been struck down by a brain tumor, and as he was dying, he turned reflective. "My illness," he wrote, "helped me to see that what was missing in society is what was missing in me. A little heart, a lot of brotherhood." There were more important things than power and wealth, Atwater concluded. "It took a deadly illness to put me eye to eye with that truth."

Hillary, too, had experienced a kind of epiphany, this time at her father's bedside. She, too, talked to her audience about the "spiritual vacuum at the heart of American society—this tumor of the soul." In her concluding remarks—clearly shaped by the extraordinary experience of sitting by her dying father—she declared that "we need a new politics of meaning. We need a new ethos of individual responsibility and caring . . . [We need] a society that fills us up again and makes us feel that we are part of something bigger than ourselves." After months of demonizing the enemy and casting herself in the role of savior for righteous liberals, Hillary Clinton had come to a set of insights much more consistent with the spiritual leadership she had learned with Don Jones than with the warrior role she had taken on as First Lady. Suddenly, she had become what Michael Kelly called, in *The New York Times*, "Saint Hillary."[33]

How to reconcile the two Hillarys, the one thoughtful, sensitive, caring about the ultimate concerns of the human condition, the other derisive, at war with an enemy who deserved no tolerance or respect? It was a lifelong tension. There were, in fact, two Hillarys. One dominated the period from Bill Clinton's election through the first months of his administration. The other brought an entirely different perspective to the public sphere, reacted with forgiveness toward one's enemies, and emphasized a sense of the common ground that brought people together who otherwise might see themselves only as mortal enemies. Unfortunately, in 1993 the Hillary who prevailed turned out not to be the one who gave the Liz Carpenter Lecture.[34]

By late spring, Bill Clinton knew he was in deep trouble. An editorial column in *U.S. News & World Report* captured his own sense of disarray. "Whoooooosshhhhh," it started. "To paraphrase Ross Perot, that sucking sound . . . is the air rushing out of Bill Clinton's balloon as he ends his first 100 days in office . . . [I]n an orgy of harsh assessments, friends and foes alike have been sticking in so many pins that his presidency is losing altitude at an alarming rate." The author was David Gergen, former White House adviser to Richard Nixon, Gerald Ford, Ronald Reagan, and George Herbert Walker Bush. But Gergen's column was not a Republican rant. Although Gergen acknowledged that Clinton had "brought many of these troubles on himself," his words were also full of praise. "Bill Clinton has had the courage to focus the nation on its major needs of better jobs, better education, and better health care . . . If he doesn't have all the right answers, we should stop jeering, get off the sidelines and help him find them. For the next 1,300 days, he is the only president we have."[35]

Ten days later, Clinton contacted Gergen, exploring what it would mean if Gergen were to "stop jeering, get off the sidelines," and help Clinton find the answers. Would Gergen be willing to join the White House staff as counselor to the president? Gergen took the offer seriously—indeed, he might even have been thinking about it when he wrote his column. He said yes. Clinton "made a convincing appeal," Gergen later said. "How I could serve as bridge to the press, to Republicans, and to people I respected in Washington."

Although to many staff members, Gergen's appointment seemed like inviting a Republican fox into the Democratic henhouse, the president had decided that enough was enough. It was time to put a halt to the demonization and polarization that had mushroomed between his White House and the Washington elite and press corps. Gergen could help do that, indeed was ideally suited to do it. The two struck a deal. They would try together to start anew, focusing on two or three major issues and reaching out for dialogue with those who previously had been treated like pariahs.[36]

When he arrived at the White House, Gergen found the staff situation even worse than he had imagined. Mack McLarty startled him with the revelation that for anything to get done, it needed to be signed off on by all three principals—Bill, Hillary, and the vice president. Scapegoating was rampant. In Gergen's view, there was too little loyalty to the overriding objectives of the administration and too much infighting by the respective staffs, especially those from "Hillaryland" who seemed determined to denigrate Bill's people. Gergen asked Hillary why she had not reached out to the Washington power structure, why she hated the press so much. Above all, Gergen hoped to be able to trigger a thoroughgoing reformulation of White House political strategy. "It is time," he said when he accepted his new post, "to move beyond the scorching partisanship that now pervades Capitol Hill, to move beyond the cynicism that now creeps into so much of our reporting, to move beyond old boxes for our thinking."[37]

Initially, the Gergen appointment seemed to presage positive changes. There was greater focus on building support for the big objectives and not getting sidetracked by petty, more controversial issues. Gergen proposed that the administration build coalitions of centrists, starting in the middle and then moving outward. This approach seemed particularly relevant to health care. When he first was briefed about Hillary's task force, he found it "immensely complex [and] requiring far more governmental intrusion . . . than I thought appropriate or politically viable." Negotiation was the way to go, he believed, reaching out to key figures like Senators John Chafee of Rhode Island and Daniel Patrick Moynihan of New York to ask that they develop a legislative proposal that would appeal to people in both parties. For a time, he made progress.

But Gergen was not the chief of staff. He lacked the authority to impose his will. And he was a single voice, not a spokesperson for the entire administration. "In truth," he later wrote, "the White House didn't need a Lone Ranger to come riding in; it needed a full posse of veterans from the past with experience and skills . . . and it needed stronger leadership at the top." By himself, Gergen could not turn around practices already deeply rooted in the approach of different White House factions. So, notwithstanding the different approach Gergen was intended to represent, the bitter divisiveness persisted. Hillary and Bill continued to have explosive arguments, often in front of others. Gergen recalled his embarrassment. "One felt party to a massive violation of their privacy," he wrote. "In the middle of a conversation, she would launch a deadly missile straight at his heart and just before it hit, the missile would explode, the shrapnel hitting the staff. He would respond and tempers would flare . . . Those conversations were demoralizing, deepened the divisions between the Bill and Hillary camps, and made one tiptoe around the principals."[38]

In the end, Clinton's gesture in recruiting someone like Gergen remained just that, a gesture. More would be necessary. Someone had to be in charge, preferably a CEO with a strong lieutenant ready and able to enforce orders. As it was, Gergen found himself increasingly marginalized. "The signals were pretty clear," he noted; "you begin to be shut out of meetings. The true believers went ahead. I have never seen a White House divided up like that before—I hope never to see another one." In Gergen's view, it all went back to the relationship between the two main actors. When Bill would get a call from upstairs, he wrote, "his mood would darken, his attention wander, and hot words would spew out." It was not a pretty picture.[39]

Whatever brief glimmer of hope Gergen's appointment represented, it was sent plummeting by the tragic suicide of Vince Foster in the summer of 1993. No one can ever explain a person's decision to take his own life. We know that Vince Foster was depressed, that he had gone to a doctor for help, that he had received a prescription for antidepressants but had barely started taking the pills. The night before he died, he watched a movie on television that ended with the hero putting a gun in his mouth and pulling the trigger. Foster had come to Washington to be with his best friends, Hillary Clinton and Webb Hubbell. A high achiever with an inordinate sense of personal responsibility, he quickly found himself overwhelmed. The political demands were enormous, the personal rewards minimal. An intimate friendship with Hillary had sorely eroded. From soulmates, they had become boss and employer, symbolized by Hillary barking orders like "Handle it, Vince!" What had started as an adventure ended as a nightmare.

Vince Foster had come to Washington to serve as deputy counsel to Bernie Nussbaum, who had been given his choice between a cabinet position and counsel to the president. Both men were close Hillary associates, Nussbaum from her days on the Nixon impeachment team, Foster from her decade-plus of service with him as a partner at the Rose law firm, where they lunched daily. So close were the two that Webb Hubbell, the third "amigo," confessed to feeling "jealous that she sometimes seemed closer to him than to me." Foster and his wife, Lisa, disagreed about whether the whole family should move immediately to Washington. On Inauguration Day, he left his wife and children at the curb on Pennsylvania Avenue so he could go to work in his new office at the White House. Lisa was so furious that she did not go to the inaugural ball. "I was angry at Vince about 90 percent of the time," she acknowledged, "for ignoring us and leaving us behind."[40]

Closely involved with Hillary's work at the Rose law firm, Foster had secured the waiver from the state bar association that allowed her to work for Rose as long as she pledged not to take clients who had business with the state. On numerous occasions, she had violated that commitment, and Foster was aware of that embarrassing truth. "It was a can of worms for her," he said. When the Jeff Gerst story had broken in *The New York Times*, Foster worked with the Betsey Wright mission to Little Rock to find any materials that might be sensitive or even relevant to the charges of conflict of interest, including the Whitewater mess, and tax return issues. Foster knew that Betsey Wright had moved the "delicate" files to Webb Hubbell's house. Some of them could have come to Foster as well. At the White House, he was known to be the Clintons' personal lawyer as well as deputy counsel to the president. That meant he handled their private business at the same time that he was spending most of his time doing work related to the president's official duties. As it turned out, that conflation of responsibilities proved to be a rat's nest. As a former White House lawyer commented, "the more deeply Foster was drawn into mopping up behind Hillary's political messes, the less he pleased her and the more he implicated himself. But refusing her assignments would have alienated him from the person he wanted most desperately to please."[41]

It did not take long for the old camaraderie to fade. Although Foster's office was literally only a few feet away from Hillary's in the West

Wing, the casual interactions, long lunches, and after-hours gossip sessions ceased. Early on, Hillary asked Vince to find out the identities of the Secret Service agents from the family residence who had leaked information to the press, and to get rid of them. When, because of the delicacy of the assignment, he took longer than expected to do her bidding, she made clear she was angry. Whereas once it had been "Let's talk this out," Webb Hubbell commented, "it was [now] Let's get this fixed . . . She was the boss . . . He was feeling the pressure, and it was a different relationship [than it had been]." To Foster's dismay, he had lost his role as equal and friend. His tasks varied. Sometimes, Hubbell noted, he was a fixer, sometimes a counselor, but no longer an intimate. "Hillary was completely out of his game," Hubbell said, "and the work kept piling up. And Hillary does not like things not happening when she wants them to happen. And trails were leading back to her."[42]

The last comment referred directly to Travelgate. Foster had been given the task of deleting her name from any and all references to the firing of travel office personnel. Foster complied, but he harbored severe doubts about her actions. It was all such a total departure from the way things used to be. "Fix it, Vince," she would hiss at him. And he was not sure he could. He considered quitting and returning to Arkansas. But he also wanted to stay and finish the job. "He couldn't do either," Hubbell said, "because of that thing inside him that demanded he not fail—that he always march proudly forward toward excellence and never turn back in defeat." He just could not get it right. "In the end," one source said, "I think they were both brokenhearted. He couldn't do enough for her once she became the First Lady. And she couldn't allow him to be her real friend, like he'd been, because she wasn't herself."[43]

The despair Foster was experiencing hit him with full force one night shortly before his death. Earlier that week, the "three amigos" had temporarily been reunited at a ceremony celebrating a major appointment. Just like old times, Hillary had embraced her two buddies. Hey, she said, let's go eat Italian this weekend. And so the three agreed to meet, with their spouses, at Hubbell's house for drinks, then proceed to a local trattoria for dinner. They had all been under tremendous strain, but Saturday would bring back some of that treasured camaraderie. Vince was in a good mood, despite the fact that the day before, he had been sent reeling by an editorial in *The Wall Street Journal* that singled him out, asking "Who Is Vincent Foster?" and suggesting that he had dark secrets to hide.

Except that in the middle of cocktails at the Hubbells' on Saturday, Hillary called from the White House to say there was a crisis because of a story breaking the next day. The Clintons would join the group at the restaurant, she said. Then, as they were about to order dinner, Hillary called again. They would not be able to come, she said.

Foster turned his chair away from the table, stared at the wall, and the rest of the evening refused to be part of any conversation. He was, Hubbell remembered, like "a child who had been promised quality time with a parent, only to have the parent renege when business called him away." The next day, Hubbell said, Foster called and told him, "It's just not the same." The woman he had loved was now the boss who simply said, "Fix it, Vince."[44]

The next week, Hillary went to Little Rock to see her mother. Bill, concerned with Vince's mental state, called to invite him to watch a movie with him at the White House, but Vince said he was at home with his wife. The day after Clinton's call, Foster went to work as usual. In the early afternoon, he left his office, saying he would return later. He went to a park in Virginia, parked his car, and shot himself in the head. It was night by the time the body was discovered. Bill Clinton was appearing on *Larry King Live*. The show was going so well that Larry and Bill agreed to extend it for another half hour. Then McLarty came into the room and said something had come up. Bill left the room where the cameras had been set up and learned of his childhood friend's death. He was overwhelmed. He called Hillary, who had also just heard the news and was crying. Then, with David Gergen, Webb Hubbell, and Vernon Jordan, the president went to Lisa Foster's house to comfort her.

The next day, Clinton convened a meeting of his staff to talk about what had happened. He asked them to spend more time with their families, and he encouraged people to share their thoughts and emotions. He and Hillary both reached out to their closest associates, offered to bring grief counselors to the White House, and shared with each other their bewilderment. "I did my best to convince her there was nothing she could have done," Bill said, "all the while wondering what *I* could have done . . . I was hurting . . . and feeling, as I had when Frank Aller killed himself, angry at Vince for doing it and angry at myself for not seeing it coming and doing something, anything, to try to stop it . . . Now Vince, the tall, handsome, strong, and self-assured person [all our friends from Arkansas] felt was the most stable one, was gone."[45]

The tragedy should have been a wake-up call to everyone, inside as well as outside the White House. Foster was simply a fragile human being who, like many others, could not withstand the overwhelming pressures being applied to him. His friends should have been able to celebrate his goodness, and people of wisdom should have been able to bemoan the eviscerating blows that public life too often inflicted on those who volunteered their services. Foster's death might have been a catharsis, helping to purge an evil process of some of its poisons.

But it was not to be. Instead, within days the Foster suicide became fodder for a new round of media speculation about conspiracy, death plots, and treason. Once more, the White House bore a substantial portion of the blame. The day after Foster committed suicide, Bernie Nussbaum, his boss, stopped the park police when they attempted to search Foster's office. He told them to return the following morning. When they did so, he once again prevented them from conducting their own search, instead telling them they could watch him as he went through Foster's papers. Nussbaum then separated them into three piles. The first had no "privilege" attached to them and could go directly to the police for perusal. The second consisted of personal papers that would go to the Foster family lawyers. Finally came a group of papers directly related to the Clintons and protected by attorney-client privilege. Those papers went to the family residence in the White House. Nussbaum's actions in preventing a free police search, then creating three separate files, fueled immediate suspicions. What was there to hide? Why should there not be complete and open access by law enforcement officials to whatever the papers might reveal? "You are messing this up very badly," Deputy Attorney General Philip Heymann told Nussbaum. "You're making a terrible mistake." His words were prophetic.[46]

As if to compound the mystery, six days later White House personnel discovered a suicide note that Foster had left. Then they failed to release the note immediately, holding on to it for hours, although it only helped clarify what had been going through Foster's mind. His wife had urged him to write down what was concerning him, and he did, then tore the paper into little pieces and deposited them in the bottom of his briefcase. "I made mistakes from ignorance, inexperience and overwork," he had written. "The Wall St. *Journal* editors lie without consequence . . . I was not meant for the job in the spotlight of public life in Washington. Here ruining people is considered sport . . . The public will never believe the innocence of the Clintons and their loyal staff." It was a cry for help from a man over his head in a job he could not figure out how to handle.[47]

Soon, the 24/7 news teams were grinding out conspiracy theories. *The Washington Times* blazoned the headline CLINTON PAPERS LIFTED AFTER AIDE'S SUICIDE, planting in the public mind the idea of a conspiracy to conceal Hillary's private files from the public. "Cover-up" became the word of the day for the conservative press. Rush Limbaugh went so far as to claim that Foster had been murdered in an apartment owned by the Clintons, then moved to the public park where his body was discovered. The strange sequence of events—Nussbaum's refusal to allow a search, his insistence on sorting the papers on his own authority into three separate files, the belated discovery of the suicide note—all contributed to a natural suspicion. As George Stephanopoulos later wrote, "By trying to preserve a measure of Foster's privacy, we invited more intense scrutiny. By thinking like lawyers, we risked being questioned like criminals. By emphasizing the 'mystery' of suicide, we appeared to be manufacturing a cover-up."

As later testimony in the Whitewater scandal would suggest, Hillary had orchestrated Nussbaum's handling of the Foster papers by phone from Little Rock. She helped determine the timing, and the process by which the contents of Foster's office were distributed. In multiple phone calls, she gave instructions to the aides responsible for handling the situation. Whether or not it was because there was something to hide, the circumstances provided a basis for suspicion.[48]

What had begun as a personal tragedy thus became a political time bomb. In a moment when the entire country should have come together in mourning a public servant, attention turned instead to the notion that the Clintons had orchestrated the entire episode as part of their larger effort to secure dictatorial power. Instead of ebbing, the frequency and hysteria of conspiracy rantings reached flood tide. If Bill Clinton had believed there was a way out of the demonization that flourished in the nation's capital, he now had to realize that the forces of polarization were growing stronger, not weaker, and that any victories he could secure would come at great cost.

It was all the more remarkable, then, that in the aftermath of Travelgate and Vince Foster's death, the Clintons found a means to claw their way back. It was not easy. Nor did the White House particularly distinguish itself with its ongoing series of mixed messages. Nevertheless, by early fall, pivotal pieces of Clinton's domestic agenda had fallen into place. Clinton's poll numbers were up, and there was a new sense of possibility in the air. "I think things are starting to come together," the president said.[49]

The key was Clinton's economic plan. Whatever other detours he allowed himself during that difficult first year, Clinton never lost sight of the main prize. Enacting economic reform would make or break his presidency. "Bill Clinton had bet his future on the abstraction of smaller deficits," Joe Klein wrote, and his tenacity in pursuing that goal represented, in Klein's view, an act of political courage.[50]

Clinton's initial economic plan represented a hodgepodge of different economic interests held together by the overriding theme of getting the budget under control and persuading brokers on Wall Street that it was now timely to bet on the future of the American economy. One major part of Clinton's plan—reflecting the strong influence of the Democratic Leadership Council—was to cut taxes for those earning less than $30,000 per year. But as opposed to the government handouts associated with LBJ's War on Poverty, Clinton's plan was to double the Earned Income Tax Credit. Although complicated, the gist of the EITC was to help out the poor, not by sending them a check but by giving them tax credits, thus putting cash in their pockets. A second Clinton focus was a $30–40 billion economic stimulus package designed to jump-start a floundering job market by creating new infrastructure projects concentrated in those states where employment was weakest. All during his campaign, Clinton had pledged a third initiative as well, a middle-class tax cut. But the most central element of the plan concentrated on streamlining government and cutting the deficit in half during his first term. "If I could convince Congress to pass the budget, and if it got the hoped-for response from the Federal Reserve and the bond market," Clinton said, the economy would turn around.[51]

Persuading Congress to go along was another matter. From the beginning, Bob Dole, head of the Senate Republicans, told Clinton there would not be a single Republican vote for his economic package. It all depended on Democrats. But they were divided into ideological factions. Some congressmen and senators from industrial states championed expansive government programs. Others wanted more budget cutting. The middle-class tax cut was soon dropped by Clinton himself, although the decision alienated most of the liberal members of his party—and a significant portion of his own staff. More difficult was the stimulus package. Clinton fervently wanted it. But powerful senators like David Boren of Oklahoma just as fervently opposed it. Up until then, Clinton's plan had been based on a twofold strategy: monetary policy, or getting the Federal Reserve Board to lower interest rates, and fiscal policy, or using federal spending to spur an economic upturn. But now conservatives insisted that plowing money into new government spending directly contradicted the larger goals of the economic package. So one more politically powerful dimension of the Clinton plan was axed.

There were other problems as well. At the instigation of Al Gore and the environmental lobby, Clinton had included in the economic package a provision for an energy tax (called the BTU tax) that would help reduce carbon emissions. Clinton insisted that the measure be included in the House version of the bill, and largely because of White House pressure, the House complied by a six-vote margin in late May. But the Senate caved to conservative pressures, and Clinton—after making loyalty to the BTU tax a litmus test for Democrats in the House—suddenly folded, severely undermining his reputation with House members. Congress left for summer recess with no resolution on the legislation. When the Clintons and Congress returned to the nation's capital to reconcile two different versions of the president's economic package, it was D-day for the Clinton administration.

The House situation looked bad. According to George Stephanopoulos, the White House was between ten and thirty votes short of a majority.

But Clinton got on the phones. So did Gore, Bentsen, Panetta—anyone with influence on the Hill. In the end, it came down to two members of Congress, Pat Williams from Montana and Marjorie Margolies-Mezvinsky from Pennsylvania, both in marginal districts with historically Republican majorities. Understanding fully what they were doing, the two cast the final ballots that gave the president a one-vote victory in the House.

The Senate was, if anything, more complicated. No matter how hard they tried, White House advocates could not come up with a scenario that would create a tie vote, which Al Gore could then break to create a majority. The key player was the Nebraska senator Bob Kerrey, a war veteran who had lost a leg in Vietnam. Independent, intellectually self-confident, and a longtime foe of Clinton who had competed against him in the early 1992 primaries, Kerrey struggled between his own ego and his sense of loyalty to party. On the day before the vote, Kerrey told Clinton he would vote no. A long shouting match ensued. "If you want to bring this presidency down, then go ahead," Clinton taunted. When Kerrey responded, saying, "I really resent the argument that somehow I'm responsible for your presidency surviving," Clinton ended the conversation with "Fuck you."

All that day White House aides tried to correct the damage. Moynihan talked to Kerrey. So did the billionaire investor Warren Buffett. Kerrey agreed to have breakfast with Clinton the next morning. The two talked candidly, minus the provocation of hyperbolic language. But Kerrey showed no willingness to change his intentions. The rest of that day the Nebraska senator was not reachable. He had gone to the movies. That night, as senators cast their votes, no one knew what he would do. Finally, he rose to speak at eight o'clock. "President Clinton," he said, "if you are watching now, as I suspect you are, I tell you this: I could not and should not cast a vote that brings down your presidency. You have made mistakes and know it far better than I. But you do not deserve, and America cannot afford, to have you spend the next sixty days quibbling over whether or not we should have this cut or this tax increase . . . On February 17, you told America the deficit reduction was a moral issue and that shared sacrifice was needed to put it behind us. Mr. President, you were right." After Kerrey voted yes, Al Gore broke the tie and Clinton's deficit reduction package was enacted. It was, said

White House aides, like Gettysburg—a turning of the tide. "A failed vote would mean a failed presidency," Stephanopoulos wrote. "Winning meant redemption, a second chance."[52]

After that, it was as if the floodgates opened—at least for a period. Al Gore and Hillary Clinton were still in competition as to whose priorities would go first. Hillary advocated health care, Gore the North American Free Trade Act. Clinton split the difference. He went to Congress in September to deliver a nationally televised speech on health care. Like most of his speeches, it went through multiple iterations and was completed only minutes before he left for the Capitol. Someone loaded the wrong speech into the teleprompter, so for the first three or four minutes, it played a copy of Clinton's State of the Union address until George Stephanopoulos got the right speech on the screen. But Clinton was magnificent. With passion, verve, and an extraordinary command of the policy horizon, he wowed his audience both in the House chambers and in the nation at large. Even Republican conservatives were impressed. In the first national sales talk on health care, Clinton had swept the boards, promising that within ninety days, Congress would have a bill embodying the principles he had just talked about.

In the meantime, the White House mounted a concerted effort to get NAFTA passed. First introduced by George Herbert Walker Bush to end tariffs on all products traded among Canada, the United States, and Mexico, the bill reflected long-standing Republican philosophical beliefs on free trade. Trade unions, on the other hand, strongly opposed the measure. Yet Clinton and Gore believed that in the end, free trade would benefit the American economy, particularly if the legislation contained provisions mandating protection of workers' rights in the participating countries. In the beginning, Clinton did not have sufficient Democratic votes to pass the measure. But he brought three former presidents to the White House—Bush, Carter, and Ford—to bless the effort and provide bipartisan legitimacy to NAFTA, making it seem like an issue of national unity. Clinton talked to more than two hundred members of Congress, and although a month earlier the White House had calculated that it was forty votes short, the measure passed the House 234–200 in November.[53]

In the same time period, Clinton posted other major victories. In

September he had signed a bill creating AmeriCorps, essentially a domestic Peace Corps. Under the new program, thousands of young people—and some older citizens—signed up to work on community service projects in cities across the country. Later, Clinton once again overcame substantial opposition, this time led by the National Rifle Association, to pass the Brady Bill, which required a waiting period for those who wished to purchase handguns so that background checks could be performed. Named for Ronald Reagan's press secretary, who had been seriously wounded in the assassination attempt on the president, the Brady Bill was opposed vehemently by the NRA, one of the richest and most powerful lobbying groups in the nation, with a record of successfully defeating virtually every previous attempt to control the sale of rifles, handguns, and even assault weapons. Now the bill became law, creating a run of successes that for the first time in his presidency led a majority of Americans to approve of the way Bill Clinton was doing his job.[54]

Clinton enjoyed less success in foreign policy. Led by what Joe Klein deemed "a flaccid, almost purposefully obscure foreign policy team," equivocation rather than decisiveness marked Clinton's response to a series of crises. From his consideration of lifting the United States arms embargo on Bosnia so that Muslim country could fight against racist policies being pursued by the Serbs, to whether and how he should respond to crises in Somalia and Haiti, Clinton waffled. As a group of scholars noted in early 1994, in a post–Cold War world, the president had "lost some of the moral authority that [came] almost automatically" when there were only two superpowers.[55]

With Somalia, Clinton seemed out of his depth, and he deferred to Colin Powell, chair of the Joint Chiefs of Staff, who he feared might become a Republican presidential candidate in 1996. United States forces were in Mogadishu as part of a United Nations peacekeeping operation. Powell was initially supportive of expanding the American mission, including seeking to capture the Somalian warlord Mohammed Farah Aidid. Just before Powell retired, Clinton gave the go-ahead for the mission without inquiring further into the chances of its success or failure. The results were a disaster. Eighteen American soldiers were killed, and the body of one was dragged through the streets by Somalian insurgents in a video that played across the world. Clinton faced intense pressure to withdraw all troops, and he soon did so.

A week later, national humiliation struck again. The navy sent a lightly armed vessel, the USS *Harlan County*, to Port-au-Prince to help prepare the way for the return of Jean-Bertrand Aristide, the popularly elected but militarily deposed president of Haiti. When hordes of pistol-packing Haitian rebels yelling "Somalia, Somalia" packed the dock where the ship was to land, it turned around and sailed away. It had been a "total fuckup," Clinton said. "I can't believe we're being pushed around by these two-bit pricks." As a consequence, he fired Les Aspin, his secretary of defense. But the lesson of both events was the danger of irresolute behavior that reflected a lack of planning and preparation. Worst of all, and to Clinton's everlasting regret, the United States did nothing while genocide claimed eight hundred thousand lives in Rwanda.[56]

Only on the question of Middle East peace did Clinton come out looking good—a signal of his passionate involvement on the issue that he would maintain for the remainder of his presidency. In late September—after Clinton's victory on his economic package and just before his initiative on NAFTA—Yitzhak Rabin, Israel's prime minister, called Clinton to tell him about a new agreement, negotiated in Oslo, out of the limelight, by Israeli and Palestinian diplomats. Rabin suggested that he and Yasser Arafat, the leader of the PLO, sign the accords at the White House. The night before the signing, Clinton got up at 3:00 a.m. and read the entire book of Joshua. The next day he chose a tie with blowing horns to symbolize the giant step about to be taken. Clinton presided over the historic moment, carefully orchestrating a handshake (not a kiss or a hug) between the Palestinian and Israeli leaders. That day, Clinton commenced his role as a missionary for Middle Eastern reconciliation. The same day was born his fervent and unending admiration for Yitzhak Rabin, whom Clinton viewed as the greatest leader for world peace he had ever met. At the ceremony, Rabin was eloquent. "We are destined to live together, on the same soil in the same land," Rabin proclaimed. "We, the soldiers who have returned from battles stained with blood, say to you . . . 'Enough of blood and tears. Enough!' . . . To everything there is a season and a time to every purpose under heaven . . . The time for peace has come." Inspired, Clinton identified himself with Rabin's cause. Although his hero and friend would not live to see the realization of his dream, Bill Clinton made the dream his own.[57]

Perhaps appropriately, the only greater moment that season came when Clinton returned to the best-loved cause of his life, that of civil rights and racial equality. Speaking without a text at Mason Temple in Memphis, where Martin Luther King, Jr., delivered his last sermon the night before he was assassinated, Clinton began to preach. Moving into his own rhythm, Clinton asked how Dr. King would feel about the number of black fathers who had abandoned their families. What would he think about those who dropped out of school, followed the lure of drugs, ended up in jail? His audience responded with "amens," not criticism, sensing that he was one of them, a brother. It was the best speech he ever gave, others later said. Not a bad way to convey to his audience and the nation that he was a person who had rediscovered himself, prepared to move out of despair into a new stage of delivering on his vaunted promise of greatness.[58]

Alas, it was not to be. By December the White House was once more engulfed in controversy, polarization replacing the optimism embodied in the Oslo Accords, AmeriCorps, and the Brady Bill. Where once there had been a new opening to those on the other side, now came a return to a Manichean world where suspicion and demonization took the place of conciliation.

It all started with a request from *The Washington Post* editorial board to David Gergen asking that Gergen intercede with the Clintons to secure the release of documents relating to Whitewater, including their personal tax returns. Gergen, charged with bridging the gap between the Clintons and the Washington establishment, had been carrying out his mission. He got the door reopened to the White House so that reporters could enter the West Wing to go to the press secretary's office. He had courted reporters like Ann Devroy of *The Washington Post* and Andrea Mitchell of NBC News. And now the *Post* sought him out as the ideal emissary to address the single most glaring weakness of the administration: the appearance that the Clintons had something to hide about events back in Arkansas involving the McDougals and the Rose law firm. Implicit in the *Post*'s request was the promise that if its reportorial staff found nothing in the papers to demonstrate the Clintons' complicity in illegal activities, the *Post* would help clear their name.

In Gergen's view, the request was a no-brainer. Certainly the papers, if released, might contain some embarrassing materials. Among other things, they would reveal Hillary's 1,000 percent stock market gains from investing in commodity futures. And they might disclose some questionable activities by Hillary on behalf of clients who had connections to the state. But the revelation of some minor embarrassments would be a small price to pay for getting rid of the public preoccupation with Whitewater. The gist of the problem was summarized in a dinner party conversation that George Stephanopoulos had with Katharine Graham of *The Washington Post* and Mary McGrory, one of her columnists. When Stephanopoulos told them there was really nothing to the Whitewater scandal, Graham responded, "But if they didn't do anything wrong, why don't you just release the documents or ask for an independent counsel to clear their name?"[59]

The question took on more urgency in late October and early November. On October 31, Sue Schmidt, a *Post* reporter, wrote that federal bank officials had asked the Justice Department to investigate whether money from McDougal's Madison Guaranty Savings and Loan had illegally been channeled into support of Bill Clinton's gubernatorial campaign. Subsequently, David Hale, a shady Arkansas financial figure, tried to use another Clinton story as bait to cut a deal with Justice for a reduced sentence for his own illegal activities. Hale claimed that Clinton had pressured him to lend $300,000 to Susan McDougal's phone marketing firm and that Jim McDougal had assured him that the loan "would help conceal earlier favors for the governor." Although investigators found no evidence to support this, the stories fed an ongoing appetite for dirt on the Clintons at a time when they were refusing any form of cooperation. Less than two weeks later, the NBC News reporter Andrea Mitchell reported a possible link between Vince Foster's death and the Clintons' investment in Whitewater. At the time of his suicide, Foster was allegedly working on Whitewater.[60]

Soon the crisis came to a head. Following through on the role he had been assigned by Clinton, Gergen made an appointment with the editors of the *Post*. He brought with him Bruce Lindsey, Mark Gearan of the White House communications office, and Mack McLarty. It was his hope—and intention—that the White House team would leave the *Post* with a deal: full access to the Whitewater documents by the *Post* in return for a promise of nonpartisan reporting. If the record turned up nothing suggesting criminal activity, there would be a clear conclusion that the Clintons had done nothing wrong.

But from the beginning the session was a disaster. The *Post* editors described in detail why they were frustrated by the lack of cooperation from the White House. Lindsey and McLarty refused to answer any specific questions. Lindsey accused the *Post* of "gotcha" reporting tactics. Instead of bridging the gap, the polarization intensified. "What is it with these people?" *Post* reporters asked. "Why can't they ever give you straight answers? What are they hiding?" Ann Devroy, who was still close to George Stephanopoulos, warned him that her paper "would go on the warpath unless [the administration] answered [the *Post's*] questions and released the documents."[61]

Gergen and Gearan went back to the White House intent on taking the issue directly to the president. An appointment was made. As they were about to meet, McLarty came up to them to declare, "It's already over." Clinton's lawyers had come and said no, they would not release the papers. Gergen felt betrayed. But he would not give up. The next morning he went to see Bill Clinton, along with George Stephanopoulos, who supported his position completely, as did most of the rest of the political team in the White House. Cogently they pressed their case. There was no downside, they insisted. If the Clintons had done nothing wrong, that would be the headline in the *Post*. Clinton understood their logic. He said he agreed with them. He supported their position. "I don't have a big problem with giving them what we have," he said. But Hillary—they would have to persuade Hillary before he could agree.

Reassured, Gergen proceeded to make an appointment to see the First Lady. Twice it was canceled and rescheduled. Then, two weeks after he had met with the *Post* editorial board, Gergen was informed that the next day, Bruce Lindsey would take a letter to the *Post* denying its request for the papers. Hillary and her lawyers held firm without ever giving Gergen the chance to make his case.[62]

Ultimately, Joe Klein noted, it all came down to "the relationship between the President and the First Lady." From the beginning, Hillary had run away from making her personal papers from the Rose law firm available for anyone's perusal. "These are my papers," she angrily declared. "They belong to me. I could throw them into the Potomac River if I wanted to."

Embarrassed by what the papers would reveal about her personal finances, anxious about evidence that she had violated conflict-of-interest rules, perhaps humiliated by suggestions that she had overbilled clients, Hillary simply refused to put herself at risk. Those seeking the information, she was convinced, were mortal enemies, out to destroy her and her husband. In the view of one aide, her reasoning was clear: "If we give this up, we give up everything, we'll never be able to claim privacy again . . . the questions would never end." And as Bill suggested to Gergen, it was Hillary's call to make. In his gut, Clinton knew that Gergen and Stephanopoulos were right. "But on this issue, Clinton wasn't commander in chief, just a husband beholden to his wife," Stephanopoulos wrote. "Hillary was always the first to defend him on bimbo eruptions; . . . now he had to do the same for her. Gergen and I didn't know what was in the Whitewater documents, but whatever it was, Hillary didn't want it out—and she had a veto."[63]

Immediately thereafter, *The New York Times* and *The Washington Post* announced full-scale investigations into Whitewater. From Congress and leaders throughout the country came increasing cries for appointment of an independent counsel. All of a sudden—after a near-miraculous recovery in the autumn with passage of the economic package, the health care speech, announcement of the Oslo Accords, AmeriCorps, NAFTA, and the Brady Bill, "the Clinton presidency," in Gergen's words, "was in free fall."

It all went back to the relationship between Bill and Hillary. She was in command. He could not control her.

Looking back at that moment years later, George Stephanopoulos had it exactly right. "If a genie offered me the chance to turn back time and undo a single decision from my White House tenure," he wrote in his memoir, "I'd head straight to the Oval Office dining room on Saturday morning, December 11, 1993," and get Hillary and Bill to change their minds about denying *The Washington Post* access to the

Whitewater documents. It was a moment—and a decision—that changed history. Had Gergen and Stephanopoulos prevailed, there would have been no independent counsel, no Kenneth Starr, no Monica Lewinsky case, no impeachment. Instead, Hillary made the call to say no. And the results were catastrophic.[64]

"For the first time in history," Carl Bernstein observed, "a president's wife sent her husband's presidency off the rails."[65]

NINE

The Health Care Debacle and the Emergence of Kenneth Starr

Eleven months after the White House decided to say no to *The Washington Post*'s request for the Whitewater records, the voters of America rendered their own verdict on the first two years of the Clinton administration. In November 1994, Democrats suffered a crushing defeat, losing fifty-four seats in the House of Representatives and eight in the U.S. Senate. Republicans were now in charge of both bodies. Although similar midterm reversals had happened three other times in post–World War II America, the sense of devastation in the Clinton White House was palpable. Bill Clinton could not believe his party had lost Congress. Hillary was in despair.

The election results mirrored the many mistakes the Clintons had made during the first two years. Despite the achievements of the Clinton deficit reduction package, NAFTA, AmeriCorps, the Brady Bill, and family leave, the media was dominated by stories suggesting disarray—the flap over gays in the military, the early exclusion of the press from the White House, Travelgate, the Foster suicide, and questions over what had happened to the records held in Foster's office. At the root of all these controversies were questions about the Clintons' character and intentions.

No two issues highlighted these doubts more than the debate over health care and the Clintons' avowals of innocence on Whitewater. From the beginning of the 1992 presidential race, health care for all Americans had ranked as the primary reform sought by Democrats, second only to economic growth as a domestic priority. A striking majority of Americans said they favored such reform. The only more important issue was whether the president and the First Lady could be believed when they claimed to be innocent of any wrongdoing in their real estate dealings in Arkansas. In the end, both issues became part of the same underlying story—the internal dynamics of the relationship between Bill and Hillary.

Throughout the 1992 election campaign, the Democratic candidates had vied to be seen as the most enthusiastic about seeking health care reform. That in itself represented a minor miracle. Five presidents had put forward the need for universal health care since the turn of the century, only to encounter stiff opposition and give up the fight. FDR almost included it as part of Social Security. Then Harry Truman proposed it in 1947. But the issue became toxic given the degree to which the politics of anticommunism pervaded both foreign and domestic policy debates. National health insurance, Republicans insisted, meant "socialized medicine," and anyone who supported it was "soft on communism," a "fellow traveler." Now the Cold War was over. Harris Wofford, to everyone's surprise, had been elected to the U.S. Senate from Pennsylvania largely by campaigning for health care. As a result, virtually every Democratic candidate embraced some form of health care reform, with Clinton saying he favored universal coverage for every American citizen.

But almost immediately after the election, that priority fell victim to political squabbles among Clinton advisers, especially given the doubling of the annual deficit, announced a month before Clinton took office. The emphasis on deficit reduction urged by Clinton's economic advisers automatically meant less flexibility for an expensive program on health care. Moreover, the powerful New York senator Daniel Patrick Moynihan believed, along with many others, that welfare reform should come first, giving Democrats the credibility with the public that would ease the path for health care reform.[1]

The delicate task of navigating these political waters was handed to Hillary. In the view of many, Hillary controlled health care as a quid pro quo for rescuing her husband from the Gennifer Flowers scandal and staying married. Five days into the new administration, Bill Clinton proudly announced that Hillary would chair the health care task force and ultimately bear responsibility for both the scope and content of the administration's health care proposals. Nothing—except perhaps for the location of the First Lady's offices in the West Wing beside those of the president and vice president—could validate more the degree to which this was to be a copresidency, two for the price of one.

At first the response was positive. More than 60 percent of the American people approved of Hillary's new role. But others had their doubts, especially those who also held key executive and economic roles in the administration. That dissension, in turn, would soon expose deep schisms within the ranks of those allegedly united in support of health care reform. As Leon Panetta, then head of the Office of Management and Budget, later said, "in Washington there are too many power centers, and you can't control them all." In a White House with divided priorities—and no chief of staff to exercise discipline over the competing factions—it would be difficult to forge a united front.[2]

Initially, the White House thought it had an easy answer: Richard Gephardt, the Democratic congressman and party leader from Missouri, proposed folding health care reform into the budgetary process. If universal health insurance could be incorporated into a budget resolution in the Senate, that would solve multiple problems in one swift legislative stroke. It would avoid a filibuster in the Senate, where sixty votes would be necessary to allow debate to proceed; and it would take supervision of hearings away from Moynihan's Senate committee, where the New York senator's skepticism might prove a damaging impediment. But Senator Robert Byrd, guardian of the Senate's traditions, took umbrage at such opportunism. Debate was the heart of the U.S. Senate, Byrd argued, and it would be sacrilege if the Senate's most venerated customs were violated for purposes of political expediency. That ended the possibility of a shortcut and threw the issue of how to proceed back to the Clinton White House, with both the House and Senate leaders, Gephardt and George Mitchell, warning that it would be well-nigh impossible to pass both economic reform and health care prior to 1994.[3]

Hillary was not pleased. "She was furious with the Democrats because they didn't rise up and stand with her in what she tried to do," her close friend and adviser Sara Ehrman observed. In Hillary's view, she and Bill had been elected to carry out the voters' mandate, and no one was showing sufficient deference to the political wishes that the new ruling couple embodied. Angry at all the obstacles she was encountering,

Hillary determined to proceed with her own plan. In the process she exhibited a personal decision-making style that undermined any possibility of success. She also displayed a conspiratorial view of Washington politics that could only reinforce political antagonism toward the White House itself.[4]

From the very beginning, Hillary seemed to have a clear idea of how to move forward. Modeling her plans on the successful task force on education that she had chaired in Arkansas, she envisioned a series of meetings with experts in the field, leading to development of a plan that could be presented—full and complete—to the appropriate legislative committees. Although early on some White House officials proposed sending a set of desiderata to congressional committees and asking *them* to draft a bill embodying the policy outcomes being sought, Hillary and her allies rejected the suggestion out of hand. Not only would such an approach take control of the health care issue from her hands, it would also deny her the platform from which to make her impact as a chief policy maker in the administration.

Most of the deliberations that subsequently ensued reflected Hillary's framework for a solution: An array of federal government regulations over private insurance companies would be developed, allowing health care reform to be implemented through marketplace mechanisms. Such a plan could never be denounced as "socialized medicine." Employers would pay the vast majority of the costs, with the government subsidizing small businesses that could not afford to pay the entire bill as well as providing insurance for the unemployed and those locked in poverty. But private companies would provide the care. To implement her plan, she chose Ira Magaziner as chief of staff for the health care task force. Magaziner had been a fellow Rhodes scholar with Bill Clinton. Now a multimillionaire, he was known for his organizing skills and management expertise.[5]

Soon enough, however, both Magaziner and Hillary would be known even more for their obsession with secrecy and their dedication to a set of deliberations that minimized open discussion about the issues, particularly with legislators. The two established thirty-four different working groups to consider the seven major issues as they defined them. They recruited five hundred different experts and held countless closed-door meetings, pledging that at the end they would have a solution produced by the best and brightest policy minds of their generation. Instead, the primary product of the task force meetings was suspicion about what Clinton and Magaziner were up to. For all his vaunted expertise, Magaziner came across as a policy wonk with no political instincts. "Ira was arrogant, rude [and] dismissive," Donna Shalala, secretary of health, education, and welfare, noted, conveying to most the notion that he and Hillary alone had the brains to come up with the right answer, with no help needed from anyone else, either inside or outside the administration.[6]

Making matters worse, Hillary conveyed the same impression. Although she assured her colleagues at the White House that she wanted a process that was "open and participatory," the opposite turned out to be the case. Many of the president's most powerful advisers were never consulted. Lloyd Bentsen, Clinton's secretary of the treasury, whose congressional experience made him an expert on health care, was never asked for his views. Nor was Donna Shalala, the cabinet officer most directly involved with health care. Joycelyn Elders, the surgeon general, was not consulted. From the beginning, Shalala said, most people around the president "thought that . . . the whole [task force] system Hillary was setting up . . . was crazy." Indeed, according to one aide, Robert Rubin "was terrified that [Hillary] was going to drive the country over the cliff" with her grand vision of health care.[7]

Convinced that the Democrats could pass health care without any Republican support, the First Lady insisted on an absolutist position, refusing to even discuss areas where compromise seemed possible. Carol Rasco, the head of Clinton's Domestic Policy Council, emphasized repeatedly the importance of making deals. "It is better to present a proposal and be willing to change," she noted, rather than have something set in stone not pass. But that was not the road Hillary walked down. Repeatedly, she burned bridges to potential allies, even in her own party. Appearing at a retreat of the Senate Democratic Caucus, she rejected all talk of seeking a middle ground. Instead, she told her fellow Democrats, the party should "demonize" Republicans who pledged to fight health care reform. "That was it for me in terms of Hillary Clinton," New Jersey's senator Bill Bradley said. "The arrogance. The assumption that people with questions are enemies! The disdain!" From that point forward, Bradley and New York's senator Daniel Patrick Moynihan— both pivotal figures who believed in bipartisan negotiation—viewed Hillary's political talents with profound skepticism. To them, and to many others, she seemed tone-deaf and strategically blind.[8]

Perhaps most important, Hillary dismissed those who raised questions about her plans. Her response to Laura Tyson, chief of Clinton's Council of Economic Advisers, when she criticized some of the implications of Hillary's approach delivered a chilling message to potential dissidents. "Why should we get into this?" other staff members asked. The division between Hillary's team of advisers and those on the president's staff simply widened the gap. Caught in the middle of all this, the president bowed out of the conflict. Quietly, many of Clinton's own team brought their concerns to the president, but quickly it became clear that he would not intervene. "I suspect," one aide said, "that there was a level at which he knew that [Hillary's approach] was really a dangerous idea . . . [But] he was president in no small measure because she stood by him in the Gennifer Flowers mess. And he had to pay her back. This is what she wanted, and he couldn't figure out how not to give it to her." "The Bill Clinton I saw," David Gergen has written, "needed the emotional approval of his wife on a daily basis. He depended on her . . . and acted as if she were his Rock of Gibraltar." Clinton would bow to his wife's wishes, no matter how destructive they might prove to be to his own legislative ambitions.[9]

In the words of one former presidential aide, as reports came back to Bill about the political mistakes Hillary was making, he would sit there with "the passivity of a Buddha . . . He's like the little kid who's been told to go to his room. Mom will handle everything. Knowing that the little kid will probably screw up again, even if she hides the cookie jar." With prescient insight, the aide had gone to the core of the dynamic governing the Clintons' interactions. Once the pendulum had swung to her side, he was powerless to speak. And so the president stood by the bargain he had struck with the First Lady. "The more you see them," another adviser said, "the more you get why she withholds the approval he seems to need, at times desperately." As long as she could threaten the peace of their mutual accommodation, he would go along, repressing his own better judgment in order to hold together their partnership.[10]

In the early fall of 1993, although Hillary's task force was still completing its work, the president and First Lady decided it was time to reveal their broad proposal to the American people. Clinton had just succeeded in securing passage of his deficit reduction package, along with final approval for NAFTA. In the midst of this ascending curve, Clinton decided to go before Congress and in a national address to the American people explain why health care was a priority for the nation and his administration. He was "on" that night, George Stephanopoulos later wrote, "like a jazz genius jamming with his pals. He poured his whole body into the speech, swaying with the rhythms of his words. Losing himself in a wonky melody, soaring from the text with riffs synthesized from a lifetime of hard study and sympathetic listening."[11]

Hillary soon followed with an equally impressive set of presentations to the various House and Senate committees that would be most involved in considering health care legislation. She presented herself as a prototypical American citizen. "[I am] here," she told the congressional committees, "as a mother, a wife, a daughter, a sister, a woman." Over and over again, she invoked her mother and the memory of Eleanor Roosevelt in her plea to see the issues of health care from the perspective of the average family. Dan Rostenkowski, the Illinois congressman who chaired the key House committee, kissed her hand and declared that "in the very near future the President will be known as your husband," echoing the response she had received a decade earlier from Arkansas state legislators when she appeared to testify on behalf of education reform. Hillary even disarmed her archfoe, the Republican leader Richard Armey of Texas, who had called her health care initiative a "Kevorkian prescription for the jobs of American men and women," invoking the name of the doctor who had participated in assisted suicides for people who chose to die. When Armey opened the hearings by saying he would try to make the day exciting, Hillary responded: "I'm sure you will, you and Dr. Kevorkian." The only response Armey could make was that of surrender. "I have been told about your charm and wit," he said, "and let me say, the reports of your charm are overstated and the reports on your wit are understated." Reviewing her appearance before five different congressional committees, *The New York Times* concluded that she had "dazzled" the legislators "in the most impressive testimony . . . anyone could remember . . . raising hopes that

an issue that had stymied Congress for fifty years was now near solution." As Hillary's biographer Carl Bernstein concluded, "[That] week may
have been the pinnacle of her career as first lady."[12]

The euphoria was short-lived. Once the president's speech and the First
Lady's testimony were over, the humdrum reality of the health care
endeavor reasserted itself. Despite promises of early delivery of a bill to
consider, the task force labored on, taking weeks more to complete its
task. All during that time, criticism mounted about the secrecy of its
deliberations, the dogmatism of its approach, and the turgid, bureau-
cratic manner in which it was proceeding. When the end result appeared—a 1,342-page bill that defied anyone's effort to summarize
quickly and crisply—the voices of dissent multiplied.

There could have been an alternative. In early fall, the administration considered once again simply sending an outline of health care
priorities to the appropriate congressional committees for them to
translate into legislation. But by that time, Hillary's stance—"my way or
no way"—had become the norm. Yet neither the president's staff nor
Hillary's had prepared the ground by briefing Congress and getting it
on board. As one of Hillary's aides noted, they failed to bring Congress
even a broad outline. Instead, there was "this ludicrously complex
thousand-page document [that] had something in it to piss everybody
off. So by the time it goes up the hill, it's DOA." Moynihan accused
Hillary of using "fantasy figures," and a leading congressman criticized
the measure for its "house-of-cards kind of financing that is going to fall
apart when people start to poke at it."[13]

Immediately, the Republicans piled on. A memo written by William
Kristol, a former aide to Vice President Dan Quayle, warned all Republicans that any indication at all of support for the Clinton bill would
destroy Republican chances for electoral victory in the 1994 midterm
elections. Enactment of health care reform, he wrote, would "re-
legitimize middle-class dependence . . . on government spending," re-
viving the reputation of the Democratic Party "as the generous protector
of middle-class interests." In Kristol's view, passage of health care legislation would permanently tie middle-class voters to the Democrats.
Hence, it must be defeated at all costs, invoking fear of state control

over private lives and promulgating the claim that health care was an instrument for taking the right to privacy away from the average citizen.[14]

Immediately, the opposition adopted Kristol's strategy. Robert Dole lambasted the Clintons for trying to turn over "one-seventh of our economy to the U.S. government." Newt Gingrich, the up-and-coming Republican leader of the House, decried the consequences of enacting health reform. "If you've seen public housing," Gingrich declared, "you've seen public medicine, and it's not a pretty picture." Soon the American Medical Association (AMA) sent out notices to seven hundred thousand doctors and medical students warning that the Clintons' plan would take away patient rights, deprive individuals of the freedom to choose their own physician, and ultimately "undermine the quality of medical services and lead to federal control of medical education and the physician workforce." The red flag of "socialized medicine" had reappeared, only in a more nuanced version. In a series of "Harry and Louise" ads paid for by the Health Insurance Association of America, a typical American couple was shown sitting at their kitchen table bemoaning the plot by the government to take away their right to make their own decisions about choosing a family doctor. If the ad campaign oversimplified the issues to the point of absurdity, the 1,300-plus-page bill that the White House had sent forward helped make the caricature credible.[15]

Disarray and dissension pervaded the White House. Tensions were rife between the First Lady's staff and that of the president. When David Gergen first saw the task force plan, he was overwhelmed by its density and unworkability, yet when he tried to raise questions, he was stifled. Alice Rivlin, another top economic adviser, took the plan home to show her husband, a professor at the Wharton Business School. After taking one look at the charts, he just laughed. "It's just over-organized, over-everything. He was absolutely right. I mean the process was laughable!" Lloyd Bentsen and others reiterated their doubts. But instead of being flexible, Hillary approached her task with a "holier than thou" attitude. "We [gave] the right kind of advice," Donna Shalala later recalled. "She just didn't take it." As the journalist Joe Klein later described the scene, "A know-it-all smugness became the operational style." Those who proposed an incremental approach were scorned, and if anyone raised a critical question in a White House meeting, "the First

Lady would, with cold fury, tell the questioner to stuff it—their plan was *the* plan."[16]

Despite clear evidence that disaster was forthcoming, the president refused to take over. "This was not a team effort," observed Judy Feder, a legislative liaison. "The President was out—and the rest of the Administration hated [the bill] like the plague." David Gergen, perhaps the most acute observer of the presidential partners, noted that "President Clinton was not fully himself in this fight. He was not as engaged, politically and intellectually, as I saw him in the budget and NAFTA struggles." Always choosing deference to Hillary over confrontation, Clinton, Gergen concluded, had explicitly elected "not [to] exercise his own independent judgment in the formulation, presentation, or final resolution of the plan. Even though he had signed off each step of the way, he did not take full ownership of the endeavor, nor did he personally marshal the resources of the administration for its success." Unwilling to break the pact he had made with Hillary lest he lose her approval, the one person who might have been able to save health care from defeat became part of the process ensuring its demise.[17]

The personal dynamic between Bill and Hillary helps explain why repeated possibilities for compromise were persistently rebuffed. When Daniel Patrick Moynihan suggested incremental reforms that could start the journey to universal coverage by insuring 91 percent of the population, Bill Clinton expressed interest. But Hillary rejected the compromise out of hand. Her husband, she insisted, would veto anything less than the complete package. Similarly, the Republican senator John Chafee offered a substitute "individual mandate" plan that Bill Bradley supported and that was endorsed by twenty-four Republican senators. It, too, could have been the basis for a negotiated compromise between the two packages. Fundamentally, Chafee was as committed to health care as Hillary was. But once again, the White House chose not to begin conversations that might lead to a "deal." For a time, even Bob Dole, who understood that government-supported health care had saved his life, seemed willing to compromise, telling the First Lady one night, "if you can sell it to Sheila (his legislative aide), you can probably sell it to me." But in the end, Hillary chose to stick to her plan—all or nothing—and by that time, Dole said, "opposition to *any* plan [had started] building up within my party."[18]

The president could not go where Hillary would not let him go. Notwithstanding the powerful start made on health care by the president's speech in early fall and the First Lady's initial testimony before congressional committees, the wind had gone out of the sails of health care. Caught in a deadly stalemate of their own making, health care advocates had nowhere to go but down. Ultimately, it was a story of self-made disaster. Only a dramatic change of tactics held any hope of rescue.[19]

Any remaining possibility of a turnaround in health care fortunes was torpedoed when other parts of the Clintons' interpersonal drama hit the airwaves. In mid-December, a story appeared in the *American Spectator* claiming that Bill Clinton had repeatedly used Arkansas state troopers to procure women for him. For the first time, a woman named Paula was mentioned in the story. The *Spectator* article appeared at almost the same time Hillary decided to deny *The Washington Post* access to her Rose law firm files on Whitewater. That decision, in turn, went hand in hand with her increasingly "all or nothing" approach to health care. Both *The Washington Post* and *The New York Times* decided to launch a massive investigation into the Clintons' lives in Arkansas and the entire Whitewater "scandal." The multiple threads of each disparate tale suddenly came together. The integrity of both the president and the First Lady was on the line. If the events of early December boded ill for the prospects of health care, those of early January seemed to suggest that the entire Clinton presidency was in peril.

The "Troopergate" stories were largely the creation of Clinton's old nemesis Cliff Jackson. The relationship between Clinton and Jackson was tortured. Both had been brilliant students, but while Jackson chose to shoot for his star at the University of Arkansas, Clinton pursued his dream at Georgetown. Each ended up at Oxford, Clinton on a Rhodes scholarship, Jackson on a Fulbright. They were friends, but also antagonists; while remaining engaged intellectually and emotionally, they developed different political orientations, especially about issues like the Vietnam War. Nevertheless—and ironically—Jackson provided some of the most direct and tangible assistance Clinton received in his quest to avoid the draft. By the time of Troopergate, however, Jackson's admiration intermixed with jealousy toward Clinton had decidedly turned into envy and anger.

In later years, Jackson gave a series of interviews that emphasized his ambivalence about Clinton, calling him "the very best politician this country *has ever seen*" and seeking to put the best face possible on his role in Troopergate. The fact remains, however, that Jackson orchestrated the entire attack, using right-wing money from groups like the Scaife Foundation to tar the president as a satanic figure without a hint of morality. Jackson contacted the state troopers who claimed they had procured women for Clinton; facilitated the personal contact between the troopers and David Brock, the *American Spectator* reporter who wrote the Troopergate article; and used his funding sources to make assurances to the troopers that they would be amply rewarded for their cooperation. And in case his *American Spectator* story fell through, he developed close ties with a *Los Angeles Times* reporter working on Troopergate and arranged a televised interview on CNN with two of the state troopers forty-eight hours before the *Spectator* article was to appear.[20]

But the story gets even more complicated. Bill Clinton learned about the conversations Brock and Jackson were having with the state troopers well before the article finally appeared on December 19. Danny Ferguson, one of the troopers who had initially cooperated with Jackson, alerted friends in the Clinton administration, and soon the president himself became involved in conversations with Ferguson and others. "All [of them are] mad because I didn't give [them] jobs," Clinton scrawled on a notepad. "Troopers being talked to by lawyers—offered big $." In response, Clinton called Jim Guy Tucker, the present governor of Arkansas and an old ally, to ask for his help in suppressing the story. When George Stephanopoulos found out about these back-channel conversations, he was incredulous. "*How could he be so reckless?*" Stephanopoulos later wrote. "*He's so sure he can talk his way out of anything that he doesn't even think about the consequences . . . Why can't he just leave these things alone?*" In Stephanopoulos's judgment, "a few stupid presidential phone calls now transformed an old Arkansas story into an Oval Office scandal."[21]

None of the president's attempted interventions worked, and the article finally appeared a week before Christmas. "[It] hit the Presidency like a ton of bricks," one insider told the journalist Gail Sheehy. The author was David Brock. "I threw in every titillating morsel and dirty quote the troopers served up," Brock later said. Full of late-night Clinton adventures in which the state troopers provided women for the governor to sleep with, perhaps the story's greatest long-term consequence was a side story in which Brock mentioned in passing that Clinton had tried to seduce a government aide named Paula while speaking at a conference in Little Rock two days after giving his "New Covenant" speech to the Democratic Leadership Council. No last name was given, no details provided. But within a short time, the name of Paula Jones would reverberate across the nation. Brock's story, soon followed up by another in the *Los Angeles Times* and preceded by the CNN interview with state troopers, became a defining moment. As the *New Yorker* correspondent Elizabeth Drew later wrote, "[it was] the most bizarre day thus far in this and perhaps any other administration." More to the point, as Betsey Wright later observed, when it came to the basic facts of the story, "the troopers were telling the truth."[22]

But the long-term consequences of the *Spectator* story did not end there. The fact that Bill and Hillary Clinton knew far ahead of time that the story was in the works shaped other presidential decisions of great portent. The Clintons' discussion of how to handle Troopergate occurred at the same time that Bill and Hillary were deciding whether to accede to David Gergen's initiative with *The Washington Post* to make available Hillary's records on Whitewater.

Most important, Clinton's submissiveness to Hillary on denying the *Post* access to the papers reflected a now common pattern in their relationship: renewed guilt—and weakness—accompanying pending revelations of his sexual escapades. "You could almost feel Hillary's power coming back in full force," one insider said. "She now had the moral high ground." Another person close to the First Couple noted, "Hillary gave [Bill] hell for months . . . She beat up on him so badly, he just sat on his hands." At just the moment when a series of issues, including health care, were coming to a head, Bill Clinton was cowed and demoralized, unable—and unwilling—to assert his power as president.[23]

Clinton's resolve was about to be weakened further: after years of fighting cancer, his mother died a few days into the new year of 1994. The president knew his mother was dying; doctors had recently told him she had only three months to live. But Virginia insisted on living life to the fullest. She rejected any attempts to talk directly about her pending death. Even as she approached her final moments, on New Year's Eve, she journeyed to Las Vegas, where she was a special guest of Barbra Streisand at a concert during which Streisand dedicated a song to the president's mother. Virginia called Bill that night to share her joy and excitement. On his last trip to see her in Little Rock, they had stayed up late to talk, but during their entire three-hour conversation, Clinton wrote, "we talked about everything except the fact that she was dying." The other most important woman in his life was now gone. Clinton was devastated. It did not help that the day after Virginia's death, as he journeyed to Little Rock for her funeral, the Republican leader Robert Dole unleashed a bitter political attack, accusing Clinton of systematically hiding the truth about the misdeeds of his administration. "The guy wouldn't even let me bury my mother," Clinton later said to Taylor Branch.[24]

It would be hard to imagine a more difficult winter. On all sides—whether the issue was health care, sex scandals, or internal relations at the White House—an air of crisis pervaded the administration. But things would get worse before they got better. Stories about Troopergate melded quickly into concerns over Whitewater. Those concerns in turn led to a concerted cry for appointment of a special counsel to investigate the Clinton White House. There was not a good sign to be seen.

The link between Troopergate and Whitewater was organic. Although in theory the two stories were worlds apart—one about the sexual recklessness of Arkansas' former governor, the other about whether the law practice of Arkansas' former First Lady involved a conflict of interest—the two were joined by one common theme: mistrust of Bill and Hillary's ethical integrity. During the same period when every paper in the country contained stories about how many women Clinton had slept with in Little Rock, they also blazoned headlines about Hillary making a fortune through speculation in stock futures and resisting disclosure of her law firm records, capped off by revelations that Vince Foster's files had been given to the Clintons' attorneys rather than to the Justice Department.[25]

A cry for appointment of an independent prosecutor quickly ensued. There were simply too many unanswered questions, too many evasive answers, too little forthright disclosure. By the end of January, nine leading Democrats, including Bill Bradley and Daniel Patrick Moynihan (not coincidentally, the principal senators Hillary had crossed during her handling of the health care task force), had joined the ranks of Republicans calling for a special prosecutor. In the White House itself, more and more of Clinton's political team came to the conclusion that appointment of an independent counsel was their only political option. "There's an air of inevitability to this," George Stephanopoulos said. "I know we didn't do anything wrong, but it looks like we did because we're not being forthcoming." He took the next logical step, noting that Whitewater in particular "is going to kill health care if we don't get it under control."[26]

To which Hillary exploded with rage and tears. "You *never* believed in us," Hillary screamed. "In New Hampshire it was just me and Susan [Thomases] and Harold [Ickes] who believed in us . . . We were out there alone, and I'm feeling very lonely now. Nobody is fighting for *me*." In tears, she yelled, "I don't want to hear anything more. I want us to fight. I want a campaign now!" Then to Stephanopoulos: "If you don't believe in us, you should *just leave*."[27]

Hillary, her devoted friend Bernard Nussbaum (White House counsel), and her personal lawyer, David Kendall, were adamantly opposed to seeking an independent counsel. Mark Gearan, David Gergen, and most of the White House political team saw no choice but to do so. Clinton was overseas, depressed over his mother's death, politically and emotionally drained by the turmoil raging around him. In a long conference call, Clinton heard out all the parties, gave voice to his own despair and helplessness, and at the end asked everyone else but Hillary and Kendall to leave. Feeling he had no choice, Clinton gave in and announced he would ask the attorney general to appoint an independent counsel. When Hillary told Bernie Nussbaum the next day, he responded, "Why are you going to put your head in that noose?"[28]

The White House had embarked on the road that would eventually lead to impeachment. It started with the decision to turn down *The Washington Post*'s request for access to the Whitewater documents. Six months later, it would lead to the appointment of Kenneth Starr as special prosecutor. Never again could the White House get back its own independent platform. By the middle of March, the three major television networks had devoted 222 minutes to stories covering Whitewater and related events, more than three times the total footage devoted to health care reform. Try as hard as he might, Bill Clinton became captive to his own and his wife's refusal to be forthcoming in their response to requests for information on Whitewater—the inevitable price exacted by the dynamic between them, by the parallel lives that persisted through their marital partnership.[29]

Once he had made the decision, Clinton asked Attorney General Janet Reno to appoint an independent counsel. On January 20, exactly one year after Clinton's inauguration, Reno responded by naming Robert Fiske, a New York Republican who had been a widely respected prosecutor as a U.S. attorney, with a reputation for toughness and integrity. Insisting on a broad mandate for his work, Fiske set out to investigate the suicide of Vincent Foster and all the issues related to the Whitewater deal. Casting further suspicion on the First Lady, reporters discovered her 1,000 percent return in Arkansas from speculating in cattle futures. The suspicion deepened further when Webb Hubbell, her other close associate in the Rose law firm, resigned as deputy attorney general and was indicted for overbilling and for defrauding the law firm of more than $500,000 in unjustified expense account claims. A new poll showed that 50 percent of the American people believed Bill and Hillary were lying about Whitewater, with 33 percent thinking they had done something illegal. The pressure mounted for Hillary to release all documents for review, with the newly appointed White House counsel, Lloyd Cutler—who had replaced Bernie Nussbaum—leading the charge.[30]

Instead, Hillary dug in her heels. Fixated on hiding any excess billing or conflict-of-interest violations, she would not budge, and Bill was in no position to overrule her. "It was Hillary," Beverly Lindsay, a White House aide, later noted, "who made the decision to [keep resisting even though] the staff realized it wasn't working."[31]

Yet with each denial, the public impression that the Clintons had something to hide simply increased. Despite a sixty-eight-minute press conference by Hillary at which she tried to answer any and all questions, the suspicions did not abate. The First Lady, her old friend Robert Reich reported, "felt hurt and bewildered," as if the whole world were seeking retribution against her. In her memoir, Hillary wrote that the entire Whitewater episode was really an attempt at "undermining the progressive agenda by any means . . . If you believed everything you heard on the airwaves in 1994, you would conclude that your President was a Communist, that the First Lady was a murderess and that together they had hatched a plot to take away your guns and force you to give up your family doctor . . . for a Socialist health care system." Hillary's view of the opposition persecuting her was not fantasy. Yet what she failed to understand was how her own decisions and behavior reinforced suspicion and mirrored the opposition's conspiratorial view of the world. Hillary would not—perhaps could not—recognize how many average citizens had good reason to want straightforward answers to legitimate questions. As Hillary's biographer Carl Bernstein noted, the "remarkable clumsiness of [Bill and Hillary] playing fast and loose with the facts" simply energized the forces arrayed against them.[32]

Still, there was some good news. Robert Fiske proceeded in a reasonable and expeditious manner. He subpoenaed White House staff members, focusing initially on the president and on Vince Foster's death. Within a few months he concluded that Foster had committed suicide, with no evidence to suggest either a cover-up or complicity by anyone. When he questioned Clinton at the White House, the interview went well. Clinton was gregarious, self-confident, at ease, and effective in his responses. Appropriately, Clinton appeared more concerned with the impact of the independent counsel on Hillary than on himself. "After all," he later wrote, "I had learned how to lead parallel lives as a child: most of the time, I could shut out all the accusations and innuendo and go on with my work." Compartmentalization had worked for Clinton before; it would do so again. Most White House staffers felt comfortable with Fiske's fairness, his evenhandedness, and his efficiency. As long as he remained in charge, they believed, the Clintons would survive.[33]

But that complacency was soon shattered. In July, Clinton had signed a reauthorization of the Independent Counsel Act, as he had promised to do. He and nearly everyone else on the White House staff assumed that Fiske would be reappointed under the terms of the new act. After all, he was a Republican prosecutor who was well respected.

Lloyd Cutler assured Hillary and Bill that Fiske would not be replaced. He would "eat his hat," he said, if that were to happen. Hillary disagreed. She urged her husband not to sign the Independent Counsel Act, convinced that the judiciary would find some way to replace Fiske with an anti-Clinton ideologue.[34]

Although White House staffers thought the First Lady was "paranoid," she was right on target. Under the terms of the legislation, the choice of a special prosecutor rested in the hands of a three-judge panel from Washington, D.C. The panel was headed by David Sentelle, a close friend of Jesse Helms and Lauch Faircloth, deeply conservative senators from North Carolina, and a longtime ally of William Rehnquist, the equally conservative Chief Justice of the United States Supreme Court. Sentelle had excoriated "leftist heretics" who, he claimed, wanted an America that would be a "collectivist, egalitarian, materialistic, race-conscious, hyper-secular, and socially permissive state." Janet Reno, the attorney general, requested that the three-judge panel reappoint Fiske. The judges had other ideas. Republican antagonists, displeased with the ruling in the Vincent Foster suicide, were claiming that Fiske was in the back pocket of the Clinton administration. They sought a whole new inquiry into Foster's death. Sentelle heeded their wishes. Having just had lunch with Helms and Faircloth, he and his two conservative colleagues removed Fiske as special prosecutor and appointed Kenneth Starr, a former solicitor general during the presidency of George H. W. Bush and someone well known for his conservative views. Starr had filed a brief opposing Clinton in a new lawsuit that had been filed on behalf of Paula Jones, a fact that most judges would have seen as evidence that Starr had a conflict of interest and could not be impartial as a special prosecutor. But Sentelle and his colleagues ignored that inconvenient problem. From that moment on, the White House staff knew there was trouble ahead. Hillary had been paranoid, and rightly so.[35]

As in a classic Greek tragedy, the players in the drama acted out the parts that fate seemed to have assigned them. George Stephanopoulos had been prescient in seeing *The Washington Post* matter as a turning point. Once Hillary said no to the request for total disclosure, everything else fell into place. Right-wing conspiracy theorists concocted new and ever more horrible scenarios about how the evil Clintons had lied their way to the White House, buried their past crimes, and then committed new ones, including murdering one of their oldest friends. Hillary reciprocated, perceiving an ideological plot to destroy her and all the progressive ideas that she and Bill had brought to Washington. Their enemies would invent crimes she had not committed and seek to convict them by searching through all their private records. Fueling the fateful battle were deep suspicions that the Clintons were contemptuous of the Washington establishment, consistently relied on evasive half-truths, and were never willing to be candid with the press. "Even the most responsible newspapers and networks," Joe Klein concluded, "appeared obsessed" with the Clintons' personal failings. It was all a recipe for tragedy, fed on each side by choices that, after *The Washington Post* decision, seemed fated.[36]

Inevitably, the outcome of health care reform was inseparable from the unfolding story of Whitewater. Although in terms of substance the two issues were as far apart as the Atlantic and Pacific oceans, in terms of politics they were intertwined. The same dynamics was at work in each. Hillary's adamant refusal to release any information about her Rose law firm records reflected the same mind-set that shaped her refusal to entertain any form of compromise with Moynihan, Bradley, or Republicans in thinking about an incremental approach to health care. Only a decisive intervention by the president could change the direction both crises were taking. But was such intervention possible, given the nature of the partnership that Bill and Hillary had agreed upon in their planned "copresidency"?

The answer seemed clear when Bill Clinton delivered his State of the Union address in January 1994. Health care was in trouble—had been in trouble for months—and there were enormous countervailing pressures on how to proceed. Some Republicans, like John Chafee, and some Democrats, including Daniel Patrick Moynihan and Bill Bradley, still favored an incremental approach that might cover 91 to 95 percent of those needing health insurance. But Hillary still opposed any compromise. So she and her allies insisted that Clinton include in his State of the Union address a commitment to veto any legislation that provided less than 100 percent coverage. David Gergen and Speaker of the

House Tom Foley begged Clinton not to throw down the gauntlet in that fashion. To do so, they argued, would render credible the opposition's argument that the Clintons were absolutists. But whatever Bill Clinton's doubts, the stories of Troopergate had only deepened his subservience to Hillary. His philandering had humiliated her. If he were to have any hopes of returning to her good graces, he must do whatever she asked. "Bill would not risk her further ire," Carl Bernstein noted. "He would challenge her on nothing remotely in her [sphere]." And so the Clintons painted themselves even further into a corner. Later, Bill Clinton wrote, "It was an unnecessary red flag to my opponents in Congress. Politics is about compromise, and people expect Presidents to win, not posture for them" As a politician, Bill Clinton undoubtedly knew this at the time. But the husband to Hillary was in no position to act on his insight. Instead, he drove one more nail into the coffin of health care reform.[37]

An air of being under siege started to permeate the White House. "They think people are out to get them," one cabinet officer said, "this right-wing conspiracy. They feel sorry for themselves. They talk about it all the time." And no one complained more than the First Lady's staff, whose West Wing headquarters was dubbed the "Intensive Care Unit." When Hillary took her show on the road with a nationwide bus tour called the Health Security Express, she—and the press—were overwhelmed by the hostility they encountered from people carrying posters denouncing her as a "socialist" who was seeking state-controlled health care. "I had not seen faces like that since the segregation battles of the sixties," she said.[38]

As approval for the health care initiative plummeted in public opinion polls, a majority of the American people now said that Hillary exercised "too much influence on her husband." The ad campaign against health care grew more vicious. One TV spot featured a screaming baby crying for help only to have his mother told that "the government health center is closed now." "Why did they let the government take over?" the ad concluded. A new consensus developed. Even "balanced" media commentators like CNN's Bill Schneider ended up denouncing the Clintons for their "awesome political stupidity. [They] turned health care reform over to a 500-person task force of self-anointed experts, meeting for months in secret, chaired by a sinister liberal activist and a driven

First Lady. Who elected them? They came up with a 1,300-page document that could not have been better designed to scare the wits out of Americans. It was the living embodiment of Big Government—or Big Brother."[39]

Still, the First Lady resisted compromise. When the Health Insurance Association of America offered to withdraw the "Harry and Louise" ads if the administration would agree to negotiate, she defiantly said no. David Gergen, probably the most centrist of the Clinton advisers, found himself increasingly left out of Hillary's counsels. "The signals were pretty clear," he said in an interview. In the eyes of many, Bill Clinton seemed to be walking through a minefield. Yet when he tried to intervene, he got slapped down. After Clinton gave a speech indicating that he was ready to consider Senate Majority Leader George Mitchell's plan to provide health coverage to 95 instead of 100 percent of the American people and eliminate an employer mandate, the First Lady was on the phone lambasting him the minute he left the stage. He returned meekly to the White House to reassess the position he had just taken.[40]

No one was in the least surprised, then, when health care went down to a crushing defeat in late August 1994. Although Clinton had achieved numerous legislative victories, most people believed his administration was plummeting. "Health care was once Bill Clinton's poster child," the Republican pundit Bill Kristol said. "It is now becoming his tar baby." It was not for lack of compromise proposals that health care reform went down to defeat. A group called the Mainstream Coalition tried to fashion an alternative bipartisan plan; George Mitchell came up with his own compromise measure; and Rhode Island's Republican senator John Chafee continued trying to organize Republican support. But it all flew in the face of Hillary's determination to stand firm. Finally, on August 26, George Mitchell announced that no further debate over health care would take place. The measure died without a vote even being taken.[41]

Smelling blood, Republicans in Congress swarmed for the kill. Newt Gingrich, an aggressive Republican congressman from Georgia with a Ph.D. in history, seized on the vulnerability of the president's falling popularity. Instead of simply attacking Clinton, Gingrich proposed a Republican "Contract with America." The party would return to greatness by establishing a compact with the American people to balance the budget and create a line-item veto; enact an anticrime package; pass welfare reform and end the issuance of welfare checks after a period of two years; increase defense spending; cut capital gains taxes; and institute congressional term limits. It was, Gingrich insisted, a blueprint for returning to Ronald Reagan's "morning in America." Few Americans could list the multiple items in the Contract; and most had no idea that Bill Clinton endorsed welfare reform and the tightening of child support. All they knew was that the Contract sounded like a visionary plan, that Gingrich was a leader, and that compared with Clinton, he seemed to know where he was headed.[42]

Clinton's pollsters told him he was in trouble. Stan Greenberg warned that he would lose the House and that the Senate was in question as well. "No way, not the Senate," Clinton retorted. Dick Morris, doing his own polling, confirmed Greenberg's skepticism and advised Clinton to stay "presidential" and not get involved in local races. Against Morris's advice, Clinton threw himself into the fray, appearing all over the country for Democratic candidates. On Election Day, the results were worse than even the most dire predictions. The Democratic Party lost eight Senate seats, fifty-four House seats, and eight governorships— the worst trouncing any president had received since Harry Truman in 1946. In Texas, George W. Bush defeated the incumbent governor, Ann Richards, even though her approval rating was 60 percent. In New York, even the giant Mario Cuomo fell. Amazingly, Speaker of the House Tom Foley—supposedly in a "safe" seat—also lost. The National Rifle Association boasted of defeating nineteen of the twenty-four people on its "hit list." Only four times since the Civil War had such losses been experienced by the party in power.[43]

Despair pervaded the White House. Clinton "was extremely distracted," David Gergen noted. "He would lash out, but then he would pull back. He seemed lost." Donna Shalala observed that it took "three or four months before we regrouped." In the meantime, the president was "almost incoherent." Clinton admitted as much. "I was profoundly distressed by the election," he wrote in his memoir. Melancholic, withdrawn, pensive, it was like a return to 1980 when for months Clinton had wandered the streets of Little Rock asking people what had gone wrong, where he had failed. Recognizing the parallel, Clinton noted that "somehow I had forgotten [that] searing lesson . . . You can have good policy without good politics." In his memoir, Clinton implicitly drew the parallel even further. Back in his first term as governor, he had tried to do too much, proposed too many changes, allowed himself to get "off message," confusing people with the plethora of reforms he sought to implement. Now, as he reviewed his first two years in the White House, he concluded that once again, as in 1980, he had tried to do too much.[44]

But Bill was not the only one in despair. Hillary was devastated. She was "deeply depressed," Gergen observed, more so than at any time since her father's death, and seemed to go "into a downward spiral." Virtually everyone in the White House agreed. Even more than the president, the First Lady seemed disconsolate. Every week, she met with her own support group—dubbed "the Chix"—that included her chief of staff, Maggie Williams, her speechwriter, her scheduler, and all those closest to her on a day-to-day basis. Breaking down in tears at the meeting after the election, Hillary declared that she was going to end her role as a public policy advocate. No, you can't do that, her team said; women all over the nation were counting on her. "You're a role model," her speechwriter Lissa Muscatine said. "What kind of message would you be sending if you stopped being actively involved?" But for months thereafter—even longer than for Bill—Hillary seemed unable to recover. She felt profoundly, as David Gergen saw it, that "not only [had] her policy advice . . . failed, but she was politically at fault [as well]."[45]

Most Washington observers agreed. She *was* more responsible than anyone else for the resounding defeat of health care and the administration's downward spiral in public opinion. Joe Klein, one of the most insightful of Washington's reporters, blamed the plunging poll numbers directly on Hillary's "unwillingness, from the very start, to listen to opposing points of view in White House staff meetings, and then her unwillingness to compromise [on health care] until it was too late." Although Hillary continued to believe that the entire Whitewater fixation was basically a right-wing conspiracy aimed at "undermining the progressive agenda by any means [available]," she also began to have some sense of how her own intransigence played into the hands of her foes. The copresidency dynamic did not sit well with people. "The more she

seems strong," Dick Morris noted, "the more [the president would] inevitably be seen as weak." From the late fall of 1993 to the election of
November 1994, tension between the two had grown. He never wished
to draw lines in the sand; she insisted that the lines be drawn. The almost schizophrenic contentiousness between them weakened everyone.
Summarizing prevailing opinion, one senior Senate aide declared that
Hillary had "destroyed the Democratic Party" by her unwillingness to
compromise with major constituencies.[46]

That assessment too easily let Bill Clinton off the hook. He was the
one, after all, who created the interpersonal dynamic that led to Hillary's intransigence by his reckless misbehavior. "Playing around" with
women procured by Arkansas state troopers was not simply a compartmentalized sexual fixation. His indiscretions mattered, the reporter
Michael Isikoff wrote, "because private misbehavior on Clinton's scale
required routine, repetitive, and reflexive lies to conceal [it] . . . If lies
were needed to avoid political embarrassment, then lies—or at least
extremely mangled versions of the truth—would be told. A culture of
concealment had . . . infected his entire Presidency."

Although Isikoff seemed preoccupied with Clinton's sex life, his
observations about its meaning for the Clinton presidency were on target. By his own example of concealment, Bill Clinton helped validate
Hillary's pattern of hiding her own past at the Rose law firm. And by
making himself eternally indebted to Hillary for forgiving his infideli-
ties, he bore fundamental responsibility for the virtually unlimited—
and unconstrained—authority that Hillary had been granted over
health care.[47]

By the end of 1994, the promise of a new spring in politics that Bill
Clinton had heralded in his inaugural address of January 1993 seemed
as far away as Mars. A profound disconnect existed between the hopes
the Clintons brought to Washington and the doubts and suspicions that
now seemed endemic. Yes, there had been extraordinary achievements
with deficit reduction, family leave, AmeriCorps, the Brady Bill, and
NAFTA. But somehow, all these victories faded into oblivion. Sensational stories about "Don't Ask, Don't Tell," Travelgate, Vince Foster's
suicide, and the culture wars between establishment Washington and

the Clinton White House dominated the airwaves. More important, these sensational stories were rooted in political realities. Rather than being temporary distractions, they reflected an ongoing dynamic in the ruling structure of the country that shaped in fundamental ways the story of the first two years of the Clinton administration.

At the heart of that dynamic was the personal partnership the president and First Lady had negotiated in their political lives, and the consequences for the nation when the terms of that partnership went awry. As health care and Whitewater came to dominate, Hillary's authority simply grew. In a profound way, the early Clinton presidency turned out to be shaped more by the First Lady than by the president himself. Not only did she icily dismiss critics, she did so with a dogmatism that was frightening in its lack of sensitivity to other points of view. Robert Boorstin, a former *New York Times* reporter who joined the health care task force as its media relations expert, cut to the chase: "I find her," he said, "to be among the most self-righteous people I've ever known in my life . . . It's her great flaw. It's what killed health care."[48]

She had not always been that way. As an activist in college and at Yale Law School, Hillary had gone out of her way to avoid extremes. She hewed to the middle, worked with the people in power, and tried to stay in touch with advocates on all sides. Even in the governor's mansion in Little Rock and the White House in Washington, she retained some of that political skill. Her advocacy of education reform in Little Rock had won the praise of a spectrum of political leaders. Her speech in Austin seeking a new "politics of meaning," as her father lay dying, raised hopes for a more inclusive and welcoming kind of advocacy.

But the norm in Washington became anger and absolutism rather than grace and mediation. Like a lightning rod, Hillary became for some a focal point for fervent devotion, but for many others an object of intense hatred.

From Hillary's point of view the whole struggle was ultimately about defending her "turf." She had marked out her territory from the first day of the administration. She would have an office in the West Wing alongside Bill's and Al Gore's. She would hire her own staff, as good if not better than theirs. She would command her own policy arena, refusing to let others invade her space or tell her where she was wrong. Literally, to cede any part of the ground she occupied to others would undermine everything she had fought for and cared about.

The same issue of turf governed her approach to the Whitewater files. This was her career, her private life. To let anyone in was not only to lose control but also to open her entire character to judgment by others. From childhood onward, Hillary Rodham thought of herself as moral, virtuous, beyond reproach. To now give someone permission to invade her private papers was existentially unacceptable—literally a violation of the most sacred part of her being. It all came down to a question of defending oneself and one's freedom. There was no higher responsibility.

Thus, Hillary chose to explain the opposition she attracted by portraying herself as a symbol of progressive social change. "I know I'm the projection for many . . . wounded men," she told Gail Sheehy in an interview after the 1994 election. "I'm the boss they never wanted to have. I'm the wife who went back to school and got an extra degree and a job as good as theirs. I'm the daughter who they never wanted to turn out to be so independent. It's not me, personally, they hate—it's the changes I represent."

Conveniently, this argument shifted criticism for the defeat of health care reform away from Hillary and onto larger social transformations sweeping the country. As she observed in *Living History*, "While Bill talked about social change, I embodied it." Hillary elaborated this focus on gender as the primary agent in these political developments during a speech she gave in India a year later. Quoting from a poem by a woman student in New Delhi, she said: "When a woman gives her love, as most do generously, it is accepted. When a woman shares her thoughts, as some women do, graciously, it is allowed. When a woman fights for power, as all women would like to, quietly or loudly, it is questioned . . . Yes, there must be freedom, if we are to speak. And yes, there must be power, if we are to be heard. And when we have both [freedom and power], let us not be misunderstood." Through such quiet pondering, Hillary helped point to the tectonic shifts occurring in women's roles in the world. In such moments, the angry, defiant Hillary became someone to empathize with and talk to, not yell at.[49]

But the angry, defiant Hillary was the person most people saw, the person who dominated daily life at the White House. One aide who served throughout the nineties believed that Hillary had been unhappy most of her life. She reserved a particular kind of wrath for herself for the compromises she had permitted herself to make. In this person's view, the culture of the nation's capital simply compounded the anger, intensifying her sense of isolation. Betsey Wright, who knew the Clintons better than almost anyone, believed the real source of Hillary's anger was not Bill—she had, after all, married him knowing he was a philanderer—but rather the fact that people in Washington dared to question her personal integrity. Her whole life had been lived in dedication to the social precepts of the Methodist church and the commitment to serve people that she had learned at the feet of Don Jones. Now she felt under "siege," her very character under assault by a Washington culture that seemed bereft of anything moral or decent.[50]

Whatever the combination, the ingredients had all come together to create a profound imbalance between the president and the First Lady. Their personal relationship extended to the worlds they controlled inside the White House. In the state of perpetual war that existed between Bill's staff and hers, she more often came out on top, berating Bill's advisers as second-class and immature while praising hers as devoted and disciplined. The same divisions occurred over the public policy issues they faced, and on the two most critical ones— health care and Whitewater—Hillary held sway. When David Gergen had persuaded nearly every political adviser that it was necessary to turn over the Whitewater records to *The Washington Post*, Hillary demurred, and Bill Clinton never raised a peep. When, repeatedly, senators from Chafee to Moynihan pleaded with the White House to back off from 100 percent health care coverage and accept 95 percent as a viable first step, the president showed interest, but then Hillary quickly intervened. "If the shadow of his past had not hung over his relationship with his wife," David Gergen wrote, "[Clinton could] have passed a bipartisan reform plan."

The mistakes were horrendous. And the dynamic of their relationship was responsible. Stan Greenberg reported in 1994 that focus groups had concluded that Bill was "over his head," "indecisive," "immature." Hillary, by contrast, had a stronger self-image. As Dick Morris observed, "the more powerful she seemed, the weaker he seemed."[51]

In areas where Hillary played little role and claimed no stake, Bill distinguished himself by decisive thinking. In early January, Robert Rubin, one of his top economic advisers, came to the president to tell him that the Mexican peso was about to implode. Engulfed by debt, the state treasury was teetering on collapse. If Clinton did not act immediately and bail out Mexican banks with billions of dollars of emergency relief, the whole continent—and potentially the world's economy—would fall apart. Within minutes, Clinton had mastered the economics of the situation and made a decision. At whatever risk, the United States must act, immediately and aggressively. Alerting all the key congressional figures, Clinton proceeded to intervene, single-handedly resolving the crisis.

Similarly, Clinton—against all odds and the overwhelming sentiment of the American people—chose to prepare, then launch, an invasion of Haiti in the fall of 1994 to return Jean-Bertrand Aristide, the elected president of the country, to power. Once more, Clinton made the hard decision. In the end, he was assisted by a last-minute mission to Port-au-Prince by the former president Jimmy Carter, Senator Sam Nunn, and General Colin Powell. But the military commander who had taken control in a coup d'état decided to leave the country only after learning that the invasion force had been launched. Two episodes, two decisive actions, two bold exercises of presidential power—both enormously successful.

But on the far more sensitive issues of health care reform and Whitewater, Clinton proved unable and unwilling to exercise independent power. He was entrapped in a cage of his own making. By the terms of the partnership he had negotiated, on these two issues, the most critical for his entire early administration, he would defer to Hillary's judgment. The results were disastrous.

Bill Clinton had been there before. Few had given him a chance to come back as governor of Arkansas after 1980. When Gennifer Flowers and the draft scandal hit the headlines in early 1992, most considered him dead in the water. Bill Clinton had political skills that no one else could touch. And Hillary had been instrumental in every success he had achieved. Could they do it again? Time would tell.

TEN

Comeback Number Three

Following the stunning defeats of 1994, the president and First Lady reevaluated their respective political roles. They backed off from visionary legislative goals and instead pursued "niche" reforms, geared to satisfy well-defined constituencies. Rather than challenge traditional values, they worked hard to place themselves within the cultural mainstream, whether the issue was gender roles or fiscal conservatism. If they did not engage in a total remake—an explicit rejection of what they had advocated before—they came close, and the result was a near-miraculous political recovery.

Appropriately, this shift reflected a pattern from the past. After the Arkansas defeat of 1980, a similar reassessment occurred. Then, too, Bill Clinton was depressed, immobilized, and lost. Then, as well, the interior dynamic of their relationship needed radical reshifting. Once again, Bill's parallel lives posed a pivotal challenge, as did how Hillary would respond. In the months after the 1980 election, Bill and Hillary had reengaged rather than withdrawing, full of ideas for how to hone their political strategy and modify their legislative objectives. Now, once more, they faced a similar test. The 1994 election had shaken the administration to the core. Neither oblivious nor indifferent, Bill and Hillary were committed to recovering their lost momentum. They were willing to try new patterns—at least for a while. Self-preservation required it. So did their common dream as partners to change the world. Whether older patterns would reassert themselves would only be evident if and when the listing ship was righted.

The crucial point of continuity between 1980 and 1994 was Dick Morris, the New York–born political operative who had redefined

Clinton in 1980, forced him to "apologize" to Arkansas voters, and molded his stunning electoral victory in 1982. Now the First Lady turned once again to Morris. Soon he became the most powerful—and controversial—figure in White House councils. A careful strategy evolved, remarkably similar to that which Morris had developed in Arkansas fourteen years earlier.

For the first few months of 1995, a ghostly presence wandered the halls of the White House, exercising mysterious powers. It would appear in pages of manuscript the president took out of a manila folder and handed to his speechwriter to incorporate in a speech he was about to make. Or in a meeting, when a secretary appeared to tell Clinton "Charlie's on the phone." To the press office, there seemed an apparent disjuncture. First, there would appear a press release they had seen before as it went through drafts and redrafts in the hands of Clinton's staff. Then a totally new set of paragraphs would suddenly emerge, saying much more conservative things—things such as "We must not ask the government to do what we should do for ourselves." Where had *that* come from?[1]

Initially, the Clintons intended that the mystery of "Charlie" continue. Hillary had always disliked Bill's staff, denigrating their unreliability and penchant for leaking to the press. More recently, Bill had adopted her critical approach as his own. On more than one occasion he attributed the disastrous election defeat to the fact that he had a bunch of "immature" kids running his office. Clinton's unease with his staff became evident when in June 1994 he replaced Mack McLarty as chief of staff with Leon Panetta, head of the Office of Management and Budget. While Clinton never would blame McLarty, his boyhood friend, for any of his early mistakes, he had finally recognized the need for more toughness in the West Wing. Panetta was a huge improvement, yet in the eyes of both Clintons, too many of the old "campaign heads" were still running around on their own, pushing liberal Democratic ideas at a time when Clinton was leaning more and more toward a return to his "New Democrat" days.

Hillary made the first call to Morris. They had always been close, much closer than the president and Morris had been. Morris agreed to her terms. His role would remain a secret. He would come to the White House late at night. No records would be kept. When he called, it would be as "Charlie." From the beginning, Al Gore was in on the secret. He approved, as long as his own priorities were protected. "We need a change around here," Gore noted to Morris, "a big change, and I'm hoping and praying that you're the man to bring it." The president agreed, of course. The result was the existence of two White Houses from December to April, one representing a continuation of the staff and ideas that had prevailed in the West Wing for the first two years, the other a radically different White House with a dramatically different strategy, worldview, and style. As George Stephanopoulos later wrote, "The President had engaged [Dick Morris] to run a covert operation against his own White House—a commander's coup against the colonels." The result was bewilderment among those people caught in the middle.[2]

Eventually, of course, the truth emerged. Panetta had no stomach for deception, or for what it signified for his own authority. More to the point, Morris's personality almost immediately divided people into camps, with virtually everyone opposed to him. Imperious, egotistical, and domineering, Morris acted as though no one else in the room had the right to voice an opinion. Indeed, many noted that Bill Clinton, for all his tremendous grasp of politics and policy, became strangely silent when Dick Morris occupied center stage. To many, Morris's presence represented the antithesis of what they envisioned government to be about. Harold Ickes, Morris's old nemesis from West Side New York politics, noted that Morris "*is* the underside of politics." John Harris, a reporter for *The Washington Post*, had a complementary but even deeper insight. Morris, he said, was a "living extension . . . of Clinton's realism . . . Their collaboration carried an aroma almost of prostitution . . . at once intimate and impersonal, driven by mutual need with an overlay of shame." That was perhaps the reason that Clinton barely mentioned Morris in his memoir and only rarely acknowledged the relationship in his lengthy interviews with his old comrade Taylor Branch, in which, theoretically, he let out his innermost thoughts.

Another reason for the embarrassment was that in the years after Morris had worked with Bill Clinton in Arkansas, virtually all his clients had been Republicans. At the time that he responded to Hillary's phone call, Morris was the chief political adviser to Trent Lott, soon to be the Republican majority leader in the Senate. ("Hell," Lott told Morris, "you'll run the White House and I'll run the Senate . . . But don't ask me to get mixed up with his wife.") Morris even bragged about his role in defeating Democrats. When asked about the infamous Willie Horton ad in 1988 that suggested Michael Dukakis was responsible for the rape of a white grandmother by a black criminal, Morris gleefully announced: "I wrote it." Almost no one in the Clinton White House had a good word to say about Morris.[3]

Once Morris's presence was known, therefore, it was inevitable that an all-out civil war would erupt between Clinton's staff, led by Stephanopoulos, and Morris's people. In Morris's view, most of the Clinton people were proceeding as though the election of 1994 had never happened. Together with liberal Democrats in the Senate and House, they intended to "push on" with the already existing agenda, not even acknowledging the need to move toward the middle. But following Hillary's lead, Clinton had become more and more disenchanted with Stephanopoulos. He blamed Stephanopoulos for a West Wing culture that produced massive leaks to the press, and he was particularly angry at him for providing much of the background interview material for Bob Woodward's searing portrayal of chaos in the White House during Clinton's first year in his book *The Agenda*. Leon Panetta shared Clinton's unease with Stephanopoulos's excesses, but also worried deeply about Morris's influence, denouncing his "cynical ethic of expediency." Panetta was profoundly offended that Clinton seemed willing to turn over executive policy making to this two-bit political consultant (who worked for Republicans, no less). Panetta threw down the gauntlet, letting Clinton know in late spring that he would resign before accepting Morris's dictates. "I'm an adult human being," Panetta told Clinton, "and I'm not going to take this squirt running around, gumming up the works."[4]

In classic Clinton fashion, the president rendered a split decision that allowed each protagonist to feel vindicated. He embraced Morris's overall advice that he move toward the center. "[I know] Dick can be pushy," Clinton said, "very pushy . . . [But] he knows my thinking, and he knows what I want . . . He and I have a track record together. I need to throw long, Leon. We've got a lot of yardage to make up here, and I've got to throw long. I'm bringing Dick in to throw long, and I need you to help him." But at the same time, Clinton made crystal clear that Morris had to work through Panetta, not go around him. Panetta was in charge, he was the chief of staff, and if Morris wished his advice to become policy, he must respect that line of authority. Panetta, who more than Stephanopoulos recognized the need for a change in political direction, accepted Clinton's Solomon-like judgment. Determined that Morris would never again try to step around him, he required that Morris secure his permission before speaking to any other members of the White House staff. Shortly thereafter, Morris struck a similar deal with Stephanopoulos. Morris and Stephanopoulos would talk each day (often several times), reconcile their opposing political strategies, and work as partners to promote the Clinton comeback.[5]

With order at least partially restored, Clinton proceeded to implement the comeback strategy that he and Morris had devised. At the heart of the effort were two words: "centrism" and "triangulation." Throughout his career, Bill Clinton had been more a "New Democrat" than an old one. His decades-old emphasis on "opportunity, responsibility, community" highlighted his profound commitment to traditional values of individualism and personal responsibility. If every person enjoyed the opportunity to realize their potential and accepted the responsibility to redeem their obligations, the community that resulted would benefit everyone. Hence, Clinton (and Morris) saw nothing to be gained by demonizing Gingrich's "Contract with America." Many of its ideas, such as fiscal responsibility and welfare reform, were at the heart of Clinton's own platform, as reflected in his deficit reduction package and the study group he had set up on welfare reform at the very inception of his administration. Rather than denounce Republican ideas, therefore, Clinton moved to embrace those parts of their agenda that he agreed with while highlighting only those parts he found unacceptable, such as Medicare cuts. Of course, Clinton opposed the part of the "Contract with America" that most Americans also opposed. No one wanted to cut Medicare, young or old. As Morris wrote to Clinton, "Medicare cuts are your single biggest weapons against the Republicans. They are hated by the public." If by deed as well as word Clinton moved toward the center, he would reestablish credibility, deprive Gingrich and the right of an easy foil, and put in place the ingredients for a stunning political comeback.

In fact, the move to the center was nothing new. As early as a re-treat of academics that Clinton had convened in January 1994, every-one present embraced the strategy of having Clinton deliver on small things like more police on the street, better schools, and more efficient government. They even saw a parallel with the New Deal, in which big reforms like Social Security were accompanied by "a lot of small things." In this instance, health care was the biggie. But the small things would also count. "The administration should foster more realistic expecta-tions, even as it pursues its big agenda," the academics concluded. This was, of course, before health care reform cratered. Still, it suggested that a focus on microreforms was not new in the Clinton lexicon.[6]

Yet if adopting the rhetoric of centrism was not new, it offered an extraordinarily effective way to dilute the impact of Republican victo-ries. Perhaps most important, practicing the politics of triangulation offered a critical means for making the Republicans look obstructionist while advancing the president's agenda. What was triangulation? In Morris's words, it meant creating a "third position, not just in between the old positions of the two parties, but above them as well." If Clinton could parse the differences between Republican and Democratic ideas and make the new option uniquely his, then he would create a new constituency, centrist in nature but drawing from both the left and the right. As one example, if the Republicans favored cutting taxes for everyone and the Democrats opposed cutting taxes for anyone, Clinton might argue for targeted tax cuts. He could propose a tax deduction for a family that had a child going to college, or was buying a first home, or investing in a retirement account. Each such tax cut would appeal to a broad base, fall within the "opportunity-responsibility-community" ru-bric, and yet take advantage of ideas that both Republicans and Demo-crats could endorse. As Clinton and Morris worked it out, such policies of triangulation fit together beautifully under a new label: a *middle-class bill of rights* that could become the hallmark of the Clinton admin-istration. It was not a New Deal, nor a Great Society. Such big initiatives were no longer viable. Instead, Clinton chose to move "quietly, patiently, and very, very deftly" to create a base for recovering his political legi-timacy. "It was," Joe Klein noted, "an astonishing, if subtle, display of political virtuosity."[7]

Central to the entire Morris-Clinton approach was the sophisticated use of polling and targeted advertising. With a team led by Mark Penn and Doug Schoen, Morris polled the living daylights out of every question on the national agenda. Each night, he and his colleagues would tweak the wording of the questions they asked until they found a formulation that served their political ends. What might happen if the term "middle-class" were inserted in front of the phrase "tax cuts," for example, in terms of voter response? By zeroing in on diverse niche constituencies, it was possible to identify a series of issues on which a highly focused presidential initiative might produce a sizable electoral dividend. Soon, the whole approach had become de rigueur in the Clinton White House. As George Stephanopolous later noted, "during the Morris era, it seemed more and more as if we were polling first, proposing later."[8]

Morris also persuaded Clinton to embark on a series of targeted advertising initiatives that would nurture, over time, a constituency in key states. Morris had done the same thing in Arkansas after 1980, marketing TV ads in which Clinton apologized for his mistakes and thereby neutralized opposition allegations against him. Now, once again using polling data on phrases and concepts that voters responded positively to, he devised a series of ads that could be shown in key swing states such as Washington, Colorado, and New Mexico. Functioning "under the radar," these ads cultivated core constituencies in pivotal states, even though they were ignored by the opposition since they did not play in major media markets. But the end result was that they created a favorable audience for 1996. By the time the election came around, opinion surveys showed Clinton doing far better in states where the ads had run than in comparable states where they had not.[9]

By the late spring of 1995, then, Dick Morris and Bill Clinton had thoroughly refashioned the president's political profile. Returning to his pre-presidential determination to redefine the Democratic message, Clinton now totally embraced the centrist ideology of the New Democrats. With difficulty, but great skill, Clinton resolved the poisonous staff tensions that had accompanied the introduction of Dick Morris into the world of White House politics. By the summer of 1995, Bill Clinton had reasserted political control over his administration. As the pendulum swung in his direction, it moved away from Hillary.

The First Lady, of course, had been the one to call Morris, hoping that in 1995, as in 1981, he could provide the foundation for a political revival by her husband. But ironically—and perhaps not unexpectedly, from her point of view—one of the glaring things Morris discovered in his polling about Bill Clinton's unpopularity was that Hillary was the main problem. This came as no surprise to most people around Clinton, who for months had bemoaned Hillary's tactics and the president's refusal to call her to task for her political blunders. But it meant that one of Morris's first pieces of advice to the First Couple was that Hillary carve out a new role for herself and cease to be copresident.[10]

Hillary had already recognized the problem. After her devastating defeat in health care, 54 percent of Americans disapproved of her. "She literally withdrew," Harold Ickes observed. "I mean you just didn't even see her . . . Even I, who was as close to her as anybody on the President's staff, hardly saw her at all . . . I don't know what she was thinking. It must have been a stinging time . . . She didn't [even] talk to the White House staff." When Panetta first came on board as chief of staff, she insisted on meeting with him once a week. So intimidated was he by her authority that he prepared for those meetings more carefully than for any others. But then she said the meetings were no longer necessary. Similarly, once the election was over and the White House started weekly Wednesday-night strategy sessions with Gore, Morris, and others, the First Lady dropped out. It was as though a funeral shroud had dropped over the First Lady and her staff. "The trauma of the '94 defeat was so profound," Bill Curry, a White House aide, observed, "[that] no one even wanted to [hold] a meeting about health care." Gail Sheehy, who interviewed Hillary in early 1995, believed that her "season of despair" lasted for a full nine months.[11]

As though she were following literally Dick Morris's advice to carve out a new role for herself that was more acceptable to the American people, Hillary gave a series of interviews depicting herself as the quintessential supportive wife. "My first responsibility," she told *Newsweek* magazine in a February 1995 interview, "is to do whatever my husband would want me to do that he thinks would be helpful to him . . . Whatever it takes to be there for him . . . It may be something of great moment, but more likely it's just to kick back, have a conversation or even play a game of cards and listen to him ruminate . . ." The Hillary Clinton of one year earlier saying such things beggars the imagination. It was all reminiscent of the *Life with Father* episode in which the wife—when asked whether she has ever regretted not pursuing a career—tells her woman doctor friend (unmarried) that no, her entire life has been blessed by serving her husband. It was as if Hillary were embracing exactly the perspective that she had devoted her entire life to repudiating.[12]

In truth, she was confused—miserably so. "You know," she told Dick Morris in a more accurate reflection of her state of mind, "I just don't know what works anymore. I mean everything we're trying is screwed up. I just don't know how to do it." Entering a phase of reflection, self-examination, and repositioning, Hillary no longer automatically embraced the role of copresident. Rather she had become at best a junior partner, searching for some answers in a world that had been blown to smithereens.[13]

The First Lady's activities during the ensuing months reflected her quest, sometimes halting, to find a new voice and a more comfortable stance. For the first time, she traveled alone as First Lady to foreign countries, touring Denmark, India, Nepal, Pakistan, and Sri Lanka with Chelsea. Beginning with her appearance at the U.N. World Summit for Social Development in Copenhagen, Hillary focused primarily on human rights, particularly those of women and children. The same emphasis persisted through her tour of South Asia. It also dominated many of her activities at home. She inaugurated the Mother Teresa Home for children in Washington, D.C., spoke out against Newt Gingrich's call for more orphanages as "big government interference," and strongly endorsed greater availability of mammograms for women. In all her work, children's rights and women's rights predominated, with a focus on sustaining the traditional social values of the family. "It is the family, it is religious belief and spirituality that guide us," she said.

Yet Hillary had not abandoned her commitment to feminism. At a Beijing international conference on women, she delivered a stirring defense of the rights of women. Walking a delicate line between intervention in Chinese domestic affairs and the embrace of universal ideals, she denounced the practice of depriving baby girls of sustenance while also criticizing the practice of genital mutilation in Africa and elsewhere.

"Human rights are women's rights," she declared to wild applause. "And women's rights are human rights, once and for all." Hillary was beginning to find her voice again.[14]

Hillary also returned to her quest for spiritual enrichment. At Renaissance Weekend, which the Clintons had attended for much of their married lives, Hillary met three women deeply engaged in New Age explorations into the life of the spirit—Marianne Williamson, who embraced the idea of women finding God through the love that existed in their own hearts; Jean Houston, who ran a foundation focused on the life of the mind; and Mary Catherine Bateson, the daughter of Margaret Mead. All were taken aback by Hillary's tormented sense of despair. They formed a bond, and Hillary arranged a retreat at Camp David at which they could probe more deeply their shared interests. There, Hillary talked about her feelings of spiritual closeness to Eleanor Roosevelt, who, like herself, struggled to be heard in a world dominated by men. She recounted conversations she had in her head with Eleanor, revolving around such queries as "How did you go on day to day, with all the attacks . . . hurled your way?" Houston encouraged Hillary to stay in spiritual touch with Eleanor, learn from her wisdom, and be sustained by her example. Returning to the spirituality rooted in her Methodist faith was one avenue Hillary was clearly willing and anxious to pursue.[15]

In many ways, the main project Hillary took on in 1995—writing her book *It Takes a Village*—encapsulated all these themes. Focused on the issue of children's nurture and development, the book argued that rearing healthy and spiritually whole young people required more than just economic security and doting parents. It took a village of concerned people engaged in one another's well-being. Working together with Barbara Feinman, a writer suggested by her publisher, Simon and Schuster, Hillary wrote pages each day in the White House living quarters. Often, it seemed as much an autobiographical exploration as a book on the well-being of children. Channeling her mother and her own marriage, Hillary argued that it was imperative that parents not take the easy way out of marital difficulties by opting for divorce. Instead, they should give marriage "their best shot." She and Bill, she pointed out, had experienced difficulties, but they had "worked hard" at holding things together and had found the rewards inestimably greater than separating. Similarly, she argued, if people wanted to create a stable society, with healthy children, they needed to "pitch in and help one another. Service is an obligation of citizenship."[16]

Ironically, in the midst of writing her paean to marriage and family, David Maraniss's book on Clinton's career prior to the White House was published and once more laid bare the tensions Bill's philandering had caused in her own marriage. Hillary exploded in fury. What angered her the most was that both Dick Morris and Betsey Wright had shared details of the Clintons' problems with Maraniss. Wright had confirmed the accuracy of all the stories about Bill's repeated sexual transgressions, and Morris had indicated that the couple had considered divorce in 1989. So upset was Hillary by the stories, Morris later said, that "she turned frosty on the president for several weeks and refused to talk to him or sleep in the same bedroom with him." For the first time, Morris said, Chelsea turned on her father. By that time, the Paula Jones lawsuit, brought by one of the people mentioned in the *American Spectator* story, had become front-page news, and the Maraniss revelations simply redoubled the tension already present in the White House. Bill was furious as well, feeling betrayed by Betsey Wright, and he and his attorney, Robert Bennett, put enormous pressure on Wright to issue a statement denying what she had actually told Maraniss. In fact, Maraniss had read to Wright the material he attributed to her, and she had confirmed its accuracy to him. The integrity of the book was never seriously questioned. Yet the entire episode attested once more to the volatility of the Clintons' relationship, and how quickly Hillary could strike fear into Bill's heart when the issue of his infidelity went public.[17]

Despite this reminder of the central dilemma their partnership faced, Hillary had nevertheless emerged during the year after the 1994 election as a different, chastened person. Rather than persisting in seeking to function as a copresident, she retreated into prolonged introspection. While her statements in early 1995 suggesting that a wife should live only to serve her husband would never be repeated, the fact that she uttered them at all spoke to how profound the shock of the preceding two years had been. In their aftermath, she had entered into a process of reevaluation, trying to figure out where to place her emphasis and refine her message. Clearly women's rights and children's rights were at the top of her list. So, too, was an international role as champion for women. Perhaps most intriguing was her reengagement with issues of the spirit. But it was all a work in progress, and, as the David Maraniss episode underscored, it could be disrupted at any minute by external events.

Bill Clinton, meanwhile, continued his own path out of despair. It was not an easy climb. For weeks after the election, Clinton remained severely depressed, sometimes slipping off to sleep in the midst of late evening interviews with Taylor Branch, sometimes launching into "towering rages" against the press and Washington insiders. His political enemies gave him cause. Jesse Helms called him "unfit" to be commander in chief, and Newt Gingrich, on *Meet the Press*, claimed that the Clintons were "counterculture McGovernites" and that up to a quarter of the White House staff had used drugs in the previous four or five years. Although the Joint Chiefs of Staff rallied to Clinton's defense to rebut Helms's charges, and Gingrich apologized, the feeling of being under siege never abated.[18]

A partial comeback started with Clinton's annual State of the Union address. These were always high points for Clinton, even when he was in the throes of profound personal and political crises. Weeks in preparation, the speeches were his time to speak directly to the American people and get his message across unimpeded by the media's interpretations. This time, unbeknownst to most of those in the White House, half of Clinton's address had been written by "Charlie"— the nom de guerre of Dick Morris. Many White House staffers hated the final product. Leon Panetta thought it was far too long, a "debacle." But the American people loved it, and those listening in the Capitol interrupted ninety-six times with applause.[19]

In fact, the speech *was* far too long. But that was because it included all the Republican-type ideas that Morris had added. Masterfully, Clinton played on the New Democrat themes of opportunity, responsibility, and community, celebrating "the values and voices that speak to our hearts as well as our heads, voices that tell us we have to do more to accept responsibility for ourselves, and our families, for our communities." Clinton boasted that America had more "houses of worship than any other country in the world," championed the role of parents as they tried "to teach their children the difference between right and wrong," and pleaded with people with different viewpoints to put the good of the whole above partisan self-interest. "The truth is," he declared, "we have got to stop seeing each other as enemies just because we have different views . . . [Our greatness] has always been our ability to associate with people different from ourselves and to work together to find common ground." Morris was flushed with satisfaction at how persuasively Clinton was implementing his advice. For the moment, Clinton was back on top.[20]

It was a brief sojourn. Despite the success of the speech itself, Gingrich remained the politician who seemed in charge in Washington. Under his leadership, the House enacted virtually all the planks of his Contract with America. The media treated him with almost deferential respect. In reality, Gingrich had a personal history almost as controversial as Clinton's. He had an affair with one of his high school teachers, and eventually married her. Subsequently, he had other sexual liaisons, including with his own staff. He divorced his former teacher, discussing the terms of their settlement in the hospital as she was recovering from cancer surgery. His second marriage was no more successful, it, too, being marred by repeated philandering. But the press paid little attention, focusing instead on Gingrich's newfound political clout. Clinton seemed almost an afterthought. When he called a mid-April press conference, only a single national network saw fit to cover it live. One reporter—reflecting the mood of the time—even dared ask Clinton whether he still felt "relevant" to what was going on in the nation's capital.[21]

The next day, the federal office building in Oklahoma City blew up, the target of a terrorist bombing. More than 160 people died, many of them children in a day care center used by federal workers. Never again would the "relevance" of Bill Clinton be questioned. Now, in a role he was almost created to play, Clinton demonstrated at each step a sensitivity, skill, and compassion that gave him command once more of the political landscape. At the retreat for academic leaders in January 1994, those present emphasized the importance of Clinton "leading a national discourse on values." Now he had his chance. "The President's religiosity is natural and integral to his role," the retreat had emphasized, and never would that be more evident than now.

Immediately, officials knew this was the work of a terrorist bomber. In light of a similar terrorist attack by Islamic extremists two years earlier at the World Trade Center in New York, it was natural for many people to assume that this, too, was the work of Muslims. But Clinton discouraged that assumption, urging people to wait until the facts were in. "This is not a question of anybody's country of origin," he said in a presidential statement. "This is not a question of anybody's religion. This was murder. This was evil. This was wrong. Human beings everywhere . . . will condemn this out of their own religious convictions." By making religious belief a vehicle for unity rather than division, Clinton had taken the first step toward focusing on those values that brought Americans of diverse faiths together in one community.[22]

Clinton's instincts were correct. The vehicle identification number of the truck containing the bomb led officials to Timothy McVeigh and Terry Nichols, two members of a Michigan militia group with more than ten thousand members. Soon a string of evidence emerged linking the two militia members to the bombing. As it turned out, the timing for the terrorist attack was no accident. The bombing occurred two years to the day after the federal raid on the Branch Davidian sect in Waco, Texas; it had been an act of revenge, by right-wing Americans, against their own government.[23]

Clinton united his fellow citizens by his personal demeanor during the crisis. Like Ronald Reagan after the *Challenger* space shuttle exploded, he became a national healer, ministering to a bereaved people. More than that, he used the occasion to bring people together with a new sense of what linked them to each other. Freely using the language of religion, he addressed the full spiritual dimensions of the attack. "This terrible sin took the lives of our American family," he told a nationally televised memorial service in Oklahoma City. But Americans should not respond with hate, but rather with love. "When there is talk of hatred, let us stand up and talk against it. In the face of death, let us honor life. As Saint Paul admonished, let us not be overcome by evil, but overcome evil with good." By using the occasion of national mourning to bring together a divided people—and then by identifying himself with those religious values he had invoked—Clinton took a giant step not just toward healing a wounded nation, but toward placing himself at the center of the healing process. "For the first time in a long time,"

Cabinet Secretary Henry Cisneros noted, "people really . . . connected with the president, and what he was trying to do." More than 84 percent of Americans approved of Clinton's response.[24]

Clinton did not let the moment pass. Instead, he seized on it to drive home the message of opposing extremism. It was not an easy decision. There were risks in taking on the right wing. But Clinton sensed that momentum was on his side. Thus, at the University of Iowa, he urged his fellow citizens to stand up against incendiary rhetoric. "Words have consequences," he declared. "To pretend they do not is idle." And in a University of Michigan commencement address, he confronted directly the right-wing conservatives who had fed on him for two years. "If you say violence is an acceptable way to make change, you are wrong," he declared. "If you say government is a conspiracy to take your freedom away, you are just plain wrong . . . I say to you . . . there is nothing patriotic about hating your country, or pretending that you can love your country but despise your government." With a rising level of confidence, Clinton had decided to engage his political foes directly.[25]

This was where the Morris strategy of triangulation came into play. Clinton had already established the framework for his new initiatives in an April 1995 education speech in which he rejected the "old labels of liberal and conservative" and declared that "what matters most is finding practical, pragmatic solutions . . . We have to stop pointing fingers at each other so we can join hands." Now he moved to demonstrate what he meant. As part of their promise to trim government spending, Republicans had proposed cutting 15,000 AmeriCorps positions, eliminating funding for 1.2 million summer jobs for young people, and cutting school lunch and infant nutrition programs. It was a political gift. Safely, he could pledge to veto what seemed like mean-spirited Republican initiatives. But at the same time, Clinton proposed a series of his own small-bore programs. While Republicans were taking aim at school lunches, Clinton was advocating more money for mammograms for middle-aged women to protect against breast cancer, Alzheimer's programs for the elderly suffering from dementia, and tax breaks for parents sending a child to college.

The new Clinton approach was clever. It isolated his Republican foes, making them look like nasty penny-pinchers going after programs like nutrition for children, while allowing his own team to look like reasonable, fiscally responsible incrementalists, making small changes that would benefit core constituencies and support programs widely valued by the American people. Under Morris's guidance, each idea was tested in polls to see which would garner the most support, and again and again, Clinton took a middle position. After engaging in a well-publicized review of affirmative action programs, for example, Clinton acknowledged the concerns that many Americans had expressed about racial favoritism in hiring processes. But in the end he pointed to the many benefits that affirmative action had produced. The way to proceed, he concluded, was to "'mend it, but don't end it.'" Throughout, these middle-of-the-road positions garnered significant support. As his press secretary, Mike McCurry, noted, the new Clinton approach might not be "the New Deal, but it ain't bad."[26]

In the meantime, a debate raged within the administration. Should Clinton just let the Republicans implode, destroying themselves with their efforts to roll back popular programs? Or should the president launch his own proposals for reform, consistent with Republican ideas, but allowing the administration to preempt and control the political debate? It was not a simple question. Indeed, the divisions inside the White House highlighted ongoing questions about Clinton's political character, and his definition of what it meant to be a New Democrat.

Most of the older White House staff favored doing nothing and letting the Republicans commit hara-kiri. By all accounts, the American people were not impressed with Republican proposals for slashing the budget. Moreover, Democratic leaders of the House and Senate, not ready to jettison traditional Democratic programs, were adamantly opposed to having Clinton propose his own plan for a balanced budget. As one White House staffer said, "They will go ballistic on the hill." The House leader, Richard Gephardt, even refused to take Clinton's phone call, which led Clinton to call him "an asshole." Dick Morris, of course, was on the other side. He argued that according to the polls (the polls, again!), most Americans did not believe that Clinton favored a balanced budget. To build on the gains he was making in his own credibility ratings with the American public, Morris contended, the president had to convince them.[27]

That left it up to Clinton. There should never have been any doubt. When the chief of staff, Erskine Bowles, asked Clinton directly what

his plan was, the president told him. Bowles, in turn, told Stephanopoulos: "Damn it, George, the President has made a decision. He
wants a ten-year budget. Let's give it to him." To people like Robert
Reich, the decision was a "cave-in that brings us halfway down the slippery slope. Bill has thrown in the towel." In truth, Clinton had always
wanted to get out in front, to control the debate. What better way to do
that than give a major speech where he came out for his own specific
plan for balancing the budget? In doing so, he could make a credible
case for his commitment to fiscal responsibility while at the same time
assuring people that he intended to save the vital social programs they
had come to count on. In fact, the two proposals were quite similar.
The Republicans proposed to balance the budget in seven years, Clinton in ten. The difference lay in what would get lost. The Republican
path to ending deficits meant stark blows to programs such as job training, Medicare, and education, while Clinton promised to keep those
programs intact while moving forward on additional reforms such as
wider availability of mammograms. Speaking in Philadelphia on June
13, 1995, Clinton dazzled his audience with the power of his presentation while dramatizing the gap between the two parties' approach. The
gist of his message: "They don't [really] want to balance the budget;
that's just an excuse. What they . . . really, really want is to end all
middle-class entitlements." By his own proposals, Morris said, "Clinton
had taken away the Republican camouflage." Joe Klein agreed. The
June speech was a turning point.[28]

The stage was thus set for the budget showdown of 1995. Neither
side was totally united. Many Democrats in the White House—and in
Congress—were convinced that if the Republicans applied enough
pressure, Clinton would cave. Hence, they went out of their way to
avoid circumstances in which Clinton might be alone with his legislative adversaries, lest his instinct for conciliation take control. Republicans also experienced deep divisions. Bob Dole was ready on numerous
occasions to make a deal. But Gingrich and his chief aides, who had
ridden to power on an ideological wave of polarization, seemed incapa-
ble of pulling back from confrontation. Thus the die was cast.

The first clash began in October. Dole and Gingrich refused to act
on any of the thirteen budget bills pending in Congress that were required to continue running the government. Based on the assumption

that Clinton would give in, Gingrich demanded cuts in Medicare and Medicaid. Panetta and Clinton made a partial concession, agreeing to minimal cuts if the Republicans would pass a budget. Dole was willing to go along, but Gingrich insisted on total capitulation and threatened to shut the government down. Angrily, Clinton refused.[29]

In the midst of the showdown, word reached the White House that Yitzhak Rabin had been assassinated in Jerusalem by a right-wing Jewish extremist. No world leader meant more to Clinton. As one reporter said, "Clinton was as stricken as subordinates had ever seen him." The president wept openly and immediately called Hillary, who came downstairs to his office. The two held each other as they mourned the loss of one of their greatest friends. "By the time he was killed," Bill later wrote, "I had come to love him as I had rarely loved another man." Bill and Hillary immediately left for the funeral, where Clinton made one of the most eloquent speeches of his life in praise of his "dear friend," using exactly the right Hebrew phrase, which moved millions of Israelis to tears.

The Clintons had taken congressional leaders with them on *Air Force One* as part of the funeral delegation, including Gingrich and Dole. When the plane landed back in Washington, the two Republicans left by a rear exit. Two days later, Gingrich went on national television to complain. The president, he said, had refused to talk with them during the trip and forced them to leave from the back of the plane. "Shoddy" was a gentle word for Gingrich's performance. The White House soon displayed photographs of Clinton talking with Gingrich and Dole on the plane. Reporters already knew that it was simple protocol that only the presidential party exited *Air Force One* through the forward door. Commenting on the Speaker's behavior, the Democratic congresswoman Patricia Schroeder of Colorado observed that Gingrich had "sewn up the category of best performance by a child actor this year. There's only one problem. The Speaker is not a child."[30]

Back in Washington, the budget crisis came to a head. When the Republican Congress passed a balanced budget bill that included the cuts Gingrich had demanded, Clinton vetoed it on November 13, 1995. He was willing to compromise on particulars, Clinton said, but not at the expense of denying 380,000 children access to Head Start programs, drastically cutting the college loan program, or slashing Medicaid and Medicare. Immediately, the government was forced to shut down. Hundreds of thousands of employees were put out of work, Social Security and Medicare payments held up. Morris continued with his polling. Every day the president's figures climbed while Gingrich's spiraled downward. Clinton especially gained credibility because he defended Medicare while Gingrich was telling reporters that Medicare would "wither on the vine" and Dole boasted that he had voted against its establishment in 1965. Soon public pressure forced a temporary solution. The government reopened six days later on a monthlong continuing resolution financing its operations.[31]

Still the Republicans refused to compromise. Pressured by the ideologues in their own ranks to do nothing that would help Clinton, and hopeful that he might yet choose to cave, they once more demanded cuts in Medicare and Medicaid as the price for passing a budget. "You've got to understand," the House majority whip, Tom DeLay, said, "we are ideologues. We have an agenda. We have a philosophy." Though other House lieutenants including John Boehner told the Speaker, "Newt, this isn't going to work," Gingrich persisted. Clinton announced to reporters that he had cut off negotiations. "They said they would not even continue to talk unless we agreed right now to make deep and unconscionable cuts in Medicare and Medicaid. That's unacceptable." It was a poker hand hard to beat. Howard Kurtz, a *Washington Post* columnist, observed that "Gingrich might be *Time* [magazine's] man of the year, but he looks like the thug of the week." It was almost unimaginable how the events that had started in Oklahoma City had transformed the political equation. For the first four months of 1995, Newt Gingrich had been king of the hill. Now he was the "Gingrich who stole Christmas." Although the government shut down once more for two weeks over the holidays, it opened up again after the first of the year, this time with fifty-four Republicans abandoning their leader to end the shutdown. As Dick Morris observed, "most people don't commit suicide twice, but Gingrich did."[32]

To an observer from another planet, it would have been almost impossible to comprehend the shift that had taken place in the political climate in the nine months since the press conference in April at which Clinton had been asked if he was "still relevant." By January, polls showed that the American people viewed Clinton as better, on both balancing the budget and fighting crime, than the Republicans. Clinton's approval rating hovered around 60 percent—the same as Gingrich's disapproval rating. Nothing displayed the impact external events could have on America's political process better than the Oklahoma City terrorist attack. Bill Clinton, however, had been ready to respond. With the tactical arrows of Dick Morris in his quiver, he moved to unite the country around traditional spiritual values that brought people together. At the same time, he inaugurated a series of microreforms, from school uniforms to college tuition tax benefits, that appealed to wide swaths of the citizenry. "Triangulation" became a new buzzword in America's political vocabulary. No one could gainsay either the impact of the external events or the brilliance of Clinton's political response. But in the end it had been the self-inflicted wounds of the Republicans that restored Clinton to a place of primacy.[33]

The problem that would not go away was Whitewater. No matter how the White House bobbed and weaved, or Hillary Clinton engaged in obfuscation to deny her involvement in anything illegal, the questions kept coming.

Although Hillary clearly spent much of 1995 intensely reexamining her political priorities, her spiritual needs, and her role as a woman, she seems never to have entertained second thoughts about her Whitewater stance. "If we [give in on] this," she told one aide, "then they're going to [ask for something else], you know, fuck 'em." Although in her memoir she suggested that she had little to do with the Whitewater response team, in fact she ran it from the beginning. "Hillary was clearly orchestrating it," said one lawyer on her legal team. "She was the conductor of it." Each day she convened a conference call with Jane Sherburne, Mark Fabiani, David Kendall, and political aides. Frequently, according to Fabiani, she ended up screaming about what was in the newspapers. She was particularly intent on devising a plan to attack *The Washington Post*. That effort, Fabiani noted, "went fairly far down the road before some of us succeeded in stopping it." As usual, Hillary did not take well to people pushing back. "A lot of times it felt like she was going to eat you alive," Fabiani said. In the eyes of at least some, Hillary was tone-deaf as well as stubborn on Whitewater. "We had a joke," Fabiani said, "that all we had to do was ask her, 'What would you do?' and then do just the opposite . . . because almost always her instincts were wrong, backwards."[34]

Kenneth Starr refused to leave any lead unexplored. Deeply suspicious of Hillary's evasiveness, he tried every method possible to bring more pressure on the Clintons. At this point, his emphasis was more on Hillary than on Bill, with her legal records the pot at the end of the rainbow. Starr indicted Susan McDougal and her husband, Jim, in the summer of 1995, seeking to turn them into witnesses against Hillary. Starr also probed other avenues of vulnerability, using threatened indictments against David Hale, the Little Rock promoter, to induce negative testimony against the Clintons. Starr even extended his multi-front offensive to the White House, reopening the investigation on Vincent Foster's death even though Robert Fiske, his predecessor in the special prosecutor's office, had already declared unequivocally that Foster had committed suicide. Hillary remained intent on resisting at all costs.[35]

But by the late fall and winter of 1995–96, the pressure on Hillary ratcheted up to a new level. Senator Alphonse D'Amato, a deeply partisan New York Republican, had initiated hearings in the summer on all aspects of Whitewater, including the records removed from Vince Foster's office. The tone was confrontational, the questions often framed with a presumption of guilt. The White House did not help itself, first claiming to have released all the documents on the Clintons' finances only to subsequently acknowledge that David Kendall had withheld papers showing that the Clintons' losses on Whitewater were far less than previously stated. The withheld documents also contained a note, in Vince Foster's handwriting, that Whitewater was a "can of worms you shouldn't open." Once again, charges of a White House cover-up gained credibility, while attention focused even more fiercely on the First Lady.[36]

Two events at the turn of the year shattered any remnants of calm in the White House. On December 29, the Whitewater legal team discovered a memo written by David Watkins that documented in devastating detail Hillary's leadership role in the Travelgate firings. Then, just four days later, Carolyn Huber, of the First Lady's personal White House staff, "discovered" in the White House living quarters the billing records from Hillary's time at the Rose law firm that had long since been subpoenaed but could not be located at the time. The possibility that Hillary Clinton might well be indicted for obstruction of justice became increasingly likely, even from the perspective of White House officials.

Watkins, a former member of Foster's staff, had written his memo as a kind of "soul-cleansing—my first attempt to be sure the record is straight, something I have not done in previous conversations . . . where I have been as protective and vague as possible." His clear intent was to come clean, to escape the burden of guilt incurred by having earlier been part of the effort to obscure any role Hillary might have played in the firings. Not only did Watkins confirm that the second floor of the White House residence had actively participated in Travelgate; he went on to say that Hillary herself had stated that there would be "hell to pay" if people in Foster's office did not "take swift and decisive action in conformity with the First Lady's wishes." In light of the White House's earlier complete denials of Hillary's involvement, the memo was dynamite, and on January 3, 1996, it was turned over to the D'Amato committee.[37]

The very next day, Huber disclosed her discovery of the Rose law firm billing records. To many, the timing seemed hardly coincidental. Maggie Williams, Hillary's chief of staff, had already spent hours testifying before the D'Amato committee, denying that she had been involved in taking Hillary's records from Foster's office on the night of his death. A Secret Service agent on duty that evening testified that he had seen Williams carrying folders out of Foster's office around 11:00 p.m. Still, it was clear that the billing records were part of the "personal" papers turned over at some point to the Clintons under attorney-client privilege. Then they had disappeared—until Huber "rediscovered" them. They had been "misplaced," Huber said, and were found only when some furniture was moved from her office. In the view of many, the discovery of the Watkins memo had helped "focus" Huber's search. The story got even more complicated when it was revealed that David Kendall had come to see the records immediately upon their discovery but led Jane Sherburne, his colleague, to believe that he was seeing them for the first time five hours later when he went with her to assess the documents.[38]

Depending on how the billing records were interpreted, they either buttressed Hillary's claim to have been only minimally involved in

Whitewater-related matters or demonstrated that she had been a great deal more involved than she had ever acknowledged. To start with, she had billed for sixty hours of work, including more than thirty conferences and phone calls on fifty-three different days. Essentially, that added up to an hour per week over a year. More to the point, the records indicated that she had done substantial work on Castle Grande, a sham real estate deal orchestrated by Madison Guaranty Savings and Loan that involved Webb Hubbell's father-in-law, Seth Ward. Hillary had told Barbara Walters that she "never did work for Castle Grande," but billing records documented fourteen meetings or conversations with Ward. The later disclaimer that she knew the deal under a name other than Castle Grande was less than persuasive. If the billing records contained no smoking gun, they did suggest that Hillary's involvement was far greater than she had claimed and that there were details of the Castle Grande deal that might not easily pass an ethics test.[39]

It was not surprising, then, that in January, Kenneth Starr subpoenaed the First Lady to appear before the federal grand jury impaneled in Washington, D.C., to investigate Whitewater. Starr and his team had become convinced, not without reason, that Hillary had sought to conceal or obscure evidence that had been in Foster's possession when he died and that might be relevant to Whitewater. William Safire, a former speechwriter for Spiro Agnew and then a New York Times columnist, had written that the First Lady was a "congenital liar." Although the D'Amato hearings arguably turned out to be more helpful than harmful to Hillary—most people felt that the Republicans had been unfair in their questioning—the fact was that Whitewater remained a daily item in the news, and speculation mounted that Starr would try to indict the First Lady. "When I say there was a serious fear that she would be indicted," Mark Fabiani recalled, "I can't overstate that." The First Lady had orchestrated everything after Foster's death, including "what you are going to do with the documents, and who's going to search the office . . . [And] then she had denied it." That, in conjunction with the lost billing records, provided the basis for a charge of obstructing justice.[40]

Just as Bill Clinton was garnering kudos for his amazing political comeback, therefore, the First Family was quaking in the face of a Ken Starr onslaught that had a good chance of ending in an indictment of

Hillary Clinton. Once subpoenaed, she was shaken to the core—understandably. "I can't take this anymore. How can I go on?" she asked. For more than a week before her testimony, she found it difficult to eat or sleep, losing more than ten pounds. All the fears generated by years of speculation and harassment came crashing together in one horrific confrontation—with a man she detested, and over an issue she desperately wanted to be free of.[41]

On the day of her testimony, Hillary looked poised and assured. She was to be deposed in a downtown courtroom, a fact that infuriated her husband, who believed it was a calculated insult. Starr was forcing Hillary to go downtown and face crowds of onlookers rather than give her testimony in the White House via television camera. But Hillary turned a negative into a positive. Refusing to use a basement entrance, she strode through the crowd, looking proud. In front of the grand jury, she handled the independent counsel's questions with respect and care. She, too, was confused about what had happened to the billing records, she said. She was eager to cooperate. She conveyed an impression of trying hard to answer all the questions. Although inwardly enraged at Starr, who dared to continue receiving a million-dollar-plus salary from his private law firm while serving as the government's independent counsel, she showed none of this in her exchanges. When she left, walking once more through the gathered crowds, she told reporters: "I, like everyone else, would like to know the answer about how those documents showed up after all these years. I tried to be as helpful as I could." Hillary had achieved her primary goals: denying the prosecutors any additional information that might seal the case against her, while impressing the public—and presumably jurors as well—with her gracious demeanor.[42]

In the end, Kenneth Starr determined that he did not have enough evidence to indict Hillary Clinton. Examples of disingenuous statements, evasive disclaimers, and outright obfuscation were abundant. *Something* irregular, improper, and perhaps illegal had taken place in Arkansas, with the First Lady, much more than her husband, at the heart of it. Whether because of incompetence, the thinness of evidence, or the cleverness of their key witness, the prosecutors lacked the decisive testimony on which to proceed. For now at least, Hillary Clinton could breathe a sigh of relief.

Hillary's grand jury testimony coincided with the publication of *It Takes a Village* and a national book tour during which she hoped to sell hundreds of thousands of books and speak to millions of people through televised interviews. She sold the books, but at each interview, questions about Whitewater kept coming up amid discussions of what a community must do to raise physically and spiritually healthy children. *Newsweek* magazine's cover story on the book featured the question "Saint or Sinner?" Even in the midst of promoting the new image she had chosen as a defender of women's rights and children's rights, the First Lady could not escape that question. Sadly, and to her lasting consternation, even Democratic friends were not rushing to her defense. When she asked why, an aide responded: "People are nervous about taking a position that may not hold up . . . You know, we don't have answers for people. We can't tell them where these billing records were. We can't tell them why it took two years to find them." On the night of her testimony, Senator Chris Dodd of Connecticut was the only party leader to call with words of praise and support.[43]

Bill Clinton was enraged at the treatment Hillary was receiving. All through the health care crisis he defended her to the limit. The hullabaloo about the billing records infuriated him. He insisted that the records simply supported Hillary's case. But however angered he was by Starr's tactics—in his words, "creating the illusion of something deeply sinister and conspiratorial"—he was most incensed by the press. He continued to believe the media were engaged in a vicious conspiracy to destroy him and his family. Indeed, interviewing the president during this period, his old friend Taylor Branch was deeply disturbed by Clinton's volatility. "The peaks and valleys were so close together," he said. "It was jarring and painful to see him so overwrought." Branch even speculated that Clinton "knew Hillary faced indictment from some discovered secret."[44]

Branch had identified the key theme of the year that had followed the electoral and legislative defeats of 1994: "The peaks and valleys were so close together." Just when the Clintons thought all was lost, a miracle would happen and a comeback begin. Similarly, just when the good news seemed totally to outweigh the bad, a downward spiral would begin, whether because of a forgotten memo on Travelgate or billing records that were supposedly lost. Both the peaks and valleys would continue, each speaking to the underlying dynamic in the Clinton relationship. Which would dominate remained the crucial question.[45]

For the moment, at least, Bill Clinton seemed to be peaking.

At virtually the same time that Hillary Clinton was facing off with Ken Starr before a Washington grand jury, Bill Clinton was preparing to give his annual State of the Union address. As he had the previous year, Clinton hit all the right buttons on the American voters' switchboard. Poll data indicated that 65 percent of voters believed that issues like crime, controls over tobacco advertising, TV violence, and children's behavior in schools were important. These were all questions of social values, precisely the focus that Clinton now adopted. In his speech, the president listed the challenges the American people faced: to protect families and children; to streamline government; to reduce crime; to improve education; to restore a healthy environment; and to retain leadership in the worldwide fight for freedom. Clinton's agenda was in perfect sync with the priorities of average Americans (and, not coincidentally, reflected Dick Morris's polling).

But most important, Clinton framed his address in ways that resonated with conservative values. Taking the Republicans' slogan right out of their mouths, the president began his address by declaring that "the era of big government is over." How bold! How daring! How Republican! But also how clever, defanging his enemies and making them look like a pale imitation of himself. But Clinton then went a step further, saying with equal vehemence, "But we cannot go back to the time when our citizens were left to fend for themselves." In short, Clinton was promising to give centrist/conservative Americans their cake while guaranteeing them that they could eat it, too. He would streamline government, reduce the nation's deficit, and at the same time assure that programs like Social Security, Medicare, Medicaid, and support for education would remain in place. "Every eight-year-old must be able to read," Clinton said. "Every twelve-year-old must be able to log on to the Internet; every eighteen-year-old must be able to go to college; and every adult American must be able to keep learning for a lifetime." Then, to show he was not just mouthing clichés, Clinton committed himself to working for national teaching standards, preschool education, and tax deductions for parents of college students. To cap it all off, Clinton pledged to bring the budget into balance in five years.[46]

The coup de grâce came when Clinton turned to a government civil service worker sitting in the balcony next to Hillary. The man, Richard Dean, came from Oklahoma City. Clinton praised him for risking his life three times during the Oklahoma City bombing to rescue people in danger. Republicans and Democrats alike rose to give a standing ovation of gratitude for the hero's sacrifice. Clinton then went on to thank the man further for staying at work during the government shutdown, a wonderful example of patriotism. Then to his peroration: "On behalf of Richard Dean . . . I challenge all of you in this chamber: Let's never, ever, shut the federal government down again." It was a master ploy, deftly designed to undermine the tactics and basic message of the Republican Party.

The response to Clinton's address was even better than he might have hoped for. His approval rating shot up ten points to 60 percent. Commentators praised both his style and bearing. "Clinton appeared robust, youthful and forceful," the TV critic Tom Shales observed, "and [he] delivered the speech with virtual flawlessness." Republicans, in turn, were dumbfounded. The GOP lawmakers, one Republican observed, "looked as if they had been forced to sit through a long banquet speech—and then had dinner snatched out of their mouths. From V-chips [to control TV content for children] to beefed-up prison sentences, [Clinton] stole so many items off the Republicans' plate that they were left with little more than the bitter gruel served by Bob Dole in his [televised] response [to Clinton]."

Indeed, Dole's task in presenting the Republican rebuttal was nearly impossible. Already viewed as laconic, dry, and often boring, he weakly lashed out at Clinton as the "rearguard of the welfare state." But the charge lacked credibility. Clinton's embrace of most Republican ideas, from crime control to welfare reform, left them with only the issues that they were against—gay rights, abortion, single mothers. By contrast, Clinton was known for what he was *for*—a balanced budget, safe TV for kids, more police on the street, and welfare reform.[47]

On that list, no issue was more important—or controversial—than welfare reform. For years, Clinton had been known for his thoughtful critique of the existing social welfare safety net. In Arkansas he had sought innovative, nontraditional ways of handling poverty and giving people a helping hand to get a job. Reform of the welfare system was at the heart of his New Democratic agenda. It was time, he repeatedly said, to stop giving poor people a "handout" and start giving them a "hand up." From the beginning of his administration, a welfare reform task force had worked on devising legislation that would incentivize people to seek jobs and remove the rewards for remaining dependent on public support. Tellingly, after the health care debacle, Clinton repeatedly stated that he should have placed welfare reform first.

Once more, the political debate revolved around how far Clinton would go to satisfy Republican demands—and where he would draw the line against dismantling the New Deal welfare state. While he presented his own bill on welfare reform in the summer of 1994, Republicans insisted on enacting their more draconian version. With almost no debate inside the administration, Clinton vetoed the first bill passed, arguing that it gutted basic, nearly sacrosanct Democratic commitments to the poor and unemployed with no compensatory measures to make jobs more available. He did the same with a second act passed in January. But six months later, a third bill came to his desk that represented much more of a compromise between his ideas and Republican demands. The bill provided many of the items that Clinton had long fought for: expanded funds for day care for children of working parents, an increase in Medicaid support for the poor, appropriate work requirements and time limits on how long a person could remain on welfare, and emergency funds to come into play if an economic downturn occurred. Healthy people would be required to look for jobs after two years on welfare. During that time, the government would provide training, child care support, and food stamps. Many of those provisions were in the June legislation. "It's not a bad bill," Clinton said at the time. But Clinton had been counting on cutting a deal with Trent Lott, via Dick Morris, to leave out of the bill amendments that were patently offensive to Democratic values, the most outrageous of which would cut all benefits for most legal immigrants and eliminate nutrition supplements for low-income working families. "I had given him to believe that Lott would produce a somewhat better bill," Morris acknowledged. "I was wrong."[48]

That created one of the most divisive White House battles in the history of the Clinton political resurgence. Most of the Clinton team believed he should veto the bill. Wendell Primus, a leading official in Health and Human Services, predicted that as many as one million children might go without food or shelter if the bill became law. Donna Shalala and Henry Cisneros weighed in against it. Leon Panetta was furious at the decision to deny basic support to legal immigrants, seeing it as pure nativist prejudice. Stephanopoulos viewed the bill as a repudiation of Democrats from FDR to LBJ, making the Democrats "the prisoners of conservative rhetoric." The speechwriter Michael Waldman called it "the death of liberalism at its own hands." And Robert Reich was appalled. "You don't need to hurt people this way," he said. "You don't need to settle for this piece of shit." All of this simply echoed the views of liberals outside the White House. Marian Wright Edelman, Hillary Clinton's first sponsor for her work with children in the 1970s and the head of the Children's Defense Fund, claimed the bill would push millions of poor children even further into poverty. *The Guardian*—the *New York Times* of England—agreed. The bill, it argued, would constitute "a betrayal of the Democratic party's heritage." Daniel Patrick Moynihan, the Democratic "guru" on welfare, declared that signing the law "would be the most brutal act of social policy since Reconstruction." On the other side stood Dick Morris and his polls. Morris insisted that if Clinton signed the bill, he would soar to a 15-point lead over Robert Dole, his putative Republican opponent, while if he vetoed it, he would fall behind by 3 points.[49]

Clinton, torn, in the end decided to sign the bill into law, in large part because the two most important people in his administration— Hillary and Al Gore—came down on the side of moving forward. Despite her long friendship with Marian Wright Edelman and her own concern with protecting children, Hillary concluded, with her husband, that it would be better to sign the bill into law now and seek corrective amendments later rather than to risk a standoff with Congress that would ultimately redound to the Republicans' benefit. Gore offered similar arguments. "The system is fundamentally broken," he said. "You won't get another chance to do this. If you don't sign, the issue will fade away and it will be a missed opportunity." The president, having kept his silence while listening carefully to all the arguments for vetoing the bill, now made his choice, to the lasting despair of many in the room.

Insisting that he would secure repeal of the odious portions of the bill in the next session (which he did), he preferred to put into effect a bill that reflected many of his most deeply held convictions, even though many perceived it as a betrayal of New Deal democracy. No single act, except perhaps his first-year budget-reduction package, more powerfully exemplified Clinton's dedication to being a New, not an Old, Democrat.[50]

Having added welfare reform to his string of victory notches for triangulation and centrism, Clinton eagerly awaited the '96 presidential campaign. Notwithstanding his successes, numerous Republicans announced their candidacy, confident that Clinton was beatable. Lamar Alexander from Tennessee, Pete Wilson from California, Phil Gramm from Texas, and Richard Lugar from Indiana all threw their hats into the ring. But the only candidate Clinton feared was Colin Powell, the black former head of the Joint Chiefs of Staff. Powell had the prestige, the aura, the magnetism to be a superb candidate. Clinton was convinced that the media treated Powell with kid gloves. "He comes on TV like a saint, and those white liberal guilty reporters are so awestruck . . . they won't ask him a damn question." But Powell refused to be a candidate, leaving Robert Dole as the best bet to secure the nomination. Dole faced political difficulty from the start. Always more willing to compromise with Clinton than Gingrich, he was caught in the middle. "He knew he couldn't have any daylight between himself and Gingrich and the right-wingers [and still] get the nomination," the White House staffer Doug Sosnick said. "But he also knew that Gingrich was driving him off a cliff."[51]

In the meantime, Clinton continued to score victories, big and small. Taking a strong stance against vicious Serbian attacks on Bosnia, he authorized a series of air strikes that finally forced the Serbian president, Slobodan Milošević, into peace talks in Dayton, Ohio, orchestrated by Richard Holbrooke and Secretary of State Warren Christopher. While most Americans initially opposed any U.S intervention in the conflict, Clinton's strong national address explaining his reasons—basically, that the Serbs were committing genocide—turned public opinion around. At the same time he piled up additional "micro" victories on issues that felt good to millions of Americans. In September, Congress passed legislation that guaranteed forty-eight hours of hospital care to mothers who had just given birth, as well as to children of Vietnam War veterans who were born with spina bifida. By the time the campaign rolled around, Clinton could boast of having increased Head Start funding by 250 percent, child care support by 300 percent, and the Earned Income Tax Credit, aimed at the marginally poor, by 250 percent. The *New York Times* columnist Maureen Dowd might deride Clinton as "President Pothole, a fixer of tiny things," but the tiny victories added up. As Norm Ornstein, a pundit at the American Enterprise Institute, said, "[Clinton] was far more effective than any other President, by far, in using the budget process to get what he wanted . . . He would retreat, delay, come back with another proposal—get a half of what he wanted, a quarter, or an eighth. But he'd almost always get something," and the beneficiaries of his victories were bound to notice.[52]

As the election unfolded, Bill Clinton had every reason to feel confident. To the dismay of many on her staff, Hillary played a low-key role in the campaign. She emphasized her role in helping her husband coordinate policies to improve the lives of children and families. Consistent with that message, she rallied the delegates to the convention by doing her own riff on "it takes a village." What does it take to raise a child? she asked. "It takes teachers. It takes clergy. It takes business people. It takes community leaders . . . Yes, it takes a village . . . [And] it takes a President . . . a President who believes not only in the potential of his own child, but of all children; who believes not only in the strength of his own family, but of the American family . . . It takes Bill Clinton." Roaring their approval, the delegates stood and cheered their president— someone who, by the testimony of the First Lady, not only provided the leadership the country needed, but also embodied the family virtues so dear to people's hearts.[53]

Ironically, Hillary's paean to Bill as a family man at the Democratic convention came just after Dick Morris, the adviser most responsible for shaping Clinton's comeback, was forced to resign in disgrace for conducting a lengthy affair with a prostitute. Every time Morris came to Washington to see Clinton, it turned out, he entertained a highly paid mistress at his Mayflower Hotel suite. Sherry Rowland, the woman in question, recounted how Morris had her listen in on his telephone conversations with the president. Rowland concluded that Morris was a little crazy. He was certainly full of himself. *Time* magazine had run a cover story called "The Man Who Has Clinton's Ear." Indeed, Morris subsequently claimed that Clinton had told him, "I don't think any president has ever had someone as close as you are to me." Now a tabloid that had been shadowing Morris published front-page photos of Morris and Rowland on the balcony of his hotel suite, baring the whole story of his love affair. The headlines appeared as Morris checked in to his suite, on the same floor as Clinton's, at the convention hotel. Shortly thereafter, Erskine Bowles, Clinton's chief of staff, marched to Morris's room and demanded that he resign.[54]

With the Republicans struggling to find a theme with which to attack an incumbent who increasingly seemed untouchable, Morris seemed dispensable. The more Clinton cleaved to issues like tax cuts for parents of college students, hospital stays for new mothers, and parental safeguards so that children could not watch violent TV shows, the more he looked like Mr. America. Elizabeth Dole, the Republican candidate's wife, did a brilliant job at the Republican convention, walking the floor and interacting with delegates as she gave a rousing speech in support of her husband. But then Bob Dole followed with a meandering, overly partisan, and boring acceptance speech. Haley Barbour, chair of the Republican National Committee, summed up the contest succinctly: "Bob Dole is a plainspoken, humorous man. [But] he is not the television personality Bill Clinton is and never will be. Bill Clinton could sell Fords to Chevrolet dealers. He is the first politician in history who has perfected the ability to cry in just one eye." Dole might be droll and ironic, but that was not what the American people were looking for. He could attack the welfare state, but Bill Clinton had enacted welfare reform. Dole called for a 15 percent across-the-board reduction in taxes, but Clinton had actually passed tax cuts for the parents of children going to college and for small businesses who hired former welfare recipients. When Clinton claimed that he was a bridge to the future, while Dole was a bridge to the past, Americans believed the metaphor. It was not just the difference in their ages, their affect, or their personal style. It was also the difference in their positions.[55]

Dole had little room to maneuver. In large part because of his own character issues (his past included an affair), as well as years of abiding by the rules of civility in the Senate, Dole refused to comment on Bill Clinton's ethics in the first televised debate between the candidates.

Even when by the end of the campaign he began excoriating Clinton's character, his heart did not seem to be in it. More to the point, he just could not gain traction on the issues. Dwarfed by Clinton's personality on the one hand and the president's mastery of the policy landscape on the other, he could only plug along, as though stuck in a rut.[56]

By the end of October, it was no longer a contest. Clinton's character was the only issue, and even that seemed to have gained little traction. More than half the American people might agree that Clinton did not have "high personal moral and ethical standards," and 52 percent felt he was not "honest and trustworthy," but in the same poll, these voters gave Clinton a 14-point lead over the Republican. "Where's the outrage?" Dole asked. The answer was, there was none. The only reason the election was not a landslide was Ross Perot's late third-party candidacy. Despite arguing (prophetically, as it turned out) that Clinton would spend most of the next two years "staying out of jail," Perot never had a chance of changing the outcome of the race. Though he kept Clinton from winning an absolute majority of the popular vote, in the end the margin of victory was decisive. Clinton won the electoral college 379 to 159. In the popular vote, he prevailed over Dole 49 percent to 41 percent, with Perot receiving the final 10 percent. The Comeback Kid was back on top.[57]

The events of 1994–96 suggested numerous lessons about the long-term political and personal partnership of Bill and Hillary Clinton as well as about the politics of the nation. In the eyes of many, the Clinton administration marked the beginning of a polarization in America's political culture that threatened paralysis in government, undermined the possibility of bipartisan agreement on pressing national priorities, and destroyed civility. "An irrational fever [had] engulfed the entire community," the journalist Joe Klein observed, "the governmental equivalent of the Salem witch trials . . . a form of madness choreographed by the most extreme elements in both parties and cheered on by a happily voracious press." Klein was right. There was a new poison in the political air, and it would not dissipate.[58]

Much of that poison came from personal antipathy on the part of conservatives, and a portion of the media establishment, toward the president and First Lady. Bill and Hillary Clinton were loved by many. But they were hated in a visceral and personal way by their enemies. Bill was not called "Slick Willie" for nothing. With a facile tongue and an unmatched capacity for ambiguity, he quickly lost the trust of reporters as well as many politicians by the slippery way he eluded hard questions. While less clever at it, in many respects Hillary was even worse than Bill. She refused to meet the press, except on very rare occasions; persistently denied access to her own records; haughtily dismissed those who disagreed with her; and presumed the authority to make decisions about what was or was not the right of the public to know. In a profound sense, the president and First Lady earned the scorn and skepticism they encountered. Their intransigence both encouraged and enabled the right, which went after the Clintons with no sense of restraint, little respect for the White House, and a callous disregard for rules of evidence or procedure. The sick reality of the situation was well summarized when Alan Simpson, the retiring ultraconservative senator from Wyoming, told Clinton in 1996 that of course the Republicans knew he had committed no crimes, but this was all payback for Watergate.

As always, the Clintons as a couple remained at the heart of this political and personal dynamic. On their twentieth anniversary, Bill gave Hillary a diamond ring—to "mark a milestone in our lives and to make up for the fact that when she agreed to marry me, I didn't have enough money to buy her an engagement ring." Hillary wore the ring, he wrote, "as a reminder that, through all our ups and downs, we were still very much engaged." But notwithstanding such verbal cleverness, there was nothing stable about the personal relationship. While many friends and aides reported how affectionate the couple were, just as many spoke of strained silences and angry words. Hillary may for the moment have accepted a public role as junior partner in the White House, but that did not mean she was at peace with her place, or with her relationship.

Bill, meanwhile, rebounded brilliantly, putting his political foes on the defensive and succeeding in painting his enemies into a corner. Through triangulation, he essentially went over the heads of both his own party and the Republicans to speak to the country in a language that mirrored their own values and priorities. In effect, he returned to his New Democratic roots, but in a manner that seemed both fresh and different. At heart, Clinton was always a centrist, not a liberal. Now he had the genius to give definition to his policy instincts through his series of microreforms—targeted tax cuts for the middle class, more money for preschoolers, V-chips for parents to regulate the TV watching of their children, mammograms for women, special programs for Alzheimer victims, a hundred thousand new police officers on the streets to reduce crime. Many of these initiatives seemed "nickel and dime." But all were popular. And with welfare reform, Clinton went big-time and took a huge risk. The bottom line was that triangulation worked. Clinton occupied 70 percent of the political spectrum, leaving disgruntled liberals and angry conservatives alone at either end.

Yet if there was anything about Bill and Hillary Clinton that was a constant, it was the changeability of their personal and political relationship. Nothing was certain, and anyone who counted on stability was likely to be confounded. In a partnership long characterized by roller-coaster twists and turns, the real question was whether they had now found agreement on a direction that would allow them to fulfill their shared dreams.

ELEVEN

The Roller Coaster Plummets

The year began well. The president's inaugural address, in which he spoke of building a "bridge to the twenty-first century," resonated. The economy grew with an energy not seen since the early 1960s. The administration made steady progress on its march toward a balanced budget, each quarter bringing better news about higher-than-expected growth rates, larger revenues, and an ongoing expansion of employment. The dot-com revolution was at its height. The country had seen the biggest increase in aid to college students in fifty years. NATO was expanding. The Kyoto Accords addressing climate change were almost ready to submit to Congress for ratification. Clinton was in control, and collaboration with Republicans had reached a point where the entire Clinton family journeyed to Bosnia, together with Bob and Liddy Dole, to press for greater progress toward reconciliation and peace in the Balkans. The First Lady was getting ready to host a series of "Millennium" lectures in which scholars and pundits would talk to the nation about all that the past century had meant for America. It all seemed so positive.

Too positive, in fact. For just as the Clintons ascended to the heights, the president's recklessness brought him crashing down to depths even he had never before imagined. The story was not new. It had happened repeatedly. But the context was different, making this chapter of Bill and Hillary's partnership the most stunning of their life together.

Her name was Monica Lewinsky. A twenty-three-year-old recent college graduate, she had used her family's connections to White House fundraising efforts to secure a position as a White House intern. From the beginning, she had a "crush" on Bill Clinton. They had made eye contact a number of times. "It was this look," she later said. "When it was time to shake my hand, the smile disappeared and we shared an intense but brief sexual exchange. He undressed me with his eyes." Other women had reported similar experiences. As often as she could, Lewinksy hung out around the Oval Office. During the confrontation with Republicans over the shutdown of government operations in the fall of 1995, White House staffers were working even harder than usual. One night, delivering papers to the Oval Office, she found herself alone with the president. Wearing thong underwear, she revealed her buttocks to Clinton in what she later called a "subtle flirtatious gesture." He asked if he could kiss her. She said yes. "What an incredible, sensual kisser," he told her. "I knew one day I would kiss you." Two hours later, she returned and they had their first sexual contact. She performed fellatio on him, while he put his hand in her pants and brought her to orgasm. Although he would not let himself come to climax—he needed to "wait until he trusted me more," she remembered his saying— the president did tell Lewinsky it had been a long time since he had enjoyed something like that. Two nights later, they had a similar rendezvous. "I'm usually around on weekends," Clinton told her; "no one else is around, and you can come and see me."

There developed a pattern of meetings, including on New Year's Eve. Often there was little conversation. In fact, Lewinsky frequently had oral sex with Clinton when he was on the phone with senators or congressmen. Three months into the relationship, they had their first lengthy conversation. "I have an empty life except for work," Clinton confided to her. He even suggested, "I might be alone in three years." To Lewinsky that meant only one thing: "I just knew he was in love with me." Clinton tried to call a halt to the affair in February, but six weeks later he resumed the relationship, which now included phone sex, sometimes as early as 6:00 a.m. On Easter Sunday, the president went to church with Hillary, then came back to the White House and had a sexual encounter with Lewinsky while on the phone with a U.S. senator. A long hiatus in the relationship then ensued, with no private contact for almost nine months. But then the affair started again, with exchanges of gifts and late-night or weekend rendezvous. On one such occasion in February 1997, Clinton again resisted coming to a climax. "He said he didn't want to get addicted to me," Lewinsky later said, "and he didn't want me to get addicted to him." But when they resumed their lovemaking, Clinton did have an orgasm. Lewinsky was wearing a blue sheath dress, which now bore some of Clinton's semen.[1]

One of the unanswered mysteries is whether this was the first time Clinton had "wandered" since becoming president. There were different, conflicting impressions. Clinton himself often said he had "retired" from an active sex life outside marriage. At different times he dated the start of his "retirement" to when he was forty or to when he began his presidential campaign. But Clinton had a pattern of lying about such things. Indeed, his most serious love affair—the one with Marilyn Jo Jenkins that almost led to his divorce in 1990—took place well after he turned forty. And there were stories of various sexual escapades in the White House. One revolved around a former flight attendant on Clinton's campaign plane with whom he had openly flirted. She became a White House receptionist after the election, and, according to Linda Tripp, at that time an assistant to Vince Foster, she bragged, "I have my twenty minutes . . . every morning with the President." Then there was Kathleen Willey, the wife of a big donor to the Democratic Party. According to a later deposition, she went to see Clinton one day about the terrible problems her husband was having. She claimed that during that encounter, he touched her breasts, put her hand on his penis, and kissed her. Others said that when she left the Oval Office, she was blushing, her hair was awry, and her clothes seemed rumpled. Still others talked of secret visits to the White House by Marilyn Jo Jenkins. But these and other stories simply became part of the Clinton mythology, with no direct evidence that they had occurred.[2]

The person most directly concerned, of course, was Hillary Clinton. After the near-divorce prompted by Clinton's intense affair with Marilyn Jo Jenkins, Hillary had insisted that the two enter prolonged marital therapy. She believed that her husband had changed as a result, that his days of indiscriminate, random sex were in the past. This conviction was only reinforced by the circumstances of their new life. After all, the White House was a virtual prison. Secret Service agents held the president and his family under twenty-four-hour surveillance. Even were he so inclined, there would be little opportunity for Bill to act out.

The round-the-clock scrutiny buttressed Hillary's belief that Bill's days of wandering were past.[3]

Nevertheless, alert eyes sensed that Lewinsky might be a problem. Why was she always wandering the halls outside the Oval Office? Secret Service agents began making note of her frequent appearances. Harold Ickes commented on her quick departures when other people came into the area. No one knew more than Betty Currie, Clinton's personal secretary, but she did not share her views with others. On the other hand, Nancy Hernreich, another secretary, and Steve Goodin, Clinton's personal assistant, became suspicious of Lewinsky and attempted to keep her away from the president. Finally, a Secret Service agent went to Evelyn Lieberman, Hillary's chief lieutenant, known, according to George Stephanopoulos, as "the Mother Superior of the West Wing." Lieberman quickly concluded that Lewinsky was a potential time bomb.

Immediately, Lieberman made sure that Lewinsky and her office mate were transferred out of the White House to the Pentagon. An unforeseen consequence was that once there, she soon met and became fast friends with Linda Tripp, also recently moved from the White House to the Pentagon. For the moment, at least, there would be no more casual encounters in the hall between the intern and the president. Presumably, if there was a potential problem, it had been solved by Lieberman's intervention. But that underestimated Bill Clinton's ardor and Monica Lewinsky's persistence. In fact, the affair lasted sixteen months before Clinton finally broke it off, and not before involving countless others including the presidential aide John Podesta, Bill Richardson, and Vernon Jordan in trying to find Lewinsky a decent, well-paying job.[4]

In the end, of course, it all blew up. Bill Clinton might act on the premise that his parallel lives would never intersect with each other and explode; indeed, for months, he had no reason to think otherwise. For more than two years, no one knew about, or connected, Lewinsky and Clinton. But someone eventually did make the link, and more important, placed Bill Clinton's relationship with Monica Lewinsky at the center of the broader investigation into whether Bill Clinton had violated the law in the Whitewater scandal. There was patently no relation between a real estate deal in Arkansas and the president having a sexual affair with a White House intern. But that did not deter Kenneth Starr, or Bill Clinton's other enemies.

Tellingly, Clinton's initial romance with Lewinsky had coincided with the worst days of Hillary's encounter with Kenneth Starr. Then, when Starr found himself lacking the pivotal piece of evidence that would allow him to indict Hillary Clinton, he found himself without a target. If he was to get the Clintons, he would have to turn elsewhere. Which is what he did, but not without an extraordinary, circuitous route that first of all led back to another of Bill Clinton's "scandals," his relationship with Paula Jones. It was all bizarre, even unfathomable—but ultimately, proof of the dictum "What goes around, comes around."[5]

Public discussion of the Paula Jones episode went back to the *American Spectator* story about Clinton's sexual escapades in Arkansas. Although initially no last name was given to the "Paula" described in the article, enterprising reporters soon identified Jones as a low-level state employee working at a welcoming booth in the Excelsior Hotel in Little Rock, where Clinton was addressing a conference. Allegedly, Clinton sent a state trooper to invite the young secretary to join the governor in a private room upstairs. "You make his knees knock," the trooper reportedly told Jones. According to her subsequent claims, when Jones went to the room, Clinton fondled her, lowered his trousers, and asked for oral sex. Encouraged by a right-wing Arkansas group pursuing Clinton, Jones and her husband soon hired a legal team to sue Clinton for his "odious, perverse and outrageous conduct," claiming as well that Jones's subsequent career as a state employee was irrevocably damaged as a result of Clinton's sexual harassment. Reporters from *The Washington Post* and elsewhere soon glommed on to the story, which seemed all too plausible given Clinton's past history and the testimony of the state troopers. As the reporter Michael Isikoff wrote, "The charges against Clinton—running from [Gennifer] Flowers and the troopers to Paula Jones—pointed to something more fundamental: a continuing pattern of reckless and even compulsive behavior that if true, would surely affect the course of his presidency." Although Clinton's lawyers offered to settle the lawsuit for $700,000—admitting no sexual misconduct by Clinton—the deal fell through.[6]

In the ordinary scheme of things, Bill Clinton's encounter with Paula Jones would rank as singularly unimportant. Assuming that Clinton did meet Jones in the room at the Excelsior Hotel in Little Rock, and even that he propositioned her, nothing happened as a result. She rebuffed Clinton's overtures. Although she claimed to have suffered sexual harassment, she never even looked at her personnel records to discover whether she had been denied a pay increase or promotion because of pressure from above. Instead, the case became a tit-for-tat exchange in which surrogates became more important than the principals. Jones's husband, Steve, rejected the $700,000 settlement offer because he felt it did not sufficiently affirm his wife's innocence. Bill Clinton could not go further than to deny that a sexual exchange had occurred, because to even admit he had invited Jones to his room was humiliating to the First Lady. Moreover, Hillary was violently opposed to any deal. If the White House settled, she claimed, "the lawsuits would never end." Thus, Jones's lawsuit became a psychodrama of political protagonists seeking to make a point, regardless of what had happened in the hotel room.[7]

Like a nagging cough that refuses to go away, the Paula Jones lawsuit lurked in the political background from February 1994 onward. After initial efforts to arrive at a settlement failed, the president's lawyers sought to defer any hearings on the case until Clinton left office, arguing that pressing government business made it difficult, and perhaps against the national interest, for the president to divert his energies to a private legal matter. When the Supreme Court unanimously rejected that argument (in what most commentators have since recognized as a disastrous and ill-conceived opinion), the Jones case once more burst into the headlines. Then, in September 1997, Susan Webber Wright, the Arkansas judge in charge of the case, dismissed two of the four charges. "I want you to get the thing settled," she told the parties. "It just screams for settlement." To Jones's lawyers she stated further, "I think it's unlikely . . . that a jury will find for her if this matter goes to trial . . . The way it looks now, more likely than not, she will fail."[8]

Faced with Judge Wright's opinion and the reluctance of Steve Jones to pursue a settlement any further, Jones's legal team resigned, presenting her with a bill for $800,000. But to anti-Clinton forces on the right, Jones still represented a potent weapon. Soon her case was

taken up by John Whitehead of the Rutherford Institute, a conservative
legal think tank devoted to the Christian right. Rutherford then bank-
rolled a Dallas legal team known for its hostility to Bill Clinton, homosexuality, and sexual promiscuity. Reenergized, the Jones legal onslaught
went into high gear in preparation for hearings that Judge Wright would
convene on the case starting in January 1998. Among the witnesses
subpoenaed to testify under oath was William Jefferson Clinton.[9]

It was at this point that the convoluted paths linking the Paula
Jones case to the independent counsel's prosecution of the Whitewater
investigation finally intersected. The two cases had no relation to each
other. All of Kenneth Starr's energies had gone into securing an indictment of Hillary Rodham Clinton for improper conduct at the Rose law
firm. That trail had petered out. Now his attention had turned to Bill
Clinton, whose primary vulnerabilities were twofold: he obfuscated all
the time, and he was reckless in his sex life. That combination eventually translated into two words: Monica Lewinsky. Although the White
House intern and the former Arkansas secretary had never met, they
had one thing in common: each claimed to have had a sexual encounter
with Bill Clinton. If in the course of being questioned in the Paula
Jones deposition, Bill Clinton could also be asked about his relationship
with Monica Lewinsky, a legal trap might be sprung on Clinton. If the
president lied under oath, he would commit perjury, which constituted
a crime under the Constitution and might possibly be an impeachable
offense. Ironically, Kenneth Starr who had never heard of or met Monica Lewinsky, now became totally dependent upon her for achieving
his objective. And the key intermediary was the woman named Linda
Tripp.

The sequence of events setting up this process of legal entrapment
almost defies comprehension. Linda Tripp was at the center of everything. Previously a secretary in the George Herbert Walker Bush White
House, she stayed on after the Clinton election and worked for Vince
Foster, then deputy counsel to the president. Tripp was one of the last
people to see Foster on the day he committed suicide. A Republican
who detested Clinton's politics, she soon moved to the Pentagon as a
high-level administrative secretary. There she met Monica Lewinsky,
who had recently been transferred from her White House internship at
the behest of Evelyn Lieberman. Tripp befriended Lewinsky, and soon

the two—more than twenty years apart in age—were seeing each other regularly for long, intimate conversations. Before long, Lewinsky confided in Tripp all the details of her relationship with Bill Clinton, something she had already done with her mother and other friends, even telling one friend at a Catskills resort about Clinton's refusal to have an orgasm. She also anticipated Clinton's own future rationale for denying that he and Lewinsky were having a sexual relationship. Sex, she said, meant intercourse, so they were not having a "sexual relationship." But she shared all the details of the interactions they did have, including her own orgasms and Clinton's placing a cigar in her vagina.

Most important, Tripp tape-recorded the conversations without Lewinsky knowing it. When they were at a bar, the recorder would be in her pocketbook. At home, she had a machine attached to her phone. Lewinsky eventually showed Tripp the blue dress she was wearing the night that Bill Clinton allowed himself to have an orgasm, which Tripp persuaded her not to get cleaned. At some time, Tripp advised, Lewinsky might need the dress as proof of her relationship with Clinton.[10]

All along, Tripp was in frequent conversation with conservative friends about the explosive nature of Lewinsky's revelations. Lucianne Goldberg was a literary agent closely connected to a group of right-wing lobbying groups and publishers. She also had links with the people financing the get-Clinton activities going on in Arkansas. Adamant that they use the Tripp tapes to bring Clinton down, Goldberg helped lay the groundwork that would round the circle, getting Kenneth Starr's office involved. Before becoming independent counsel, Starr had already been indirectly involved in the Paula Jones case, preparing an amicus curiae brief for her initial lawsuit. If he could now secure permission from the attorney general to broaden his mandate to include potential perjury charges against the president of the United States, he could acquire the pivotal missing ingredient in his mission to get the president.

All the key components were in place. Tripp arranged to tell her story to Jackie Bennett, Starr's chief aide, and to share with him all her tapes. Jones's attorneys had already subpoenaed both Lewinsky and Bill Clinton to testify in the Jones case. The Lewinsky subpoena specifically requested that she turn over to the court "all gifts and communications from Bill Clinton, including any and all accessories, jewelry and/or hat pins." It was a dead giveaway. Someone had been talking. Only Clinton, Lewinsky, and Betty Currie, Clinton's secretary, knew about the gifts, including the hat pin that Clinton had given Lewinsky the previous Christmas. When Clinton found out about the subpoena, he immediately suggested to Lewinsky that she find a way to get rid of the gifts by asking Betty Currie to hold them for her. But by now, everyone's suspicions were alerted. Clinton's lawyers wanted to know how Lewinsky's name got on the witness list. Who was she, anyway? Despite having seen Lewinsky that very same day, Clinton answered unambiguously, "Bob, do you think I'm fucking crazy? . . . No, it didn't happen. I'm retired. I'm retired." Reassured, his lawyer Robert Bennett offered a final lecture. "The only thing you have to worry about," he told Clinton, "is if you lie in there. The crazies will come after you. They will try to impeach you if you lie. That's the only thing you have to worry about."[11]

The stage was thus set for the beginning of the worst personal scandal ever to rock the White House. It had been a strange autumn. Clinton had secured a budget agreement on his terms, achieved a middle-class tax cut, and—planning ahead—had arranged for a balanced budget by 2002. But there was also a sense of unease. Chelsea had gone off to Stanford, leaving the Clintons as empty nesters. The president remained furious at Ken Starr, particularly for his persecution of Susan McDougal, whom Starr had sent to a windowless cell wearing leg manacles and a waist chain in an effort to force her to buy her freedom by denouncing Clinton. Clinton also continued to excoriate the press, believing they were intent on persecuting him by raising the specter of corrupt White House fundraising. In fact, Clinton was vulnerable. The Center for Public Integrity accused Clinton of turning the White House into a "Fat Cat Hotel." Nearly a thousand individuals had stayed in the White House residence overnight, most of them big donors. Particular attention focused on Clinton's alliance with the Riady family and its association with an Indonesian conglomerate, the Lippo Group. Frequently, people associated with the Riady family showed up at Clinton "coffee hours" where they could ask questions before coughing up their checks. On another occasion, Charles Trie, a Chinese American restaurant owner from Little Rock, brought with him $460,000 in money orders, all filled out in the same hand although allegedly from different donors. No criminal charges were ever filed, but a sense of ethical ambiguity was pervasive. "The whole mess reeked," Carl Bernstein said.[12]

But the subpoena to testify in the Paula Jones case crystallized the unease. On January 12, five days before the deposition, Linda Tripp turned over her tapes to Starr's office. Four days later, Starr went to Janet Reno to ask that his mandate be expanded to include the potential charge of perjury or obstruction of justice. Reno agreed. The same day, Starr's office arranged to plant a microphone on Linda Tripp for her scheduled lunch with Monica Lewinsky. At the end of the luncheon, federal agents whisked Lewinsky away, placing her under their control and pressuring her to cooperate immediately. She resisted the agents until she could reach her mother, who came from New York to take her home that evening. The next day, knowing none of this, Clinton went to the deposition being conducted by Judge Wright on the Paula Jones case. He was to be questioned by Jones's lawyers, who were fully knowledgeable about the Lewinsky tapes.

At the beginning of the deposition, the lawyers gave Clinton a list of criteria for what constituted "sexual relations." It included "contact with the genitalia, anus, groin, breast, [or] inner thigh . . . with an intent to arouse or gratify the sexual desire of any person." Significantly, only fifteen minutes of the questioning involved any mention of Paula Jones. Instead, it focused on Lewinsky. The first question to the president was whether he had carried on an "extramarital sexual affair" with Lewinsky. Clinton said no, he had not. His reasoning: In his opinion, sexual intercourse represented the essence of a "sexual affair." Since Clinton had never engaged in intercourse with Lewinsky, he believed that he was telling the truth according to the law as he knew it and had not perjured himself. Amazingly, the Jones lawyers refrained from asking specific questions. Had one of the attorneys asked straightforwardly whether Lewinsky had ever performed oral sex on Clinton, he would have had to lie outright, making his perjury indisputable. But they never did. Instead, for hours they probed around the edges of the relationship. It was enough to terrify Clinton, but not enough to force him into an outright lie.[13]

Nevertheless, Clinton understood immediately the depth of the crisis he now faced. Canceling a dinner that he and Hillary had scheduled with Erskine Bowles and his wife, Clinton went back to the White House and brooded for hours. Although he did not yet know about the Linda Tripp tapes or the involvement of the independent counsel's office, he could sense what was coming. In his memoir, Clinton wrote: "What I had done with Monica Lewinsky was immoral and foolish. I was deeply ashamed of it and I didn't want it to come out. In the deposition, I was trying to protect my family and myself from my selfish stupidity. I believed that the contorted definition of 'sexual relations' enabled me to do so, though I was worried enough about it to invite the lawyer interrogating me to ask specific questions. I didn't have to wait long to find out why he declined to do so."

But if Clinton did not yet know precisely where this was going, he knew enough to call Betty Currie and ask her to come in on the weekend. In their meeting he "coached" her, suggesting to her that she had never seen him alone with Monica, that there was nothing suspect about their relationship. It was one of the more reprehensible examples of Clinton's abusing his power to manipulate people close to him in order to protect his reputation, even if at their own expense.[14]

But Clinton's first instinct was to call Dick Morris to assess his vulnerability. "You poor son of a bitch," Morris said in response. Clinton insisted: "I didn't do what they said I did, but . . . I may have done enough so that I don't know if I can prove my innocence . . . There may be gifts . . . And there may be messages on her home answering machine . . . You know, ever since the election, I've tried to shut myself down . . . sexually . . . But sometimes I slipped up, and with this girl, I just slipped up." It was the first—and only—time that Clinton told the truth over the next seven months. Clinton told Morris he was not sure he could survive the week after the news broke. The Internet already had the story. He feared he would be forced to resign. Hence, his request to Morris was simple: Could Morris devise a poll to test whether Americans would forgive their president if he confessed to wrongdoing? Morris took the assignment and soon enough called Clinton back. The answer was no. His polling showed that although it was conceivable that Americans might accept an admission of adultery, they would not accept his having lied under oath. "Well," Clinton responded, "we'll just have to win."[15]

If nothing else, the Morris episode highlighted how aware Clinton was of his predicament. Interestingly, he appears to have considered coming clean as one option. The self-doubt about how to proceed would make itself evident numerous times over the next few days. How long could he carry on this charade? Did it not make more sense to tell the truth and get it over with? But that was not where Clinton came down. As George Stephanopoulos wrote, instead of the truth, "Clinton chose to follow the pattern of his past. He called Dick Morris. Dick took a poll. The poll said lie. It was out of Clinton's hands." The journalist Joe Klein said the same thing more eloquently. "This nauseating revelation," he subsequently wrote, "seemed to encapsulate all the worst aspects of the Clinton administration: the President was a man who would actually poll whether or not he should tell the truth."[16]

In the meantime, the news was hitting the streets with a speed and force that seemed out of control. The Internet, with all its blogs, led the charge. The Drudge Report, a conservative site that sometimes had problems with accuracy, began to disclose pieces of the Lewinsky story, including the blockbuster news about the semen stains on Lewinsky's blue dress. When ABC broadcast the same story, Erskine Bowles, Clinton's chief of staff, leaped to his feet and left the room, saying, "I think I'm going to be sick." Unlike the Gennifer Flowers story, which had stayed underground for more than a week, every paper in the country headlined the Lewinsky scandal. Clinton's instinct that publication of the news would bring immediate demands for his resignation was confirmed. "Clinton is a cancer on the culture," Andrew Sullivan wrote in the *New Republic*, "a cancer of cynicism, narcissism and deceit. At some point, not even the most stellar of economic records, not even the most prosperous of decades, is worth the price of such a cancer metastasizing even further. It is time to be rid of it." Clinton's presidency, the conservative ABC commentator George Will declared, is "deader really than Woodrow Wilson's after he had a stroke." The Clinton White House was under siege.[17]

Knowing what was coming, Clinton woke Hillary the morning after his deposition to alert her. She responded with questions. Who was this

woman, and how often had he seen her? Clinton answered that Lewinsky was a needy person who came to him for advice, and he insisted
that nothing improper had taken place. He claimed to have spoken only
a few times with Lewinsky.[18]

What actually went on in Hillary's mind that morning is unknown.
In all likelihood, she experienced a surge of conflicting emotions. She
knew all too well her husband's history of repeated infidelity. On the
other hand, she believed that their marital therapy had generated a permanent change in his behavior—reinforced in no small measure by the
twenty-four-hour-a-day surveillance that existed in the White House.
Had Evelyn Lieberman ever mentioned Lewinsky to her as a potential
danger? Was she aware of other stories, such as that of Kathleen Willey?
Some White House aides stated that Hillary "acted as if she knew" and
was furious. But others—perhaps most—thought that Hillary believed
Bill's story. "He ministers to troubled people all the time," she told her
close friend Sidney Blumenthal. "He does it out of religious conviction
and personal temperament. If you knew his mother you would understand it." In her memoir, Hillary declared that she believed Bill because
in the past he had so often been falsely accused of similar behavior.
Besides, it was undeniable that outside forces were trying to destroy
them. In the midst of such pressures, Hillary made a decision. She
would stand by her husband.

"How could Hillary buy that [story]?" George Stephanopoulos
asked. "How could she not? . . . She had to believe that he wouldn't risk
their life's work for a fling with an intern only a few years older than
their daughter. She had to believe that he loved her enough not to humiliate her. She had to do what she had always done before: swallow
her doubts, stand by her man, and savage his enemies." Everything was
on the line, all that she had ever worked for and hoped for. "For Hillary," Carl Bernstein observed, "the investment in the truthfulness of
Bill's explanation was nothing less than a lifetime's savings."[19]

Whatever her motivation, Hillary had made a command decision
that transformed the world around her. Just as in the Gennifer Flowers
case, she rescued her husband from political annihilation. Even those
who thought she secretly recognized the likelihood of an affair found
her commitment to do battle absolute. No matter what, one friend
noted, "she was going to fight to the death to save his presidency." But

the overwhelming impression from the beginning was that she did believe Bill. This was a political battle, she insisted, energized by right-wing partisans who could not bear to think of a successful Clinton presidency.[20]

In the end, Hillary's adamant insistence on fighting back proved instrumental in stiffening Bill Clinton's backbone. Indeed, it helped create the inexorable pressure that drove him toward complete denial. Arguably, there were moments in the beginning when Clinton not only considered coming clean about the Lewinsky affair, but may also have considered resigning. The first day after the deposition, Clinton seemed thoroughly flummoxed, unsure of what direction to take or how to proceed. "I had never seen him this off-balance before," Sidney Blumenthal, a White House aide, said. Clinton had called Blumenthal, a close associate of Hillary's, to his office to talk, hoping he would help assuage any doubts that Hillary might have. Lewinsky, Clinton told Blumenthal, had made a sexual demand on him. "But I've gone down that road before. I've caused pain for a lot of people, and I'm not going to do that again." Calling Lewinsky a "stalker," Blumenthal recalled, Clinton described himself as "being at the mercy of his enemies, uncertain about what to say or do. In that Oval Office encounter, I saw a man who was beside himself."

The same impression of uncertainty struck the entire nation when Clinton appeared on a previously scheduled interview with Jim Lehrer on public television. Throughout, Clinton appeared uneasy, tentative, as if his entire being were in disarray. He looked like a man on a hot seat. When Lehrer brought up the issue of the Lewinsky deposition, Clinton did the strangest thing, declaring, in the present tense, "there *is* not a sexual relationship"—not "there has never been a sexual relationship," or "I never had sex with Monica Lewinsky," but "there *is* not a sexual relationship." It was as though Clinton had no clue what to do, his body language and terminology a mirror of the self-doubt and anxiety he was experiencing. Everyone noticed. Harry Thomason, a close friend of both Bill and Hillary and a Hollywood producer, was astonished at Clinton's apparent weakness, and he immediately hopped on a plane to come to the White House, where he resided for the next thirty-four days. Clinton almost "marinated in his sense of victimhood," the legal commentator Jeffrey Toobin noted.[21]

That was the context in which Hillary put steel in his spine. By her own example, she literally pushed him into a more declarative and passionate denial of the affair. Harry Thomason arrived at the White House intent on persuading Clinton to go on the offensive against Ken Starr. Hillary reinforced that message, urging Bill to more emphatically deny the very idea of an affair. He acted immediately on their advice. After appearing with Hillary at the White House in a joint presentation on child care, Clinton returned to the platform. "I did not have sexual relations with that woman, Miss Lewinsky," he declared, vigorously. "I never told anybody to lie . . . These allegations are false. Now I need to go back to work for the American people." A somewhat better denial.

But the next day was the turning point. Hillary had agreed to go on NBC's *Today* show, to be interviewed by Matt Lauer. The most popular morning TV show in America, *Today* always had a huge audience, but this morning, viewership reached new heights. Prior to the trip to New York, Sidney Blumenthal had briefed the First Lady on his conversations with David Brock. The author of the *American Spectator* "Troopergate" article, Brock had now changed sides and told Blumenthal about all the right-wing foundations and lobbying groups who were plotting to "get" Clinton. The First Lady was primed. Poised and confident, she began by expressing her faith in her husband and denying that he had been guilty of sexual infidelity. "We know everything about each other," she assured the audience. She had no doubts of his claims to innocence.

But then she moved on. "I guess I've just been through it so many times," she told Lauer. "I mean Bill and I have been accused of every-thing, including murder, by some of the very same people who are be-hind these allegations . . . The great story here for anybody willing to find it . . . is this vast right-wing conspiracy that has been conspiring against my husband since the day he announced for president." Neither strident nor irrational, she calmly placed on the table the serious sug-gestion that all of the scandalmongering was really a carefully plotted attempt to destroy Bill Clinton. It was a tour de force.[22]

Hillary's strength in that moment closed off any possibility that Bill Clinton would waffle on the Lewinsky matter. Instead of appearing uncertain, mixing up his tenses, and engaging in obfuscation, he had no choice but to become decisive. Whatever his previous doubts, a former press secretary noted, Clinton "knew [now] there was no going back."

He denied, absolutely, any sexual liaison, insisted that he had never urged anyone to lie for him, and declared that his only concern was to work nonstop for the American people. Privately, he acknowledged that Hillary's defense of him heightened his shame. But publicly he responded not with shame, but with vigorous, renewed affirmation of his innocence. Hillary had *forced* his new defiance by the strength of her own response.[23]

Clinton rode his newly invigorated political persona to new heights, even in the midst of tabloid headlines about dress stains and secret rendezvous. Nowhere was the president's unique talent for compartmentalization put on better display than with his 1998 State of the Union address. Delivered in the middle of the Lewinsky news cycle, Clinton had already decided not to even mention the scandal. Instead, he trumpeted his dedication to the gospel of being a New Democrat. He began by forecasting the first balanced budget in thirty years. But he could also boast of multiple initiatives he had achieved despite the balanced budget: $30 billion in new tax credits for higher education; $24 billion for a children's health program to cover every child whose parents could not pay for insurance; the restoration of welfare support to legal immigrants. "We have moved past the sterile debate of those who say the government is the enemy," he declared, "and those who say government is the answer . . . We have found a Third Way. We have the smallest government in thirty years, but a more progressive one." Even Republicans applauded. Then came Clinton's coup de grâce. With the budget surplus that would be forthcoming, he declared, we must "save Social Security first." No support for cutting taxes first, none for other Republican favorites. All these were preempted by the "Save Social Security First" banner.[24]

The president was by no means out of the woods. But in the face of attacks that would have debilitated anyone else, he responded with a massive show of strength. His State of the Union address was interrupted 104 times by applause. A *Chicago Tribune* poll showed Clinton's approval rating at 72 percent, while a *Wall Street Journal* / CNN poll had it at 79 percent. "The big news that night," Clinton later told Klein, "was that I was standing there." Michael Waldman, Clinton's speechwriter, called it "the most incredible moment of the presidency . . . Not so much because Clinton had managed to . . . outflank the Republicans in the midst of the Lewinsky scandal, but because in that moment you could just see one trillion dollars moving from their side of the ledger to ours, from tax cuts to Social Security." Hillary's intervention had refocused attention away from Lewinsky and onto the "vast right-wing conspiracy." By doing so she had created a whole new playing field, one where attention could turn to Starr's tactics as much as Clinton's shenanigans and the president had an equal shot at winning those who ultimately were the key players—the American people. In one more example of her capacity to rescue her husband and keep their collective dreams alive, Hillary had altered the terms of the public discussion yet again.[25]

Clinton's staff and cabinet were harder to win over. Vice President Al Gore offered complete public support of Clinton, but his wife, Tipper, was very dubious, and Gore himself was skeptical. Erskine Bowles, Clinton's chief of staff, was sickened by the scandal. Once Clinton's primary golf partner, Bowles never played golf with Clinton again. Mike McCurry, Clinton's press secretary, felt manipulated, as he was called on to deny stories that he really did not think were deniable. "Maybe there'll be a simple innocent explanation," he told the *Chicago Tribune*. "I don't think so, because I think we would have offered that up already." In a fit of inebriated glee, McCurry was once seen riding in an open convertible through Chicago screaming "He didn't do it!" The president himself seemed distant, removed, "out of it." Most painful, Chelsea Clinton let it be known that she did not want her father anywhere near the Stanford campus.[26]

All the while, Kenneth Starr proceeded apace with his plan to charge Bill Clinton with perjury and obstruction of justice. That meant Clinton's fate rested in the hands of Monica Lewinsky. Would she testify against the president? What would she say? Clearly, the tapes indicated that a sexual relationship had existed, but did Clinton ask her to lie? Were others implicated? Did Clinton use associates like Vernon Jordan to secure a job for Lewinsky in order to keep her quiet? Each of these queries involved multiple levels of complexity. There was little evidence that Clinton had urged Lewinsky outright to lie, though he had told her she could compose her own statement to the Jones hearing denying a sexual relationship, which she did. The president had also asked numerous associates to help Lewinsky in her job search, but these interventions had occurred before there was any evidence she might be the subject of investigation on the part of the independent counsel. It was difficult, therefore, to suggest that he was seeking to compromise a potential witness. Ultimately, then, it all came down to whether Lewinsky would testify, and how damning her revelations would be.

Starr and his staff conducted themselves poorly with Lewinsky from the start. They got off on the wrong foot when they detained her after her lunch with Linda Tripp and held her virtually incommunicado for more than eight hours. Clearly, their strategy was to intimidate the twenty-three-year-old. She was terrified, as well as bitter. But worldly wise, she knew she had some rights. While Starr's people tried to prevent her from calling a lawyer, they recognized that she was entitled to use the phone and eventually permitted her to call her mother. After that, Lewinsky's situation stabilized. She knew her mother was coming to get her and that she could outwait the various efforts of Starr's staff to force incriminating disclosures from her.

But the real failure of the Starr team came during the following month, when they sought to reach an immunity agreement with Lewinsky under which she would agree to testify against Clinton if she herself were not prosecuted. In the view of many, the Starr team was not exactly lit up with legal luminaries. Hickman Ewing, Starr's chief counsel, was a conservative Vietnam War veteran who had spent his entire legal career in Memphis. Jackie Bennett was also a hard-core conservative, without nuance or diplomatic skill. Robert J. Bittman, nicknamed "Bulldog," was direct, harsh, uncompromising, and without subtlety. For days the Starr staff sought to negotiate an immunity agreement with William Ginsburg, Lewinsky's lawyer. Ginsburg had become a media star, appearing one Sunday morning on all five major news shows defending his client while on the side letting reporters know that there had indeed been a sexual relationship with Clinton. Finally, two more experienced members of Starr's staff, Bruce Udolph and Mike Emmick, arrived at an agreement with Ginsburg and Lewinsky. In return for a ten-page written description of her relationship with Clinton, and her agreement to testify that the president had suggested to her that she deny the relationship, the government would grant Lewinsky immunity. Ginsburg and Lewinsky signed the faxed document and sent it back to Washington.

There, to the astonishment of Udolph and Emmick, the Starr staff rejected what the government had committed to. Taking the most hard-line position they could, Bittman, Bennett, and Ewing insisted that Lewinsky do an oral "proffer" of the testimony she would give instead of the written one that Udolph and Emmick had accepted. Emmick and Udolph kept returning to square one: There was no case without Lewinsky's testimony. Who cared if Ginsburg was a jerk? The issue was proving their case! But in the end, Starr went with his inner staff, vetoing the deal that his own people had negotiated. "Starr's decision on February 3," wrote Jeffrey Toobin, author of the definitive book on the Clinton case, "marked the precise moment when Bill Clinton's survival in office became assured . . . If Starr had agreed to the immunity deal that day, he would have had the ammunition—in testimony and in conclusive genetic evidence—to prove that Clinton had lied. He could have had an impeachment report for Congress in a month or less. Instead, Starr's obsession with toughness led him to disaster. In attempting to punish Ginsburg, he merely damaged himself. In believing the reports about Ginsburg's incompetence, he only established his own."[27]

Just a few days before, Bill Clinton had made a calculated bet. Told by his pollster that the country would not accept the president's lying under oath and conducting a sexual affair with an intern, he made the decision to lie. Fearing that he might well be forced to resign by the initial surge of public condemnation of his behavior, he decided to buy time by denying the relationship with Lewinsky. Then Hillary rushed to his rescue, as she had exactly six years earlier when the Gennifer Flowers scandal hit the tabloids. Now, as then, she defended her husband's integrity. Rejecting the allegations, she did more—pointing to the "vast right-wing conspiracy" out to get Bill Clinton and thereby shifting people's focus, at least in part, toward those leveling the charges rather than the person accused. Her intervention was crucial, but it was also double-edged. Because now Bill Clinton had to become an absolutist in his own defense, insisting that he had never done anything wrong. Clearly, that claim would not withstand careful examination. But *Clinton had bought time*. With the help of his archenemies, he avoided the immediate embarrassment of Monica Lewinsky's testimony while the scandal was still at fever pitch. Now he and all the others would simply have to wait while the remainder of the tragedy unfolded.

•

Ken Starr was persistent. He subpoenaed Monica Lewinsky's mother to testify, against her will. He offered "transactional immunity" to Kathleen Willey, meaning that if she testified against Clinton she would not be prosecuted for other lies she had told under oath. Conversely, he indicted Julie Hiatt Steele, a friend of Willey's, who had initially fabricated a story in support of Willey's tales of sexual harassment in the White House only to withdraw it later. Starr even attempted to question the legality of Steele's adopting a baby from Romania. The number of papers and commentators questioning his tactics steadily grew, and by February, according to an NBC poll, only 26 percent of the American people believed he was conducting an impartial inquiry. Continuing to pressure Webb Hubbell to turn state's evidence, Starr indicted him (and his wife) a second time for the same tax evasion charge for which he had previously been imprisoned, and he went after Susan McDougal once more for obstructing justice—again, the same charge for which she had already served eighteen months in prison. He even violated the ground rules of presidential security—something George Herbert Walker Bush warned him against—by insisting that Secret Service agents be questioned about Clinton's daily activities.[28]

But the heart of Starr's effort focused on Lewinsky and on Clinton himself. After blowing the chance to get an early immunity agreement with Lewinsky in February, Starr accepted more or less the same terms in July. He scheduled Lewinsky to testify before the grand jury on August 6, and he subpoenaed Clinton on August 17. In the meantime, he sent medical authorities to the White House on August 3 to take a sample of Clinton's blood in order to match the president's DNA with the semen stain on Lewinsky's blue dress.[29]

Clinton could almost feel the noose tightening. "When they took the blood from his arm," a close friend said, "that's when it really hit home." Aides had already noted a chill in the air between the First Couple. While in the spring they had often held hands or hugged, now they seemed to avoid each other, moving in opposite directions. "She deliberately did not want to be anywhere near him at all," an aide said. "She wanted nothing to do with him." Whether the cooling in relations between the Clintons preceded David Kendall's telling them about the Lewinsky immunity agreement and the summons to the president is not clear, but to everyone, it was obvious that events were coming to a crisis. Under intense personal pressure, Clinton searched desperately for some way out. Kendall urged him to refuse to testify on the grounds that a person who was the object of a criminal investigation should never have to go before a grand jury. In Kendall's opinion, Clinton should invoke the Fifth Amendment. But in almost no one's judgment was that course politically viable.[30]

Desperately, Clinton sought to prepare Hillary for what was coming. On the Friday before he was to testify, a story appeared in *The New York Times*, clearly planted by a White House source, suggesting that Clinton was contemplating admitting sexual contact with Lewinsky. According to Joe Klein, the story represented an effort by people in the know, close to the president, to deliver a message to Clinton: "Stop dawdling, Mr. President. Face the facts. Tell your wife and staff." Clinton evidently got the message. That same day, he asked Linda Bloodworth-Thomason, one of the First Couple's closest friends, to talk to Hillary about Lewinsky, preparing her for the worst. She flatly refused. Finally, that night, Bob Barnett, a political confidant, went to see Hillary. "What if there's more to this than you know?" he asked. "I don't believe there is," she responded, "I've asked Bill over and over again." At that point, Barnett pressed the point further. "You have to face the fact that something about this might be true." To which she replied, "Look, Bob, my husband may have his faults, but he has never lied to me." Hillary's resistance to facing the truth was almost as fanatical as Bill's.[31]

Finally there was no choice but to confess. That Saturday morning, Bill woke Hillary and told her what had happened. Sticking to his age-old conviction, he insisted it was not sex. They had not slept together. Only fellatio. "I could hardly breathe," Hillary wrote of the confession in her memoir. "Gulping for air, I started crying and yelling at him, 'What do you mean? What are you saying? Why did you lie to me?' I was furious and getting more so by the second. He just stood there saying over and over again, 'I'm sorry. I'm so sorry. I was trying to protect you and Chelsea.'" What could Bill say? Would it have done any good to go over all the rationales he had devised since January, all the convolutions in his thinking about the political—and personal—consequences of telling the truth from the beginning? No, that would not help. All he could do was face the realities right now. "She looked at me as if I had punched her in the gut," he wrote in *My Life*, "almost as angry at me for lying to her in January as for what I had done." Even worse, she insisted that he be the one to tell Chelsea, who "had to learn that her father not only had done something terribly wrong, but had not told her or her mother the truth about it." It was the worst moment of his life, repeating myriad similar episodes in the past, but this time deeper, more terrifying, more scandalous than ever before.[32]

Hillary was devastated. Despite her recent coolness toward Bill, most of her friends believed she had accepted his denial of any relationship with Lewinsky. "Anyone who thinks Hillary knew what happened before the two of them had their conversation wasn't there that weekend," Linda Bloodworth-Thomason said. Others agree. "That was the epiphany," another friend said. "Public deniability would no longer be possible. Her nose would be rubbed in it." She was heartbroken. "Hillary had hoped against hope that her husband had reformed himself," Sidney Blumenthal said, "that whatever agony she had gone through earlier in her marriage had been resolved. Now she was discovering that it was not over."[33]

Where would she find the resources to respond? How could she come back from this, the most stunning humiliation of her life? No challenge had ever been greater, no pain more excruciating.

There were two north stars in her personal firmament that had guided her through every other crisis. The first was her religion. In her memoir, Hillary talked of going immediately "deep inside myself and my faith to discover any remaining belief in our marriage, to find some path to understanding." So she turned to John Wesley's prayer, which encouraged her to "live every day doing as much good as you can, in every way you can" and struggle with "what theologians have described as the push of duty and the pull of grace." The second lodestar was the example set by her mother. Dorothy Rodham later said that Hillary was able to survive this "because she had a commitment to her daughter—somebody outside of her own problems that she [could be] strong and positive for"—just as she had been with her daughter, Hillary, when faced with her own husband's abuse. Hillary was determined to protect Chelsea at all costs.[34]

In the meantime, Bill faced his next huge challenge—the grand jury. Clinton's lawyers had persuaded Starr not to force Clinton to come downtown, as he had the First Lady, in what many saw as an effort to humiliate her. Instead, the president would testify in the White House, his responses videoconferenced back to the grand jury. But Starr insisted that the session be videotaped, confident that release of the testimony to the general public would embarrass the president before the entire country. It did not take long to get to the heart of the matter, despite Clinton's obsession with legal detail as he sought to deflect the independent counsel's questions.

Within minutes, Clinton got to his major point. Yes, he said, he had been guilty of "inappropriate intimate contact" with Monica Lewinsky, but that activity did not consist of sexual intercourse, and therefore, in his reading, it did not "constitute sexual relations" as defined by Jones's attorneys. There he stopped. He would answer no specific follow-up questions. To do so, he said, would be an act of disrespect to the "dignity" of the office of the president. When Robert "Bulldog" Bittman asked how Clinton's admission of "inappropriate intimate contact" could be reconciled with his lawyer, Robert Bennett's, claim that "there is no sex of any kind in any manner, shape or form," Clinton went into a complicated parsing of grammar. "It depends on what the meaning of 'is' is," he declared. "If 'is' means is and never has been, that is one thing. If it means there is none, that was a completely true statement." Nor did he end his obfuscation there. When asked about oral sex and the definition of sexual relations given by Jones's lawyers, Clinton pontificated, "if the deponent is the person who has oral sex performed on him, then contact is not with anything on that list, but with the lips of another person." But equally insulting were the repeated questions, posed by Starr's team about personal issues, that almost every American would find offensive. Starr's team, Clinton later wrote, "did their best to turn the videotape into a pornographic home movie [so that] the American people . . . would demand my resignation." It was hard to know which of the contending parties was more infuriating. But Clinton achieved his primary goal of admitting only what he wanted to admit. The president was still in control.[35]

He was also furious. All the anger that had been boiling up in him against Starr and his tactics came spewing out as he left the grand jury session. He had booked time on all three networks the evening of his grand jury testimony to come clean to the American people. But he refused to do what virtually every adviser told him to do. Paul Begala,

James Carville, and Rahm Emanuel had written a speech that represented the conventional wisdom in the White House: a combination of self-blame, accountability, confession, and repentance. But Clinton had his own handwritten version that he had been drafting for days, venting his spleen at Starr. A remarkable mixture of egomania and self-justification, it turned the blame outward, not inward. Although all his advisers took exception to Clinton's approach, he proceeded anyway.

When he asked Hillary, who had been crying during his deposition, for her opinion, she responded, acerbically, "Well, it's your speech. You're [still] the President of the United States—I guess." Engulfed by self-righteous anger, Clinton began his speech to the nation by admitting he had done wrong. But then he immediately launched into an attack on Starr, blaming the entire disaster on him, claiming Starr had "found no evidence of wrongdoing by me or my wife." Virtually every newspaper in the country condemned the speech, aghast at its hubris. It was "an utter disaster," *Newsweek* magazine pronounced. "Too angry, too lawyerly, and he never apologized." Most on target, though, was the comment of George Stephanopoulos. "Blinded by his own self-pity," he later wrote, Clinton "had never displayed his flaws more clearly or in front of a bigger audience."[36]

Then came the inevitable consequence of overstepping the boundaries of responsible behavior: withdrawal, isolation, introspection, and a change in course. No one will ever forget the now iconic photograph of the Clintons leaving the next day for their family vacation on Martha's Vineyard. Chelsea stood in the middle, holding her mother's hand on her left, her father's hand on her right, as they walked somberly across the White House grass toward the White House helicopter. It was a stunning depiction of separation and despair. "You could [almost] feel the deep gasps, the strain, the personal anguish," one of Hillary's aides, Melanne Verveer, recalled. With Chelsea devoting herself to taking care of her mother, Bill and Hillary pursued their own separate paths. He slept downstairs on the couch, played golf with Vernon Jordan and others, and conferred with aides. Hillary spent time with the novelist William Styron, who had written about, and suffered from, deep depression. She struggled to maintain her composure. Diane Blair, one of Hillary's closest friends, observed that Hillary "could not talk to anyone [for days]."[37]

Halfway through their retreat from Washington, Bill flew back to coordinate, then announce to the nation, a missile attack on al-Qaeda training camps in Afghanistan and a pharmaceutical factory in Sudan. For years, but especially since the bombing of the World Trade Center garage in 1993, Islamic revolutionaries had been an obsession of U.S. intelligence agencies. Now al-Qaeda had mounted coordinated attacks on the American embassies in Tanzania and Kenya, killing scores of African citizens and some United States personnel as well. The CIA believed it knew the location of a meeting called by Osama bin Laden, al-Qaeda's chief, in Afghanistan, so Clinton came back to the White House for final meetings on the missile attacks. Ultimately, they failed to achieve their objectives. Bin Laden had left the Afghan village an hour before the missiles hit, and controversy raged as to whether the Sudanese factory actually manufactured material that could be used in biological warfare. But Clinton had reasserted himself in a leadership role, and even though Republicans claimed he was simply trying to divert attention from his personal scandal, enough generals and intelligence officials spoke in support of his military intervention that the American people overwhelmingly backed the president's action.[38]

In Martha's Vineyard, meanwhile, the passage of time led slowly toward reflection and the possibility of healing. Hillary reached out to her spiritual mentor, Don Jones, who sent her a copy of the theologian Paul Tillich's sermon "You Are Accepted," a meditation on the meaning of grace and forgiveness. For Tillich, the essence of Christianity was the concept of unconditional love, or *agape*. Christ's crucifixion embodied God's effort to overcome the separation of man from God through an act of absolute love—sacrificing his son. Tillich's message meshed with Hillary's own instincts. Later, she recalled that her time with Bill on the Vineyard, even in conditions of estrangement and pain, had reaffirmed her commitment to him. When Diane Blair and Betsy Ebeling, two dear friends, visited Hillary at the White House a couple of weeks after their return from the Vineyard, that commitment was evident. "I mean it's love," Blair said, "but it's also [that] they're dependent upon each other, and have been for over twenty-five years in ways the rest of us can only begin to understand if we have that kind of marriage ourselves." Although Hillary remained angry, she had begun the move toward reconciliation. "I wanted to wring his neck," she wrote in her memoir, "but he was not only my husband . . . he was also my President."[39]

Bill, too, used the time to reflect and refocus. Ashamed, he now seemed to realize the hubris of his post-grand-jury speech to the nation. With the passage of each day on Martha's Vineyard, he recognized the need for contrition. At the national prayer breakfast shortly after the family's return from the Vineyard, Clinton unabashedly said, "I don't think there is any fancy way to say that I have sinned." The night before the breakfast, Clinton barely slept. "Legal language," he told the assembled ministers, "must not obscure the fact that I have done wrong." Clinton now sought ministerial counseling on a regular basis. "The pastors took me past the politics into soul-searching and the power of God's love," he wrote in his memoir. The new posture of accountability seemed genuine. "To be forgiven," Clinton said, "more than sorrow is required. First, genuine repentance, a determination to change and to repair breaches of my own making . . . And if my repentance is genuine and sustained . . . then good can come of this for our country, as well as for me and my family."

Clinton "hit all the [right] buttons," one minister said. His repentance also touched Hillary. "I never heard him say that before," she told the minister. "And you know what we've been through." When asked how she was doing in terms of forgiving him, she told the pastor, "I think I'm getting there." Others followed suit. In Clinton's moment of crisis, John Lewis, the civil rights leader and congressman from Atlanta, called Clinton a "friend and a brother." And Nelson Mandela, president of the newly liberated South Africa, declared to a White House dinner, "Our morality does not allow us to desert our friends. And we have got to say tonight, we are thinking of you in this difficult and uncertain time in your life." If Nelson Mandela could offer forgiveness, Hillary said, she, too, could try.[40]

The response of Clinton's cabinet was less kind, at least at first. In some ways it was the "old" Clinton—the unrepentant one—who walked into the room on September 10 to apologize for lying to them. But once again, he immediately laid into Starr. One of the reasons he had fallen down, he said, was that for four years he had been angry. It was all so self-justifying—and so oblivious to the sense of betrayal that his loyal followers felt. They had put themselves on the line for him. He had lied to them, used them, exploited them. When Clinton cited his rage at

Starr as an excuse, many in the room were incredulous, especially the women. Donna Shalala told Clinton that his comments were "self-justifying nonsense." She had fired professors for what Clinton had done. "I can't believe that you don't [feel] an obligation to provide moral leadership," she scolded. Clinton only compounded his error. "By your standards," he responded, "we should have elected Nixon instead of Kennedy." Even those who were sympathetic found that retort inexplicable. He still had not grasped the degree to which he had injured those who worked most closely with him. "Listening to my cabinet," he finally wrote, "I really understood for the first time the extent to which the exposure of my misconduct and my dishonesty about it had opened a Pandora's box of emotions in the American people."[41]

Yet the combination of self-pity and contrition seemed to work for the average voter. Ever since the first stories of the Lewinsky affair had broken in January, Clinton's approval ratings had remained high. Dick Morris's poll data in January telling him he should not confess turned out to have been correct, politically. By lying for six months, he bought time, and by July, more and more people had gotten accustomed to the idea that the president might have had an affair with his intern. The rationale that "even if it did happen, it doesn't matter" had taken hold. Ironically, Clinton now was helped—not hurt—when a month after his testimony, Starr and House Republicans pressed to have the videotape of his grand jury testimony released. Instead of generating anger toward Clinton, the videotape triggered widespread sympathy for the president and anger toward Starr.

Notwithstanding his legalistic machinations with the meaning of the word "is," Clinton now came off as sympathetic, complicated, and normal, while Starr and his lawyers looked monomaniacal. More than eighty of their questions were about sex, not one about Whitewater. As Carl Bernstein observed, "there was something prurient about what Starr and the Congress were doing that seemed to offend more people than Clinton's conduct had." As more and more media outlets began to question Starr's impartiality, more and more of the American people became supportive of Clinton (now more than 60 percent) and dismissive of the idea of impeachment.[42]

•

Yet if the public opinion polls suggested that congressional Republicans should shift tactics, an all-consuming political hatred propelled most in the opposition party to pursue nothing short of impeachment. Newt Gingrich sounded the charge. "Mr. President," he told Clinton, "we are going to run you out of town." The day after Kenneth Starr delivered his 445-page report to Congress, the Republicans voted to release it to the general public—before anyone had really had a chance to read it.[43]

Nothing more starkly highlighted the tactics of the independent counsel's office. Starr featured every lascivious detail that it was possible to mention, from Clinton masturbating in his secretary's office after a Lewinsky visit to his inserting a cigar in her vagina. While in 1974 Leon Jaworski had written a "facts only" indictment of Richard Nixon after Watergate, Starr consciously packed his report with embarrassing details. Each sexual contact between Clinton and Lewinsky was described not just once but three or four times. The word "sex" appeared 581 times, the word "Whitewater" only four. When some members of Starr's staff questioned the report's tone and its almost pornographic details, Starr responded, "I love the narrative." To millions of Americans, however, Starr's approach seemed over the top. As Jeffrey Toobin, the widely respected legal commentator for CNN, observed, "such details had no conceivable relevance to Congress's duty, but were rather designed to humiliate Clinton." Suddenly, the president had become the underdog, courageously resisting a schoolyard bully who had neither good taste nor good manners.[44]

Equally important, Hillary Clinton became a national heroine for the steadfast courage she displayed in standing by her husband. Clearly, she was the aggrieved party. But once more, as she had with Gennifer Flowers in 1992 and during the first publicity blast about Lewinsky in January 1998, she resolved to respond as the wronged wife who placed country and family first. Bill Clinton, she said, was not only her husband but also her president, and she was not about to let all the good things that he—and she—stood for be destroyed by a partisan witch hunt. Every time Kenneth Starr or the Republicans raised a sensational charge about her husband's sexual offenses, Hillary's quiet tenacity, by contrast, shone through. And the American people responded far more enthusiastically to the long-suffering wife than to the irascible, sex-obsessed prosecutor. Hillary's approval rating soared to more than 70 percent; Starr's dropped to less than 30 percent.

Still, millions of people remained outraged by what Clinton had done, including leaders of his own party. Many of Clinton's advisers feared that momentum might build within the party to desert him. What if the "feminist" wing in the cabinet chose to resign in protest?— not an inconceivable thought given Shalala's response to Clinton's presentation to the cabinet. Giving substance to the fear, Kent Conrad, a leading moderate Democrat from North Dakota, called the White House to say "you are about three days from having the senior Democrats come down and ask for the President's resignation." Senator Joe Lieberman of Connecticut had already condemned the president as "immoral" in a speech from the Senate floor while Clinton was in Ireland. In the House, Richard Gephardt was convinced Clinton should be asked to resign if the evidence of wrongdoing was sufficient, and David Obey, a leading liberal, told Gephardt: "We have to get rid of this guy. He will destroy the Democratic party for a generation." The Virginia congressman Jim Moran telephoned Hillary and blasted the president, labeling him a "philanderer" and a "liar." "[I'm] offended at what he's done to you," Moran said, "not to mention all the people who supported him." Not surprisingly, the Washington "establishment" shared a similar view. Clinton's old *Washington Post* "friend" Sally Quinn weighed in with a column about the pervasive discontent in the capital over Clinton's behavior. "The scope and circumstances of [Clinton's] lying enrage Establishment Washington," she wrote. "If Washington is a tribe, then the president is a tribal chief. He cannot be seen to dishonor the tribe." Hence, the chief should resign to spare the tribe "any more humiliation."[45]

But once more the Comeback Kid rallied. On the one hand, Hillary raced to the rescue, as she had so many times before. When Congressman Moran berated her husband mercilessly in his telephone call to the First Lady, she quieted his rage by telling him she was supporting Bill against the Republican onslaught and had become the general in charge of his defense. On the other side, the Republicans kept shooting themselves in the foot. If some Democrats thought about joining the anti-Clinton movement in 1998 as Republicans had joined the anti-Nixon forces in 1974, they quickly had second thoughts in the face of the

polarizing partisan rhetoric of the Republican Party, whose leaders es-
chewed even small gestures of bipartisanship.

Any fear of Democrats becoming turncoats ended definitively with
the midterm congressional elections of 1998. It was a rule of thumb that
the party in power would lose between 15 and 25 seats in the House
in the midterms. Clinton had lost more than 50 seats in 1994, Truman
81 in 1946. Not since 1822 had the party in power actually won seats
from the opposition in midterm races. Just days before the election, Gingrich predicted that Republicans would pick up 22 seats. But Clinton
rallied the Democrats, Hillary went out and campaigned, and the Democrats actually took 5 seats from the Republicans. It was stunning. By
casting their ballots against the Republicans, the voters seemed to mirror the recent public opinion polls about the impeachment process.
Clinton's poll ratings were still at 60 percent, two-thirds of all Americans opposed impeachment, and a majority favored a far less onerous
response such as congressional censure.[46]

But the Republicans were not through acting on their capacity for
self-destruction. In the aftermath of the congressional election, Newt
Gingrich resigned both his seat in Congress and his post as Speaker of
the House of Representatives. Gingrich, who had carried on numerous
affairs during his first two marriages and was now about to get married
for a third time, having carried on a long-term affair with a staff member, faced criticism within his own party. Just as the Republicans were
about to elect Robert Livingstone as Gingrich's successor, he disclosed
that he, too, had carried on an extramarital affair and followed Gingrich
in resigning from the House, pausing only to suggest that the president
would be well advised to follow his example.[47]

In August, Bill Clinton had worried that he would be forced to resign
within a week; by November, he was once more a viable player in an ever-
evolving political drama. Hillary had done it again. In what was the most
important of her many efforts to rescue her husband, she paved the way
for his comeback. If she could bring herself to forgive him for the Lewinsky affair, perhaps the American people would follow her example. The
Republicans and Kenneth Starr, for their part, made Hillary and Bill's
task far easier by their extreme tactics and their rejection of all forms of
accommodation with Democrats. It was not a pretty scene. But it was
the one most likely to work for Bill and Hillary Clinton.

•

Every time Bill Clinton became secure politically, it seemed, he acted out sexually, apparently oblivious to what this might mean to his career, his family, and his chance for greatness. It had happened in Arkansas over and over again, Gennifer Flowers being only the most visible example. Now it had occurred all over again. "[I] never believed that Bill Clinton would actually risk his presidency," his former press secretary Dee Dee Myers wrote in *Time*, "a job he had studied, dreamed about, and prepared for since he was a kid—for something so frivolous, so reckless, so small." How could the same man who spent endless hours trying to get right the formula for an economic growth package be so heedless? "Here you had the most tactical, risk-averse President we've ever had," one White House aide observed, "all that polling and market-testing before he'd even propose the tiniest of Dick Morris's 'bite-sized' social programs. And at the same time, for reasons that are inexplicable to me, he takes these huge, absurd personal risks and throws it all away."[48]

Bill Clinton—and his wife—often blamed his childhood. "It pained me," Clinton wrote in his memoirs, "to face the fact that my childhood and the life I'd led since growing up had made some things difficult for me that seemed to come more naturally to other people. I also came to understand that when I was exhausted, angry, or feeling isolated and alone, I was more vulnerable to making selfish and self-destructive personal mistakes about which I would later be ashamed. The [Lewinsky] controversy was the latest casualty of my lifelong effort to live parallel lives . . . There was no excuse for what I did, but trying to come to grips with why I did it gave me at least a chance to finally unify my parallel lives." Hillary often fell into the same pattern of blaming his childhood and mother for creating Bill Clinton the philanderer.[49]

But somehow that explanation was too easy. Yes, the "parallel lives" argument made sense. The metaphor helped to explain the "secrets" Clinton harbored, and the existence of another self, not visible on the surface. But the rationale worked only to a limited degree. It was transparently self-indulgent. Claiming that one could not help one's actions because of certain life conditions was too easy a way out. It removed all personal responsibility. In the "parallel lives" world, free will essentially disappeared. Everything was predetermined, a matter of fate rather than choice. It was all too convenient for Clinton and his self-image. Which was why Donna Shalala called Clinton's explanation to his cabinet about the Lewinsky lie pure rubbish.

Some other dynamic was at work, beyond the ability of either Bill or Hillary to see. When he acted out sexually, he knew he owed her. Whenever she became aware of his transgressions, the debt rose exponentially. As one person close to Bill observed after the Lewinsky affair broke, "in deed and expression, you could see he was trying to do everything he could to make it up to Hillary . . . Whatever Hillary wants, Hillary gets." She, in turn, had something to give. Her forbearance and love permitted him to survive, even to "come back." No one else could rescue him as she could. No one else could make right what was wrong. The exchange even worked romantically. When she was in charge of defending him, they were a team once more, affectionate with each other, sensitive to each other's feelings. "It was hand-holding," one of the White House lawyers said, "arms around one another, lots of eye contact." In some respects, their partnership achieved a new intimacy and camaraderie when she stood by him in the face of his misbehavior. Thus, in the strangest of ways, Clinton's reckless sexual behavior actually enhanced their personal ties. It made their relationship more functional and productive. Arguably—and in the strangest irony of all—it was at the heart of their partnership, the centerpiece that made it work.[50]

Whatever the case, the two were once more a team as they fought the final months of the impeachment wars. Hillary was back in command. She also was more free than she had been for years. Their time in the White House would end soon, no matter what. Having now performed the ultimate act of rescuing her husband from shameful humiliation, Hillary could think of her own future. Her approval rating stood at 70 percent, a new high. On the Friday after the November election, Daniel Patrick Moynihan announced he would retire in 2000 as U.S. senator from New York. That night, the New York congressman Charles Rangel called Hillary to tell her she should run for Moynihan's seat. Others, including the chairwoman of the New York Democratic Party, said the same thing. Perhaps she might think about it.

TWELVE

Survival—and a New Beginning

By the time the House committee chaired by Henry Hyde began its impeachment hearings, it was clear that Republican chances of toppling the president were slim. Public opinion polls had tilted dramatically toward Clinton. The electorate had already given its verdict.

But that did not concern either Hyde or the Republican leadership. They intended to wage a scorched-earth campaign against Clinton, regardless of public opinion. Even if they could not force him from office, they would shame him forever, while demonstrating that Republicans were in control. To most observers in November 1998, the impeachment drama seemed largely over, but the Republicans were determined to play out their hand.

One of the critical remaining issues was what role Hillary would play as the impeachment process unfolded. All along she was the decisive variable. If she chose to distance herself from the president, finally fed up with his outrageous behavior, things could change. Some cabinet members would likely join her, and at least some leading Democrats were open to turning negative. By his behavior, their president had betrayed them. But in the most agonizing decision of her life, Hillary chose to stand by her husband, swallowing her rage and rescuing his career one more time, for the good of her family as well as her country.

There was one more consideration as well. Whether or not it was explicitly part of her calculation, she understood that in the end, she needed him for her political future as much as he needed her. It was in her self-interest as well as his that the Clinton presidency survive. If the Lewinsky affair was more severe on the Richter scale by a factor of ten than anything that had gone before, it nevertheless represented a familiar pattern. The stakes may have been higher, but so, too, were the rewards. If he went down, she would go down with him. Their fates were tied together.

As it turned out, Hillary not only saved her husband but also liberated herself. In fact, she required a successful conclusion to the impeachment scandal to pursue her own goals. If she were once again to become her own person, returning to the political persona that twenty-five years earlier had led Betsey Wright to predict that she would become the first woman president, that could happen only if the Clinton presidency remained intact.

Ironically, no one helped her achieve that goal more than Kenneth Starr. If Bill and Hillary Clinton had a secret weapon in the impeachment struggle, it was the independent counsel himself. At every turn, Starr and his staff rejected dispassionate analysis, opting instead for lascivious sensationalism. These tactics did not sit well with the American people, and by the time the impeachment process came to an end, the Starr operation had left a bitter taste in the mouths of most Americans. All in all, it was a scenario that boded well for the Clintons, and especially for Hillary.

The Hyde committee began its impeachment deliberations in October. Much of the initial bickering revolved around what the Constitution meant when it said the president could be deposed for "high crimes and misdemeanors." Did lying about a sexual affair reach the bar of being called a "high crime"? How did one define "obstruction of justice" or "perjury," especially if the circumstances surrounding the charges were ambiguous? Even though the November elections soon showed Hyde and other Republican committee members that the voters had little tolerance for Republican tactics, the committee plowed on as though voters had never gone to the polls, convinced that shaming Bill Clinton represented a higher political goal. In effect, Hyde and his allies had placed the partisan objective of destroying Clinton ahead of the political opportunity to simply embarrass and wound him. At any time, they could have achieved a bipartisan majority to censure the president for his behavior. But that was not enough. They wanted—they needed—to take it all the way.[1]

The skewed nature of the hearings became clear as soon as Kenneth Starr took the stand. First, Starr agued that Clinton had been guilty of "high crimes and misdemeanors" for lying under oath about his affair with Monica Lewinsky in the Paula Jones deposition; second, he had "obstructed justice" by asking Vernon Jordan to find Lewinsky a job in New York City, in return for which, Starr claimed, Lewinsky would refuse to testify against him. But when the Massachusetts Democrat Barney Frank began his cross-examination, Starr's certainty crumbled. Starr admitted that his office had illegally leaked material from the grand jury to the press, and he acknowledged that he had misled (if not outright lied to) the public when he denied trying to get Monica Lewinsky to wear a wiretap for possible meetings with the president.

Starr further diminished his credibility when he admitted that his office had already concluded that there were no grounds for impeachment in the Travelgate investigation. When had they come to that conclusion? Frank asked. "Several months ago," Starr responded. Then why had they not announced that finding to the public? Starr had no answer. It became apparent that while the independent prosecutor was perfectly willing to release negative information on Clinton, he was not willing to make public any positive findings. Moreover, under cross-examination by Clinton's lawyer, David Kendall, Starr acknowledged that he himself had taken no role in questioning witnesses in the case: Hence he had no first-hand knowledge of the quality of the evidence being presented. Astonished by Starr's performance, Sam Dash, who had been chief counsel to the Watergate committee chaired by Senator Sam Ervin, immediately submitted his resignation as "ethics adviser" to Kenneth Starr. His new "boss," he suggested, had forfeited any claim to ethical integrity.[2]

Slowly, the Democratic strategy became clear. Democratic leaders would highlight the partisan nature of the process, plant seeds of doubt in the minds of the American people, and thus prepare the ground for eventual victory in the Senate. As the House leader, Richard Gephardt, said to Abbe Lowell, his chief counsel, "Abbe, we're going to win by losing."[3]

From the beginning, the heart of the Democratic case centered on the partisan nature of the impeachment process. In the debates at the Constitutional Convention, Alexander Hamilton had commented that impeachable offenses "are of a nature which may with peculiar propriety be denominated POLITICAL, as they relate chiefly to injuries done immediately to the society itself." The operative words were "injuries done . . . to society." Clinton's sexual affair certainly had political consequences, but it was personal and involved no "injuries" to society. In 1974, the Nixon impeachment committee had chosen not to indict Nixon for cheating on his income taxes, because that action was personal, not political. Instead, the Nixon impeachment process zeroed in on *criminal* activities by the president, thereby garnering bipartisan support. Applying the same logic, no basis existed for indicting Clinton for personal recklessness. Democrats were thus able to argue cogently that the facts did not support impeachment. Instead, the whole process was a partisan exercise to "get Clinton," nowhere better manifested than in the Hyde committee's party-line vote to send a recommendation for impeachment to the House. As Jeffrey Toobin noted, "in an odd way," the president's accusers, like Clinton himself, "were blinded by lust—in their case, for one man's downfall."[4]

In a perverse way, both sides were living parallel lives. Clinton's secret demons drove him to acts that threatened his political survival. Yet if he could contain the damage done by his personal demons and be a successful president, he might still retain the confidence of the American people. The GOP, as well, lived in two political worlds. If they focused on simply embarrassing the president, they would both score political points and justify their own integrity. But if they chose the path of all-out attack, they risked drawing suspicion on themselves for being overly partisan, thus undermining their political viability.

In all of this, Hillary Clinton continued to play a pivotal role. Her own reactions were a combination of personal humiliation, deep self-examination, and careful consideration of her own and her family's long-term well-being. Hence, while publicly supporting her husband, she also displayed pain and anger. For two months after his August 15 confession, Bill Clinton slept on a couch outside the couple's bedroom. Often, aides and friends sensed tension. Clearly Hillary had decided to defend her husband when asked, yet she rarely attended the weekly White House strategy sessions on how to fight back. Those conversations were too painful for her. Indeed, Hillary was still working her way through how she would resolve the tensions in her personal life. Greg Craig, an old family friend and powerful Washington attorney who had come on to help defend Clinton against impeachment, remarked that during this time "she was pretty much detached." It was as if she were still processing the impact of Bill's revelations, carefully weighing how to pursue her commitment to him, to their collective political mission, and to her own independent future.

Yet however complex this process, Hillary decisively reinforced Bill's case whenever it was important to do so. As the House vote on impeachment approached, Hillary publicly urged people to practice reconciliation rather than retribution. Most important, when Richard Gephardt asked her to come to Congress to speak to the Democratic caucus before the impeachment vote, Hillary rallied with a powerful, emotional speech imploring House Democrats to stand by their leader. "[I am here] as a wife who loves and supports her husband," she said spiritedly. "Certainly I'm not happy with my husband. But impeachment is not the answer." The words mirrored almost exactly her thought process. First came commitment, then an acknowledgement of pain, and finally a conclusion. Impeachment was not the answer, either for her husband or for herself.

After the House voted to impeach Clinton along strict party lines, Hillary followed up quickly by inviting the House Democrats back to the White House for a rally of solidarity. The tension between the First Couple was palpable before the rally began. But as they walked from the Oval Office to the gathering of congressional Democrats, they tightly gripped each other's hand. Hillary thus helped turn a dismal day of defeat into an affirmation of party resilience in the face of potentially mortal attacks from the Republican opposition. As a result, the story turned out to be as much about Democratic solidarity as about a divided Congress demanding the president be removed from office. A quarter century earlier, Republicans had joined Democrats to impeach Richard Nixon. By contrast, not a single Democrat crossed party lines to join Republicans in impeaching Bill Clinton. It was a story of two radically different political moments.

Al Gore seized the occasion to highlight the partisan nature of the Republican approach. The House, he declared, "has done a great disservice to a man I believe will be regarded in the history books as one of our greatest presidents." Inexorably, the Richard Gephardt strategy seemed to be working—we will win by losing. It was not a bad conclusion to a day that began with a resolution of impeachment. And in shaping that conclusion, Hillary Clinton had played a pivotal role.[5]

Bill Clinton, meanwhile, carried out his part in the overall strategy: Be a good president even as your enemies seek to destroy you. He did so by tackling—effectively—a variety of challenges, both foreign and domestic. While Republicans were acting in a manner that made them seem more concerned with partisan triumph than with the nation's well-being, Clinton took advantage of the opportunity to appear ever more presidential. If part of the Clintons' strategy was Hillary's staunch defense of her husband, the other part was Bill's determination to show he was working for the American people and doing a damned good job of it. To the degree he was able to rack up impressive achievements, both at home and abroad, the Republican attack on him seemed increasingly motivated solely by vindictiveness.

Ironically, the world had become more rather than less perilous since the end of the Cold War. Whereas once there had been just two superpowers and a world divided by the simple question of whether a nation was pro–Soviet Union or pro–United States, now loyalties and responsibilities were far more opaque. Clinton found himself right in the middle of trying to be a broker in this new world. The former Yugoslavia offered a perfect example. Divided into separate ethnic entities, the former independent Communist state experienced constant civil wars, none more vicious than that between Serbia and Bosnia. Through the superb diplomacy of Richard Holbrooke, Clinton had helped create temporary stability in the area with the Dayton Accords, but a long-term settlement proved elusive, and threats of genocide were never far from the surface. The breakaway nation of Kosovo soon became the primary point of contention, with incessant threats by Serbia to wipe out the Muslim population. Clinton demonstrated critical leadership there. Throughout the months when impeachment was being considered, Clinton devoted endless hours to trying to find a way to end the Serbian assault and provide a modicum of stability—and safety—for minorities otherwise subject to murder and mayhem.

Of even greater concern was the emerging nuclear threat in South Asia. The largest democracy in the world, India was also on its way to becoming one of the fastest-growing economies as well. More and more

Western jobs were "outsourced" to India—more often than not, an "800" telephone call from the United States was answered in Delhi or Mumbai. Adept at playing the United States off the Soviet Union during the Cold War, India now had become a power in its own right, detonating a series of nuclear bombs to show its military muscle. India's greatest obsession, however, was with Pakistan. Whereas a clear majority of Indians were Hindus, Pakistan was a Muslim nation. Both countries traced their origins to the struggle for independence from Britain, but they had two very different political systems. Prone to military dictatorships and fanatical about confronting India, Pakistan devoted substantial resources to fighting for domination over Kashmir, a province dividing the two countries. In the spring of 1999, moreover, Pakistan also developed nuclear weapons. One of the most dangerous spots on the globe suddenly became one of the likeliest for all-out nuclear war.

But no trouble spot loomed larger than the Middle East, where for half a century, Israelis and Palestinians had engaged in ferocious conflict. Throughout his presidency, Clinton had devoted himself to bringing peace to the area. No world leader had been closer to him than Yitzhak Rabin. Ironically, the current leader of Israel, the Likud Party leader, Benjamin Netanyahu, had favored Clinton's election in 1992, in large part because George Herbert Walker Bush had openly favored Rabin. Bush had also been the first American president to cut American financing for Israeli security as a means of pressuring Israel into peace talks with the Palestinians. Now Clinton became more and more deeply involved. Angry at Netanyahu for not allowing an industrial park to be built in Palestinian-controlled Gaza, he pushed to put in place the building blocks for peace in the Middle East. On the day articles of impeachment arrived on the House floor, the Clintons journeyed to Gaza to cut the ribbon for a new airport. While he was in the city, the Palestinians, by prearrangement, publicly removed from their charter a clause calling for the destruction of Israel.[6]

Finally, the rise of terrorism among Islamic fundamentalists represented an ongoing threat. Ever since the 1993 attack on the World Trade Center, when the truck bomb was detonated in the building's parking garage, Clinton had made Muslim extremism a priority concern. The intelligence community zeroed in on Osama bin Laden, the son of a Saudi Arabian billionaire who had once fought alongside Western forces in

Afghanistan when they sought to end the Soviet occupation there but who now saw the United States as the embodiment of evil in the world. To achieve his goals, Bin Laden had mobilized a far-reaching underground operation of Islamic fundamentalists dedicated to using terrorist violence to expel America from the Middle East and to wipe out, once and for all, the nation of Israel. After the attacks on the U.S. embassies in Tanzania and Kenya by al-Qaeda terrorists (and during the week after his grand jury testimony), Clinton had authorized missile attacks that sought to kill Bin Laden. Each day, he was briefed on the threat from al-Qaeda, and he focused intently on America's vulnerability to terrorist attacks. He was committed to acting preemptively to destroy al-Qaeda.

Clinton also had not forgotten about Iraq. Although he knew there was no relationship between Saddam Hussein in Iraq and Bin Laden's al-Qaeda operation, he was deeply concerned by Hussein's persistent effort to avoid U.N. inspections and the bravado of his challenge to the rule of international law. Here, too, the Clinton approach was measured yet decisive. He sought above all to restore Iraq's willingness to abide by the terms under which George H. W. Bush's Desert Storm operation had ended. But when Hussein systematically flouted that accord, Clinton ordered a four-day bombing raid on Iraq. As a result, Hussein once more agreed to accept the inspectors.[7]

But Clinton experienced the most success with his domestic policy initiatives. Already his economic program, launched with his 1993 deficit reduction package, had helped spark one of the longest economic booms in the nation's history. He could boast of helping to generate 19 million new jobs; balancing the budget, with pending surpluses to be used to buttress Social Security and Medicare; and supporting, through college tuition credits, a 10 percent increase in the number of young people going to college. Each of these gains may have been incremental, but in total, they added up to significant progress on critical issues. And all of this was happening in the midst of, and in spite of, the impeachment crisis.[8]

The combination of Hillary's strong support and Bill's effective conduct of his presidential duties proved critical to public response to the impeachment crisis. If Hillary had at any point turned against him, Bill would have been dead in the water. Conversely, if Bill had stumbled repeatedly in carrying out his job, the GOP attacks on him would have gained traction. As it was, the Bill and Hillary partnership came through again. She prevented his personal recklessness from taking them down, and he exercised his political gifts to reinforce his viability as president.

It was clear from the beginning of the Senate trial that unless new information surfaced, there was little chance of securing the two-thirds majority necessary to remove the president. Numerous Democrats would have to vote to convict Clinton—not likely after Starr's disastrous performance before the House committee. Indeed, Republican defections seemed much more plausible. In part this reflected the age-old differences between the Senate and the House. Although the upper chamber had also become more partisan in the nineties, the club atmosphere and slower pace of the hundred-person Senate created a measure of camaraderie that still differed dramatically from the mood of the House. The tactics of the Hyde committee simply accentuated the partisan divide, which to at least some Republicans in the Senate was an embarrassment they had no desire to emulate. Richard Shelby, a conservative Alabama Republican and a former prosecutor, confided that he saw the case against Clinton as objectively weak. Indeed, Trent Lott, the Republican leader (and former Dick Morris client), wanted informally to take a test vote, and if two-thirds of the Senate were not in favor of finding the president guilty, to end the trial. House Republicans rebelled, and the Lott plan never came to fruition. What was remarkable was that it had been considered at all.[9]

Hyde and his colleagues thus bore a heavy responsibility in presenting their case against the president. They were not up to the task. Their brief was partisan, with little nuance or evidentiary detail. Moreover, since so much of the House case rested on the sensationalized Starr report, the House team began with little credibility among the press corps or the public at large. Having failed to expand the Starr findings in any way, the Hyde committee faced a hard slog in persuading the Senate or the public to find against the president.

Clinton's defense team, by contrast, represented the best legal minds in the country. Headed by Charles Ruff, a legendary advocate confined to a wheelchair (his disability actually made him more effective, winning people's sympathy), they could pursue all the weaknesses in the prosecution's case without having to deal with any additional charges. Greg Craig worked closely with Ruff, as did Cheryl Mills, a black attorney who pointed out to the assembled senators that most of those leading the Republican charge had voted against the civil rights legislation that permitted her to be there in the first place to defend the president. Effectively, the Clinton attorneys highlighted the differences between Nixon's lies about the Watergate break-in of Democratic Party headquarters, Reagan's "lies" about Iran-contra, and Clinton's testimony about a private sex act.

Perhaps most powerfully, Charles Ruff blew out of the water the idea that Vernon Jordan had acted on Clinton's instructions to "obstruct justice." In what Jeffrey Toobin called a "Perry Mason moment that few lawyers ever have the opportunity to savor," Ruff pointed out that Jordan's intervention on Lewinsky's behalf had come well *prior* to Lewinsky's receiving a summons to testify in the Jones case—hence it could not have been prompted by the subpoena. Indeed, Jordan was out of the country on a trip to Amsterdam when the subpoena was issued.[10]

Given the circumstances, the final Senate vote was almost anticlimactic. With sixty-seven votes needed for conviction, Republicans never came close to reaching the bar. On the obstruction of justice charge, the Senate split down the middle, 50–50. Five Republican moderates, including four New Englanders (James Jeffords from Vermont, Olympia Snowe and Susan Collins from Maine, and John Chafee from Rhode Island), voted not to convict. On the perjury count, the vote was 55–45, but still never in doubt. When Richard Nixon left the Oval Office, the new president, Gerald Ford, had declared, "our long national nightmare is over." Clinton's impeachment had likewise been a nightmare, but unlike the situation with Nixon, its conclusion was not cathartic. Although they had blown the case with their own partisan tactics, Republicans were not appeased. The country breathed a sigh of relief, but the political poison that had been administered did not soon go away.[11]

Bill Clinton had again escaped. The partnership had prevailed. Hillary's help was crucial. Her decision to stand by him saved him from being thrown to the dogs by people in his own party. He had also helped save himself. Just as in the past when he had been rescued by Hillary, he came through with a stellar performance that restored his credibility with the public.

The pattern was by now familiar. Clinton, by his own admission, had a sex addiction. Hillary was an enabler who actually acquired power, and husbandly affection, when she came to his aid. Both features of their partnership were evident in the Lewinsky affair. In that context, the GOP's reckless partisanship made the Clintons winners.

"I almost wound up being grateful to my tormentors," Clinton later wrote. "They were probably the only people who could have made me look good to Hillary again." His family had come back during the struggle. "In the midst of all the absurdity," he said, "we were laughing again, brought back together by our weekly counseling and our shared determination to fight off the right-wing coup." In the complicated world of Bill Clinton's parallel lives, his proclivity for acting out his sexual impulses had once more functioned as an instrument for bringing Hillary and him together.

But the key winner was Hillary. She alone had read the situation for what it was, recognizing that her fate even more than his was tied up in preserving the Clinton presidency.[12]

Unfortunately, Clinton's retrospective assessment of the impeachment crisis reflected a self-righteous egomania. He scapegoated others as a means of defending himself, almost as if his political enemies were the only guilty parties. In Clinton's reconstruction, he was the victim. "The New Right Republicans," he wrote, "wanted an America in which wealth and power were concentrated in the hands of the 'right' people . . . They also hated me because I was an apostate, a white southern Protestant who could appeal to the very people they had always taken for granted . . . I was glad that, by accident of history, I had had the good fortune to stand against this latest incarnation of the forces of reaction and division, and in favor of a more perfect union." In this version of history, Clinton reigned as hero, his sexual affair with Lewinsky an "accident of history" that allowed him to fight "the forces of reaction and division," and, à la Abraham Lincoln, seek "a more perfect union." "When it came to the politics of personal destruction," he commented, "the New Right Republicans were in a class by themselves . . . [They] believed that might makes right, and they didn't care what they put the country through." Clinton's binary world was a mirror image of Gingrich's and Rush Limbaugh's. He was the innocent victim, they the embodiment of evil.[13]

Both Clinton and his adversaries were capable of massive delusions. But Clinton had the advantage of being able to counterbalance his recklessness with consummate political skill. That balance did not exist in either Starr or Hyde. Politically, they were tone-deaf. At every turn, they persecuted potential witnesses, distorted evidence, and violated professional ethics, all to pursue in the most partisan way the objective of removing the president of the United States from office. In the end, they overreached. Yet Clinton ignored the degree to which he had brought on himself all the prosecutor horrors he spent so much time enumerating. In the end, Bill Clinton caused his own crisis, and that responsibility would remain his forever.

One of those who benefited most from the crisis was Hillary Clinton. A direct relationship existed between the Lewinsky affair and Hillary's future political career. All her life, she had lived with Bill's infidelity. She knew it from the beginning, taking the calculated risk that the benefits of their partnership would outweigh the sacrifices. As Betsey Wright said repeatedly, Hillary understood that Bill was not really interested in the women he sought out regularly for sexual satisfaction. At some level she was willing to accept that pain as the price she would have to pay for the opportunity to fulfill their mutual dream. Only in the case of Marilyn Jo Jenkins had Wright's prediction proven wrong, and that affair nearly led to Bill and Hillary's divorcing. The Lewinsky scandal was the final—and most humiliating—test she would endure as a consequence of his sexual addiction.

But on this occasion, her decision to rescue Bill also represented her liberation from him, the vehicle by which she could become the singular figure that Wright and others had always hoped she would be. In a fundamental way, Hillary understood the equation: Her sacrifice for Bill opened the door to freedom for herself. "The most difficult decisions I have made in my life," she wrote in her memoir, "were to stay married to Bill and to run for the Senate from New York." She claimed they were two separate decisions; in reality, they were one. This was the reward she had earned. When she closed the door on the option of leaving Bill in 1998, she opened the door to the option of becoming a powerful politician in her own right.[14]

The idea had always been there. In the 1972 McGovern campaign, Betsey Wright was convinced that Hillary would become the country's first woman president. Everyone recognized her talent. Networking with people of different backgrounds at Wellesley and Yale, staying close to the center, winning the approval of authority figures, she understood instinctively the ground rules for her own political advancement. But when she entered her partnership with Bill, she changed course, tying her dreams to his, becoming complementary to him rather than proceeding solely on her own.

The decision was transparent and mutual. They both calculated that they could achieve their goals more effectively as a team than independently. Now the idea of pursuing her own career returned. When, after the Democratic victory in 1998, Daniel Patrick Moynihan announced he would not seek another term in 2000, people rushed to promote Hillary's candidacy. It became the ideal response to the existential reality she faced, a way of healing the searing humiliation she had just endured, of once again becoming her own person. Significantly, Hillary's decision to explore a New York race came well before the denouement of the impeachment trial. The script up to then had been a familiar one. Bill screws up; she suffers but rallies to his defense; they elude disaster. But this time she opted for an escape route as well. Timing and opportunity joined to open the way to her own career. And she took it. "She's moved on," a friend of Hillary's said. "She's thinking of herself rather than him . . . They both know it's time for him to do right by her." Appropriately—and symbolically—at the same moment that the Senate was voting on the two resolutions to convict her husband and remove him from the presidency, Hillary was meeting with Harold Ickes to plan her New York senatorial race. She had entered her own orbit.[15]

Hillary had considered other options. At her thirtieth college reunion, she talked about becoming a college president or starting her own foundation. But nothing rang as true to her instincts as the idea of becoming a United States senator. Bobby Kennedy had run for the New York Senate seat in 1964, even though he came from Massachusetts; so why should Hillary not do the same thing in 2000, even though she came from Illinois and Arkansas?

To start the process, she embarked on a series of "conversation" tours of New York State. By contrast with her appearances as First Lady, these were unscripted trips on which she met with people to listen to their concerns. As opposed to telling people what she thought, Hillary emphasized learning what *they* thought. The trip was a banner success, suggesting this was someone who cared about her potential constituents and wanted to be informed about their needs. Rather than coming across as imperious, didactic, and all-powerful, Hillary appeared as a person genuinely interested in what other people thought, whatever their differences from her. Consistent with political etiquette, she went to the Moynihan farmhouse in upstate New York to receive their blessing. Neither Moynihan nor his wife had felt particularly comfortable with the Hillary of health care days, but now they gave her their blessing, appreciating the degree to which she seemed a different person. When a young student at a lab school introduced her at a rally, she whispered in her ear, "Dare to compete, Mrs. Clinton. Dare to compete."[16]

No one proved more enthusiastic about Hillary's candidacy than her husband. Twenty-five years earlier, he pointed out, he was "taking her away from her life—the most gifted person I had known." Now Clinton said he was thrilled that she was finally doing what she might have done then. "For twenty years," he told one audience, "we've gone where I wanted to go and done what I wanted to do . . . [Now] I'll give [her] the next twenty years. And if I'm still alive after that, we'll fight over the rest." Hillary's expression on hearing those words, a friend said, "was one of pure bliss, true love." Perhaps the partnership could still work. But this time it would be different. It would be on her terms.[17]

Although she made mistakes during the campaign, Hillary used her poise, grace, and attentiveness to other people's concerns to win over even those who had begun as skeptical critics. Her biggest faux pas came in the Middle East when she kissed the wife of Yasser Arafat on the cheek after she had denounced Israel for using poison gas against the Palestinians. But she quickly recovered. Her race was made far easier when Rudolph Giuliani, the popular mayor of New York City, decided to withdraw because of prostate cancer. (He also had been guilty of a brazen extramarital affair.) Giuliani's replacement was Rick Lazio, a conservative Republican from Long Island. During a televised debate, Lazio alienated moderate voters when he aggressively strode over to Hillary's podium and demanded that she sign, right there, a pledge not to take money from political action groups. Responding calmly, Hillary highlighted by her poise the extent of Lazio's unseemly behavior.

By election night, it was no contest. Hillary prevailed by 55 to 43 percent. She was sworn in as the junior United States senator from New York even while she still lived in the White House. The aura of insurmountable crisis had given way to the miracle of victory. Now it was Hillary who was back, but on her own. Although Bill and Hillary were still a team, no longer did her fate hang on his or his on hers.[18]

Just as Hillary Clinton had set out to seek redemption after the Lewinsky affair through her senatorial campaign, Bill Clinton sought the same end, in his case working incessantly for peace in the Middle East. Free of the stresses of the impeachment trial, he now sought to conclude his presidency with as much success as possible. No goal meant more to him than peace between Israel and its neighbors.

From the beginning of his administration, Clinton understood the centrality of resolving the Arab-Israeli dispute. Yitzhak Rabin had been his closest friend, followed by Jordan's King Hussein. It was not just the statesmanship of the two. There also existed a couples relationship. King Hussein was dying of cancer. He and his American-born wife, Queen Noor, struck up an intimate relationship with the Clintons. The same was true of the Rabins, never more clearly highlighted than in Clinton's moving remarks at Rabin's funeral after he was assassinated. Clinton understood the role that individual leaders could play in the delicate diplomacy of Israel-Palestine relations. Although he had trusted Rabin implicitly, he felt less comfortable with Rabin's eventual successor, the Likud Party leader, Benjamin Netanyahu. Clinton found Yasser Arafat to be perplexing, enigmatic, and unpredictable. But in a private conversation with Taylor Branch, he confided that anyone replacing Netanyahu would be an improvement, while anyone replacing Arafat would be a setback. Playing the hand he was dealt, Clinton did his best to push forward the possibilities of peace, knowing even better than members of his own foreign policy team the details about neighborhoods, West Bank villages, and Israeli settlements that were at the heart of the discussions.[19]

Although there had been near-breakthroughs before, the final, most passionate drive for ending the conflict came in the summer and fall of 1999, and then the whole year of 2000—the period after Clinton had been acquitted by the Senate in his impeachment trial. Netanyahu had been replaced as prime minister by the Labor Party leader, Ehud Barak. Although never as close to Clinton as Rabin had been, Barak was a person of courage who recognized both the risks and possible rewards of seizing the moment. He and his wife came to Camp David in July 1999 and talked with Clinton until three in the morning. Complications arose over whether there should be a prior deal with Syria on the Golan Heights. President Assad of Syria proved remarkably flexible, given the past history of the region, but then Barak pulled back from a deal, to Clinton's lasting consternation, and the Syria portion of the talks broke down.

The main event started in the summer of 2000, when Arafat joined Clinton and Barak at Camp David for a summit that was to last more than two weeks. Arafat began by feeling like the odd man out, angry that the Syrian issue had seemed to take precedence over his own agenda for Palestinian independence. His primary objectives were the same ones that had shaped the Palestinian position for decades: (a) 100 percent Arab control of the West Bank and Gaza; (b) control over the Temple Mount (one of the centerpieces of Islamic religious life) and East Jerusalem, except for Jewish neighborhoods there; and (c) recognition of the principle, enunciated by the United Nations since 1948, of the right of Palestinian refugees to return to their native land. Clinton told Arafat that he would have to compromise, but he was pleased by the commitment of both sides to the process. He especially appreciated how the staffs of the two negotiating partners related to each other. Every night, they had dinner together, talking informally. The White House staff helped make them feel comfortable, with Hillary's aide Huma Abedin, a Muslim, working with both sides.

With acute insight, Clinton noted the culture clash that existed between the negotiating styles of the two principals. Barak held back from putting offers on the table, assuming he could decide the appropriate time to put his last, best proposal forward and have it discussed. Arafat and his team preferred an ongoing give-and-take, with abundant discussion about items big and small so that trust could be built over

time, leading to convergence on the biggest questions. The disconnect
in modes of negotiation made it more difficult to arrive at benchmarks
of progress and put an even greater burden on Clinton, who was scheduled shortly to go to a G8 summit meeting in Okinawa.

Under pressure, Barak finally came through with his best offer,
which he expected Arafat to accept. Arafat refused to play, taking a
traditional first-move negotiating stance of being negative in the hopes
of generating further concessions on the other side. Clinton told the
Palestinian leader he would close down the talks unless Arafat showed
more flexibility. Arafat told Clinton that if he (Arafat) could be satisfied
on the Jerusalem question, he would give Clinton the authority to propose a final land settlement between Israel and the Palestinians based
on what Clinton saw as fair and just. In conversations that lasted halfway through the night, Clinton worked on Barak. The Israeli leader
seemed unwilling to go as far as his aides had already gone in informal
discussions. But finally Barak gave Clinton the same kind of carte
blanche that Arafat had, authorizing him to try to work out a deal acceptable to both sides on Jerusalem and the West Bank. Clinton was
encouraged. "Barak's sense of timing and his enormous courage had
kicked in," he later wrote.

At that juncture, the power of symbolic issues dividing the two
sides burst to the fore. Clinton proposed a settlement giving Arafat
control over 91 percent of the West Bank, a Palestinian capital in East
Jerusalem, and sovereignty over the Muslim and Christian quarters
of the old city (Jerusalem's old city is divided into Muslim, Christian,
and Jewish sectors, cheek by jowl with one another). But while Clinton
was willing to cede the Palestinians custodial authority over two of the
most sacred holy places in the Old City—the Temple Mount and Haram
al-Sharif—he was not willing to grant them *sovereignty* over these holy
sepulchers. Arafat once more went negative, and it appeared that the
peace efforts would come to naught. Clinton now had to travel to Okinawa for the summit, but before he left, he pleaded with Arafat and
Barak to remain at Camp David and continue talking. They agreed.

Unfortunately, when Clinton returned, there had been little progress. Arafat remained fixated on sovereignty over the Temple Mount
and East Jerusalem. "It was frustrating and profoundly sad," Clinton
said. He understood that Arafat's strategy was to hold out until the last

minute, but that time had arrived, and Clinton could not fathom his reluctance. In his public statement closing down the talks, he singled out Barak for his "particular courage, vision, and an understanding of the historical importance of this moment." He knew the Israeli leader had put himself way out on a limb, and he still hoped that the momentum that had been generated at Camp David might lead to a peace agreement.[20]

Hope did in fact rekindle in September. Ehud Barak called Arafat and invited him to dinner at his home. That night, the two talked by phone with Clinton and agreed to resume the three-way negotiations. At just that moment, however, a tragic misstep occurred. Barak's political foe Ariel Sharon decided to go to the Temple Mount, ignoring the long-standing understanding between Jews and Palestinians that neither party would violate the other's most sacred sites. Protests greeted Sharon, violence followed, and once more chances for peace seemed imperiled.

But then Clinton journeyed to the Egyptian seaside resort of Sharm el-Sheikh and presented a plan for moving forward, including an end to all violence, a fact-finding commission involving Kofi Annan and the United Nations, and a resumption of peace talks. Arafat and Barak agreed. In his office, Clinton told Arafat that this was his last chance. If Arafat was going to sabotage the talks, Clinton said, he owed it to Clinton to tell him so then and there. Arafat demurred, suggesting that he was ready for Clinton to proceed based on the progress made over the preceding months.

Now Clinton held the ball. He knew it was up to him to force a peace by setting terms that involved compromise on each side. His premise—and passionate hope—was that if he could make each side give up enough, they could agree to a common solution.

Clinton's ultimate plan was brilliant. The Israelis would give back to the Palestinians 94 to 96 percent of the West Bank, with Israeli settlers to live in blocks of land retained by Israel. The Israeli army would withdraw from all Palestinian territory over a three-year period, and an international peacekeeping force would take their place. Palestinians would develop their own security forces, but with no army. Palestine would control Arab neighborhoods in Jerusalem, while Israelis would control Jewish neighborhoods. Palestine would retain sovereignty over the Temple Mount, Israel over the Western (Wailing) Wall. And a new UN Resolution would ratify the settlement. "I knew the plan was tough for both parties," Clinton wrote, "but it was time—past time—to put up or shut up." With consummate skill, Clinton had threaded a needle with an eye so narrow that hardly anyone else could even have attempted it.

Clinton called each Arab leader to let them know the stakes. In Israel, there was strong difference of opinion on how much was being asked. But in the end the Israeli cabinet embraced the parameters of Clinton's proposal. Now it was up to Arafat. He had toyed with peace for years, weaving and bobbing like a boxer seeking to avoid a final clinch. Clinton told him and everyone else that this was now it. There would be no better bargain, no chance for a superior deal, and the world was watching. To show how much he cared, Clinton canceled a trip to North Korea during which he was to finalize a treaty banning the development of long-range missiles. Still Arafat waffled. To Clinton, he "seemed confused, not wholly in command of the facts . . . not . . . at the top of his game." After his final meeting with the Palestinian leader, Clinton said, "I still had no idea what Arafat was going to do. His body language said no, but the deal was so good I couldn't believe anyone would be foolish enough to let it go."

In the end, Arafat did say no. Forsaking his last best chance for peaceful coexistence with the Israelis, he opted for ongoing hostilities. Some said he feared assassination if he said yes. Others thought he was bluffing one more time, hoping against hope for one additional set of concessions. Clinton warned that he was single-handedly ensuring the election of Ariel Sharon as Barak's replacement—a prediction that came to pass. It was "an error of historic proportions," Clinton later wrote. The president had done everything to make happen what no one else had been able to achieve. And Arafat had destroyed his dream.

Just before Clinton left office, Arafat called him on the phone. "You are a great man, and a great president," Arafat said. No, Clinton replied, "I am a failure, and you made me one." In a presidency full of both triumphs and tragedies, this was perhaps the disappointment that hurt the most.[21]

Domestically, success stories were more frequent. Clinton had not only balanced the budget; he could now boast a $200 billion surplus that could be used to save Medicare and Social Security. Over the seven-plus years of his presidency, more than 20 million jobs had been created; unemployment reached its lowest level in thirty years; welfare rolls continued to diminish; poverty rates had plummeted; and crime had fallen to the lowest level in a quarter of a century. Teen pregnancies were in decline, more and more children were going to pre-school classes, and 150,000 young people were serving in AmeriCorps. If these economic trends continued, America for the first time since 1835 would be totally free of debt by 2013. It was hard to question the enormous progress reflected in such figures, and nothing did more to bolster Clinton's image as an effective president. Whatever his personal weaknesses, few if any could match his political skills or his practical achievements.[22]

But Clinton hungered for more. None of the progress he had made matched his aspiration for the kind of transcendent victory he had been seeking in his quest for peace in the Middle East. Throughout his presidency, Clinton had aspired to greatness. But as *The New York Times* and countless columnists suggested, greatness required engaging with—and surmounting—a huge crisis like war, depression, or a foreign attack. Clinton had dealt brilliantly with many challenges, from deficit reduction to welfare reform. But in the end, the worst crises he had faced were of his own making—the failure of health care, the imminent threat of impeachment because of his sexual recklessness. The only external crisis that rose to the level of giving him a chance for greatness was the Israeli-Palestinian conflict. He had given it his best, doing more than anyone preceding or following him to find the answer. But in the end Arafat denied him the victory he needed.[23]

Appropriately, as the administration wound to an end, a new stage developed in the Clintons' relationship. For years, they had been inextricably tied together, shaping each other's daily behavior. But now things were different. Through her New York Senate race, Hillary became an independent figure, listening carefully to the opinions of others, making sure not to alienate established powers, and using centrist politics to advance her moral concerns. These became the foundation for her election. She was in charge and it was her campaign, not his.

Staff members in the White House noted the change. One aide

believed that Hillary had been unhappy during most of her time with Bill. She bore an abiding grudge toward him, angry at his unreliability but also mad at herself for the compromises she had made for the sake of their partnership. "Does [Bill] need her?" the aide asked. "Yes. Does he like her? Yes. And there are times when he's almost embarrassingly affectionate toward her. But the ambivalence is there on both sides. He acts out by fucking around. She's unhappy, and angry a lot of the time, and lashes out at people." But Hillary now had a way out. While his flaws required her support if he was to retain his political viability, she was less dependent on him for her advancement politically.[24]

A new act in their mutual drama had begun, this time with her as the star. She became the expert driving the campaign bus. The questions they considered together were a product of her experience, not his. Hillary's race for the Senate offered the perfect occasion for restructuring their relationship, but not on the same old terms. She was away for six days at a time. She would send him memos, "B—what do you think of this?" and he would respond to her inquiries—but as a supportive, not a dominant, presence. People noted a new level of affection between the two. As Bill had stated in his remarks when she entered the race, this was something that she had wanted to do for more than twenty-five years, something she had given up for him. The fact that she was returning to her earlier aspirations put new wind in her sails, which in turn provided a new and different structure for their relationship. They were already in marital counseling once a week, and he in pastoral counseling. Perhaps in this new act of their drama, the debilitating swings back and forth would finally come to an end.[25]

Even as Clinton's term in office drew to an end, the debate over his legacy decisively shaped ongoing events. The 2000 presidential election between Al Gore and George W. Bush should have been a shoo-in for Gore. But while Hillary had been able to remove her political fate from Bill's political standing through her New York Senate race, Al Gore was more inextricably bound to the Clinton legacy, both good and bad. He had been an instrumental part of an administration that had helped create the greatest number of jobs in a single decade since World War II, with advances in education, the environment, and family issues that resulted in a public approval rating of well over 60 percent. But as Clinton's personal flaws took center stage, Gore was inevitably affected. Anyone tethered to Clinton's successes was also associated with his failures. In the months after the Lewinsky affair, Gore distanced himself from Clinton. His wife, Tipper, was furious with the president. After repeatedly defending the president, Gore himself felt betrayed. No longer did the two talk on the phone each day or have a private lunch once a week. Instead of claiming ownership of the Clinton-Gore record, the vice president purposefully disassociated himself from Clinton.

Nothing symbolized the gap between Gore and Clinton more than Gore's choice of Joe Lieberman as his vice presidential candidate—the same Joe Lieberman who had denounced Clinton as immoral from the Senate floor. Clinton was enraged. Had Bill campaigned for Gore in Arkansas, Tennessee, and Missouri, it might have made the difference that would have ensured victory for Gore. But a fundamental breach had now occurred between the two. As Clinton told Taylor Branch, "The whole world thinks Gore ran a poor campaign from a strong hand. Yet Gore thinks he had a weak hand because of [me] and ran a valiant campaign against impossible odds." Clinton was right. If Gore had run on their joint record, in all likelihood he would have won. Yet Clinton bore the ultimate responsibility for having driven him away. Nothing more painfully encapsulated the harm Clinton had done to his own legacy than the defeat of his vice president in the 2000 presidential election.

At the very end of his presidency, Clinton compounded the damage to his personal reputation by issuing a pardon to Marc Rich. A multimillionaire, Rich had been indicted for evading tens of millions of dollars in taxes. He made business deals with enemies of America, befriended Israel, and renounced his U.S. citizenship while going into exile to avoid serving a prison sentence. In the meantime, his wife, Denise, donated more than a million dollars to the Democratic party, contributed $100,000 to Hillary's Senate campaign, purchased furniture worth $7,000 for the Clintons' new house in New York, and gave nearly half a million dollars to the Clinton library. During the final two years of the Clinton administration, she visited the White House on ninety-six separate occasions. Despite the fact that the Israeli government advocated for the Rich pardon, in the opinion of virtually everyone, there was no justification for granting it—except the fawning persistence of Denise Rich.

As the journalist Joe Klein noted, a disturbing similarity linked Denise Rich and Monica Lewinsky. The two, Klein wrote, were "of a piece—desperate to please, desperate for attention, and easy to exploit." In Klein's judgment, "Clinton's eagerness to exploit them . . . was imperious and manipulative; his willingness to be exploited in turn, and the certain knowledge that the exploitation was bound to be exposed, was downright weird." Klein believed there was something pathological about Clinton's weakness in the face of both Lewinsky and Rich. "He not only had a compulsion to please others," Klein commented, "but also to be fawned over himself. Indeed, that may have been the real quid pro quo of the Marc Rich pardon. It was a favor granted in return for indulgences." He still believed he could get away with anything, it seemed.[26]

And then there was Clinton's other side—his roots, and the way he returned to them for solace and inspiration. If Clinton's flaws were persistent, so were his strengths. Nothing ever meant more to Clinton than his closeness to black Americans. From his time as a boy in his grandfather's store in Hope playing with black friends to his sitting at the "black table" at Yale Law School, Clinton reveled in his ties to America's most repressed minority. "Toni Morrison once said I was the first black president this country has ever had," he told the Congressional Black Caucus in 2000, "and I would rather have that than a Nobel Prize, and I'll tell you why. Because somewhere, in the deep and lost threads of my own memory, . . . there was a deep longing to share the fate of the people who have been left out and left behind . . . I don't exactly know who . . . I have to thank for that. But I'm quite sure I don't deserve any credit for it, because whatever I did, I really felt I had no other choice." After walking across the Pettus Bridge on the thirty-fifth anniversary of the march from Selma to Montgomery, he recalled: "I loved that day. Once again I was swept back across the years to my boyhood longing for an America without a racial divide. Once again, I returned to the emotional core of my political life . . . As long as Americans are willing to hold hands, we can walk with the wind, we can cross any bridge. 'Deep in my heart, I do believe, We Shall Overcome.'" The emotional core of his political life. What Bill Clinton really cared about.

This Bill Clinton conveyed a powerful sense of the possibilities and limits of the human journey. "Our job," he wrote, "is to live as well as we can, and to help others do the same . . . The river of time carries us all away. All we have is the moment." Clinton recalled going to black churches as a young politician. "For the first time," he said, "I heard people refer to funerals as 'homecomings.' We're all going home, and I want to be ready." With gratitude he called out the names of those who had made his career possible. "I have been privileged," he said, "to spend every day working for things I believed in since I was a little boy hanging around my grandfather's store. I grew up with a fascinating mother who adored me, have learned at the feet of great teachers . . . I have built a loving life with the finest woman I've ever known, and have a child who continues to be the light of my life." In sharing these thoughts, Clinton displayed his ability to distill the most important re-alities of the human condition.

When Clinton spoke in these terms, he brought a new level of meaning to the world of politics. No one could rival his capacity to gal-vanize the idealism, faith, and engagement of the American people on behalf of "opportunity, responsibility, and community." Arguably, when at his best, Bill Clinton was as good a political mind as America has ever produced.

Clinton brought it all together at the Democratic convention in 2000—the roots, the family, the commitment. "My friends," he told the delegates, "fifty-four years ago this week I was born in a summer storm to a young widow in a small southern town. America gave me a chance to live my dreams. And I have tried as hard as I knew how to give you a better chance to live yours . . . Remember . . . keep putting people first. Keep building those bridges. And don't stop thinking about tomorrow."

The question is which Bill Clinton would be most remembered— the one whose favorite memory was crossing the Pettus Bridge in Selma in honor of "the emotional core of [his] political life," or the one who succumbed to the sexual advances of a young intern and the fawning devotion of a rich wife seeking a pardon for her husband.

THIRTEEN

What If?

How could a president so intelligent, so compassionate, so public-spirited, and so self-conscious of his place in history act in such a stupid, selfish, and self-destructive manner?   —George Stephanopoulos, *All Too Human*

Bill Clinton is a mass of contradictions. He is one of the smartest men ever elected president and has done some of the dumbest things . . . He can be the most caring of friends. But [he] has a habit of using people and throwing them away . . . [His] central problem has been the lack of an inner compass. He has 360 degree vision, but no true north.   —David Gergen, *Eyewitness to Power*

Sometimes clarity is enhanced by asking what did not happen rather than what did. History focuses on what transpired at a given point in time. Yet to understand how and why something happened, it can be instructive to explore the roads not taken.

What if, for example, Bill Clinton had appointed a strong chief of staff at the beginning of his transition to the presidency—someone like Sherman Adams under Dwight Eisenhower, or James Baker under Ronald Reagan—to be the "in charge" person who would discipline the presidential staff, order priorities, keep the administration's eye on the prize, and squelch competing interests?

What if the Clinton administration, after making deficit reduction its first order of business, had turned to welfare reform as its first major domestic initiative? Al Gore, Leon Panetta, Lloyd Bentsen, and others argued strenuously that showing a willingness to bring the welfare state under control would establish the administration's bona fides as a responsible manager of the nation's economy. With that kind of credibility, they might have garnered the political chips to proceed with even bolder—and more expensive—reforms such as health care.

What if the door between the White House press room and the office of the press secretary in the White House had not been sealed for the first six months of the administration's term? Would the maintenance of easy access to White House aides have resulted in less suspicion among reporters toward the president and First Lady? If the Clintons had adopted an atmosphere of trust and congeniality with the press corps, would that approach have been reciprocated, creating a foundation of mutual respect on which to build future relations rather than one of recrimination and hostility?

What if Vince Foster had insisted that Hillary Clinton maintain the same relationship of equal respect and candid communication with him that they had shared as partners in the Rose law firm in Little Rock? Might that have allowed Foster to confront Hillary on the explosive potential of the Whitewater records (that "can of worms," as he called it)? And would Foster then have been able to fight back when Hillary insisted that he do everything possible to cover up her involvement in Travelgate or protect files that were potentially embarrassing?

What if the president and his lawyers had settled the Paula Jones case as soon as it was filed, thereby removing—at however high a temporary price—a fundamentally minor irritant that eventually occupied the headlines from 1994 to 1999 and resulted in the impeachment of the president of the United States? When it first surfaced in the *American Spectator* piece by David Brock, the Jones episode seemed negligible, similar to countless other anecdotes about Bill Clinton's wandering eye. It could easily have been handled. What if a discreetly arranged legal settlement had been negotiated, as Clinton's lawyers advised?

What if the president and First Lady had followed through on David Gergen's suggestion that the First Family turn over to *The Washington Post* all records relating to Whitewater, trusting that an honest newspaper with objective reporters would accurately report whether there was anything in those records suggesting criminal behavior? Might such an action have forestalled the feverish speculation that then ensued about what the records contained? Would it have provided the opportunity to put an end to the Whitewater controversy once and for all?

What if the entire approach to health care reform had been different? Would bringing congressional leaders into the process from the
beginning have eased the tensions between the executive and legislative branches? What if a bipartisan approach that emphasized compromise had been adopted from the beginning? Was the threat of a veto for
anything other than 100 percent coverage a move that encouraged, or
discouraged, legislative action?

Finally, what if Bill Clinton had resigned in the face of the Lewinsky
scandal? What might the consequences have been for his administration, for his wife, for his legacy, for Al Gore, and for the nation's history?
If Clinton had apologized for disgracing the presidency and then resigned, Al Gore would have become president. Would that have tipped
the 2000 presidential election to Gore? Would Gore as president have
handled the terrorist threat differently than George W. Bush? Would
he have initiated war with Iraq, or tripled the nation's deficit?

Obviously, such contingencies describe a world that never happened.
Yet it is useful to contemplate how a different set of responses might
have changed the Clinton White House. If nothing else, such an exercise helps highlight those dynamics that were most pivotal in determining the history that did unfold.

A strong chief of staff, for example, would never have permitted
the issue of gays in the military to define the first weeks of the new
administration. Nor would a knowledgeable White House operative have
risked offending the entire press corps by arbitrarily removing a right of
access to the White House that had been taken for granted for decades.
A strong chief of staff would have snuffed out the vicious infighting that
broke out among White House aides and would have imposed a uniform
code of conduct on those who worked in the West Wing, whether for
Bill Clinton, Hillary Clinton, or Al Gore. Anyone who violated the code
would have been subject to immediate punishment or removal. The difference between a White House governed by a strong and a weak chief
of staff is palpable. Bill Clinton, for example, was a policy wonk. He
knew every detail about every policy issue that came before him. Ronald
Reagan, by contrast, knew almost nothing about the specifics of *any*
policy issue. But the Reagan White House under Jim Baker ran like a

streamlined locomotive, while the Clinton White House under Mack McLarty heaved to and fro in constant tension between multiple warring parties, paralyzed by having no clear sense of direction.

If after enacting deficit reduction legislation the Clinton administration had moved directly to welfare reform, it would have co-opted mainstream conservative values, building up political credit so that it could move forward to health care reform. Clinton cared passionately about changing the welfare system. Throughout his twelve years as governor, he thought long and hard about the problem. More than any other single issue, it embodied his philosophy as a New Democrat. One of his first actions as president was to set up a welfare reform study group in the White House. In Clinton's view, changing the welfare system lay at the heart of his "opportunity, responsibility, community" mantra. Nothing spoke more clearly to his desire to win the loyalty of America's mainstream. If he had pushed welfare reform first, he would have demonstrated the conservative side of his credentials, making it impossible for his political opponents to tar him as a left-wing liberal. Then, with welfare reform behind him, he could have used the political capital he had accumulated to seek health care reform as the next step to take in implementing his "New Democratic" credo.

Proactively releasing the Clintons' personal files on Whitewater and settling the Paula Jones case would have cleared the decks of the most nettlesome issues that eventually dominated, then paralyzed, the Clinton presidency. What might have been possible if these controversies had been decisively lanced in the beginning—something that a strong chief of staff would have insisted upon? What other new initiatives, foreign and domestic, might then have dominated the headlines? Instead, the Paula Jones case and Whitewater were kicked down the road. Rather than remaining tiny blips on the radar screen, soon forgotten, each became a history-defining scandal that titillated a worldwide audience and inspired multiple conspiracy theories. Acting preemptively would certainly have caused the Clintons—especially Hillary—significant momentary discomfort. But decisive immediate action would have limited the pain and prevented years of ever-growing damage to the political system.

If there had been no Whitewater scandal or Paula Jones case, a different political approach might easily have secured health care reform.

When the administration came into office, health care reform, in principle, had the support of more than 60 percent of the American people. More than twenty Republicans signed on to the Rhode Island senator John Chafee's proposal to extend medical coverage to between 91 and 95 percent of the American people. If welfare reform had been passed first, and with the kind of centrist coalition Chafee represented, it should have been possible to forge a compromise between the 100 percent coverage that Bill and Hillary Clinton supported and the slightly lower level of coverage advocated by moderate Republicans. As late as March 1994, Bob Dole wrote Daniel Patrick Moynihan asking if the time had come for a Moynihan-Dole bipartisan health care reform bill. Tragically, it never happened.

Had even *some* of the above "what ifs" been realized, the trajectory of the Clinton administration would have been dramatically altered. Both Clintons would today be associated primarily with legislative benchmarks equal to the enactment of Social Security and labor reform under FDR and civil rights and Medicare under LBJ. With NAFTA, AmeriCorps, family leave, deficit reduction, health care, and welfare reform, the Clinton administration would have been hailed as one of the most productive of the twentieth century.

Perhaps most important, there would have been no impeachment. And no final "what if." If Bill Clinton had chosen to resign to atone for the shame of the Lewinsky scandal, another New Democrat, Al Gore, would have taken over. But that was an act of surrender that Bill Clinton was not prepared to make.

Why did none of these "what ifs" come to pass? The answer to that question, and with it all the others, rests with the partnership between Bill Clinton and Hillary Rodham. The history—good and bad—of the Clinton administration reflects the degree to which their internal dynamics shaped the choices they made at every turn.

Hillary assumed substantial responsibility for selecting White House aides. She had no interest in a strong chief of staff, someone that might obstruct her power within White House inner circles. Just as during Bill's first term as governor in Arkansas, having multiple voices and decision makers improved her own ability to wield decisive influence.

Dick Morris had persuaded her that becoming Bill's chief of staff in the White House was unworkable. But if she could not have that job, it was important that no one of comparable strength should ascend to it. That way, she could not be impeded in her own plans by a power structure in which someone else exercised executive authority. The same rationale helps explain the importance she placed on having her own office in the West Wing, as well as hiring an independent staff fully competitive with her husband's and Vice President Al Gore's. She would brook no diminution of her own executive power.

That power also gave her the right to act, autonomously, on issues that often were not even brought to Bill Clinton's attention. The closing of the White House to the Washington press corps was carried out at her instigation, and with no apparent input from the press secretary, George Stephanopoulos, or other Oval Office aides. Similarly, the decision to fire the travel office staff originated in a discussion she had with Harry Thomason and Linda Bloodworth-Thomason; no wider consultation occurred. The First Lady ordered immediate action, and then, when a furor erupted, she took every step possible to obscure the pivotal role she had played in the entire affair.

In all of this, her chief instrument of action was Vincent Foster, perhaps the closest friend she had in the world, whom she had brought with her from the Rose law firm in Little Rock to be deputy counsel to the president. But rather than be a comrade to Hillary as he had been in Little Rock, Foster became submissive, and his chief duty in the White House was to do the First Lady's bidding. With growing agitation, he tried to obey her wishes, disguising her involvement in Travelgate and seeking to protect the privacy of her records on Whitewater, her personal investments, and the lobbying she had done with government officials in Arkansas on behalf of Rose law clients. A relationship that once had been a model of mutual respect and transparency turned into one of hierarchical authority. "Let's go to lunch" had been replaced by "Fix it, Vince."

When Foster's depression led him to take his own life, Hillary once more assumed direct command, ordering another old friend, the presidential counsel Bernie Nussbaum, to bar the park police from going through Foster's papers, insisting instead that Nussbaum decide which papers should go to the police and which to her private files in the

White House residence. Predictably, when this became known, conspiracy theories were the result.

In perhaps the most portentous decision of Bill Clinton's first term,
Hillary's refusal to share Whitewater documents with *The Washington
Post* virtually guaranteed the appointment of a special prosecutor. It
should have been a no-brainer. The president's entire staff recognized
the wisdom of taking the chance. If there was nothing to hide, what
could be lost? Saying no was a slap in the face of the most important
political voice in the capital other than Congress. Yes, there were legal
concerns; but compared to the political stakes involved, and the opportunity to deflect the crusade for an independent prosecutor, such concerns were small potatoes. It was a moment, as George Stephanopoulos
said, that changed history—the one decision, of all that were made,
that he wished could be made over again.

Nothing encapsulated the melodrama of Hillary's role during these
first two years more than her decisions on health care. She insisted that
her task force be given priority over welfare reform, even though she may
well have understood the tactical reasons for going with welfare first.
But that would have meant deferring her role as the first in line to make
policy history. Moreover, she repeatedly dismissed others in the administration who raised questions about her approach to health care reform.
Whether these questions came from the secretary of the treasury, the
surgeon general, the secretary of health, education, and welfare, or the
head of the president's Council of Economic Advisors, Hillary responded
with haughty rejection. So fervent were her own staff in support of their
boss that none of them intervened. Regardless of the furor over secret
task force hearings or the absence of public debate, no one was permitted
to have second thoughts. Even the president refused to intervene, knowing full well the political land mines Hillary was planting. Worse, he
compounded the problem by threatening—at Hillary's insistence—a
veto of any bill that did not meet fully and precisely her criteria.

In this way, the First Lady repeatedly shaped the administration's
response at junctures that in hindsight cry out "What if?" How could
brilliant political minds let this happen? Where was the common sense?
Why did no one have the courage—the integrity—to blow the whistle?

Again, the answer goes back to the dynamic at the heart of Bill and
Hillary's relationship. They had a common dream. They would be part-

ners. Together they would conquer, and better, the world. But her part in realizing the dream was tied directly to his inability to integrate his parallel lives, to discipline his sexual addictions. Hillary knew from the beginning these impulses would not disappear. Yet she took the calculated risk that she could control them enough that they would not derail the larger political dream that they shared.

Most perverse of all, Bill's penchant for womanizing animated the partnership, shaping its dynamics. When he acted out, she became more central to, and influential in, their common journey. His indiscretions invariably forced him to pacify her rage. And that required a newly contrite and attentive Bill to cede more control to her side of their partnership. In that way, Bill's addictions were central to Hillary's empowerment. They functioned as the pivot point of their partnership. As a result, she won out on multiple counts: They were happier together as a couple after his indiscretions, he paid her greater attention, and her ability to shape the partnership reached new heights.

The dynamics, in retrospect, seem transparent. Gennifer Flowers's revelations threatened to destroy Bill's candidacy. Hillary came to his rescue. She created, then coordinated his "defense team" that aggressively took charge of the counterattack. By affirming her love for her husband, she redeemed Bill in the eyes of the public but simultaneously solidified her right to the role of copresident. She could dictate the shape and direction of the health care initiative because "he owed her." Whatever objections his closest economic and political aides raised ran counter to the bargain he had struck with her. Hillary's power increased even further when news spread of the *American Spectator* story on state troopers procuring women for Bill, including a young clerical worker named Paula. In such circumstances, Clinton lost all leverage. He could not settle the Jones case, nor make a compromise on health care. When Hillary insisted that he threaten a veto of any health care bill that did not meet her requirements, he agreed—despite overwhelming opposition from his political advisers. Their dissent did not matter. Under such circumstances, Bill Clinton lost the ability to uphold his end of the partnership and use his political instincts to find the right answer.

Only in the aftermath of the health care defeat and the 1994 midterm election debacle—which in the eyes of many people were directly connected—did Bill resume a leadership role in the relationship. The pendulum had swung. Hillary herself finally recognized the degree to which she bore responsibility for the administration's downward plunge. While she did not remove herself completely, she entered a lengthy phase of reflection and withdrawal, exemplified by her temporary embrace of a more traditional wifely persona and then a role as an international spokesperson for women's and children's rights.

Hillary became a different person, at least for a time. During the first two White House years she had been everywhere at once; now she was absent. "I mean you just didn't even see her," her friend Harold Ickes noted. Although Hillary was responsible for bringing Dick Morris back into the Clinton fold, the two did not talk through the issues as they always had done in Arkansas. In Morris's view, it looked as though the president "did not speak to Hillary about anything." While clearly an exaggeration, Morris's assessment reflected a larger truth. Where once she had been a constant presence, now Hillary never even attended strategy meetings. "I couldn't see . . . Hillary's fingerprints on anything," Morris observed.[1]

In part, this period of quietude reflected the spiritual quest Hillary was on throughout her life, though at times more intensely than others. Who was she? How would her heroine Eleanor Roosevelt have acted in similar circumstances? Where and how could she be most effective in carrying forward her half of the partnership she had begun so long ago with Bill? She had always had a spiritual core. From the time Don Jones took her to hear Martin Luther King, Jr., in Chicago to her speech in Austin in 1993 pondering the questions of when life begins and when it ends, Hillary was in touch with the most fundamental questions of human existence. Often they got lost in the midst of the various crises she confronted, from Gennifer Flowers to Whitewater. But in the end, her search for a life of faith and meaning remained central to her personal journey.

Much of Hillary's activity the next year involved pursuing new answers to the question of how she could make a difference for good in her world. Her trip to India with Chelsea cast her in the role of spokesperson for universal human rights issues, particularly involving women. When she subsequently traveled to China for a United Nations conference on women, Hillary captured the world's attention as an international figure championing the rights of women and children. She also devoted hours each day to writing *It Takes a Village*, a passionate plea for people to recognize that only the combined energies and dedication of every person can assure a society in which children can grow into successful and productive citizens.

The remainder of Hillary's time was consumed by Whitewater, the can she had kicked down the road by refusing to turn over her papers to the *Post*. Now the special prosecutor—first Robert Fiske, then Kenneth Starr—was in hot pursuit of evidence as to whether Hillary had violated the law. Although both Bill and Hillary were under investigation, Hillary was the priority target. She was also the person who mobilized the legal team to defend the presidential couple. In daily conference calls she coordinated the team's work, strategized responses, and sought to keep potentially embarrassing information about her legal practices from mushrooming into a federal indictment.

Still, the one reality that more than any other determined Hillary's place in the administration during the years after health care was that Bill Clinton was on a roll. He did not want to play the part of copresident that she had assumed during the first two years. With Dick Morris as his guru, Clinton traversed the political playing field with the finesse of an All-American. The legislative victories may have been small—$30 billion in new tax credits for parents with children in college, $24 billion for new children's health programs, a hundred thousand more police on the streets, V-chips to prevent youngsters from watching violent TV programs—but they added up, and the political dividends were huge. By addressing meaningful issues for millions of mainstream Americans, Clinton reestablished his credibility as a New Democrat. Republicans, meanwhile, alienated mainstream Americans when they chose to close down the government rather than work with Clinton on budget issues. The result: Bill Clinton became a middle-class hero again. Hillary's popularity rose with her husband's. While no longer copresident, she was back in the good graces of millions of Americans, and she drew rave reviews when she presented her husband to the 1996 Democratic convention as the person who more than anyone else could save the village of America by being its community leader.

But it was only a matter of time before the pendulum swung back in Hillary's direction. At almost the same moment that Bill was scoring his greatest victory in the White House, he once again succumbed to his sexual impulses. Seemingly oblivious to the stupidity of his actions, he carried on a sixteen-month sexual relationship that was bound to be discovered. When it was, all the other skeletons came back out of the closet—Paula Jones, Troopergate, all the decisions that had created a world in which, in a moment straight out of the theater of the absurd, Whitewater and Monica Lewinsky occupied the same moment of history.

That was the occasion—the final occasion—when Hillary Clinton faced the question of whether to rescue her husband. It was the ultimate "what if" moment: whether to stand by him, fight alongside him, and work together with him to once more salvage their common vision, or to let it all fall apart and force him to resign in disgrace.

The possibility of resignation was real. It was one that Clinton felt closing around him when news of the Lewinsky affair broke. In his panicked first phone call to Dick Morris, Clinton openly speculated that he would not be able to survive in the presidency for another week. His former aide (and by then ABC News commentator) George Stephanopoulos immediately raised the issues of resignation and impeachment on his TV news show. So did the White House correspondent Sam Donaldson. The political columnist George Will declared Clinton's presidency deader than a doornail, and NBC's Tim Russert gave him only a fifty-fifty chance of survival. If, as seemed possible, Democrats and Republicans came to the White House to tell Clinton it was time to go, there was little chance he could remain.

Only Hillary could save him. She asked Bill: Who was this woman? What was the relationship? It was not sexual, Bill responded. Lewinsky needed help and came to him and he had responded. And now there was this charge of sex. It was not true. She must believe him. He had not engaged in a sexual relationship with the young intern.

Hillary Clinton had profound reasons of self-interest and self-protection to stand by her husband. Yes, she took Bill at his word, as countless friends testified; she did not believe her husband would lie to her, and besides, she trusted the security system of the White House. But she also knew instinctively that her future was tied to his survival. She would never have a chance to become a political figure in her own right if his presidency ended in disgrace. To secure her own survival, she had to fight for his.

Ultimately, then, Hillary's was less a choice than an affirmation of her original contract with Bill, of her personal aspirations to make a difference in society, of her love for her husband—and finally, of her own dreams to become the person Betsey Wright and so many others believed in. As a result, she saved her husband for the final time. Simultaneously, she freed herself to become the person she had always had the potential to be. When, as Betsey Wright commented, "she came out of her anger," she also delivered another message: "I'm going now. It's my turn."[2]

Considering the "what ifs" in the Clinton presidency highlights the degree to which any judgment of the Clinton years must consider both parties in the relationship. Bill Clinton did not exist without Hillary. Without Hillary, Bill's womanizing would eventually have upended his career. He needed her because her affirmation of his moral integrity was necessary to rescue him from dismissal as a sexual miscreant. But Hillary also needed Bill. Realization of her ambitions depended on his political ascent. Joe Klein got it right. "The quality and texture and the nature of the Clinton marriage was the . . . abiding mystery of his presidency," the backstory as well as the main narrative of his eight years in the White House.[3]

By himself, Bill Clinton was one of the most acute masters of politics ever to occupy the Oval Office, in the same league as FDR and Lyndon Johnson. However complicated the issues, he understood their nuances instinctively. In both foreign and domestic policy, he demonstrated an unparalleled intellectual grasp of both perils and opportunities.

Yet he lacked discipline and political toughness. Yes, there were exceptions—the Mexican peso crisis, the planned invasion of Haiti, granting a visa to the IRA leader Gerry Adams, pushing for NAFTA, signing the welfare reform bill. But more often than not he deferred decisive action in order to continue exploring options. Staff and cabinet members became accustomed to his taking one position only to subsequently abandon it as soon as he began to reexamine the choice he had supposedly already made. It was why Democrats were scared to death that he would cave if left alone with Republicans during the budget battles of 1995–96.

The person who put steel in his spine was Hillary. She did it in his campaigns, in how she encouraged him to preempt the womanizing rumors, and in how she coordinated the defense team in response to Whitewater. She brought the same focus to organizing staff operations in the White House and to determining policy priorities, including her own role in shaping health care. In the eyes of most, she was the central figure of both his personal and political life. "The Bill Clinton I saw," David Gergen noted, "needed the emotional approval of his wife on a daily basis . . . When they were in balance, they complemented each other well. Their partnership energized his leadership. She was the anchor, he the sail. He was the dreamer, she the realist. She was the strategist, he the tactician." As long as their relationship worked, each brought to the other a quality that was missing in the other, making the whole far greater than its two halves.[4]

But if the pendulum swung out of balance, disaster followed. When Bill's excesses went too far, Hillary ascended. Yet at such moments, when it was most crucial that Hillary recall her mother's metaphor about the carpenter's level and keeping the bubble in the middle, Hillary lost her balance. She no longer listened to other voices, she imposed her will on the president, and she insisted on getting her way, even if it meant flying in the face of political reality.

When Hillary's excesses went too far, Bill achieved some of his finest moments, though never the transcendent moment of greatness that Dick Morris and others insisted was necessary for Clinton to join the ranks of the best presidents. With the exception of welfare reform, Clinton's legislative achievements were niche initiatives, focused, with brilliant precision, on specific constituencies and designed to enhance his political strength among middle-class Americans: hence Maureen Dowd's description of Clinton in *The New York Times* as a "fixer of tiny things."

In the end, Bill Clinton was a victim as well as a beneficiary of the partnership that had brought him to the presidency. Hillary's actions helped cause the disastrous political failures of his first two years in office. Because of her decisions, the major domestic initiative of his administration imploded, costing him the chance to achieve the greatness he had dreamed of since childhood.

Yet Bill Clinton was more the beneficiary than the victim of their partnership. Hillary's presence was what allowed Bill to surmount his weaknesses in the first place, to survive the consequences of his parallel lives. Without Hillary's discipline and focus, he could never have achieved what he did. Had she not been there to rescue him, he would never have left Arkansas. If Bill lacked the steel to stand up to Hillary on matters such as compromising on health care or releasing the Whitewater papers, she possessed the steel to sustain his political viability when all seemed lost.

The ultimate "what if" question is what might have happened if Bill Clinton had kept his zipper up. Would his brilliant political instincts and his mastery of public policy have flourished, unimpeded by an out-of-control libido? A monogamous Bill working alongside Hillary would have been much more likely to have gotten welfare reform done ahead of health care, subsequently winning on health care and putting his legacy alongside FDR's and LBJ's. It would have put him in a position to pass on his presidency, cleanly, to Al Gore.

But that counterfactual scenario is the least plausible of all. There was no way for Bill Clinton to harness his erotic impulses. Everything bad that happened went back to his inability to control his secret urges. Hillary may have been guilty of inflicting grievous injuries on the administration by her actions, but Bill was the only one who came close to inflicting a mortal wound. That weakness became the crux of the political and personal partnership that made Hillary essential to his survival.

The final, more tantalizing question is whether *she* needed *him* to achieve her ambitions. She made a bet, when she married Bill Clinton in 1975, that the two of them together would have a better chance of realizing their shared dreams than if either one of them acted alone. But was the bet a good one? Did it work out in her best interest? Did he need her more than she needed him? Without Hillary, Bill would never have reached the White House. But could the same be said of her? Without him, might she have been able to achieve the dream that Betsey Wright held in her heart for her—to become the first woman president of the United States?

We will never know the answer. The Hillary Clinton career after 1999 suggests intriguing possibilities. The one reality we can be confident of is that the partnership that Bill Clinton and Hillary Rodham created was instrumental in shaping the last presidency of the twentieth century.

When historians run the final scorecard on American presidents, Bill Clinton will be rated highly. He presided over an economy that grew faster and was more prosperous than at any other time in the century. His deficit reduction package, enacted by just one vote in the House and a tie-breaking ballot cast by Vice President Gore in the Senate, helped trigger a boom by reassuring the magnates of Wall Street that this president knew what he was doing. Twenty-two million jobs later, he could leave the White House proud of what his economic team had accomplished. For the first time in decades, the government ran a surplus. An end to all national debt was in sight.

Nor was that all. He had enacted NAFTA, bolstering the forces of free trade. He had overhauled the welfare system—his second-largest domestic achievement after deficit reduction. Family leave, AmeriCorps, tax credits for higher education, more police on the streets, health insurance for children, V-chips for TV, the Earned Income Tax Credit to help poor people—all of these were sources of pride. They were not "big pieces of legislation," Stephen Hess of the Brookings Institute noted. Some even called them "scraps off the table." But as Joe Klein pointed out, the college tax credit of 1997 was larger than the GI Bill after World War II. Clinton's most important achievement, he concluded, "[was] a government that had dramatically improved the lives of millions of the poorest, hardest-working Americans."[5]

The tragedy was that it might have been so much more. The most talented political figure of his time became, in Joe Klein's words, a "mechanic," most of whose achievements amounted to small-scale reforms in "dozens of line-item skirmishes."

The secret to that tragedy resides in the partnership that shaped the Clinton years. Bill refused to take responsibility for his actions or contain his sexual impulses. And Hillary abetted the process by blaming all his problems on a "vast right-wing conspiracy," thereby allowing him to portray himself as a virtuous soldier fighting against evil, not answerable for how he had brought on himself the attacks he now deplored.

A friend of David Gergen once said, "Bill Clinton would have been a great president if he had not been who he was." That statement misses a more basic truth: Whatever Bill Clinton achieved owed as much to Hillary Clinton as to himself. Who they were together determined, for better or worse, what their partnership was able to accomplish.

Epilogue

"I'm going now. It's my turn."

With those words to Betsey Wright during the Lewinsky scandal, Hillary Rodham Clinton set out on a new path. Her moral center, nurtured by Don Jones and the Methodist Youth Fellowship of her youth, was ready to reassert itself. Long before she met Bill Clinton, she had developed her own distinctive style. Intent on making a difference, she developed a balanced approach to social conflict. Throughout her time at Wellesley and at Yale, she retained her commitment to staying in the middle, the position her mother had taught her was so important to a productive life. Even as she led student protestors at Wellesley and joined supporters of the Black Panthers at Yale, she never alienated those in power or stopped listening to people with points of view different from her own. She always had a moral anchor, but she did not use it as a weapon to impose her views on others. If people wished to make a difference, she told friends, they first had to build constituencies, win over potential allies. Alienating others was the last thing an agent of reform should do.

After Hillary met Bill Clinton, that worldview started to change. The moral core remained; indeed, some of the most powerful words Hillary Clinton spoke reflected her spirituality, as in her Liz Carpenter lecture in Texas while her father was dying. Yet that moral voice soon took on a didactic quality. Issues became less gray, more black-and-white. Enemies were to be defeated, not won over. Life became more of an us-against-them contest. Subtlety and conciliation mattered less than hammering a foe into submission.

The nature of the partnership between Bill and Hillary helps explain why she came to adopt this Manichaean view of life. When Bill acted out, she could either turn her moral wrath on her husband, or come to his rescue by directing her moral wrath on his accusers (or victims). Hillary chose the second path, seeing *them* as the source of evil, not her husband. *They* were the enemy, and if they succeeded in besmirching his reputation, the partnership she had forged with him would be undermined. The enemy could be given no quarter.

In this ever-tightening circle of good versus evil, there could be no acknowledgment of guilt or weakness. Hillary's self-image of moral probity needed to be protected as much as, if not more than, her husband's. Hence there could be no admission of misconduct. If there were files that suggested Hillary had overbilled clients, or that she had violated the bar's code of ethics by contacting officials who worked for her husband, to make them public would be devastating. Hence, she applied the same white/black binary to her own situation that she used to respond to those who circulated rumors about Bill's sexual adventures. Rejecting accommodation of any sort, she refused every request to make her records available to reporters or investigators. Nothing could be allowed to tarnish her reputation for moral rectitude.

That dynamic became its own trap. The rules of combat—*no* disclosure under any circumstances, *never* an admission of guilt— became a cage that foreclosed conciliation. Everything had to be her way. Critics' voices, even if they came from inside the Clinton camp, were rejected.

Almost every bad decision made in the Clinton White House during the first two years reflected that mind-set. Hillary's previous approach of consultation and balance had given way to a worldview in which a middle ground no longer existed. When Hillary told the Democratic Senate caucus that their task was to "demonize" anyone opposed to her health care plan, she both exhibited the myopia of her new modus operandi and cut herself off from the very people she needed most in order to achieve her goals.

In the end, what made the Bill and Hillary partnership work was also what prevented its vision from being achieved. Neither Bill nor Hillary could accomplish their goals when seeing the world as "us" against "them." It was too simple a formula. It ignored the reality of Washington's culture. And it drove away the give-and-take that represented the essence of bringing people together. The consensus approach that had defined Hillary's political lifestyle at Wellesley and Yale went into eclipse. Its disappearance foretold the problems her leadership in Washington would encounter.

When Hillary Clinton saved her husband from impeachment, she finally freed herself from that cage. It was the last act of one approach to politics and the first act of a return to the philosophy that had guided her through Wellesley and Yale. How did Hillary begin her campaign for election to the U.S. Senate from New York? By embarking on a lengthy *listening* tour of the state. What do *you* care about? she asked her future constituents. How does this issue appear to *you*? Rather than demonize her opposition, she allowed them to demonize her, in the process relearning that it was better to be open and welcoming than judgmental and arrogant. It was a different Hillary who responded to the aggressiveness of Rick Lazio, her Republican opponent for the New York Senate seat. Had he run against the Hillary who had overseen health care reform, Lazio might have had a shot. Instead, the Senate candidate Hillary repeatedly displayed her openness to multiple perspectives, her willingness to listen, her refusal to sling mud. And she coasted to victory, a consensus candidate seeking ways to move forward peacefully.

That was what made Hillary Clinton one of the most popular and effective members of the United States Senate for the next eight years. Her entire demeanor was nonpartisan. Rather than defining herself by those she chose to do battle with, she created her Senate identity by reaching out to colleagues on both sides of the aisle. She was noted for her friendship with Republicans like Arizona senator John McCain or South Carolina's Lindsey Graham. Wherever possible, she sought bipartisan compromise. The contrast with her demeanor in the White House could not have been more striking.

For most of this period, the Clintons lived more apart than together. They had two homes, one in New York, where Bill Clinton spent most of his time working on his new global foundation, the other in Washington, where Hillary carried out her duties at the Capitol. Both Clintons traveled extensively, but rarely together. Bill had his own cadre of friends, many of them wealthy, and he flew around the world in private planes to carry forward his own agenda.

Interestingly, the only time when Bill became a pivotal part of Hillary's daily political life was during her 2008 bid for the presidency. From the time she had been elected to the Senate, most Americans expected that she would seek to fulfill Betsey Wright's dream that Hillary become the country's first female president. After her decisive re-election victory as senator in 2006, the time seemed right. The Bush presidency was in serious decline. Having launched two increasingly unpopular wars in Iraq and Afghanistan, and presiding over a weakening economy, the Republicans were vulnerable. In contrast, Hillary's popularity continued to grow. Her only serious weakness as a candidate was her having voted to give George W. Bush authorization to start a war with Iraq.

Both directly and indirectly, Bill Clinton played a significant role in her presidential strategy. Hillary turned primarily to his political team to both shape and manage her campaign—people like Mark Penn, a Dick Morris associate who had become Clinton's pollster-in-chief. And to bolster her chances, she relied on her husband's advice and campaign participation to improve her appeal.

It was in these roles that the less productive side of their partnership once more came into play. No one had anticipated that a young black senator from Illinois named Barack Obama would turn the political world upside down. But he did, winning the Iowa caucuses and posing a direct threat to the former First Lady's candidacy. Bill Clinton was furious. It was Hillary's "turn" to be president, and Clinton could not abide the thought that this youthful upstart might deny her the White House. Clinton's active intervention on behalf of Hillary and in opposition to Obama increased in proportion to his anger. He made speeches in South Carolina that came close to suggesting that Obama was simply a "race" candidate. Jesse Jackson had taken the South Carolina primary twenty years earlier, focusing on the black vote, and now Clinton implied that Obama was adopting similar tactics. The results were disastrous. The more visible Bill became, the more the media centered on his role in his wife's campaign and the more Americans were reminded of the less attractive legacy of the Clinton partnership. Precisely at the point in the primary when voters should have been weighing Hillary's merits, they were forced instead to consider the prospect of a second copresidency, with both Clintons in the White House.

But over the long haul, Hillary stuck to the ideas and political approach that had defined her senatorial career. And when Barack Obama, then the president-elect, asked her to become his secretary of state, she said yes. This was a new partnership, one in which she thrived, performed brilliantly, and won nearly universal acclaim for the steadiness of her vision, the success of her efforts at coalition building, and the skill with which she ran a huge bureaucracy. Emblematic of that partnership, she made relations between the White House and the State Department a model of consultation and shared policy making.

Hillary Clinton's future in politics remains an open question. But one thing is clear: The genius Betsey Wright saw in 1972 remains unchanged, arguably more powerful and compelling than ever. Hillary Clinton has rediscovered her identity, the carpenter's level and moral compass restored to their proper place.

Notes

1. BILL CLINTON: THE EARLY YEARS

1. Virginia Kelley, with James Morgan, *Leading with My Heart: My Life* (New York: Simon and Schuster, 1994), 19–21; David Maraniss, *First in His Class: A Biography of Bill Clinton* (New York: Simon and Schuster, 1995), 21.

2. Kelley, *Leading with My Heart*, 19, 24; Maraniss, *First in His Class*, 20–22; Margaret Polk interview with Michael Takiff in Michael Takiff, *A Complicated Man: The Life of Bill Clinton as Told by Those Who Know Him* (New Haven: Yale University Press, 2010), 12.

3. Kelley, *Leading with My Heart*, 19, 20, 40; Takiff, *Complicated Man*, 11.

4. Kelley, *Leading with My Heart*, 23, 24, 28, 42, 51.

5. Ibid., 21, 28, 29.

6. Ibid., 14, 25, 28.

7. Ibid., 42, 43; Maraniss, *First in His Class*, 24–28.

8. Kelley, *Leading with My Heart*, 64; Maraniss, *First in His Class*, 24–28.

9. Kelley, *Leading with My Heart*, 54; Maraniss, *First in His Class*, 28.

10. Maraniss, *First in His Class*, 21; Gail Sheehy, *Hillary's Choice* (New York: Random House, 1999), 94–95.

11. Kelley, *Leading with My Heart*, 69, 71.

12. Myra Reese interview with Michael Takiff in Takiff, *Complicated Man*, 10; the Clinton quote is from Roy Reed, "Clinton Country," *New York Times*, September 6, 1992.

13. B. Clinton, *My Life* (New York: Alfred A. Knopf, 2004), 10–11; Maraniss, *First in His Class*, 31; Myra Reese interview with Michael Takiff in Takiff, *Complicated Man*, 10.

14. B. Clinton, *My Life*, 11–12.

15. Ibid., 11–13.

16. Ibid., 17, 18.

17. Kelley, *Leading with My Heart*, 107–109, 72–80; Maraniss, *First in His Class*, 31–35. In an interview with Michael Takiff, Hugh Reese described Roger in the following words: "[he] was of real short stature. And real nice looking. Dark curly hair. Well dressed all the time. What we'd call a high roller in his gambling. He liked to party." Takiff, *Complicated Man*, 14.

18. Maraniss, *First in His Class*, 32; B. Clinton, *My Life*, 19; Kelley, *Leading with My*

Heart, 86; Sheehy, *Hillary's Choice*, 96. Margaret Polk described to Michael Takiff Mammaw's hate for Roger: "Roger had bought [Virginia] a lot of pretty clothes . . . Edith just tied them up in the backyard and burned them . . . She didn't want Virginia to have anything to do with Clinton." Takiff, *Complicated Man*, 15.

19. Maraniss, *First in His Class*, 32; Kelley, *Leading with My Heart*, 85.
20. Kelley, *Leading with My Heart*, 90–94.
21. Sheehy, *Hillary's Choice*, 98; Kelley, *Leading with My Heart*, 91, 94.
22. Kelley, *Leading with My Heart*, 146–49; B. Clinton, *My Life*, 52. Margaret Polk told Michael Takiff about the shooting episode: "He shot at her. He missed her, but the [bullet] holes are over in that house." Takiff, *Complicated Man*, 16.
23. Roger Clinton, with Jim Moore, *Growing Up Clinton: The Lives, Times and Tragedies of America's Presidential Family* (Arlington, Tex.: Summit Publishing Company, 1995), 1–3; Kelley, *Leading with My Heart*, 134; B. Clinton, *My Life*, 44–46, 79.
24. Kelley, *Leading with My Heart*, 146–49; B. Clinton, *My Life*, 52.
25. R. Clinton, *Growing Up Clinton*, 3; Kelley, *Leading with My Heart*, 137; Maraniss, *First in His Class*, 38.
26. Maraniss, *First in His Class*, 33–37.
27. B. Clinton, *My Life*, 58.
28. Ibid., 46, 51.
29. Ibid., 40, 46–47.
30. Ibid., 149.
31. Ibid., 48, 50; Gail Sheehy interview with Carolyn Yeldell Staley, 1992, in Sheehy, *Hillary's Choice*, 99; Kelley, *Leading with My Heart*, 151–53.
32. Kelley, *Leading with My Heart*, 45; B. Clinton, *My Life*, 45; David Maraniss interview with Carolyn Yeldell Staley, 1993, in Maraniss, *First in His Class*, 46; Patty Howe interview with Michael Takiff in Takiff, *Complicated Man*, 19, 27. On the other hand, Clay Farrar, another high school classmate, said that in high school, Clinton "was a total straight arrow—no alcohol at all—basically almost shy around the coeds." Interview with Takiff in Takiff, *Complicated Man*, 26.
33. B. Clinton, *My Life*, 60–61; Maraniss, *First in His Class*, 11, 14–16.
34. B. Clinton, *My Life*, 60–62; Maraniss, *First in His Class*, 20, 42.
35. Interview with Staley in Sheehy, *Hillary's Choice*, 105; B. Clinton, *My Life*, 66.
36. Tom Campbell, "A Preference for the Future," in Ernest Dumas, ed., *The Clintons of Arkansas: An Introduction by Those Who Knew Him Best* (Fayetteville: University of Arkansas Press), 42–53. Campbell was Clinton's roommate at Georgetown.
37. Campbell, "Preference for the Future," in Dumas, *Clintons of Arkansas*, 47–48.
38. Maraniss, *First in His Class*, 53–57.
39. B. Clinton, *My Life*, 90–93; Maraniss, *First in His Class*, 83–85.
40. B. Clinton, *My Life*, 84–85; Maraniss, *First in His Class*, 75.
41. B. Clinton, *My Life*, 64; Campbell, "Preference for the Future," in Dumas, *Clintons of Arkansas*, 49. When Clinton met Staley at the airport, she later told Michael Takiff, he was very grave. There was no big hug, just the declaration "We have a job to do." Takiff, *Complicated Man*, 35.
42. Maraniss, *First in His Class*, 56; B. Clinton, *My Life*, 97, 122.
43. Campbell, "Preference for the Future," in Dumas, *Clintons of Arkansas*, 48–49; B. Clinton, *My Life*, 117–22.

44. B. Clinton, *My Life*, 79; Kelley, *Leading with My Heart*, 163–64.
45. B. Clinton, *My Life*, 105; Kelley, *Leading with My Heart*, 165–69; Sheehy, *Hillary's Choice*, 111.
46. Maraniss, *First in His Class*, 64–68; Campbell, "Preference for the Future," in Dumas, *Clintons of Arkansas*, 45; letter from Bill Clinton to Denise Hyland, August 11, 1965, in Maraniss, *First in His Class*. David Maraniss interviewed Hyland on three separate occasions in the spring and summer of 1993.
47. Maraniss interviews with Staley in 1992–93, in Maraniss, *First in His Class*, 64–65, 94–95, 108–109.
48. Staley interview in Maraniss, *First in His Class*, 116–17; Staley interview in Takiff, *Complicated Man*, 27.
49. Maraniss, *First in His Class*, 101; B. Clinton, *My Life*, 114–16.
50. Letter from Bill Clinton to Denise Hyland, July 14, 1966, in Maraniss, *First in His Class*, 78–79.
51. B. Clinton, *My Life*, 7.
52. Ibid., 69.
53. Interview with Staley in Maraniss, *First in His Class*, 117, 218; Kelley, *Leading with My Heart*, 90–92.
54. David Maraniss interview with Jim Moore, 1993, in Maraniss, *First in His Class*, 112–13.

2. HILLARY RODHAM: THE EARLY YEARS

1. Maraniss, *First in His Class*, 249–50; Sheehy, *Hillary's Choice*, 21; Carl Bernstein, *A Woman in Charge: The Life of Hillary Rodham Clinton* (New York: Vintage Books, 2008), 11–12, 16–27; Hillary Rodham Clinton, *Living History* (New York: Simon and Schuster, 2003); Hillary Rodham Clinton, *It Takes a Village* (New York: Simon and Schuster, 1995).
2. Sheehy, *Hillary's Choice*, 20–23; Bernstein, *Woman in Charge*, 13–14.
3. Sheehy, *Hillary's Choice*, 23; Carl Bernstein interview with Betsy Johnson Ebeling, Bernstein, *Woman in Charge*, 15–16, 21–22.
4. Bernstein, *Woman in Charge*, 13–16.
5. Ebeling interviews in ibid., 28–30; Gail Sheehy interview with Dorothy Rodham, 1992, in Sheehy, *Hillary's Choice*, 24–26.
6. Ebeling interview and confidential interview in Bernstein, *Woman in Charge*, 16–26; Dorothy Rodham interview in Sheehy, *Hillary's Choice*, 16.
7. Sheehy, *Hillary's Choice*, 23–24; Nicole Boxer interview with Carl Bernstein in Bernstein, *Woman in Charge*, 26.
8. Joyce Milton, *The First Partner: Hillary Rodham Clinton* (New York: William Morrow and Company, 1999), 17–25; Bernstein, *Woman in Charge*, 29–30. The bubble metaphor is from Gail Sheehy's interview with Dorothy Rodham in Sheehy, *Hillary's Choice*, 23.
9. Bernstein interviews with Betsy Ebeling and Linda Bloodworth-Thomason in Bernstein, *Woman in Charge*, 28–31; Sheehy, *Hillary's Choice*, 26–28; Edward Klein, *The Truth About Hillary* (New York: Sentinel, 2005), 53.
10. Bernstein, *Woman in Charge*, 28–33; H. R. Clinton, *Living History*, 24.
11. Bernstein, *Woman in Charge*, 34–37; Sheehy, *Hillary's Choice*, 21–23.

12. Sheehy, *Hillary's Choice*, 33–37; Bernstein, *Woman in Charge*, 34–37.
13. Sheehy, *Hillary's Choice*, 33–37.
14. Ibid., 35–37; Maraniss, *First in His Class*, 250–54.
15. Bernstein, *Woman in Charge*, 35–36; Sheehy, *Hillary's Choice*, 26.
16. Bernstein interview with confidential source in Bernstein, *Woman in Charge*, 36.
17. David Maraniss interview with Geoffrey Shields in Maraniss, *First in His Class*, 255.
18. Bernstein, *Woman in Charge*, 43–48; Sheehy, *Hillary's Choice*, 40–46.
19. Bernstein, *Woman in Charge*, 46–52; Sheehy, *Hillary's Choice*, 45–50; Maraniss, *First in His Class*, 355–57. Both Sheehy and Bernstein were able to interview Geoffrey Shields, Rodham's boyfriend at Harvard. Shields also shared with Bernstein some of the letters he exchanged with Rodham.
20. Bernstein, *Woman in Charge*, 44, 50–58; Sheehy, *Hillary's Choice*, 56–60.
21. Bernstein, *Woman in Charge*, 54–56; Sheehy, *Hillary's Choice*, 65–67.
22. Sheehy, *Hillary's Choice*, 63–70; Bernstein interview with Ebeling in Bernstein, *Woman in Charge*, 54–56.
23. Sheehy, *Hillary's Choice*, 62–64, 69. Gail Sheehy conducted interviews with David Rupert, Nancy Pietrafesa, and John Danner in 1999.
24. Sheehy, *Hillary's Choice*, 64–69; Bernstein, *Woman in Charge*, 55–58.
25. Bernstein, *Woman in Charge*, 57–59; Maraniss, *First in His Class*, 258; Sheehy interview with Allan Schechter, Rodham's professor, 1999, in Sheehy, *Hillary's Choice*, 67.
26. Bernstein, *Woman in Charge*, 58–60.

3. OXFORD AND THE DRAFT: A TEST OF CHARACTER

1. David Maraniss interviews with Robert Reich and Rick Stearns, 1993, in Maraniss, *First in His Class*, 122, 128.
2. B. Clinton, *My Life*, 117–18, 135.
3. Ibid., 118, 135, 144–45.
4. Maraniss interviews with Hannah Achtenberg and Strobe Talbott, 1993, in Maraniss, *First in His Class*, 126, 128.
5. Maraniss interviews with Robert Reich and John Isaacson in Maraniss, *First in His Class*, 129–30.
6. B. Clinton, *My Life*, 136–40; Maraniss interviews with Doug Paschal and John Isaacson, 1993, in Maraniss, *First in His Class*, 140.
7. Maraniss, *First in His Class*, 136–39.
8. Letter from Bill Clinton to Denise Hyland, January 27, 1969, in Maraniss, *First in His Class*, 145, 149; B. Clinton, *My Life*, 147–48.
9. Maraniss, *First in His Class*, 148; B. Clinton, *My Life*, 104, 151.
10. B. Clinton, *My Life*, 143–44; Maraniss, *First in His Class*, 151–53.
11. Maraniss, *First in His Class*, 190–93, 166; B. Clinton, *My Life*, 152.
12. Letter from Bill Clinton to Denise Hyland, July 8, 1969, in Maraniss, *First in His Class*, 167–69, 172.
13. Maraniss interview with Cliff Jackson, 1993, in Maraniss, *First in His Class*, 173–75.

14. Letter from Bill Clinton to Denise Hyland, July 20, 1969, in Maraniss, *First in His Class*, 174.
15. Ibid.; B. Clinton, *My Life*, 154–56.
16. B. Clinton, *My Life*, 155.
17. Letter from Bill Clinton to Rick Stearns, September 9, 1969; Maraniss interview with Stearns, 1993, in Maraniss, *First in His Class*, 179–80.
18. Letter from Bill Clinton to Rick Stearns, September 9, 1969; B. Clinton, *My Life*, 149.
19. Maraniss, *First in His Class*, 179–80; B. Clinton, *My Life*, 158–59.
20. Maraniss interview with Ed Howard, 1993; Maraniss interview with Cliff Jackson, 1993, in Maraniss, *First in His Class*, 180–81.
21. B. Clinton, *My Life*, 158; Maraniss, *First in His Class*, 178.
22. Maraniss, *First in His Class*, 190–94.
23. Letter from Bill Clinton to Colonel Holmes, December 3, 1969, in Maraniss, *First in His Class*, 200–204; B. Clinton, *My Life*, 159–61. The Clinton letter surfaced during the 1992 presidential campaign just before the New Hampshire primary.
24. Maraniss, *First in His Class*, 193–94.
25. Ibid., 198–200.
26. B. Clinton, *My Life*, 151.
27. Ibid., 149, 173.

4. HILLARY AND BILL AT YALE: TWO DESTINIES INTERSECT

1. Sheehy, *Hillary's Choice*, 68–70.
2. Bernstein, *Woman in Charge*, 63–65.
3. Milton, *First Partner*, 37–41; Sheehy, *Hillary's Choice*, 77–80; Bernstein, *Woman in Charge*, 66–69. For a discussion of the Black Panthers at Yale, see Paul Bass, *Murder in the Model City: The Black Panthers, Yale, and the Redemption of a Killer* (New York: Basic Books, 2006).
4. David Maraniss interview with Greg Craig, 1994, in Maraniss, *First in His Class*, 248.
5. Bernstein, *Woman in Charge*, 65–67, 72–74.
6. Maraniss, *First in His Class*, 225–30; B. Clinton, *My Life*, 175–77.
7. Maraniss interviews with Anne Wexler, Nancy Bekavac, and William Coleman in Maraniss, *First in His Class*, 233–35.
8. William T. Coleman, "Don't You Know Whose Table This Is?" in Dumas, *Clintons of Arkansas*, 53–62.
9. Sheehy interview with Bekavac in Sheehy, *Hillary's Choice*, 76–78; B. Clinton, *My Life*, 181.
10. Maraniss, *First in His Class*, 246–50; B. Clinton, *My Life*, 181–82.
11. Bernstein interviews with Nancy Bekavac and Robert Reich in Bernstein, *Woman in Charge*, 76–81; Sheehy, *Hillary's Choice*, 76, 83.
12. Maraniss, *First in His Class*, 263–64; Bernstein interview with Sara Ehrman in Bernstein, *Woman in Charge*, 86.
13. Bernstein, *Woman in Charge*, 85; Maraniss interviews with Steve Cohen, 1994, Don Pogue, 1993, and Nancy Bekavac, 1993, in Maraniss, *First in His Class*, 247–48, 264.
14. Bernstein, *Woman in Charge*, 83–84; B. Clinton, *My Life*, 182–84.

15. B. Clinton, *My Life*, 182–85.
16. Maraniss interviews with Brooke Shearer, Strobe Talbott, Mike Shea, and John Isaacson, 1993, in Maraniss, *First in His Class*, 259–61; B. Clinton, *My Life*, 187–88.
17. Maraniss, *First in His Class*, 259–60.
18. Letter to Cliff Jackson, December 1971; Maraniss interview with Greg Craig, in Maraniss, *First in His Class*, 261–62.
19. B. Clinton, *My Life*, 188.
20. Ibid., 188; Bernstein, *Woman in Charge*, 84–87.
21. Maraniss, *First in His Class*, 265–77; B. Clinton, *My Life*, 190–200; Bernstein, *Woman in Charge*, 86–87; Sheehy, *Hillary's Choice*, 84.
22. Maraniss interviews with Billy Carr, 1992 and 1994, and with Rick Stearns, in Maraniss, *First in His Class*, 265–77.
23. Bernstein, *Woman in Charge*, 85–86; Maraniss, *First in His Class*, 269–71.
24. Bernstein interview with Sara Ehrman in Bernstein, *Woman in Charge*, 85–86.
25. Bernstein interview with Taylor Branch in ibid., 86–87; Maraniss, *First in His Class*, 277.
26. Maraniss interviews with Taylor Branch, Betsey Wright, and Sara Ehrman in Maraniss, *First in His Class*, 270, 275–77; Bernstein, *Woman in Charge*, 86–87.
27. Maraniss, *First in His Class*, 275–77.
28. Maraniss interview with Nancy Bekavac in ibid., 284–86.
29. Maraniss, *First in His Class*, 288–91; Milton, *First Partner*, 59–61.
30. B. Clinton, *My Life*, 201; Sheehy, *Hillary's Choice*, 86; Bernstein, *Woman in Charge*, 89.
31. B. Clinton, *My Life*, 200–201.
32. R. Clinton, *Growing Up Clinton*, 28; Sheehy, *Hillary's Choice*, 87; Kelley, *Leading with My Heart*, 192.
33. Kelley, *Leading with My Heart*, 192–200; Sheehy, *Hillary's Choice*, 87–88; Bernstein, *Woman in Charge*, 90–91.

5. THE ARKANSAS YEARS, PART ONE: 1973–80

1. David Maraniss interview with Mort Gitelman, a law school colleague of Hillary Rodham's, in Maraniss, *First in His Class*, 293.
2. Maraniss, *First in His Class*, 293–95; B. Clinton, *My Life*, 204–205.
3. B. Clinton, *My Life*, 213–15; Maraniss, *First in His Class*, 294–97.
4. Maraniss, *First in His Class*, 301–306, 321–25; B. Clinton, *My Life*, 211–15, 218–25.
5. Bernstein, *Woman in Charge*, 102–103; Maraniss, *First in His Class*, 307–11; B. Clinton, *My Life*, 210–11.
6. Bernstein, *Woman in Charge*, 96–97, 101–103; Sheehy, *Hillary's Choice*, 91; Maraniss interview with Terry Kirkpatrick, 1994, in Maraniss, *First in His Class*, 316.
7. Bernstein interview with Bernard Nussbaum in Bernstein, *Woman in Charge*, 95–97.
8. Bernstein, *Woman in Charge*, 97–98.
9. Maraniss interview with Paul Fray in Maraniss, *First in His Class*, 319–21; Bernstein interview with Betsey Wright, 1998, in Bernstein, *Woman in Charge*, 106–107.

10. Bernstein interview with Sara Ehrman in Bernstein, *Woman in Charge*, 106–107; Donnie Radcliffe, *Hillary Rodham Clinton: A First Lady for Our Time* (New York: Warner Books, 1993), 136.

11. Maraniss, *First in His Class*, 319–21, 327; Bernstein, *Woman in Charge*, 113.

12. Bernstein, *Woman in Charge*, 112–14; E. Klein, *Truth About Hillary*, 83, 87; Sheehy, *Hillary's Choice*, 113; Doug Wallace, undated memo, in Douglas Wallace Papers, cited in Maraniss, *First in His Class*, 335.

13. Bernstein, *Woman in Charge*, 114–15; Maraniss interviews with Paul Fray, Doug Wallace, and Neil McDonald in Maraniss, *First in His Class*, 327, 335–37; Sheehy, *Hillary's Choice*, 110–15.

14. Bernstein, *Woman in Charge*, 110–13, 116–23; Woody Bassett, "The Clinton Factor," in Dumas, *Clintons of Arkansas*, 73–74; Sheehy, *Hillary's Choice*, 120–25.

15. Bernstein, *Woman in Charge*, 109–13; Sheehy, *Hillary's Choice*, 123–26.

16. Sheehy interview with Hillary Rodham Clinton, 1992, in Sheehy, *Hillary's Choice*, 121–23.

17. Sheehy interview with Betsey Wright in ibid., 121–23; B. Clinton, *My Life*, 234–35.

18. B. Clinton, *My Life*, 234–35; Maraniss, *First in His Class*, 344–45.

19. Maraniss, *First in His Class*, 346–49; Bernstein, *Woman in Charge*, 124–26.

20. Doug Wallace memo on the 1976 election, in Douglas Wallace Papers, cited in Maraniss, *First in His Class*, 351, 340.

21. Bernstein, *Woman in Charge*, 130–31.

22. Ibid., 129–32; Webb Hubbell, *Friends in High Places* (New York: Morrow, 1997), 4, 60–65.

23. Dick Morris, *Behind the Oval Office: Getting Reelected Against the Odds* (Los Angeles: Renaissance, 1999), 7, 43, 55–61. The author worked on campaigns in New York City during the period at the same time Morris organized his group of college political activists. These paragraphs are based on the experience of interacting with him at that time.

24. B. Clinton, *My Life*, 258.

25. Bernstein, *Woman in Charge*, 138–41; B. Clinton, *My Life*, 255–58.

26. Bernstein, *Woman in Charge*, 140–43; Maraniss, *First in His Class*, 353–57.

27. Bernstein interview with Rudy Moore in Bernstein, *Woman in Charge*, 140; Bernstein interview with Stan Greenberg in ibid., 84.

28. Maraniss, *First in His Class*, 358; Roy Reed, "I Just Went to School in Arkansas," in Dumas, *Clintons of Arkansas*, 105; Bernstein interview with Dick Morris in Bernstein, *Woman in Charge*, 275.

29. Maraniss, *First in His Class*, 358–60; B. Clinton, *My Life*, 262.

30. B. Clinton, *My Life*, 262–63; Maraniss interview with Dick Morris, 1994, in Maraniss, *First in His Class*, 360.

31. Rudy Moore, Jr., "They're Killing Me Out There," and Bobby Roberts, "Everyone Will Do the Right Thing," in Dumas, *Clintons of Arkansas*, 125, 88; B. Clinton, *My Life*, 266; Maraniss, *First in His Class*, 363.

32. Moore, "They're Killing Me," in Dumas, *Clintons of Arkansas*, 93; Maraniss, *First in His Class*, 361–65.

33. Maraniss, *First in His Class*, 364–65; B. Clinton, *My Life*, 266; Moore, "They're Killing Me," in Dumas, *Clintons of Arkansas*, 88–89.

34. Moore, "They're Killing Me," in Dumas, *Clintons of Arkansas*, 91–92; B. Clinton, *My Life*, 266.

35. Stephen A. Smith, "Compromise, Consensus, and Consistency," in Dumas, *Clintons of Arkansas*, 9; Moore, "They're Killing Me," in Dumas, *Clintons of Arkansas*, 92; Milton, *First Partner*, 13; Maraniss, *First in His Class*, 361.

36. Maraniss, *First in His Class*, 376–81; B. Clinton, *My Life*, 266–72.

37. Maraniss, *First in His Class*, 376–80; B. Clinton, *My Life*, 274–82.

38. B. Clinton, *My Life*, 272; Bernstein, *Woman in Charge*, 149–51.

39. B. Clinton, *My Life*, 272; Bernstein, *Woman in Charge*, 148–52; Diane Blair, "Of Darkness and Light," in Dumas, *Clintons of Arkansas*, 62–71; see especially 65–66.

40. Maraniss, *First in His Class*, 373–75; B. Clinton, *My Life*, 273; Bernstein, *Woman in Charge*, 149–51.

41. Bernstein, *Woman in Charge*, 135–38; Maraniss, *First in His Class*, 371–75; Milton, *First Partner*, 107.

42. Bernstein, *Woman in Charge*, 148; Milton, *First Partner*, 107–8; Maraniss, *First in His Class*, 370–72; E. Klein, *Truth About Hillary*, 94; Sheehy interview with Nancy Pietrafesa, in Sheehy, *Hillary's Choice*, 149; Connie Bruck, "Hillary the Politician," *New Yorker*, May 30, 1993.

43. Moore, "They're Killing Me," in Dumas, *Clintons of Arkansas*, 85–94; Morris, *Behind the Oval Office*, xix; Sheehy, *Hillary's Choice*, 18.

44. Bernstein, *Woman in Charge*, 155; Maraniss, *First in His Class*, 376–79; B. Clinton, *My Life*, 286; Carl Whillock, "Change Has Never Been Easy," in Dumas, *Clintons of Arkansas*, 82.

45. Bernstein, *Woman in Charge*, 140–41; B. Clinton, *My Life*, 280–86.

46. B. Clinton, *My Life*, 282–85; Maraniss interview with Dick Morris in Maraniss, *First in His Class*, 384.

47. Bernstein, *Woman in Charge*, 156–63; Maraniss, *First in His Class*, 387.

48. Moore, "They're Killing Me," in Dumas, *Clintons of Arkansas*, 90–92.

49. Bernstein, *Woman in Charge*, 144, 162–64.

6. THE ARKANSAS YEARS, PART TWO: 1980–91

1. B. Clinton, *My Life*, 287.

2. Maraniss, *First in His Class*, 391–92. Significantly, Clinton fails to mention the fight in his memoir.

3. E. Klein, *Truth About Hillary*, 96; B. Clinton, *My Life*, 285, 296; Maraniss, *First in His Class*, 392–94, 399–400.

4. Maraniss, *First in His Class*, 396–97.

5. David Maraniss interview with Dick Morris in Maraniss, *First in His Class*, 407–10; Morris, *Behind the Oval Office*, 10–11, 45–48.

6. Maraniss interview with Morris in Maraniss, *First in His Class*, 391–92.

7. Morris, *Behind the Oval Office*, 45–52; Maraniss interview with Morris in Maraniss, *First in His Class*, 397–99; B. Clinton, *My Life*, 295.

8. Morris, *Behind the Oval Office*, 52–54 ; Maraniss, *First in His Class*, 399; B. Clinton, *My Life*, 295.

9. Morris, *Behind the Oval Office*, 52–54; Maraniss, *First in His Class*, 401–403.

10. B. Clinton, *My Life*, 295–99; Bernstein interview with Morris in Bernstein,

Woman in Charge, 164–67; draft remarks by Jim Johnson, 1980, Jim Johnson Collection, Arkansas Historical Commission, box 39, folder 16.

11. Maraniss interview with Morris in Maraniss, *First in His Class*, 403.
12. B. Clinton, *My Life*, 300; Maraniss, *First in His Class*, 403–404.
13. B. Clinton, *My Life*, 301–303.
14. Milton, *First Partner*, 144–45.
15. Maraniss, *First in His Class*, 412–14; B. Clinton, *My Life*, 309–10; Milton, *First Partner*, 152–58.
16. Milton, *First Partner*, 151–57; Maraniss, *First in His Class*, 414; B. Clinton, *My Life*, 309; Bernstein, *Woman in Charge*, 170–73; Paul Greenberg, "His Finest Hour," in Dumas, *Clintons of Arkansas*, 117.
17. Bernstein, *Woman in Charge*, 172–75; B. Clinton, *My Life*, 309–12.
18. Milton, *First Partner*, 161–65; Bernstein, *Woman in Charge*, 174–75.
19. R. Clinton, *Growing Up Clinton*, 31–39, 43–45.
20. Maraniss, *First in His Class*, 419–22; Milton, *First Partner*, 167–69; B. Clinton, *My Life*, 315–16.
21. Maraniss, *First in His Class*, 420–22; Milton, *First Partner*, 168.
22. Milton, *First Partner*, 169–70; Maraniss interview with Carolyn Yeldell Staley in Maraniss, *First in His Class*, 421–24.
23. Maraniss, *First in His Class*, 427–33; Bernstein, *Woman in Charge*, 175–78; Milton, *First Partner*, 169–70, 176–79; Sheehy, *Hillary's Choice*, 165–67.
24. B. Clinton, *My Life*, 319–22; Sheffield Nelson to Bill Clinton, August 30, 1985, Jim Johnson Collection, Arkansas Historical Commission, box 52, folder 14.
25. Sheffield Nelson to Bill Clinton, August 30, 1985, Jim Johnson Collection, Arkansas Historical Commission, box 52, folder 14; Maraniss, *First in His Class*, 437–38; B. Clinton, *My Life*, 319–26.
26. Bernstein, *Woman in Charge*, 176–78; Maraniss, *First in His Class*, 438–40; B. Clinton, *My Life*, 332.
27. Bernstein, *Woman in Charge*, 178–80; Maraniss interview with Dick Morris, 1994, in Maraniss, *First in His Class*, 440–41.
28. Maraniss interview with Betsey Wright, 1993, in Maraniss, *First in His Class*, 440–42; Bernstein interview with Betsey Wright in Bernstein, *Woman in Charge*, 177–79; B. Clinton, *My Life*, 333–35.
29. Maraniss, *First in His Class*, 442–44; Bernstein, *Woman in Charge*, 179–80; B. Clinton, *My Life*, 335.
30. Maraniss interview with Betsey Wright in Maraniss, *First in His Class*, 445–47; Bernstein interviews with Betsey Wright in Bernstein, *Woman in Charge*, 181–83; B. Clinton, *My Life*, 340–44.
31. Bernstein interviews with Betsey Wright in Bernstein, *Woman in Charge*, 181–84; Milton, *First Partner*, 194; Maraniss interview with Betsey Wright in Maraniss, *First in His Class*, 450.
32. Bernstein interviews with Betsey Wright in Bernstein, *Woman in Charge*, 183–84, 187; Maraniss interview with Betsey Wright in Maraniss, *First in His Class*, 450.
33. Bernstein interview with Betsey Wright in Bernstein, *Woman in Charge*, 184–85.
34. Ibid., 184–87.
35. H. R. Clinton, *It Takes a Village*, 34.

36. Bernstein interviews with Betsey Wright and with a confidential source in Bernstein, *Woman in Charge*, 187–88.
37. Bernstein interview with Dick Morris in ibid., 188–89; Maraniss interview with Dick Morris in Maraniss, *First in His Class*, 452–53.
38. Maraniss interview with Dick Morris in Maraniss, *First in His Class*, 452–53; B. Clinton, *My Life*, 356–57.
39. B. Clinton, *My Life*, 357; Bernstein, *Woman in Charge*, 188–90; Sheehy, *Hillary's Choice*, 12–13.
40. B. Clinton, *My Life*, 359–60.
41. Morris, *Behind the Oval Office*, 64; Maraniss, *First in His Class*, 455–60; B. Clinton, *My Life*, 370.
42. B. Clinton, *My Life*, 365–66.

7. "THERE IS A PLACE CALLED HOPE"

1. Bernstein, *Woman in Charge*, 192–94; B. Clinton, *My Life*, 369–84; Maraniss, *First in His Class*, 458–64.
2. J. Klein, *The Natural: The Misunderstood Presidency of Bill Clinton* (New York: Doubleday, 2002), 38–39; Maraniss, *First in His Class*, 458–59; B. Clinton, *My Life*, 365–67.
3. Leon Panetta interview in Jeff Gerth and Don Van Natta, Jr., *Her Way: The Hopes and Ambitions of Hillary Rodham Clinton* (Boston: Little, Brown, 2007), 9, 57. The authors argue, based on the Panetta interview, that the Clintons had an explicit twenty-year compact to win the White House, with him going first. The Panetta interview is their only hard source, and though the argument is plausible, it is not backed up by any other comparable documentation.
4. *Vanity Fair*, May 1992, 44; Gil Troy, *Hillary Rodham Clinton: Polarizing First Lady* (Lawrence: University of Kansas Press, 2008), 1; Bernstein, *Woman in Charge*, 476–78.
5. Bernstein, *Woman in Charge*, 196–200. For his book, Carl Bernstein was given access to the voluminous materials Diane Blair had compiled on the 1992 campaign before her untimely death.
6. Troy, *Hillary Rodham Clinton*, 32; Donnie Radcliffe, *Hillary Rodham Clinton*, 229; Bernstein, *Woman in Charge*, 213
7. Radcliffe, *Hillary Rodham Clinton*, 229; Bernstein, *Woman in Charge*, 213.
8. B. Clinton, *My Life*, 374–75; George Stephanopoulos, *All Too Human: A Political Education* (Boston: Little, Brown, 1999), 29–30.
9. Bernstein, *Woman in Charge*, 197; B. Clinton, *My Life*, 375–77.
10. Bernstein, *Woman in Charge*, 128–29, 204–205, 352–54; Gerth and Van Natta, *Her Way*, 63–64, 72–73, 106–19.
11. B. Clinton, *My Life*, 372; Bernstein, *Woman in Charge*, 195–97; Gerth and Van Natta, *Her Way*, 92, 94.
12. The quotation from Clinton is reported by David Ifshin, interview with Gerth and Van Natta, Jr., *Her Way*, 94.
13. Bernstein, *Woman in Charge*, 199–203; B. Clinton, *My Life*, 379–84.
14. Michael Isikoff, *Uncovering Clinton: A Reporter's Story* (New York: Crown Books, 1999), 31; Bernstein, *Woman in Charge*, 197.

15. Bernstein, *Woman in Charge*, 200.
16. Sheehy, *Hillary's Choice*, 199–201; Bernstein, *Woman in Charge*, 201–202.
17. Stephanopoulos, *All Too Human*, 62–68; B. Clinton, *My Life*, 385–86.
18. B. Clinton, *My Life*, 386–91.
19. Isikoff, *Uncovering Clinton*, 27; Gerth and Van Natta, *Her Way*, 97–99.
20. Stephanopoulos, *All Too Human*, 74–82.
21. Ibid., 74–75.
22. B. Clinton, *My Life*, 388–89; Gerth and Van Natta, *Her Way*, 7, 106–109; Sheehy, *Hillary's Choice*, 205–207.
23. Sheehy, *Hillary's Choice*, 205–207; Gerth and Van Natta, *Her Way*, 107–10.
24. Sheehy interview with Jane Sherburne in Sheehy, *Hillary's Choice*, 205–207; Gerth and Van Natta, *Her Way*, 109–11.
25. Bernstein, *Woman in Charge*, 206–209; Gerth and Van Natta, *Her Way*, 111.
26. Sheehy interview with Betsey Wright in Sheehy, *Hillary's Choice*, 18, 188; Bernstein, *Woman in Charge*, 476; the Morris quote is from the *New York Post*, December 5, 1998. See also Nigel Hamilton, *Bill Clinton: Mastering the Presidency* (New York: Public Affairs, 2007), 10.
27. B. Clinton, *My Life*, 393–410; Stephanopoulos, *All Too Human*, 81–83.
28. B. Clinton, *My Life*, 418–24.
29. Ibid., 425–28; Stephanopoulos, *All Too Human*, 91, 95.
30. B. Clinton, *My Life*, 426, 433; J. Klein, *The Natural*, 42.
31. Hamilton, *Bill Clinton*, 24–30; David Halberstam, *War in a Time of Peace* (New York: Simon and Schuster, 2001), 169; Dan Balz, *Washington Post*, November 8, 1992.
32. Bernstein, *Woman in Charge*, 210–13.
33. Stephanopoulos, *All Too Human*, 205; Hamilton, *Bill Clinton*, 39.
34. J. Klein, *The Natural*, 117; Bernstein, *Woman in Charge*, 209–13.
35. Bernstein, *Woman in Charge*, 214; John Harris, *The Survivor: Bill Clinton in the White House* (New York: Random House, 2005), 5–7.
36. Hamilton, *Bill Clinton*, 41, 43.
37. Harris, *Survivor*, 3–5.
38. J. Klein, *The Natural*, 28–29.
39. Bernstein, *Woman in Charge*, 215–17; Harris, *Survivor*, 4–5.
40. Harris, *Survivor*, 8.
41. Ibid., 4–9.
42. Hamilton, *Bill Clinton*, 68.
43. Ibid., 8–13; Harris, *Survivor*, 13.

8. THE FIRST YEAR

1. Harris, *Survivor*, 14–15; Hamilton, *Bill Clinton*, 46–47; Stephanopoulos, *All Too Human*, 109–11.
2. Hamilton, *Bill Clinton*, 46; Taylor Branch, *The Clinton Tapes: Wrestling History with the President* (New York: Simon and Schuster, 2009), 5–7; Harris, *Survivor*, 15–18.
3. Harris, *Survivor*, 14–16; Hamilton, *Bill Clinton*, 43–45.
4. Bernstein, *Woman in Charge*, 266–70; B. Clinton, *My Life*, 488–89.

5. On the welfare reform task working group, see assorted memos to Carol Rasco of the Domestic Policy Council, in boxes 10 and 11, Domestic Policy Council Papers, William Jefferson Clinton Presidential Library, Little Rock, Arkansas; Bernstein, *Woman in Charge*, 214–16, 262; Harris, *Survivor*, 191; B. Clinton, *My Life*, 482.

6. J. Klein, *The Natural*, 108–10; Hamilton, *Bill Clinton*, 17; Harris, *Survivor*, 19–22.

7. Bernstein, *Woman in Charge*, 262; Harris, *Survivor*, 19–24; Robert Rubin, interview with Chris Bury, "The Clinton Years," PBS TV, in Hamilton, *Bill Clinton*, 17–20, 74, 108; J. Klein, *The Natural*, 52.

8. Harris, *Survivor*, 23; Hamilton, *Bill Clinton*, 109–17; Elizabeth Drew, *On the Edge: The Clinton Presidency* (New York: Simon and Schuster, 1995), 107–109; J. Klein, *The Natural*, 62; Lawrence Summers interview in Hamilton, *Bill Clinton*, 64.

9. Hamilton, *Bill Clinton*, 102–108; David Gergen, *Eyewitness to Power: The Essence of Leadership, Nixon to Clinton* (New York: Simon and Schuster, 2000), 273; Stephanopoulos, *All Too Human*, 286–88.

10. Branch, *Clinton Tapes*, 11. See also Jonathan Gill, "The First 100 Days," in box 12, Domestic Policy Council Papers, William Jefferson Clinton Presidential Library, Little Rock, Arkansas.

11. Bernstein, *Woman in Charge*, 202; Branch, *Clinton Tapes*, 11.

12. B. Clinton, *My Life*, 497–99; Hamilton, *Bill Clinton*, 90–92.

13. Hamilton, *Bill Clinton*, 135, 137, 140; B. Clinton, *My Life*, 523–24.

14. Stephanopoulos, *All Too Human*, 166–75; Harris, *Survivor*, 59–60.

15. Bernstein, *Woman in Charge*, 248–49; J. Klein, *The Natural*, 106; Troy, *Hillary Rodham Clinton*, 121–22; Harris, *Survivor*, 146–47.

16. Harris, *Survivor*, 35–37.

17. Sally Quinn, "Beware of Washington," *Newsweek*, December 28, 1992; Hamilton, *Bill Clinton*, 9–10; Harris, *Survivor*, 3–4; Branch, *Clinton Tapes*, 21.

18. Bernstein, *Woman in Charge*, 316–20; Harris, *Survivor*, 99.

19. Quinn, "Beware of Washington"; Bernstein, *Woman in Charge*, 321.

20. Bernstein, *Woman in Charge*, 278–81; Harris, *Survivor*, 33–34.

21. Bernstein, *Woman in Charge*, 244–45, 271.

22. B. Clinton, *My Life*, 467–68; Bernstein, *Woman in Charge*, 322. Later, Bill Clinton reflected that "the real problem with the staff was that most of them came out of the campaign in Arkansas, and had no experience working in the White House or dealing with Washington's political culture." As a result, he concluded, there was too little understanding about how to manage issues like gays in the military or Zoe Baird in a world totally different from that of Arkansas.

23. Bernstein, *Woman in Charge*, 324–31; Troy, *Hillary Rodham Clinton*, 122–24; Stephanopoulos, *All Too Human*, 145; Harris, *Survivor*, 38–40.

24. Troy, *Hillary Rodham Clinton*, 65–69; Bernstein, *Woman in Charge*, 219–21.

25. J. Klein, *The Natural*, 65–67; Bernstein, *Woman in Charge*, 220. The president seemed, on more than one occasion, to see the point of putting welfare reform first. Welfare reform, he said at a press briefing in June 1994, was different from health care "because it plays into the American people's desire to support work and family and independence and their desire to change the way government works," whereas health care was harder to understand and played into the preju-

dice that "government can't do anything good." *New York Times*, June 15, 1994; see also Domestic Policy Council Papers, Bruce Reed, Welfare Reform Series, box 2, Clinton Library.

26. Bernstein interview with confidential source in Bernstein, *Woman in Charge*, 217, 249–51; Harris, *Survivor*, 3–4.
27. Hamilton, *Bill Clinton*, 62; Bernstein interview with Donna Shalala in Bernstein, *Woman in Charge*, 218–19, 222–24.
28. Bernstein interview with confidential source in Bernstein, *Woman in Charge*, 218–23; Hamilton, *Bill Clinton*, 62.
29. Hamilton, *Bill Clinton*, 62; Gergen, *Eyewitness to Power*, 300; Bernstein, *Woman in Charge*, 289–91; Harris interview with Jake Siewert in Harris, *Survivor*, 97–98; Stephanopoulos, *All Too Human*, 302.
30. Troy, *Hillary Rodham Clinton*, 68–69, 74, 78–79; J. Klein, *The Natural*, 106, 118.
31. Bernstein interview with Wendy Smith in Bernstein, *Woman in Charge*, 331–32; Gergen, *Eyewitness to Power*, 298–99.
32. Bernstein, *Woman in Charge*, 328; Troy, *Hillary Rodham Clinton*, 122–24.
33. Bernstein, *Woman in Charge*, 297–98; Troy, *Hillary Rodham Clinton*, 83; J. Klein, *The Natural*, 147.
34. Bernstein, *Woman in Charge*, 298.
35. David Gergen, "After 100 Days, a President in Distress," *US News & World Report*, May 3, 1993.
36. Bernstein, *Woman in Charge*, 332–34; Gergen, *Eyewitness to Power*, 268–71.
37. Gergen, *Eyewitness to Power*, 268–71.
38. Ibid., 298–99.
39. Gergen interview with Gail Sheehy, 1999, in Sheehy, *Hillary's Choice*, 251; Gergen, *Eyewitness to Power*, 274.
40. Sheehy, *Hillary's Choice*, 232–33; Bernstein, *Woman in Charge*, 227, 253, 281–83, 292–93, 323–30; Peter J. Boyer, "Life After Vince," *New Yorker*, September 11, 1995.
41. Bernstein, *Woman in Charge*, 453–55; Sheehy, *Hillary's Choice*, 233.
42. Bernstein, *Woman in Charge*, 338–40; Webb Hubbell, *Friends in High Places* (New York: William Morrow, 1997), 212, 231–32.
43. Bernstein, *Woman in Charge*, 339–40; Hubbell, *Friends in High Places*, 231–35.
44. Hubbell, *Friends in High Places*, 234–35, 239, 259; Bernstein, *Woman in Charge*, 336–40, 343–45.
45. Bernstein, *Woman in Charge*, 340–42; B. Clinton, *My Life*, 531.
46. Bernstein, *Woman in Charge*, 342; Harris, *Survivor*, 75. Heymann's words are quoted in *The Final Report of the Independent Counsel In Re: Madison Guaranty Savings and Loan Association*, vol. III, March 20, 2002, 207–10.
47. Hamilton, *Bill Clinton*, 153; B. Clinton, *My Life*, 531–32; Bernstein, *Woman in Charge*, 339, 345. When doctors prescribe antidepressants, they often warn their patients that sudden suicidal impulses may accompany the onset of treatment, and urge them to stop taking the pills and call their physician immediately if such feelings occur. We do not know whether this happened in Foster's case.
48. B. Clinton, *My Life*, 586; Bernstein, *Woman in Charge*, 365; Stephanopoulos, *All Too Human*, 186–87.

49. Stephanopoulos, *All Too Human*, 197.

50. J. Klein, *The Natural*, 57.

51. B. Clinton, *My Life*, 458–63; J. Klein, *The Natural*, 44–46.

52. Hamilton, *Bill Clinton*, 160–71; B. Clinton, *My Life*, 534–36; Harris, *Survivor*, 83–90; Stephanopoulos, *All Too Human*, 176–81.

53. J. Klein, *The Natural*, 57; Hamilton, *Bill Clinton*, 177; Stephanopoulos, *All Too Human*, 270; Harris, *Survivor*, 101–2.

54. B. Clinton, *My Life*, 547, 557–58; Stephanopoulos, *All Too Human*, 197.

55. Harris, *Survivor*, 44–46; J. Klein, *The Natural*, 65–67; Branch, *Clinton Tapes*, 92; B. Clinton, *My Life*, 512. In January 1994, a group of distinguished academics held a retreat on the Clinton presidency convened by the White House. It was in that context that they observed there was no longer in foreign policy matters "the same kind of moral component [as existed during] the Cold War." See a memo from Stan Greenberg to Bill Clinton, Al Gore, Hillary Rodham Clinton, Mack McLarty, David Gergen, and George Stephanopoulos, January 4, 1994, in the Domestic Policy Council Papers, Carol Rasco, box 3, Clinton Library.

56. Harris, *Survivor*, 121–23, 127; Hamilton, *Bill Clinton*, 194.

57. B. Clinton, *My Life*, 541–45; Stephanopoulos, *All Too Human*, 194–95.

58. B. Clinton, *My Life*, 559–60.

59. Gergen, *Eyewitness to Power*, 295–99; Harris, *Survivor*, 105–106; Stephanopoulos, *All Too Human*, 239.

60. Bernstein, *Woman in Charge*, 351–53; Isikoff, *Uncovering Clinton*, 33.

61. Isikoff, *Uncovering Clinton*, 35; Gergen, *Eyewitness to Power*, 286; Bernstein, *Woman in Charge*, 335.

62. Gergen, *Eyewitness to Power*, 288–90.

63. J. Klein, *The Natural*, 111; Bernstein, *Woman in Charge*, 357; Stephanopoulos, *All Too Human*, 226.

64. Stephanopoulos, *All Too Human*, 251; Gergen, *Eyewitness to Power*, 290.

65. Bernstein, *Woman in Charge*, 9.

9. THE HEALTH CARE DEBACLE AND THE EMERGENCE OF KENNETH STARR

1. Bernstein, *Woman in Charge*, 290. For a discussion of Clinton administration planning on welfare reform, see the memos of the working group on welfare reform in the papers of the Domestic Policy Council, Carol Rasco, boxes 11 and 12, Clinton Library. Welfare reform, it should be noted, was very much tied in to other Clinton priorities, such as the Earned Income Tax Credit, which so effectively helped people with low incomes.

2. Hamilton, *Bill Clinton*, 32–33; interview with Leon Panetta, 2006, in Gerth and Van Natta, *Her Way*, 120.

3. Bernstein, *Woman in Charge*, 294.

4. Hamilton, *Bill Clinton*, 100; Carl Bernstein interview with Sara Ehrman in Bernstein, *Woman in Charge*, 294.

5. Bernstein, *Woman in Charge*, 284; Troy, *Hillary Rodham Clinton*, 78–79.

6. John Harris interview with Donna Shalala in Harris, *Survivor*, 116; Bernstein, *Woman in Charge*, 284–85; Troy, *Hillary Rodham Clinton*, 78–79.

7. Bernstein interview with a confidential source in Bernstein, *Woman in Charge,* 223, 255; Hamilton, *Bill Clinton,* 62, 225; Bernstein interview with Donna Shalala in Bernstein, *Woman in Charge,* 218.

8. Bernstein, *Woman in Charge,* 287–88; Bernstein interview with Bill Bradley in ibid., 304. For Rasco's views, see a paper by Kevin MacMillan and Jennifer Cable, May 9, 1994, in the Domestic Policy Council Papers, Carol Rasco, box 11, Clinton Library. Rasco went on to ask if it was worth it "to fight tooth and nail for an issue and maybe not to have it pass," or whether it was more advisable to accept something for signature that went partway and was "better than nothing."

9. Troy, *Hillary Rodham Clinton,* 79–82; Bernstein interview with a confidential source in Bernstein, *Woman in Charge,* 218–19; Hamilton, *Bill Clinton,* 58–62; *Newsweek,* October 9, 1993.

10. The aides' quotes are from unattributed interviews cited in Gail Sheehy, "Hillary's Choice," *Vanity Fair,* January 1999; Bernstein, *Woman in Charge,* 289.

11. Stephanopoulos, *All Too Human,* 202–203.

12. Troy, *Hillary Rodham Clinton,* 86; Bernstein, *Woman in Charge,* 395–96.

13. Sheehy, *Hillary's Choice,* 252; the Hillary Clinton adviser was Robert Boorstin, quoted in Bernstein, *Woman in Charge,* 396. For the remarks of Moynihan and the Democratic congressman (Jim McDermott), see Karen Tumulty, "Health Care Math Leaves Critics Puzzled," *Los Angeles Times,* September 11, 1993.

14. Bernstein, *Woman in Charge,* 399; Hamilton, *Bill Clinton,* 264–65.

15. Bernstein, *Woman in Charge,* 399.

16. Gergen, *Eyewitness to Power,* 300; Bernstein, *Woman in Charge,* 308; Hamilton, *Bill Clinton,* 226; J. Klein, *The Natural,* 121.

17. Nigel Hamilton interview with Judy Feder in Hamilton, *Bill Clinton,* 221–24; Gergen, *Eyewitness to Power,* 307–309.

18. J. Klein, *The Natural,* 122–24; Bernstein, *Woman in Charge,* 397–99.

19. J. Klein, *The Natural,* 124.

20. Troy, *Hillary Rodham Clinton,* 113–14; Hamilton interview with Cliff Jackson in Hamilton, *Bill Clinton,* 201–208, 240–41; Sheehy, *Hillary's Choice,* 248; Bernstein, *Woman in Charge,* 365–66.

21. Hamilton interview with Jackson in Hamilton, *Bill Clinton,* 210–12; James Stewart, *Blood Sport: The President and His Adversaries* (New York: Simon and Schuster, 1995), 351–52; Stephanopoulos, *All Too Human,* 228.

22. Hamilton interview with Jackson in Hamilton, *Bill Clinton,* 237–48; Bernstein, *Woman in Charge,* 365–66; H. R. Clinton, *Living History,* 206; David Brock, *Blinded by the Right: The Conscience of an Ex-Conservative* (New York: Random House, 2003).

23. Hamilton, *Bill Clinton,* 241–45; Gergen, *Eyewitness to Power,* 309; the quotes are from Sheehy, *Hillary's Choice,* 249, one from an anonymous Washington "power-broker close to the Clintons," the other from an "insider" quoted in a Washington financial newsletter.

24. Bernstein, *Woman in Charge,* 370–71; Branch, *Clinton Tapes,* 104–106; B. Clinton, *My Life,* 567–68.

25. Stephanopoulos, *All Too Human,* 228–30.

26. Ibid., 229; Bernstein, *Woman in Charge,* 373.

27. Stephanopoulos, *All Too Human,* 229.

28. B. Clinton, *My Life*, 573–74; Bernstein interview with Bernard Nussbaum in Bernstein, *Woman in Charge*, 372–74.
29. Seeking an independent counsel, Clinton wrote in his memoir, "was the worst presidential decision I ever made, wrong on the facts, wrong on the law, wrong on the politics, wrong for the presidency and the Constitution." The passage of time had clearly produced a wisdom visibly absent at the time. "What I should have done," Clinton said, "is release the records, resist the prosecutor, give an extensive briefing to all the Democrats who wanted it, and ask for their support." But the insight of looking backward could not undo the tragedies that ensued.
30. Bernstein, *Woman in Charge*, 374–80; B. Clinton, *My Life*, 574, 584–90.
31. Bernstein, *Woman in Charge*, 366–68.
32. Ibid., 350, 380–82; H. R. Clinton, *Living History*, 245.
33. B. Clinton, *My Life*, 584.
34. Ibid., 606–607.
35. Bernstein, *Woman in Charge*, 389–92; B. Clinton, *My Life*, 612–14.
36. J. Klein, *The Natural*, 9–11.
37. Troy, *Hillary Rodham Clinton*, 116–17; Bernstein, *Woman in Charge*, 360–61; B. Clinton, *My Life*, 577.
38. Hamilton, *Bill Clinton*, 301–303; Harris, *Survivor*, 144–50, with the Hilary Clinton quote from 150; Sheehy, *Hillary's Choice*, 226. The cabinet member's comment is from Haynes Johnson and David Broder, *The System: The American Way of Politics at the Breaking Point* (Boston: Little, Brown, 1996), 280.
39. Troy, *Hillary Rodham Clinton*, 128–29, 133; B. Clinton, *My Life*, 594–95.
40. Sheehy, *Hillary's Choice*, 249–51; Gergen interview with Sheehy in ibid., 251; B. Clinton, *My Life*, 612.
41. B. Clinton, *My Life*, 619; Stephanopoulos, *All Too Human*, 303; Hamilton, *Bill Clinton*, 264, 301–303.
42. Hamilton, *Bill Clinton*, 347–48; B. Clinton, *My Life*, 621–22.
43. B. Clinton, *My Life*, 628–29; Bernstein, *Woman in Charge*, 406.
44. Bernstein, *Woman in Charge*, 208–209; B. Clinton, *My Life*, 630–32.
45. Bernstein interview with David Gergen in Bernstein, *Woman in Charge*, 408–409; the Muscatine quote is from H. R. Clinton, *Living History*, 261.
46. J. Klein, *The Natural*, 126; Bernstein interview with Lawrence O'Donnell in Bernstein, *Woman in Charge*, 403, 407; H. R. Clinton, *Living History*, 257.
47. Isikoff, *Uncovering Clinton*, 168.
48. Bernstein interview with Boorstin in Bernstein, *Woman in Charge*, 394.
49. Sheehy, *Hillary's Choice*, 265–66.
50. Bernstein interviews with a confidential source and with Betsey Wright in Bernstein, *Woman in Charge*, 310–11.
51. Gergen, *Eyewitness to Power*, 315; Bernstein, *Woman in Charge*, 400.

10. COMEBACK NUMBER THREE

1. Morris, *Behind the Oval Office*, 94, 115; Stephanopoulos, *All Too Human*, 328–30; Bernstein, *Woman in Charge*, 410.
2. Bernstein, *Woman in Charge*, 410–11; Sheehy, *Hillary's Choice*, 258; Morris, *Behind the Oval Office*, 116; Stephanopoulos, *All Too Human*, 329.

3. Stephanopoulos, *All Too Human*, 399; J. Klein, *The Natural*, 133–34; Harris, *Survivor*, 161–64; Branch, *Clinton Tapes*, 176. Interestingly, Clinton scoffed at reports that Morris had been involved in writing any of his speeches.

4. J. Klein, *The Natural*, 132–24; Morris, *Behind the Oval Office*, 123–35; Sheehy, *Hillary's Choice*, 258–59; Harris, *Survivor*, 218–20.

5. Morris, *Behind the Oval Office*, 125–28; Harris, *Survivor*, 218–20; Stephanopoulos, *All Too Human*, 330–41.

6. Morris, *Behind the Oval Office*, 91–92; recommendation of the academics retreat convened by Clinton in January 1994, in the papers of the Domestic Policy Council, Carol Rasco, box 3, Clinton Library. Attending the retreat were William J. Wilson, Alan Brinkley, Samuel Huntington, Theda Skocpol, Charles Hamilton, and Robert Kuttner. From the administration, those attending included Robert Rubin, Mandy Grunwald, Paul Begala, David Gergen, Carol Rasco, and Stan Greenberg.

7. Harris, *Survivor*, 164–65; Morris, *Behind the Oval Office*, 82–84; J. Klein, *The Natural*, 138–40.

8. J. Klein, *The Natural*, 136–38; Morris, *Behind the Oval Office*, 82–84; Stephanopoulos, *All Too Human*, 413.

9. Morris, *Behind the Oval Office*, 139–40, 144.

10. Bernstein, *Woman in Charge*, 412.

11. Carl Bernstein interview with Harold Ickes in ibid., 409; Hamilton, *Bill Clinton*, 547–50; Gail Sheehy interview with Bill Curry in Sheehy, *Hillary's Choice*, 259; Bernstein, *Woman in Charge*, 423.

12. The *Newsweek* interview is quoted in the *Atlanta Constitution*, February 18, 1995; Troy, *Hillary Rodham Clinton*, 140.

13. Carl Bernstein interview with Dick Morris in Bernstein, *Woman in Charge*, 410.

14. Bernstein, *Woman in Charge*, 420; Troy, *Hillary Rodham Clinton*, 142; Sheehy, *Hillary's Choice*, 277. See also a memo from Bill Galston to Carol Rasco on October 28, 1993, and a letter to Bill Clinton from six congresswomen on August 5, 1993, both in anticipation of the need for the United States to be a world leader in the fight for women's rights, in the Domestic Policy Council Papers, Carol Rasco, box 26, Clinton Library.

15. Bernstein, *Woman in Charge*, 415–17; interview with Houston in ibid., 472.

16. Bernstein, *Woman in Charge*, 418, 447; H. R. Clinton, *It Takes a Village*.

17. Bernstein, *Woman in Charge*, 423–27; Hamilton, *Bill Clinton*, 426; Sheehy, *Hillary's Choice*, 260; Morris, *Behind the Oval Office*, 111.

18. Branch, *Clinton Tapes*, 208–18; Hamilton, *Bill Clinton*, 371–74.

19. Hamilton, *Bill Clinton*, 413–17.

20. Ibid., 418–21.

21. Ibid., 333–38; Harris, *Survivor*, 178.

22. Hamilton, *Bill Clinton*, 437–43. See also the recommendations of the retreat for academic leaders in January 1994, Domestic Policy Council Papers, Carol Rasco, box 3, Clinton Library.

23. Hamilton, *Bill Clinton*, 442–43.

24. Leon Panetta interview with Chris Bury, "The Clinton Years," PBS TV, in Hamilton, *Bill Clinton*, 444–48; Branch, *Clinton Tapes*, 238; Harris, *Survivor*, 178–79.

25. Hamilton, *Bill Clinton*, 450–51; J. Klein, *The Natural*, 143.

26. Hamilton, *Bill Clinton*, 430; B. Clinton, *My Life*, 646–47, 663–64; Morris, *Behind the Oval Office*, 165; Harris, *Survivor*, 246–50.

27. J. Klein, *The Natural*, 144; Morris, *Behind the Oval Office*, 162; Bernstein, *Woman in Charge*, 474; B. Clinton, *My Life*, 659.

28. Morris, *Behind the Oval Office*, 165, 173; J. Klein, *The Natural*, 145.

29. Hamilton, *Bill Clinton*, 520; Branch, *Clinton Tapes*, 297, 300, 313.

30. Branch, *Clinton Tapes*, 308; Hamilton, *Bill Clinton*, 522–24; Harris, *Survivor*, 212; B. Clinton, *My Life*, 678–80.

31. Branch, *Clinton Tapes*, 313; Morris, *Behind the Oval Office*, 183.

32. Hamilton, *Bill Clinton*, 548–49, 563–66, 569–71.

33. Stephanopoulos, *All Too Human*, 403–8.

34. Bernstein interview with Mark Fabiani in Bernstein, *Woman in Charge*, 429–31, 458–60.

35. Stephanopoulos, *All Too Human*, 227–29, 416; Bernstein, *Woman in Charge*, 351–53, 355–57, 440–41.

36. Bernstein, *Woman in Charge*, 431–41.

37. David Watkins draft memo, "Response to Internal White House Travel Office Management Review," House Government Reforms and Oversight Committee, in Bernstein, *Woman in Charge*, 439–40.

38. Sheehy, *Hillary's Choice*, 278–81; Bernstein, *Woman in Charge*, 441–44.

39. Bernstein, *Woman in Charge*, 441–44; Sheehy, *Hillary's Choice*, 278–81.

40. B. Clinton, *My Life*, 691, 699; Bernstein, *Woman in Charge*, 443, 453, 459; Bernstein interview with Fabiani in ibid., 453.

41. Bernstein, *Woman in Charge*, 453; Troy, *Hillary Rodham Clinton*, 154–55.

42. Bernstein, *Woman in Charge*, 456.

43. Ibid., 443–45, Bernstein interview with confidential source.

44. Branch, *Clinton Tapes*, 336–39.

45. Ibid., 335.

46. B. Clinton, *My Life*, 694–95, 743.

47. Branch, *Clinton Tapes*, 334; Morris, *Behind the Oval Office*, 207, 218–19; Hamilton, *Bill Clinton*, 571–78.

48. Morris, *Behind the Oval Office*, 302; Bernstein, *Woman in Charge*, 463; Harris, *Survivor*, 233; B. Clinton, *My Life*, 602; Hamilton, *Bill Clinton*, 625; Branch, *Clinton Tapes*, 368.

49. J. Klein, *The Natural*, 150–52; Stephanopoulos, *All Too Human*, 403, 411; Branch, *Clinton Tapes*, 368; Bernstein, *Woman in Charge*, 462–65; Hamilton, *Bill Clinton*, 625–26; Harris, *Survivor*, 232.

50. J. Klein, *The Natural*, 152; Harris, *Survivor*, 233–36. Elaine Kamarck, a "New Democrat" thinker who was now part of Vice President Al Gore's staff, was asked by Clinton to attend the final staff meeting on welfare reform. Not accustomed to being invited to such high-level powwows, she wondered why she had been asked. "And then it dawned on me, when I walked into the room. Clinton was going to sign the bill, and all those people were against it, and he needed a few more people . . . in the room to make his argument." Harold Ickes, she recalled, stared "daggers at me" as she entered the meeting. J. Klein, *The Natural*, 152–53. Perhaps no one was more angry with Clinton than Hillary's cherished mentor, Marian Wright Edelman. See her letters to Clinton on August 3, 1995, and January

30, 1995, among others in the Domestic Policy Council Papers, Carol Rasco, box 6, Clinton Library. After Clinton signed the bill—to Edelman's everlasting disgust—her husband, Peter Edelman, resigned his post in the administration.

51. Branch, *Clinton Tapes*, 233; Harris, *Survivor*, 207; Nigel Hamilton interview with Doug Sosnick, 2005, in Hamilton, *Bill Clinton*, 584.

52. Morris, *Behind the Oval Office*, 255; Harris, *Survivor*, 219–20; J. Klein, *The Natural*, 155–56; Branch, *Clinton Tapes*, 385; B. Clinton, *My Life*, 729.

53. Bernstein, *Woman in Charge*, 459; Troy, *Hillary Rodham Clinton*, 173.

54. Hamilton, *Bill Clinton*, 628–30; Morris, *Behind the Oval Office*, 323; Branch, *Clinton Tapes*, 382.

55. Morris, *Behind the Oval Office*, 308–13; Hamilton, *Bill Clinton*, 638.

56. Hamilton, *Bill Clinton*, 638–46.

57. Branch, *Clinton Tapes*, 385; Harris, *Survivor*, 241; B. Clinton, *My Life*, 731–33.

58. J. Klein, *The Natural*, 86–89.

11. THE ROLLER COASTER PLUMMETS

1. Hamilton, *Bill Clinton*, 540–43; Harris, *Survivor*, 223–27; Troy, *Hillary Rodham Clinton*, 151–53; Jeffrey Toobin, *A Vast Conspiracy: The Real Story of the Sex Scandal That Nearly Brought Down a President* (New York: Random House, 1999), 86, 325.

2. Toobin, *Vast Conspiracy*, 98, 107; Harris, *Survivor*, 228–29, 231–33.

3. Troy, *Hillary Rodham Clinton*, 151; Stephanopoulos, *All Too Human*, 32.

4. Harris, *Survivor*, 226–29; Toobin, *Vast Conspiracy*, 209; Hamilton, *Bill Clinton*, 605.

5. Toobin, *Vast Conspiracy*, 87; Harris, *Survivor*, 225–26.

6. Hamilton, *Bill Clinton*, 273, 275; Isikoff, *Uncovering Clinton*, 54, 60, 91; Bernstein, *Woman in Charge*, 383–87.

7. Toobin, *Vast Conspiracy*, 293; H. R. Clinton, *Living History*, 440.

8. Toobin, *Vast Conspiracy*, 208–10.

9. Ibid., 6, 127–28.

10. Isikoff, *Uncovering Clinton*, 221; Toobin, *Vast Conspiracy*, 249.

11. Toobin, *Vast Conspiracy*, 167, 216, 246–49.

12. B. Clinton, *My Life*, 759–62; Harris, *Survivor*, 268–71; Bernstein, *Woman in Charge*, 467.

13. B. Clinton, *My Life*, 772–75; Toobin, *Vast Conspiracy*, 217–27; Harris, *Survivor*, 301–3.

14. B. Clinton, *My Life*, 774; Harris, *Survivor*, 304.

15. Interview with Dick Morris in Sheehy, *Hillary's Choice*, 297; Hamilton, *Bill Clinton*, 10; Bernstein, *Woman in Charge*, 487–93; J. Klein, *The Natural*, 174.

16. Stephanopoulos, *All Too Human*, 436; J. Klein, *The Natural*, 175.

17. Toobin, *Vast Conspiracy*, 250; Bernstein, *Woman in Charge*, 494; Troy, *Hillary Rodham Clinton*, 190.

18. Bernstein, *Woman in Charge*, 484–86; H. R. Clinton, *Living History*, 440–41.

19. Sheehy, *Hillary's Choice*, 175; Toobin, *Vast Conspiracy*, 242; Stephanopoulos, *All Too Human*, 436; Bernstein, *Woman in Charge*, 485.

20. Sheehy, *Hillary's Choice*, 175; Toobin, *Vast Conspiracy*, 253.

21. Bernstein, *Woman in Charge*, 488–89; Toobin, *Vast Conspiracy*, 244.
22. B. Clinton, *My Life*, 776; Bernstein, *Woman in Charge*, 497–99.
23. B. Clinton, *My Life*, 776; Toobin, *Vast Conspiracy*, 258.
24. J. Klein, *The Natural*, 17–18; Branch, *Clinton Tapes*, 497.
25. J. Klein, *The Natural*, 19–20.
26. Harris, *Survivor*, 313–27.
27. Toobin, *Vast Conspiracy*, 264–79.
28. B. Clinton, *My Life*, 779–80, 790–91, 796; Bernstein, *Woman in Charge*, 509–10.
29. Sheehy, *Hillary's Choice*, 309; Bernstein, *Woman in Charge*, 511–12.
30. Bernstein interviews with confidential sources in Bernstein, *Woman in Charge*, 510–12.
31. Ibid., 511–12; J. Klein, *The Natural*, 167; Toobin, *Vast Conspiracy*, 310.
32. Bernstein, *Woman in Charge*, 512; B. Clinton, *My Life*, 800–801; H. R. Clinton, *Living History*, 466.
33. Sheehy, *Hillary's Choice*, 310; Bernstein, *Woman in Charge*, 513.
34. Troy, *Hillary Rodham Clinton*, 194; Gail Sheehy interview with Dorothy Rodham in Sheehy, *Hillary's Choice*, 311; H. R. Clinton, *It Takes a Village*, 15; H. R. Clinton, *Living History*, TK.
35. Harris, *Survivor*, 339–41; B. Clinton, *My Life*, 800–803; Sheehy, *Hillary's Choice*, 309–11.
36. Sheehy, *Hillary's Choice*, 312–13; Bernstein, *Woman in Charge*, 516; B. Clinton, *My Life*, 802–803; J. Klein, *The Natural*, 171–72; Stephanopoulos, *All Too Human*, 320.
37. Carl Bernstein interviews with Diane Blair, William Styron, and Melanne Verveer in Bernstein, *Woman in Charge*, 502, 508, 517, 520, 527; Sheehy, *Hillary's Choice*, 313–23.
38. Sheehy, *Hillary's Choice*, 195; B. Clinton, *My Life*, 803–804.
39. Bernstein, *Woman in Charge*, 507–508, 521, 524–25; Bernstein interviews with Diane Blair and Betsy Ebeling in ibid., 524–25.
40. Sheehy, *Hillary's Choice*, 322–23; Harris, *Survivor*, 340–45; B. Clinton, *My Life*, 805–806; Bernstein, *Woman in Charge*, 527.
41. Harris, *Survivor*, 347; Bernstein, *Woman in Charge*, 522; B. Clinton, *My Life*, 809.
42. Troy, *Hillary Rodham Clinton*, 185; B. Clinton, *My Life*, 811–14; Harris, *Survivor*, 350; Bernstein, *Woman in Charge*, 527; J. Klein, *The Natural*, 177–79.
43. Harris, *Survivor*, 334; Toobin, *Vast Conspiracy*, 330.
44. Sheehy, *Hillary's Choice*, 322; Bernstein, *Woman in Charge*, 505; Toobin, *Vast Conspiracy*, 289, 327–28.
45. Harris, *Survivor*, 344–47; Bernstein, *Woman in Charge*, 526, 529; Stephanopoulos, *All Too Human*, 330–33.
46. J. Klein, *The Natural*, 179–81.
47. Ibid., 180; Bernstein, *Woman in Charge*, 530.
48. J. Klein, *The Natural*, 173–74.
49. B. Clinton, *My Life*, 811.
50. Sheehy, *Hillary's Choice*, 302–303.

12. SURVIVAL—AND A NEW BEGINNING

1. B. Clinton, *My Life*, 813; Toobin, *Vast Conspiracy*, 345–48.
2. B. Clinton, *My Life*, 828–29; Bernstein, *Woman in Charge*, 533–34; Toobin, *Vast Conspiracy*, 349–52.
3. Toobin, *Vast Conspiracy*, 335–37.
4. Ibid., 335–38.
5. Bernstein, *Woman in Charge*, 533–37; Harris, *Survivor*, 357–60.
6. Branch, *Clinton Tapes*, 488–92, 500; Sheehy, *Hillary's Choice*, 345.
7. B. Clinton, *My Life*, 833–34.
8. Ibid., 842–45.
9. Toobin, *Vast Conspiracy*, 370; Branch, *Clinton Tapes*, 537.
10. Toobin, *Vast Conspiracy*, 378.
11. Branch, *Clinton Tapes*, 537–38; B. Clinton, *My Life*, 845.
12. B. Clinton, *My Life*, 846.
13. Ibid., 862–63.
14. Bernstein, *Woman in Charge*, 537–39; H. R. Clinton, *Living History*, 506.
15. Sheehy, *Hillary's Choice*, 340–41; Bernstein, *Woman in Charge*, 537. Harold Ickes referred to the Senate contest as Hillary's "race for redemption."
16. Sheehy, *Hillary's Choice*, 345–50; Bernstein, *Woman in Charge*, 541.
17. Sheehy, *Hillary's Choice*, 348, 350–60; B. Clinton, *My Life*, 861; Gerth and Van Natta, *Her Way*, 209.
18. Branch, *Clinton Tapes*, 533; Bernstein, *Woman in Charge*, 541–43; Sheehy, *Hillary's Choice*, 365–66, 375–77; B. Clinton, *My Life*, 927.
19. Branch, *Clinton Tapes*, 609–15.
20. Ibid., 610; B. Clinton, *My Life*, 867, 883–88, 911–16.
21. B. Clinton, *My Life*, 935–38, 943–45.
22. Ibid., 891–93, 910; Branch, *Clinton Tapes*, 583.
23. B. Clinton, *My Life*, 890.
24. Bernstein, *Woman in Charge*, 475–76; Bernstein interviews with confidential sources in ibid., 310–11.
25. Harris, *Survivor*, 379–83, 398.
26. Branch, *Clinton Tapes*, 623, 634, 641–43, 649–51; J. Klein, *The Natural*, 204–208.

13. WHAT IF?

1. Bernstein, *Woman in Charge*, 410; Sheehy, *Hillary's Choice*, 261.
2. Bernstein, *Woman in Charge*, 312.
3. J. Klein, *The Natural*, 114.
4. Gergen, *Eyewitness to Power*, 297.
5. J. Klein, *The Natural*, 160–61.

A Note on Sources

As indicated in my acknowledgments, this book would not have been possible without the extraordinary research and writing of others. The papers of the William Clinton Presidential Library and Museum have been useful, as have confidential oral history interviews that I conducted. But many of the Oval Office papers, particularly those involving the president and first lady, have not yet been released, and the multiple oral history interviews conducted by the Miller Center at the University of Virginia on the Clinton administration will not be open to scholars for some years to come. The heart of this book, therefore, is based on the work of journalists and others who have done so much to illuminate the contours and tensions of the partnership between Bill and Hillary Clinton. While the endnotes refer specifically to the materials I have used, I want to take this opportunity to single out a few authors whose insights have proved most valuable to my work.

Carl Bernstein's *A Woman in Charge: The Life of Hillary Rodham Clinton* (New York: Knopf, 2007) is an invaluable guide to the personal and political journey of Hillary Rodham Clinton. Bernstein conducted more than two hundred interviews, providing indispensable insights into the former First Lady's childhood, youth, and adult life. As a biographer and civil rights historian, I have written many books informed by extensive oral histories. Bernstein has mastered the art. With nuance, care, and deep personal insight, he has woven the myriad observations of his sources into a textured and compelling portrait of Hillary Rodham Clinton and those around her. I am deeply indebted to him for his masterful biography.

David Maraniss has done a comparable job in his brilliant assessment of Bill Clinton during the years leading up to his presidency, *First in His Class: A Biography of Bill Clinton* (New York: Simon and Schuster, 1995). Full of insights about both Bill and Hillary Clinton, the Maraniss book lays out the contours of the Clintons' story, based on both extensive personal interviews and comprehensive research in news sources in Arkansas and the nation as a whole.

Gail Sheehy brings her own set of insights to *Hillary's Choice* (New York: Random House, 1999). Sheehy conducted a series of interviews with Hillary Clinton, and also secured access to important correspondence regarding her early years, and particularly her relationship with Rev. Don Jones, the youth minister who shaped her basic values so fundamentally.

Many first-person memoirs have helped illuminate critical aspects of the Clintons' years in the White House, but two in particular stand out. George Stephanopoulos's *All Too Human: A Political Education* (Boston: Little, Brown and Company, 1999) is extraordinarily fresh, spontaneous, and direct, recounting the tensions and confusion that pervaded the White House during his four years of service there. David Gergen's *Eyewitness to Power: The Essence of Leadership, Nixon to Clinton* (New York: Simon and Schuster, 2000) is, likewise, full of trenchant observations on the relationship between Bill and Hillary Clinton and its impact on national policy.

Finally, a number of books by journalists have been helpful. These include John Harris, *The Survivor: Bill Clinton in the White House* (New York: Random House, 2005); Bob Woodward, *The Agenda: Inside the Clinton White House* (New York: Simon and Schuster, 1994), an insider's view of the first year of the Clinton administration; Haynes Johnson and David S. Broder, *The System: The American Way of Politics at the Breaking Point* (Boston: Little, Brown and Company, 1996), a careful study of the health care proposal from the Clinton administration; Jeffrey Toobin, *A Vast Conspiracy: The Real Story of the Sex Scandal That Nearly Brought Down a President* (New York: Random House, 2000), a detailed narrative of the Monica Lewinsky affair; and Joe Klein, *The Natural: The Misunderstood Presidency of Bill Clinton* (New York: Doubleday, 2002), a set of trenchant and acerbic observations by the "anonymous" author of *Primary Colors*, the "semi-fictional" account of the 1992 presidential primary campaign that highlighted the personality foibles of Bill Clinton.

As indicated, these are just a few of the outstanding books and articles that have informed this work. More detailed information on sources is contained in the endnotes.

Acknowledgments

This book would not have been possible without the assistance of countless individuals. First are all the authors and journalists who have compiled the written record that provided the basis for what is written here. While some research materials came from the William J. Clinton Presidential Library and Museum in Little Rock and from oral history interviews, virtually every page builds on the insights and discoveries first mined by others. I am deeply indebted to all those who have come before me in writing about Bill and Hillary Clinton.

A significant portion of this book came into being while I was on writing fellowships in other countries. In the fall of 2009 the Centre for Historical Research of the Australian National University invited me to spend two months in Canberra. With the exception of one or two seminar presentations, I was given total freedom to spend my days and nights writing. Good friends like Geoffrey Bartlett, Doug Craig, Pat Jalland, and Desley Deacon nourished my spirits over lunches and coffees, while morning walks by the lakeside provided a wonderful time for reflection. It was an ideal place to launch this project.

The next year I was invited to be an Erskine Fellow at the University of Canterbury in Christchurch, New Zealand. There, too, I enjoyed the company of dear colleagues like Peter Field and Maureen Montgomery, and once more was given a superb environment in which to write. I will never forget the generosity of these gifts, nor the beauty of the two countries where a substantial portion of this book was written.

There are two people more responsible for what lies between these pages than any others. The first is Jim Jones. A fellow historian, old friend, and the author of numerous prize-winning books, from *Bad Blood*, his exposé of the notorious Tuskegee experiment with victims of syphilis, to his brilliant biography of Alfred Kinsey, Jim developed an interest in writing about Bill Clinton.

We met at conventions, talked about our work, and shared insights. Then one day he told me he had decided to forgo his own Clinton book. The next thing I knew a huge box arrived on my doorstep. It contained all of Jim's notes, reams of Xeroxes from the Clinton Library, and numerous books and articles. Rarely have I experienced such generosity of spirit, or camaraderie. What Jim gave me supplemented and complemented my own work. I will always treasure Jim's act of friendship and scholarly partnership.

My second partner in this venture has been my editor, Thomas LeBien. For years I had known Thomas. We talked about various book projects, but I had never written with him before. Then I helped to get Thomas involved in John Hope Franklin's autobiography. John Hope was one of my dearest friends, and I saw how Thomas and he fused their talents. As soon as I started thinking about this book, I decided that I wanted Thomas as my editor. It was one of the wisest decisions I ever made. His penciled comments appeared on every page of the manuscript. He must have spent weeks working on it. And in almost every instance, I agreed with the changes he suggested. Thomas LeBien is the best editor I have ever met.

Another indispensable aide has been Tim Tyson. A dear friend, kindred spirit, and former student, Tim has helped transform the profession of history with his work on race, Black Power, and the struggle to integrate the personal and the political. Tim read every word of this manuscript, raising questions big and small, which sharpened immeasurably what is written here. Together with lifetime friends like Sydney Nathans, Harvard Sitkoff, Anne Firor Scott, and William Leuchtenburg, he has helped provide the spiritual support that made this book possible.

Daniel Gerstle has shepherded this book through the publishing phase with consummate skill, adding trenchant comments that have helped improve the manuscript while smoothing over every editorial glitch.

Finally, none of this could have happened without my family. My grandchildren, Lila and Jordan, inspire me with their humor, their genius, and their impulse to celebrate life. Their father and mother, my son, Christopher, and his wife, Katherine, and my daughter, Jennifer, offer sharp insights and wise observations about all of life. But most important is Lorna, who for more than four decades has nurtured my better side with her love and humor. That, and my great-grandparents' house on Harmon's Harbor in Georgetown, Maine, where the rest of this book was written, is what it's all about.

Index